# NEW DEAL COWBOY

# NEW DEAL COWBOY
## GENE AUTRY AND PUBLIC DIPLOMACY

Michael Duchemin

UNIVERSITY OF OKLAHOMA PRESS : NORMAN

Library of Congress Cataloging-in-Publication Data

Names: Duchemin, Michael, 1959– author.
Title: New Deal cowboy : Gene Autry and public diplomacy / Michael Duchemin.
Description: Norman : University of Oklahoma Press, [2016] Includes
~ bibliographical references and index.
-~-Identifiers: LCCN 2016001065 | ISBN 978-0-8061-5392-6 (hardcover)
ISBN 978-0-8061-9481-3 (paper)
Subjects: LCSH: Autry, Gene, 1907–1998. | Autry, Gene, 1907–1998—
    Political and social views. | Motion picture actors and actresses—United
    States—Biography. | Singers—United States—Biography. | Arts and
    diplomacy—United States—History—20th century. | Motion pictures—
    Political aspects—United States—History—20th century. | Country
    music—Political aspects—United States—History—20th century. |
    Popular culture—Political aspects—United States—History—20th
    century. | New Deal, 1933–1939. | United States—Foreign relations—
    1933–1945.
Classification: LCC PN2287.A9 D83 2016 | DDC 791.4302/8092 [B] —dc23
LC record available at https://lccn.loc.gov/2016001065

The paper in this book meets the guidelines for permanence and durability of the Committee on Production Guidelines for Book Longevity of the Council on Library Resources, Inc. ∞

Copyright © 2016 by the University of Oklahoma Press, Norman, Publishing Division of the University. Paperback published 2024. Manufactured in the U.S.A.

All rights reserved. No part of this publication may be reproduced, stored in a retrieval system, or transmitted, in any form or by any means, electronic, mechanical, photocopying, recording, or otherwise—except as permitted under Section 107 or 108 of the United States Copyright Act—without the prior written permission of the University of Oklahoma Press. To request permission to reproduce selections from this book, write to Permissions, University of Oklahoma Press, 2800 Venture Drive, Norman, OK 73069, or email rights.oupress@ou.edu.

*For Gene, always your pal*

# Contents

| | |
|---|---|
| List of Illustrations | vii |
| Introduction: America's Ace Cowboy | 3 |
|    1. Country-Western Hybrid Music | 18 |
|    2. Musical-Western Hybrid Film | 44 |
|    3. New Deal, New West | 66 |
|    4. The Second New Deal | 91 |
|    5. The Good Neighbor Policy | 118 |
|    6. Western Hemisphere Idea | 138 |
|    7. Youth's Model, 1940 | 164 |
|    8. Sergeant Gene Autry | 191 |
| Conclusion: New Deal Cowboy | 224 |
| Notes | 237 |
| Bibliography | 263 |
| Index | 305 |

# Illustrations

| | |
|---|---:|
| *Bells of Capistrano* lobby card | 2 |
| The Oklahoma Yodeling Cowboy, 1934 | 29 |
| *Round-Up of WLS Radio Stars,* 1934 | 30 |
| "WLS Round-Up: Gene Autry / Also Vaudeville," 1934 | 31 |
| Autry's first gold record, 1935 | 32 |
| "Nate Levine Presents Ken Maynard, 'In Old Santa Fe'" | 55 |
| *The Big Show* lobby card | 56 |
| "Gene Autry in Person" press book, 1936 | 57 |
| Autry with Martin guitar, c. 1935 | 78 |
| Autry with new horse trailer, 1937 | 79 |
| Autry and Rudy Vallee, 1937 | 104 |
| *Public Cowboy No. 1* lobby card | 105 |
| *Rovin' Tumbleweeds* lobby card | 106 |
| Autry and Champion at the Savoy Hotel, London, 1939 | 148 |
| "Céad Mile Fáilte, Gene Autry" (A Hundred Thousand Welcomes) | 149 |
| "Welcome to Dublin, Gene Autry" | 150 |
| The Autrys with Franklin Roosevelt, Jr., Herbert Yates, and Art Satherly, 1939 | 151 |

| | |
|---|---|
| "South of the Border (Down Mexico Way)" sheet music | 152 |
| *South of the Border* poster | 153 |
| "Down Mexico Way" comic | 154 |
| Autry and the Gene Autry Fan Club, c. 1936 | 176 |
| Autry with CBS microphone, 1940 | 177 |
| Autry at Melody Ranch, 1939 | 178 |
| *In Old Monterey* poster | 179 |
| With Eleanor Roosevelt and others, 1940 | 180 |
| Autry and Champion on the Capitol steps, 1941 | 181 |
| Autry and Champion, Madison Square Garden, 1941 | 205 |
| Autry and Champion at the rodeo, 1941 | 206 |
| Fans at the Gene Autry Rodeo, Fort Worth, Texas, 1941 | 207 |
| Autry with young fans at the rodeo, 1941 | 208 |
| Gene Autry, Oklahoma | 209 |
| Gene Autry's enlistment, *Melody Ranch* Radio Program | 210 |
| Autry signing U.S. savings bonds, 1941 | 211 |
| *Sgt. Gene Autry Presents His Favorite Patriotic and Hillbilly Songs* | 212 |
| Autry broadcasting from Luke Field, Arizona, 1942 | 213 |

# NEW DEAL COWBOY

*Bells of Capistrano* lobby card, 1942. © Autry Qualified Interest Trust and The Autry Foundation (BIO_033).

# Introduction
## America's Ace Cowboy

In July 1942, Gene Autry worked straight through the filming schedule to finish his scenes in *Bells of Capistrano* (1942) so that he could fly out for Chicago to join his rodeo troupe. *Bells of Capistrano* was the cowboy hero's fifty-sixth film and the last one he made for Republic Pictures before joining the U.S. Army Air Forces. The film mirrored Autry's real life as a singing cowboy headliner with a traveling rodeo troupe that drew throngs of spectators to experience exciting displays of Western sport. The premise of the film involved Autry bringing innovation to the World Wide Wild West and Rodeo with the addition of a "crooner attraction" that spiced up the traditional events. *Bells of Capistrano* dramatized an uneasy union between Western music and Western sport. Old-timers and traditionalists in rodeo did not care for the yodeling cowboy; yet they could not deny Autry's box office success. Large crowds and increased ticket sales eventually won over the most ardent opposition.[1]

Gene Autry's Flying "A" Ranch Rodeo Stampede opened at Soldier Field in Chicago on Thursday night, July 23, 1942. A raucous crowd of 28,000 spectators turned out to see the "western idol of motion picture and radio fans." Autry appeared at each performance during the weeklong show, described by Rita Fitzpatrick in the *Chicago Daily Tribune* as "a good old-fashioned rodeo with a Broadway flare." The

Flying "A" Stampede featured one hundred top-hand cowboys and cowgirls dressed in colorful costumes of scarlet, baby blue, pink, and gold. The greater purpose of these fancy duds became apparent when the stadium lights lowered and the field was flooded by a stroboscopic black-light system. The luminescent costumes of the Flying "A" riders turned the traditional stampede into a surreal new experience. Fitzpatrick wrote that "the corral seemed alive with myriad brightly colored fireflies."[2]

Gene Autry's Flying "A" Stampede coincided with a special "V-Days" campaign launched with thousands of volunteers selling war bonds and stamps throughout Illinois. During the lunch hour on July 24, 1942, Autry worked on Treasury corner—State Street and Van Buren—in Chicago's downtown loop. Autographing war stamp boutonnieres to sell for $1, he sang his latest hit, "(I've Got Spurs That) Jingle, Jangle, Jingle." Majorettes from the Flying "A" Stampede rode around the loop on the "Victory Special," a streetcar painted red, white, and blue, to stimulate war bond and stamp sales. Autry also joined with other radio and stage stars of Chicago to boost the United Service Organization (USO) by appearing at USO–American Legion booths where members of the legion auxiliary collected contributions during the Loop parade. Autry's Flying "A" Ranch Rodeo also took up collections for the nightly USO drive at Soldier Field.[3]

In addition to selling war bonds and raising funds for the USO, Autry planned a special event for the matinee performance on Sunday, July 26: his own induction as a technical sergeant into the U.S. Army Air Forces. The induction took place during a live broadcast of *Gene Autry's Melody Ranch*, the singing cowboy's nationally syndicated radio program, sponsored by Wrigley's Doublemint Gum and produced by the Columbia Broadcasting System (CBS). An estimated 2.5 million listeners tuned in from coast to coast to hear Autry take the oath of enlistment during the symbolic broadcast. Soldiers stationed around the world heard the program beamed overseas via shortwave radio frequencies.[4]

To boost morale, promote recruiting efforts, and sell more war bonds, the army brass requested that Autry be sworn in during the special Sunday broadcast. After administering the oath of enlistment and inducting the cowboy hero, Colonel Edward F. Shaifer issued a first command: "Sergeant Autry, a song." America's Ace Cowboy chuckled in response and then launched into a rendition of "Private Buckaroo," a Western folk ballad about a young cowboy recruit who joined the U.S. Army.[5]

The command for Autry to sing had come from higher-ups in the Pentagon, led by Hap Arnold, commanding general of the U.S. Army Air Forces, who worked with Wrigley and CBS to develop a public relations campaign featuring the newly enlisted singing cowboy hero. Wrigley retired *Gene Autry's Melody Ranch* and surrendered its Sunday evening time slot to the Army Air Corps for the production of a new program, *Sergeant Gene Autry*.[6] Wrigley's announcer explained the change:

> In the interest of supplying *information and entertainment* to the public and to acquaint young men of America with details of life around Army Air Forces flying fields, Sergeant Autry has been detailed to bring you dramatizations of true stories from the official records of this splendid organization. Sergeant Autry's participation in this radio program, for the time being, is a part of his regular duties in the Army Air Forces, and he receives no compensation for so doing, other than his sergeant's pay. Doublemint Gum now turns broadcast over to the United States Army Air Forces.[7]

### Public Diplomacy

This vignette of Autry's enlistment and the Army Air Corps commandeering of the *Melody Ranch* radio program serve as capstones in *New Deal Cowboy: Gene Autry and Public Diplomacy*. Showing the singing cowboy's support for Franklin Delano Roosevelt (FDR), the thirty-second president of the United States, *New Deal Cowboy* explains how Autry used his mastery of multiplatform entertainment and the techniques of transmedia storytelling to make the president's policies more attractive to the American public. Autry chose the Western genre as his modus operandi because it appealed to rural, small-town, and newly urban fans throughout the Midwest, South, and Southwest regions of the United States. Western folk songs provided the glue that held his enterprises together. Western music was the one element common to all the forms of art, entertainment, and recreation featuring the "Gene Autry" brand.

The singing cowboy's ability to reach lower-culture audiences appealed to New Dealers promoting western travel and tourism as an antidote for rebellious tendencies, reactionary conservatism, and foreign aggression in the United States. Regarding tourism as a key component for economic recovery, Roosevelt funded national advertising campaigns to stimulate cross-country travel, and he supported the efforts of business and civic leaders to promote tourism in western locales.[8] As the Second World War got under way in Europe, Autry promoted the New Deal and the "New West" in all the American cultural industries—live performance, sound recording, motion picture, radio broadcasting, and print media—with one singing cowboy persona. When the president's agenda shifted toward foreign policy, Autry promoted Americanism, war preparedness, and friendly relations with Latin America to audiences that favored isolationism. Autry helped make Roosevelt's internationalism more palatable for U.S. citizens leery about engagement in another foreign war.

Music provided the glue that held Gene Autry's multiplatform entertainments together. The combined effect elevated the singing cowboy to new heights as an international icon. By extending his persona through live performances, radio broadcasting, and music publishing, Autry created synergy within the motion picture and sound recording subsectors of the U.S. information economy. His concerted effort across multiple information media shaped a total result greater than the sum of each individual achievement. Synergy created a "Gene Autry" franchise capable by 1939 of shaping public opinion, boosting morale, and sparking patriotism within the mainstream of American culture. Autry's messaging tapped into a deep vein of Americanism that affected nearly everyone during the run-up to World War II.

The mixture of consumers sampling Autry's cultural products resembled the "quasi-folk low culture" that sociologist Herbert J. Gans first described in 1974, in *Popular Culture and High Culture: An Analysis and Evaluation of Taste*. Autry fans enjoyed the singing cowboy's combination of old-time singing and yodeling blues blended with Western folk culture and commercial low culture, borrowed from medicine shows and vaudeville. Fans found Autry's singing cowboy persona very attractive. The singing cowboy appealed to the taste culture of many lower-income people with educations that typically ended in grade school who were working in unskilled blue-collar and service jobs.[9]

In addition to the quasi-folk, Gans identified lower-class audiences, and these also numbered among Autry's rural, small-town, and newly urban fans in the Midwest, South, and Southwest. Consisting mainly of skilled and semiskilled factory and white-collar service workers, lower-culture Americans generally achieved nonacademic high school educations in the 1930s. Many dropped out of school after the tenth grade. These Americans dominated the taste culture of the United States until the 1950s, when the group rose en masse to join the ranks of the lower-middle class. Lower-culture publics usually rejected all notions of "high culture" in their arts and entertainments, sometimes with a degree of hostility.[10]

Autry presented lower-culture expressions of working-class values in his performances. Highly valued by lower-culture audiences, his musical-Western, action-comedy dramas used simple and direct expressions to portray heroic fights against crime, related violations of the moral order, and attempts to save society from natural disasters. Different from traditional Westerns depicting conflicts between cowboys and Indians in the "Old West," Republic's "Gene Autry" series represented a contemporary cowboy hero fighting Depression-era gangsters and corrupt businessmen in the New West of the 1930s. Unlike traditional cowboy heroes in Westerns produced for lower-middle-culture audiences, Autry never doubted the social usefulness of his activities or the validity of his identity.

Appealing to quasi-folk and lower-culture audiences, Autry represented a quintessential American folk hero, offering rural American folk values and important working-class behavioral norms becoming increasingly palatable within the American mainstream of popular culture. Autry remained sure of his masculinity despite the questioning of heavies who chided his fancy duds and the penchant of his goofy male sidekick to dress in drag. Unlike his movie rivals, Autry did not depend on luck and fate for success. He voiced support for the federal government and for voluntary collective action at the state and local levels.

Autry became a star by creating less expensive content of lower technical quality for large audiences to consume through sound recordings, radio broadcasts, motion pictures, live performances, and licensed merchandise. Admirers sought vicarious contact with their singing cowboy hero through radio and movie guides, fan magazines, comic books, and other mass-produced publications. Followers did not distinguish between Gene Autry the performer and the character he played in the movies. Right on cue, they blurred the line between Gene Autry the man and Gene Autry the public image, the singing cowboy.

As national advertisers developed an interest in sponsorship, record and motion picture producers revised material written for lower-middle-class audiences to fit with Autry's working-class values. National advertisers demanded new content to reach audiences with more purchasing power than the quasi-folk and lower-culture consumers alone could command. The shift in content became increasingly evident after Wrigley agreed to sponsor and nationally syndicate *Gene Autry's Melody Ranch* on the CBS Radio Network. *Melody Ranch* launched on New Year's Eve, December 31, 1939, and was followed by a song and movie with the same title, released by Republic Pictures in November 1940.[11] During this special preview broadcast for merchants selling Doublemint Gum, the *Melody Ranch* announcer explained how the Western folksinger and star of musical-Western films made his way and succeeded by contributing something unique to American culture:

> Millions go to their favorite theater to see Gene and thrill to his singing in Republic pictures. And now, Gene Autry comes to visit you: to sit around your firesides with you, swapping stories of the colorful West. Telling you his adventures and

singing you the grand songs we all love so well, here is a new program. A program to carry you out of yourselves; out of this troubled world of ours; out into the great open plains of the west; a program that brings you color, American humor, and American song—that successful interpreter of our nation's most tuneful folksongs—Gene Autry.[12]

Taking notice of Autry's newfound fame, First Lady Eleanor Roosevelt invited the singing cowboy to Washington, D.C. The First Lady asked the singing cowboy to join the president's annual birthday ball, a major fund-raising event for the National Foundation for Infantile Paralysis. While in the nation's capital, the cowboy hero accompanied Mrs. Roosevelt to the Fort Myer Horse Show. She, in turn, made a special guest appearance on *Gene Autry's Melody Ranch*.[13]

Broadcasting from Washington, D.C., on January 28, 1940, CBS produced a live simulcast using state-of-the-art information technology to include live remote broadcasts from sister stations in St. Louis; Fall River, Massachusetts; and Chicago. The Presidential Birthday Broadcast demonstrated Autry's ability to celebrate diversity as an aspect of American music while simultaneously promoting unity by harmonizing diverse musical forms. *Melody Ranch* featured musical groups performing in noticeably different styles, yet the world recognized each form as a style of American music.[14]

*Gene Autry's Melody Ranch* created a place of convergence in American culture in which content flowed across multiple media platforms, cooperative agreements brought together multiple media industries, and information circulated nationally and internationally through an active, participatory fan culture. Media convergence represented a cultural shift for Autry fans seeking new information and making connections between the disparate media content the singing cowboy created. Cultural convergence occurred within the minds of individual fans and through their social media networks. Conversations about Autry created a media buzz valued by industry insiders.[15]

Autry's support for President Roosevelt exemplified a new type of "public diplomacy" identified by Joseph S. Nye as the performance of government relations through public information media and nongovernmental organizations to influence political action. Nye saw the origins of public diplomacy in FDR's "New Deal" proclamation, broadcast in his acceptance speech at the Democratic National Convention in Chicago on July 2, 1932. Nye's book *Soft Power: The Means to Success in World Politics* (2004) explained that the Roosevelt administration developed its tendencies for public diplomacy by garnering support for its New Deal domestic agenda.[16]

Franklin Roosevelt was the first presidential candidate to convey information directly to the nation via radio transmission. Earlier candidates had simply allowed radio stations to broadcast the speeches they made to groups. Radio enabled Roosevelt to break the hold of sectionalist politicians who relied on crowd psychology to control American politics. National interest focused on the presidential election campaign during the summer of 1932. As the candidates put forth plans to mitigate the impact of the Great Depression, Roosevelt ran what is now considered the classic political campaign in the history of radio broadcasting. Long experience with the medium made FDR a candidate tailor-made for radio. Describing his campaign speeches, Ben Gross explained to readers of the *New York Daily News* that "each word, each phrase, each sentence seemed to be built . . . with the invisible audience in mind." As president, Roosevelt addressed U.S. radio audiences estimated at more than 40 million persons on at least ten occasions.[17]

*Soft Power* underscores the attractiveness of the nation as a crucial element in the U.S. government's ability to achieve desired outcomes in an age of global information. Roosevelt's willingness to share information made the federal government more appealing to citizens at home and abroad. Open access to information improved people's ability to cooperate with the Roosevelt administration, and it increased their inclination to do so. When the president decided to prepare the nation for war, access through global information media enabled FDR to develop a new, internationalist identity. President Roosevelt used "soft power" to make his internationalist stance desirable for American citizens leery about entering another foreign war.[18]

These types of activities, commonly connected to a media-savvy White House, prompted *Life* magazine executive Fitzhugh Green to proclaim Franklin Roosevelt the "Wizard of Washington." In *American Propaganda Abroad* (1988), Green marveled at Roosevelt's ability to subtly massage public opinion with soothing explanations as he moved the country toward a war footing in 1939. He documented the creation of a domestic information committee innocently labeled the "Office of Facts and Figures" (OFF) in 1941. The president calmed public concern by putting the poet Archibald MacLeisch in charge. Autry provided FDR with another means of reaching quasi-folk and lower-culture Americans in the Midwest, South, and Southwest. As the nation prepared for war the singing cowboy's message extended beyond his rural, small-town, and newly urban base into the mainstream of American popular culture.[19]

FDR created a second agency called the Coordinator of Information (COI), headed by lawyer William "Wild Bill" Donovan, to deal with foreign intelligence and covert operations. Donovan recruited the playwright and presidential speechwriter Robert E. Sherwood to launch the Voice of America (VOA), a U.S. government broadcasting agency that distributed public information directly to European listeners. Donovan also managed the president's covert operations, known as "black" propaganda, through the Office of Strategic Services (OSS). "Black propaganda" referred to U.S. programs that sowed disinformation among the news media in neutral nations to influence public opinion in Germany, Italy, and Japan. After the Japanese attack on Pearl Harbor on December 7, 1941, the president merged all these public information activities into the Office of War Information (OWI).[20]

Roosevelt's concerns regarding German propaganda in Latin America prompted the exception of Nelson Rockefeller's operations as Coordinator of Inter-American Affairs (CIAA). Wilson Dizard pinpointed this exception as the beginning of U.S. efforts to set the pace and direction of global communications. Dizard's *Digital Diplomacy* (2001) examined the spirit of Roosevelt's "Good Neighbor Policy" toward Latin America and the job Nelson Rockefeller did to make the United States more attractive to the people of Mexico and the citizens of other nations in the Western Hemisphere. Rather than creating a government-run broadcasting system, Rockefeller relied on NBC and CBS, two privately funded commercial radio networks, to beam shortwave broadcasts of U.S. news and entertainment to foreign nationals. Dizard argued that this use of commercial radio to broadcast government information marked the internationalization of U.S. public diplomacy and the beginning of a global information revolution.[21]

When Monroe Price looked at the patterns of diffusion that sent these state messages across national boundaries, in *Media and Sovereignty: The Global Information Revolution and Its Challenges to State Power* (2002), he linked studies of information flows and imagery to a history of acquiescence by the U.S. state in periods when new media for information distribution transcended established boundaries of state control. Looking specifically at international broadcasting, Price called for more in-depth study of the U.S. government's exploitation of genres, technologies, and messages: "We urgently need a far-reaching discussion about the relationship between state and imagery. We need to stop denying that such relationships exist."[22]

Conversations about the state and imagery in U.S. history center naturally in the American West. The federal government exploited no artistic genre more than the Western. As Franklin Roosevelt implemented his approach to public diplomacy, he took advantage of Westerns in every cultural form to convey information in the public interest. The president benefited from high-tech advancements in microphones, amplifiers, and loudspeakers that revolutionized the sound recording, motion picture, radio broadcasting, and live-performance industries. He profited from the support of Gene Autry, who emerged in parallel fashion as a personality larger than life—"America's Favorite Cowboy"—delivering the presidential dope through Western entertainment, providing intelligence in multiple information media, and earning the top spot among Hollywood's cowboy heroes for six consecutive seasons (1937–42).

## Public History

*New Deal Cowboy: Gene Autry and Public Diplomacy* demonstrates Gene Autry's participation in President Roosevelt's public diplomacy, using a broad range of primary sources culled from a survey of more than 15,000 records, including archives and collections of ephemera, photography, published music, sound recordings, radio broadcasts, motion pictures, rodeo sports, Western art, and artifacts, all housed at the Autry National Center of the American West in Los Angeles. The idea of Autry's association with FDR first emerged from research related to the production of *Gene Autry and the Twentieth Century West: The Centennial Exhibition, 1907–2007*. As the historian and curator of the Gene Autry centennial, I first needed to make sense of the relationship of the singing cowboy to public diplomacy. That effort began with a presentation titled "South of the Border: Gene Autry and U.S. Foreign Policy," delivered in 2006 to the Westerns and the West group at the joint conference of the American Culture Association and Popular Culture Association (ACA/PCA). Publication of "Mr. Autry Goes to Washington: The Cowboy and the New Deal" in *Convergence* magazine further developed my ideas about singing cowboy diplomacy. I developed the "New Deal Cowboy" concept at the ACA/PCA in 2010 and offered a presentation titled "A Pioneer of Multiplatform Entertainment: Gene Autry and Transmedia Storytelling" at the 2011 conference.[23]

The history museum exhibition *Gene Autry and the Twentieth Century West* established the social relevance of the singing cowboy as a major producer of Western art, entertainment, and recreation and Autry's significance as a pioneer in the sound recording, motion picture, broadcasting, and live-performance industries. In its service to the public through the museum medium, the curatorial scholarship used to produce the history museum exhibition differed from the methods of academic history in making different use of narrative, description, and analysis. The museum exhibition encompassed a much broader range of primary source materials than found in most academic histories. Considered within the chronology of Autry's career from 1932 to 1942, the wide-ranging primary sources produced an exhibition narrative derived mainly from new forms of electronic media. Sound recordings, including radio broadcast transcriptions, and motion picture productions provided more content and a broader interpretation than printed materials alone could yield.[24]

Combining art and artifacts, costumes, photography, and audiovisual assets with traditional archival resources, the method of storyboarding used to develop the history museum exhibition involved layering multiplatform entertainments with related content. The storyboard also highlighted the emergence of new forms of hybrid entertainment: country-Western music, for example, and musical-Western films. Compared to academic treatments such as Holly George-Warren's *Public Cowboy No. 1: The Life and Times of Gene Autry* (2007), the history museum exhibition offered an alternative form better equipped to present the historical artifacts of the twentieth century preserved in electronic media. The ability of "readers" to screen historical film clips, listen to period sound recordings, and hear radio broadcast transcriptions demonstrated the superiority of the history museum exhibition over the printed descriptions of live action, sound recordings, motion pictures, and radio transcriptions.

As a form of visual art, the history museum exhibition measured the differences between our own age and those of the Great Depression and World War II generations. Highlighting distinctions between then and now, the public display created historical awareness while emphasizing differences in the material conditions of American life in the 1930s and '40s. To forestall anachronism, the curatorial messaging of the interpretive displays referenced distinctions in mentality to explain how the values, priorities, fears, and hopes of an earlier generation differed from our own.[25]

History museum curatorship underscored the importance of context in history, borrowing from E. P. Thompson a method of organizing the past into a series of historical episodes. Using examples from each of the mass media mastered by the singing cowboy, the Gene Autry centennial represented cultural products in both their physical context and within a wider social context that mirrored the folk culture of rural, small-town, and newly urban Americans as their values converged into the cultural mainstream during the Roosevelt presidency. As the president's initiatives shifted from the domestic concerns of the New Deal to the security concerns of the Good Neighbor Policy and the needs of war preparedness, Autry's multiplatform entertainments reflected Roosevelt's change in governance.

Autry conveyed information in the public interest that gave meaning to these changing circumstances for tens of millions of fans at home and abroad.[26]

Borrowing from these methods of history museum exhibition, the chapters in *New Deal Cowboy: Gene Autry and Public Diplomacy* are organized into eight episodes that connect Autry's cultural products with Roosevelt's public diplomacy across multiple information media. Chapter 1 explores how country-western music became hybridized as national radio networks grew in the 1930s. Gene Autry's hybrid form of country-western music served the needs of dispossessed people struggling to resist or reshape the flows of mass media that continuously pummeled their cultural heritage. Popular with rural, small-town, and newly urban radio listeners, country-western music offered national advertisers and politicians a means to appeal to large and underserved audiences in the Midwest, South, and Southwest.

Chapter 2 looks at the hybridization of musical-Western film from the standpoint of Herbert Yates, head of Republic Pictures, who employed the singing cowboy in a strategy to control the means of transcultural consumption experienced by Gene Autry fans. As a film producer and distributor, Yates used Republic Pictures to create musical-Western star vehicles to promote the country-western recording artists whom he signed to the American Record Company. Republic's musical-Westerns offered a contemporary glimpse into the lives of rural, small-town, and newly urban Americans.

Chapter 3 probes the ways in which Gene Autry delivered New Deal messaging by incorporating country-western music into musical-Western films. Communication through Autry's multiplatform entertainments represented some of the earliest and most advanced forms of soft-power public diplomacy. Republic developed its Gene Autry series to include twenty-seven films with New Deal themes.

Chapter 4 brings into play the notion of Gene Autry as a symbol of a modern, postindustrial New West, a concept consistent with the work of scholars who pegged the emergence of this environment to the New Deal. As a westerner with ties to Texas, Oklahoma, and California, the singing cowboy recognized the New Deal as a progenitor of a new western culture, a culture different from and superimposed upon the landscape of the ancient west and Old West. Autry's New Deal filmography showcased stories promoting travel and tourism through performance of Western music, western dude ranch locations, annual rodeo spectacles, and touring Wild West shows.

Chapter 5 deals with the films in the Gene Autry series made by Republic Pictures to promote Americanism, war preparedness, and friendly relations with Latin America at a time when most of Autry's audience favored isolation. The Good Neighbor films in the Gene Autry series provided an introduction to Mexican culture for many moviegoers. American values put forth through Republic's musical-Western formula and the inclusion of ethnic Mexicans in studio productions made Autry's brand of Americanization palatable for Mexican American moviegoers while also meeting the expectations of increasingly larger and more mainstream national and international audiences. As an advocate for the Roosevelt presidency, Gene Autry symbolized heroism and character, offering hope for the millions of people who survived the hardships of the Great Depression only to face the prospects of global war.

Chapter 6 delves into the song "South of the Border, Down Mexico Way," to examine the power of music in Autry's live performances and the singing cowboy's ability to appeal to Spanish-speaking audiences as a part of Roosevelt's Good Neighbor strategy, engaging new audiences along the U.S.-Mexico border. The public diplomacy projected through Gene Autry productions demonstrated the innovative redefinition of the role played by the U.S. government in formulating a policy of international cultural activity. The focus of Autry's Good Neighbor pictures on U.S. relations with Mexico illustrated the importance of border security issues for the Roosevelt administration and the singing cowboy's ability to reach cross-cultural audiences. Herbert Eugene Bolton's idea of a common heritage throughout the Americas found a simple and direct expression in the historical figures of the cowboy, vaquero, and gaucho upon which Autry's musical-Western form drew. Autry's British tour cemented the singing cowboy's international standing. The image of an American cowboy singing a song of Mexico to audiences in Ireland while millions of British and American citizens, on the verge of global war, listened on the BBC presented a powerful symbol of harmony and unity for people on three continents.

Chapter 7 studies how radio broadcasting transformed Autry from the New Deal Cowboy of 1936 into "Youth's Model, 1940." Symbolizing Americanism, war preparedness, and hemispheric cooperation as aspects of the American Way, Autry created new forms of synergy in the Western genre to reflect the changes taking place in the American cultural and media industries. The singing cowboy's inclusion on the Hollywood A-list provides one such reflection. His gold-record sales offer another. Sold-out stadium shows with the World's Championship Rodeo provide a third mirror. Music supplied the source of synergy between motion pictures and radio broadcasting.

Chapter 8 features the song "Melody Ranch" to analyze Autry's associations with radio broadcasting within a context of war preparedness, culminating with the transformation of *Gene Autry's Melody Ranch* into the *Sergeant Gene Autry* program in 1942. As the commander-in-chief's main concerns shifted from the New Deal to the Good Neighbor policy and war preparedness, Autry's cultural products—music, sound recordings, motion pictures, live performances, radio broadcasts, and licensed merchandise—mirrored Roosevelt's move from isolationism to internationalism.

Examining Autry's oeuvre within a context created by Roosevelt administration policies, *New Deal Cowboy* reveals a process of public diplomacy at work in American media culture from 1932 to 1942. To get at the substance of public diplomacy in Autry's legacy, I used the following questions to frame the research: What information did Gene Autry productions present and how did this information relate to presidential politics? How were the singing cowboy's cultural products similar to and different from one another in terms of their ideological operations? As President Roosevelt's priorities changed over time, how did Autry's productions reflect these changes? How did audiences respond to the mixing of public information into Gene Autry productions? What values did Autry endorse?

CHAPTER 1

# Country-Western Hybrid Music

Gene Autry's reputation as a lowbrow entertainer dates back to the beginning of his career as a singer-songwriter. Autry got his start in 1929, recording knockoffs of Jimmie Rodgers's blue yodels to sell at discount prices through mail-order catalogs and other low-cost retailers. He moonlighted while working as a telegrapher for the St. Louis and San Francisco Railroad (the Frisco line). Making good money from the sale of records like "Hobo Yodel" (1930) and "A Yodeling Hobo" (1931), Autry promoted himself as "The Sunny South's Blue Yodeler." Working alone or in tandem with Jimmy Long, the two railroad men–turned–singer-songwriters modeled their performances after "The Singing Brakeman." Beside Rodgers and Long, Autry's other musical influences included Vernon Dalhart and Gene Austin.[1]

Autry and Long scored their first big hit for the American Record Corporation (ARC). Recorded on October 29, 1931, "That Silver Haired Daddy of Mine" charted as Autry's 142nd recording. Art Satherley produced "That Silver Haired Daddy of Mine," putting "Mississippi Valley Blues" on the flipside. ARC's head of artists and repertoire (A&R), Satherley marketed the song nationally using twelve different record labels and collecting half of the music royalties for each record sold. Autry and Long split the remainder, each of them earning 25 percent. Similarly, Satherley and Autry split the royalties 50–50 for two big-selling Victor recordings, "Jailhouse Blues" and "I'm Atlanta Bound," recorded a few days later. In quick succession, the trio scored two more hits: "I'm Always Dreaming of You," recorded by Victor, and "The Crime I Didn't Do," an ARC recording. As before, Satherley, Long, and Autry split the royalties for these songs 50–25–25.[2]

Stylistically and artistically, "That Silver Haired Daddy of Mine" marked a turning point in the career of young Autry. Satherley convinced the singer-songwriter to stop imitating Jimmie Rodgers's blue yodel sound and embrace the trendy old-time music favored by Jimmy Long, his boss on the Frisco Line and musical mentor. Satherley also persuaded the blue yodeler to capitalize on his Texas and Oklahoma roots by developing a singing cowboy persona, thereby launching Autry's career from Tulsa, Oklahoma, to Chicago, Illinois, and Los Angeles, California.[3]

Following a trajectory from song to live performance, sheet music, sound recording, radio broadcast, and gold record, the success of "That Silver Haired Daddy of Mine" made the singing cowboy's segue into the role of movie star appear natural. Riding a sea change in American music, Autry moved from performing in Tulsa as "The Sunny South's Blue Yodeler" to becoming "The Oklahoma Yodeling Cowboy" in Chicago and then "The Original Singing Cowboy" in Hollywood. Autry's musical-Westerns offer a glimpse into the lives of rural, small-town, and newly urban Americans in the 1930s as people dealing with the cultural transformations accompanying significant transportation improvements, communications revolutions, and steadily increasing mobility. The singing cowboy joined a group of avant-garde musicians, writers, and filmmakers doing innovative, experimental, and unconventional work, presenting new hybrid forms of "country-western" music *within* new hybrid forms of "musical-Western" films.[4]

Explanations for the hybridization of musical and motion picture genres have argued that the economic decline of 1929 influenced record companies and film studios to mash up their formulas, beginning with the combination of "country" and "Western" music. The country label included various subgenres such as "old time," "hillbilly," and "mountain" music. Western music was comprised mainly of cowboy songs compiled by John A. Lomax in *Cowboy Songs and Other Frontier Ballads* (1910)—songs like "Jesse James," "The Old Chisholm Trail," and "Whoopie Ti Yi Yo, Git Along Little Dogies."[5]

Since 1930, country-western music has grown into an important facet of the entertainment industry. Financial success led to increased status and respect for the hybrid genre, known today as country music among the popular arts of the United States. The history of country-western music and American attitudes toward the genre reflected contradictions in a growing audience segment labeled "urban hillbilly." Urban hillbillies dealt with the polarization of living between two cultures: the old world of their parents back home on the farm and the new world of their peers in the growing cities of the American South and West. Appeasement between town and country necessitated an accommodation of values expressed, in part, through the hybridization of county-Western music and the identification of a fan base comprised of urban hillbillies.[6]

In *Convergence Culture: Where Old and New Mediums Collide* (2006), Henry Jenkins showed that hybridity occurs when one cultural industry—for example, that of motion pictures—absorbed and transformed elements from other cultural mediums. As Jenkins explained, "A hybrid work exists betwixt and between two cultural traditions while providing a path that can be explored from both directions." *Convergence Culture* framed hybridity as a strategy of dispossessed peoples struggling to resist or reshape the flow of mass media into their culture—taking electronic media imposed from the outside and making those media serve the purposes of the dispossessed. Autry's singing cowboy persona met the conditions of this definition for many rural, small-town, and newly urban Americans.[7]

Jenkins also described hybridity as a corporate strategy that came from a position of strength rather than vulnerability or marginality, a strategy seeking control rather than containment of transcultural consumption. Here too, Autry met the conditions of hybridity as a multiplatform entertainer able to mash up the desires of both rural and urban audiences. Blending traditional and modern culture within a single corporate strategy, Autry took advantage of hybridity to create synergy by combining multiple information media. In this regard, Herbert J. Yates had the greatest influence over the singing cowboy. As head of Consolidated Film Industries, ARC Records and Republic Pictures, Yates shaped Autry's image as a recording artist and movie star into a transformative Western hero within a pantheon of Western heroes that included Daniel Boone, Davy Crockett, "Buffalo Bill" Cody, William S. Hart, and Tom Mix, to name but a few of the classic characters representing American culture in the media history of the United States.[8]

The mash up of country and Western music occurred simultaneously with news from national outlets revealing extreme poverty in the southern states. Franklin Roosevelt referred to Appalachia as a particularly depressed region. Americans increasingly perceived the Appalachian Mountains as a cultural site of backwardness and degradation. In response, musicians and their fans across the country turned away from urban hillbilly and embraced the classic image of the American cowboy hero, represented in motion pictures, popular fiction, Wild West shows, and rodeos. Roosevelt tapped into this sea change in American culture by announcing his favorite song was "Home on the Range." As the 1930s unfolded, hillbilly singers still sang about cabins in the mountains, now the Rocky Mountains, instead of the Cumberland Mountains. The Kentucky Ramblers became The Prairie Ramblers, backed up by Patsy Montana, and so on.[9]

Meanwhile, a new music scene surfaced in Los Angeles, held together by the movie studios producing musical-Western films. Among the singing cowboys already in Hollywood, The Beverly Hillbillies emerged as progenitors of a new sound and style of musical performance. Combining the attributes of hillbilly music with Western folksongs and cowboy trappings, The Beverly Hillbillies premiered on Los Angeles Radio Station KMPC, showcasing a new country-western format with live radio play in 1930.[10]

Seeing the sales numbers of "That Silver Haired Daddy of Mine," Herbert Yates backed the play of Art Satherley to sign Gene Autry to a long-term contract with ARC Records. They recast the yodeling bluesman as a singing cowboy with hillbilly chops. Sears, Roebuck and Company collaborated with ARC to create a line of signature merchandise featuring the "Gene Autry" name and image. Satherley made a deal with Sears to sponsor personal appearances by the Oklahoma Yodeling Cowboy on Chicago Radio Station WLS. Autry hosted *Conqueror Record Time* to promote record sales for Sears, making special guest appearances on Sears' *Tower Topics* and the *WLS Barn Dance* programs. In May 1932, when the National Broadcasting Corporation (NBC) syndicated the *WLS Barn Dance*, Autry expanded his fan base from coast to coast, making special guest appearances on the syndicated *National Barn Dance*.[11]

Moreover, Sears sponsored Radio's Singing Cowboy to appear live, in person, on concert tours with the *Round-Up of WLS Radio Stars*. The traveling troupe did live shows from remote broadcasting locations in rural, small-town, and newly urban theaters throughout the upper Midwest. Theater owners combined these localized "barn dance" programs with double features of Westerns and musical-Western films featuring Ken Maynard and other Hollywood stars. The combined effects of these live performances, radio broadcasts, motion pictures, sound recordings, and advertising provided local exhibitors with a draw powerful enough to attract a crowd during the Depression years.[12]

The licensed merchandise developed by Sears using Autry's name and image included sound recordings, sheet music, songbooks, and two guitars bearing the singing cowboy's signature. The Harmony Guitar Company made "Gene Autry Round Up" guitars and "Gene Autry Old Santa Fe" guitars for Sears. The giant retailer tied "Gene Autry" advertisements in its mail-order catalogs with Autry's personal appearances on WLS. "Gene Autry" merchandise targeted newly urban audiences of young women recently relocated from the countryside to Chicago and other Midwestern cities. Within this target market, "That Silver Haired Daddy of Mine" maintained enormous fan appeal from 1931–35. Autry's signature song served as a form of wheat paste, bonding the singing cowboy's live performances, sound recordings, radio broadcasts, motion pictures and licensed merchandise, with a large and growing fan base across multiple entertainment platforms.[13]

The growth of radio broadcasting as a new information medium stands out as the greatest influence upon the hybridization of country-western music and musical-Western films. A U.S. census map titled

"Radio Set Ownership 1930" revealed a cultural shift occurring as Autry became a star. Displaying the percentages of American families owning radio receiving sets, the map showed concentrations of listeners in and around New York, Chicago, Detroit, and Los Angeles, where more than 50 percent of households listened to radio broadcasts. The map also revealed the existence of fewer radio receiving sets in the Southern and Southwestern states. Less than 20 percent of households in these regions had access to local or national broadcasting.[14]

Limited access to electricity meant fewer radio stations and less competition for Sears in selling phonographs, sound recordings, and related merchandise in the South and Southwest. The number of households with radio receiving sets in many rural communities remained static until President Roosevelt created the Rural Electrification Administration to make low-interest loans to local electrical cooperatives in 1935. These underserved regions saw dramatic change in 1936, when the Tennessee Valley Authority (TVA), Boulder Canyon Project (Boulder/Hoover Dam), and other federal hydro projects began producing electricity. It was the late 1930s before rural cooperatives could build and operate new power lines throughout much of the South and Southwest. Many areas did not see service until after the Second World War.[15]

New Dealers promoted the American West as a destination for commercial agricultural and industrial development. Simultaneously with the development of water and power resources, the federal government literally paved the way for the expansion of travel and tourism along U.S. Highway Route 66—from Chicago to L.A.—and other highway construction projects. Improved roads, roadside attractions, and new accommodations were part of a New Deal plan to promote recreational tourism as an antidote for social divisions in American culture. The president believed that travel and tourism could temper revolutionary tendencies, right-wing reactionaries, and foreign aggression.[16]

Regarding tourism as a key component for economic recovery, Roosevelt funded national advertising campaigns to stimulate cross-country travel, and he supported local efforts of business and civic leaders to promote tourism. The themes and storylines in country-western music and musical-Western films provided incentives for

American worker-tourists with newly awarded two-week paid vacations to travel and take advantage of tourist promotions in the American West.

The hybridization of country-western music came about as national radio networks grew in the 1930s. Popular with rural, small-town, and newly urban radio listeners, country-western music offered national advertisers and politicians a means to access large and underserved audiences in the Midwest, South, and Southwest. When Republic Pictures began producing musical-Western films, the studio cross-promoted these cultural products with radio broadcasts, sound recordings, and live performances.[17]

Art Satherley understood these trends when he signed Gene Autry to a long-term contract. Satherley persuaded Autry to get out front of major changes affecting the recording industry by adding some Western flare to his yodeling blues. Two weeks after Autry recorded "That Silver Haired Daddy of Mine," the record producer arranged for the singing cowboy to premiere his new song and image before investors and advertisers in Manhattan. Dressed from head to toe in an outfit sold by Sears, the Oklahoma Yodeling Cowboy sang "That Silver Haired Daddy of Mine" before a studio audience at New York Radio Station WPCH during a live broadcast at 4:45 P.M. on Friday, November 13, 1931.[18]

Autry's new singing cowboy persona enabled Satherley to position the talented recording artist to ride a shifting tide in American media culture associated with the westernizing of hillbilly music and government promotions of western tourism and travel. The trend started in 1930, when radio programmer Glen Rice masked the hillbilly roots of one musical group with a veneer of cowboy culture. Broadcasting from Los Angeles Radio Station KMPC, Rice claimed to discover the musicians wandering in the Santa Monica Mountains, above Malibu, California. Dubbed The Beverly Hillbillies, the group used hillbilly terminology and mountain imagery, but they dressed similar to cowboys and performed songs like "When the Bloom is on the Sage," "Red River Valley," and "The Strawberry Roan." This fusion of hillbilly and cowboy styles gained notice with the rise of "Western Swing" music in Texas and elsewhere. Los Angeles grew in importance as a hotbed for musicians and radio programmers. Both Decca and Okeh paid more attention to the Southwest as they moved from recording hillbilly to country-western music.[19]

The instant popularity of The Beverly Hillbillies convinced Art Satherley to promote the broader fusion of country-western music at ARC. Combining the regional musical styles of the South and the Southwest to create a musical hybrid form, Satherley transformed Gene Autry from the Sunny South's Blue Yodeler into the Oklahoma Yodeling Cowboy. Subsequently, the A&R man used the Autry prototype to sign and record some of the biggest names in country-western music, including Bob Wills & His Texas Playboys, the Carter Family, Roy Acuff, the Sons of the Pioneers, Bill Monroe, Lefty Frizzell, and Marty Robbins.[20]

Responding to the lure of the new, country-western format, Autry signed an exclusive contract with ARC on December 1, 1931. He agreed to migrate from Tulsa to Chicago and reinvent himself as the Oklahoma Yodeling Cowboy. Satherley paid the singing cowboy a stipend of $90 a month, plus music royalties, to record high-volume, low-markup songs for ARC to sell in rural, small-town, and newly urban markets. "That Silver Haired Daddy of Mine" fit the bill as a nostalgic song, evoking tensions between the road and the old home place. Nostalgic for many rural and small-town fans, Autry's hit song simultaneously guided newly urban audiences coming to terms with the rapid lifestyle changes brought on by industrialization and the traumas of dislocation, disenfranchisement, and dispossession.[21]

Singing, "I'd give all I own, if I could but atone. . . . ," Autry expressed the lament felt by many young people who identified with urban hillbilly music. "That Silver Haired Daddy of Mine" represented the changes coming about as one means to rid Southern vernacular music of its pejorative and negative connotations. Autry conveyed respectability through his singing cowboy persona that enabled white southerners to develop a new sense of identity and opportunity associated with the American West. Peter Stanfield explained:

> The history of the singing cowboy is intimately tied up in this process of making Country music respectable and therefore

marketable. It was the image and mythology of the cowboy that provided the most accessible means of repressing the vulgarity of Southern vernacular music, while simultaneously suggesting a classless and uncontroversial image of white supremacy.[22]

A majority of white Americans with rural roots found hillbilly and mountain music attractive counterpoints to urban jazz and blues. The market share for hillbilly and mountain music accounted for 25 percent of the 65 million records sold in the United States in 1929. Record executives and journalists viewed rural white southern folk music as an outgrowth of the same rural culture that produced the blues and jazz. Record company catalogs often listed white and black rural musical selections in separate categories on facing pages, despite attempts by white musicians to distinguish their music as separate from that of black performers. When Sears adopted the "hillbilly" tag to sell records in its mail-order catalogs in 1929, Montgomery Ward followed suit a year later.[23]

Jazz music, dance crazes, and popular songs disappeared after the stock market crash on October 24, 1929. Record sales plummeted, hitting bottom in 1933 when only $5 million worth of discs were purchased nationwide. New "old time" records produced during the Depression combined with free radio play to target a subculture of performers and listeners who enjoyed rural white southern folk music throughout the Midwest, South, and Southwest. Displaced Americans and others feeling psychologically adrift enjoyed country-western songs of independence, romance, and nostalgia. Fans of country-western music preferred songs dealing with the economic issues of everyday life to the sugarcoated popular music of the day.[24]

As the Depression took hold, manufacturers and retailers increasingly employed old-time musicians to reach rural, small-town, and newly urban audiences. Henry Ford pioneered the sponsorship of fiddle contests at his dealerships. Ford promoted fiddle tunes as wholesome family fun—an alternative to the "loose morals" of jazz and the themes of sex and violence in blues music. Early recordings of rural, southern white vernacular music displayed an obsession with community and regional identity, reflected in songs about places and the values of faith and family, represented so distinctly in the music of the Carter Family.[25]

Simultaneously, the dark days of the Great Depression revealed some alternative themes reflecting the restlessness and rootlessness in American culture in songs about drifters and hoboes by Jimmie Rodgers, Goebel Reeves, and others. As the Depression wore on, the singing cowboy came to represent the tension between home and the road that agonized rural, small-town and newly urban audiences, best reflected in the title of the popular song "Home on the Range." The possibility for broad appeal attracted commercial advertisers, radio broadcasters, and record producers, especially ARC Records.[26]

ARC controlled at least thirty music labels, having merged the Cameo Record Corporation, Pathé Phonograph and Radio Corporation, Plaza Music Company, and Scranton Button Company (Emerson Records). As Autry signed on in December 1931, ARC added Brunswick and Vocalion to its catalog, leasing the labels from Warner Brothers. Controlling so many labels, ARC Records pursued high volume, low markup strategies to sell music to rural, small-town, and newly urban record buyers. The approach worked in 1932. ARC sold six million units, twice the volume of RCA Victor, the recording industry leader. ARC sold Brunswick and Columbia records for a premium at 75¢, while discounting the Melotone, Vocalion, Banner, and Perfect labels, selling these brands for 35¢, or three for one dollar. Moreover, the record company produced exclusive labels for national—"five and dime"—retail department store companies. ARC made Oriole Records for J. G. McCrory's and the McCrory Stores; Romeo Records sold by the Kress Stores; and Conqueror Records for Sears.[27]

Satherley released "That Silver Haired Daddy of Mine" on twelve different ARC labels, including Okeh, Vocalion, Perfect, Banner, Oriole, Romeo, Conqueror, Broadway, Crown (Canada), Melotone (Canada), Royale, and Sterling. The A&R man made a special deal with Jeff Shay, the record buyer for Sears. Shay took advantage of Sears' history of developing up-and-coming musicians since 1923, when he agreed to promote "That Silver Haired Daddy of Mine" and other Autry recordings through the giant mail-order enterprise.[28]

The rural retailer created an alternative to the commercial radio model, established by American Telephone & Telegraph (AT&T) at New York Radio Station WEAF in 1922. Funding Chicago Radio Station WLS through a nonprofit, Sears-Roebuck Agricultural Foundation, with call letters signifying "World's Largest Store," Sears kept advertising off the WLS airwaves by promoting WLS and WLS-brand products through its catalogs, newspaper advertisements, and store displays. Instead of using the radio station to promote products, Sears used its product catalog to promote WLS. Associating the WLS logo with high-quality popular programming, the mail-order company sold a wide variety of products, especially its best-selling "Silvertone" brand of radio receiving sets, antennas, headphones, loudspeakers, battery chargers, and power units.[29]

This was the world that Autry entered when he landed in Chicago in December 1931. Schooled in Sears' enterprising approaches to using WLS as an effective public relations tool to boost the sales of mail-order products, Autry saw how the giant retailer staffed its Radio and Electronic Goods Department with buyers who provided both goods and information to consumers. The Sears-Roebuck Agricultural Foundation employed people to produce radio programs, serve as on-air talent, and cater to public relations needs. Rural, small-town, and newly urban audiences really benefited from the Sears broadcasting model. "The farmer was truly one of radio's favorite children," claimed James Evans in *Prairie Farmer and WLS* (1969). "No one talked much about radio programs for accountants or carpenters, but the value of radio for the farmer was clear from the beginning."[30]

Recognizing that radio receivers were of little use to customers without radio programs and noting the popularity of old time music among rural and small-town audiences, Sears launched the *WLS Barn Dance* as a regular Saturday night feature in 1924. Broadcasting from a 100-seat theater, Sears made fans part of the live radio broadcasts. The giant retailer also created a traveling troubadour version of the hugely popular program, billed as the *Round-Up of WLS Radio Stars*. The *WLS Round-Up* played state and country fairs and community theaters throughout the upper Midwest.[31]

The Oklahoma Yodeling Cowboy, 1934. © Autry Qualified Interest Trust and The Autry Foundation (T87_36-260-1).

*Round-Up of WLS Radio Stars*, 1934. © Autry Qualified Interest Trust and The Autry Foundation (BIO_055).

"WLS Roundup: Gene Autry / Also Vaudeville," 1934. © Autry Qualified Interest Trust and The Autry Foundation (MARQUEE-BK).

Gene Autry receiving first gold record from Art Satherley and Herbert Yates, 1935. © Autry Qualified Interest Trust and The Autry Foundation (BIO_108).

WLS radio announcers engaged listeners to find out what fans liked and disliked about specific shows. Radio audiences gladly cooperated, sending thousands of telegrams asking programmers to play favorite songs and read messages over the air. Once the novelty wore off, letters replaced telegrams as the dominant form of fan communication. In 1927, WLS received nearly 200,000 letters from listeners all over the country and faraway places like Puerto Rico, New Zealand, Manila, England, and Hawaii. "Letters were in large degree a measure of a station's popularity," explained Edward Condon. The Sears executive noted, "No station of similar size received as many letters as WLS, and no station received the same quality of mail." By 1928, the enormously popular *WLS Barn Dance* commanded an incredible 59 percent of the market share among radio listeners in the upper Midwest.[32]

Modeling the success of WLS, the Sears-Roebuck Agricultural Foundation developed new programs for other radio stations in Dallas (WFAA), Atlanta (WSB), Memphis (WMC), and Kansas City (KMBC). Sears promoted its catalog and merchandise distribution centers in these metropolitan areas by sponsoring news and entertainment programming. Sears replicated its WLS achievements by promoting a barn dance radio format, which was in large part responsible for the advent of country-western music in each new radio market, developing new audiences and a circuit for musicians to play in the South and Southwest. The expansion of Sears into regional radio markets prompted competing stations to create barn dance programs in New York, Louisville, Cincinnati, Wheeling, Nashville, Saint Paul, Des Moines, Shreveport, Tulsa, Fort Worth, and Hollywood.[33]

By 1930, the barn dance format was hugely popular on radio stations from coast to coast. The growing number of radio stations playing barn dance music created a boon for Autry and other musicians performing in the new country-western style. Radio programmers needed local talent to air live performances. Adding radio work to a schedule of recording sessions and play dates enabled Autry to stay employed full-time. Regular radio performances helped the musician secure local concert bookings. Autry landed lucrative show dates, primarily because of his popularity on the radio. Radio exposure helped the singing cowboy cross-promote his upcoming personal appearances and stay in the public limelight.[34]

Autry got his big break when Jeff Shay booked him to perform on *Tower Topics*, a WLS morning program sponsored by Sears every weekday at 9:30 A.M. Anne Williams introduced "The Oklahoma Yodeler" during a special *Conqueror Record Time* segment, sponsored by Herbert Yates's American Record Corporation. Williams provided a big buildup to capture the imagination of Midwestern listeners who wondered about the singing cowboy's persona. Autry sang "That Silver Haired Daddy of Mine," "The Crime I Didn't Do," and other popular hits, while promoting record and sheet music sales and special mail order offers. He booked the $90 a month received from ARC as "Radio Station Salaries WLS." Regular work as a radio performer enabled Autry to join the Chicago Musicians Union in 1932. The singing cowboy paid a $100 initiation fee and quarterly dues of $4.[35]

Targeting the responses of Conqueror Record buyers, Shay developed a one-page catalog insert offering twenty Gene Autry recordings for only 21 cents per song, or five records for one dollar. Designed as a self-mailer, Shay's insert pitched: "Gene Autry, Famous 'WLS' Radio Star and Yodeler has made it possible for you to hear him whenever you wish." Customers returned the mailer to Sears with cash enclosed. Sears paid the postage for delivery orders of two dollars or more, encouraging customers to buy in bulk. Special instructions for rural route customers suggest the identity of the market targeted for this promotion.[36]

About the time Autry began working at WLS, the station installed a 50,000-watt clear-channel transmitter. Clear-channel capability enabled the radio station to reach large audiences in a six-state region surrounding Chicago that included about 10 percent of the total population of the United States. As an ever-larger fan base began to hear "That Silver Haired Daddy of Mine" and other Autry hits, the singing cowboy started to book tours with Joseph Lee Frank, also known as J. L. Frank or Joe Frank. A big promoter in the music business, J. L. Frank booked acts for WLS and dozens of other play dates for the WLS Round-Up of Radio Stars in theaters across the upper Midwest.[37]

Autry's personal balance sheet for January 1932 showed a gross monthly profit of $635, the equivalent of $11,029 in 2015 dollars, using the Consumer Price Index method of conversion. Fifty-four percent of Autry's income came from record company royalty payments, totaling $345 in the fourth quarter of 1931. He earned another $150 in radio salaries from WJJD, plus the $90 from ARC for his *Conqueror Record Time* performances. The Gayble Theater in North Judson, Indiana, provided Autry's only paying theater gig that month. Autry earned $50 for one show, and he paid Dave Kapp a booking agent commission of 15 percent. He expensed other booking agent and advertising agent commissions that month, along with advertising photographs, car expenses, and two pairs of custom-made cowboy boots. Autry's net profit for the month equaled $460, about $7,989 in 2015 dollars.[38]

Sears and ARC shaped Gene Autry, the Oklahoma Yodeler, into a benign, respectable, and modern spokesperson. The retailer and the record company cast the singing cowboy in a role eminently suitable for product endorsements, targeting newly urban female consumers with sentimental attachments to rural and small-town lifestyles. The mail-order company propelled Autry's rising star toward celebrity on February 1, 1932, when radio programmers gave the singer-songwriter, radio pitchman, and traveling troubadour his own ten-minute segment leading into the popular *Tower Topics* program on WLS. Sears promoted the singing cowboy by marketing a new "Gene Autry Round Up Guitar" for $9.95 in its mail-order catalogs. The retailer packaged the Gene Autry Round Up Guitar with a folio from music publisher M. M. Cole titled *Gene Autry's Sensational Collection of Famous Original Cowboy Songs and Mountain Ballads*. The retailer's second book using Gene Autry's name was titled *The Art of Writing Songs and How to Play the Guitar*.[39]

Offering the "Gene Autry" brand as a new and permanent presence in the lives of millions of rural, small-town, and newly urban music fans, Sears promoted a transitional cowboy hero capable of honoring nostalgic folkways while simultaneously representing a modern New West. Combining tradition and innovation, Autry helped many quasi-folk and lower-culture Americans deal with the changes brought on by deprivation, relocation, and marginalization during the Great Depression. Having turned to the West for his own reinvention, the singing cowboy encouraged his large and growing fan base to consider a similar option by crafting a new and more acceptable identity in tune with mainstream American culture during the New Deal.

Public opinion polling and electronic recording devices enabled radio advertisers to refine listening habits and listener preferences, taking much of the guesswork out of measuring the mainstream in the 1930s. In Chicago and dozens of other cities, survey organizations conducted telephone-sampling studies and compiled monthly listener ratings. Large survey organizations made millions of listener calls each year. Radio stations also distributed millions of printed questionnaires. Pollsters assembled vast files of data showing when and how long listeners tuned into programs. New methods of information gathering revealed a mesh of tie-ups between individual radio stations and specific service areas. Radio advertisers learned to use product tie-ups as part of the entertainment programming for listeners segmented by race, class, gender, age, and other criteria.[40]

Powerful interests in the United States and other countries used mass persuasion to influence public opinion and social beliefs in the 1930s. Power brokers employed radio programming and advertising instead of intimidation and coercion. In response, critics raised concerns about the effects of radio broadcasting upon popular culture. They complained that radio deliberately catered to vulgar tastes and contributed to the deterioration and eventual surrender of the listener's critical faculties. As the awe-inspiring ubiquity of radio mesmerized tens of millions of listeners, researchers studied the radio medium's enormous power and the exercise of social control by the powerful interest groups that exploited broadcasting. As public relations and advertising firms increasingly refined their techniques to manipulate mass publics, broadcasters introduced subtler forms of psychological exploitation, achieved largely through the mass dissemination of information in the public interest.[41]

A classic example of this type of manipulation was documented during the presidential election campaign in full swing during the summer of 1932. As a presidential candidate, Franklin Delano Roosevelt described the wretched living conditions in the South, especially in Appalachia, as the nation's largest economic issue. Roosevelt drew upon the perceptions of the many Americans who viewed the Appalachian Mountains as home to a culture of backwardness and degradation. As the news unfolded, a derogatory "hillbilly" stereotype took center stage in the national news cycle. Rejection of the hillbilly label in 1932 was but one in a string of name changes brought about to rid Southern vernacular music of its pejorative and negative connotations. The negative image and growing disfavor among newly urban fans caused musicians to turn away from the hillbilly blues and embrace a country-western alternative. Record companies followed the example of ARC, hybridizing the more marketable cowboy music and requisite singing cowboy form. The broad appeal of Sears attracted other commercial advertisers, radio broadcasters, and product sponsors.[42]

Voters learned of Franklin Roosevelt's "New Deal" for the American public when the presidential candidate gave his acceptance speech in Chicago at the National Convention of the Democratic Party on July 2, 1932. Roosevelt's extraordinary appearance before the national convention established a historic precedent. Going to Chicago and accepting the nomination in person, FDR broke the American tradition of candidates awaiting formal notification of their nominations. Moreover, the candidate called attention to his break with tradition by flying from Albany to Chicago in a new Ford Tri-Motor airplane operated by American Airlines. Roosevelt's decision to fly demonstrated his physical courage, stamina, and a desperately needed spirit of urgency.[43]

The familiar story of Franklin Roosevelt's 1932 presidential election campaign emphasized the economic significance of radio broadcasting, including federal licensing, national networks, metropolitan and regional super stations, radio departments in large advertising agencies, electrical-transcription companies, and individual station representatives. Roosevelt knew that a system of national spot advertising fueled growth in the radio industry. Radio advertising appealed to the candidate because he could adapt the techniques to serve the needs of public policy. FDR understood the magical quality of radio that gave him simultaneous access to a constituency of forty million Americans—an amazingly large audience compared to other forms of political debate.[44]

Polls underscored the notion of audiences embracing radio advertising as the cost of free programming. Audience acceptance made it easier for radio advertisers to add information about products and sponsors to the content of shows. Pollsters determined that rural and urban audiences shared similar tastes in the early 1930s. Housewives, high school students, and families in small cities ranked among the largest radio audience segments.[45]

Roosevelt had a long history with radio and advertising that dated back to World War I and his service with the Committee on Public Information (CPI). Using the airwaves, the candidate shared information in the public interest with the same large and underserved audiences that Autry and other country-western musicians patronized. No national politician before Roosevelt had ever reached out to these quasi-folk and lower-culture constituencies in such a meaningful way. Radio broadcasting unquestionably enabled Roosevelt to reach these audiences and ultimately to contribute to the renunciation of the incumbent Republican President Herbert Hoover.[46]

As the president-elect prepared for his inauguration in March 1933, Gene Autry was in Chicago, living uptown with his extended family, building a career as a recording artist, radio celebrity, and marquee performer. "That Silver Haired Daddy of Mine" continued to sell like hotcakes; on its way to becoming a million-seller. Inspired by the president's leanings toward "Home on the Range," Sears tweaked its "Gene Autry" promotions, rebranding the Oklahoma Yodeler as the Oklahoma Yodeling Cowboy to increase sales for records, songbooks, sheet music, and guitars. This name change signaled the complete transformation of Gene Autry from hillbilly blues singer to singing cowboy persona in 1933. As a regular on NBC's *National Barn Dance*, the Oklahoma Yodeling Cowboy developed a nationally recognizable fan base in twenty-eight states.[47]

Adding to Autry's exposure on America's number-one country music show, Sears also sponsored him as a headliner with the *Round-Up of WLS Radio Stars*. Advertising the two-and-one-half-hour show with the tag line—"*Your* Radio Favorites-*In Person*-On *the* Stage"—this traveling troupe of veteran performers included Anne Williams, the Log Cabin Boys, Jimmy Long, Sue Roberts, Smiley Burnette, Patsy Montana, and many others. Sears sponsored the live remote broadcasts of the WLS Round-Up from locations in small-town cinemas. *Radio Digest* reported, "The traveling units were the answer to countless pleas by out-of-towners who cannot come to Chicago."[48]

Rural and small-town theater exhibitors booked Hollywood Westerns to show in combination with the *WLS Round-Up*. Ken Maynard's films for Universal Pictures worked particularly well. Films like *The Strawberry Roan* relied upon a musical-Western format to showcase country-western music. As a headliner and host for the *WLS Round-Up,* Autry modeled himself after Ken Maynard in part, developing a singing cowboy persona that appealed to concert-goers, radio listeners, and movie fans alike. Years later, Autry recalled: "Most people made their money doing personal appearances in those days. I played most of the theaters and some auditoriums and fairs. I played all through Wisconsin, all the way up to the upper peninsula of Michigan. And I played all down through Indiana, Illinois, all the way down to Cairo, as we used to call it, and over into Iowa. You could play about five or six states right out of Chicago, because WLS had that 50,000-watt clear channel."[49]

The "Gene Autry" cultural products developed by ARC, Sears, and WLS exemplified the changing advertising techniques used by radio broadcasters in the mid-1930s. ARC and Sears skillfully blended their product tie-ups to increase the entertainment value for WLS listeners. Listeners understood and appreciated the relationship between the advertising and programming. They demonstrated approval by joining fan clubs, accepting give-away premiums, and buying licensed merchandise. The C. F. Martin Guitar Company of Nazareth, Pennsylvania, for example, validated Autry's rising star power by adding a new model number—D-45—to its sales catalog, a mere four days after the singing cowboy placed a custom order through the Chicago Musical Instruments Company on March 23, 1933. Subsequently, the Martin D-45 became one of the most popular acoustic guitars ever made.[50]

In 1933, the *WLS Family Album* listed Autry as a singing cowboy and regular show performer. The program highlights mentioned the universal appeal of "That Silver Haired Daddy of Mine," suggesting, "No program with Gene Autry is quite complete until he sings it." Copyright royalty statements from ARC, Southern Music Publishing, and M. M. Cole Publishing revealed that Autry's income from music publishing more than tripled within a year, from $345 for the quarter ending December 31, 1931, to more than $1,260 for the last quarter of 1932.[51]

The enormous popularity of "That Silver Haired Daddy of Mine" was largely responsible for this windfall. ARC reported sales of 20,349 copies of the record on six different labels during the fall of 1932. M. M. Cole sold 5,370 copies of *Gene Autry's Sensational Collection of Famous Original Cowboy Songs and Mountain Ballads*, which featured the big hit. Cole paid the musicians a 3¢ royalty for the songbook, which Autry and Long split, 50–50. Publishing royalties from M. M. Cole added $93 to Autry's quarterly income. Moreover, he earned an average of $400 a month from play dates at various theaters. All totaled, the singing cowboy made more than $800 a month in 1932, about $13,895 per month in 2015 dollars.[52]

To complete the development of Autry's singing cowboy persona, ARC scheduled the singer-songwriter to make his first recording of Western folk songs on January 27, 1933. Autry's first cowboy recordings featured four songs that he wrote or co-wrote and one from the public domain. Gene sang all the voice and yodeling parts, providing his own guitar accompaniment. He recorded "Louisiana Moon" (Gene Autry), "The Little Ranch House on the Old Circle B" (Gene Autry—Volney Blanchard), "Cowboy's Heaven" (Frankie Marvin—Gene Autry), "Your Voice is Ringing" (Percy Wenrich—arranged by Gene Autry), and "The Yellow Rose of Texas" (public domain). After the session, the singer-songwriter gave up his radio gigs to concentrate on live play dates for a couple of months to get familiar with the new songs.[53]

On tour, the singing cowboy promoted and sold two new songbooks, *Rhymes of the Range* (1932) and *The Art of Writing Songs and How to Play the Guitar* (1932), published by Frontier Publishers of Evanston, Illinois. Financial statements showed that Frontier Publishers paid the singing cowboy $780 for services rendered and the use of his name and image to sell publications, about $13,547 in 2015 dollars. Frontier managed to get *The Art of Writing Songs* included in the Sears catalog with advertisements featuring "Gene Autry and His Famous Round Up Guitar." A balance sheet dated April 30, 1933, documented the sale of songbooks valued at $3,130 ($54,363 in 2015 dollars). Forty-eight radio stations in twenty-eight states recorded sales. Additional sales came from magazine advertisements in *Breeders Gazette, College Humor,* and *Real Detective.* The Lyon & Healy Guitar Company and Marquette Guitar Company also sold "Gene Autry" songbooks. The financial statements of Frontier Publishers showed that Autry's exposure on WLS reached a national audience by 1933. WLS accounted for nearly 90 percent of all the Frontier sales receipts.[54]

Recognition by newspapers, radio, magazines, and Chicago theater marquees testified to Autry's stardom in November 1933, about the time he scored another huge hit with a recording of "The Last Round-Up," which peaked at No. 12 on *The Billboard* pop chart. Important enough to be singled out from the large, anonymous masses, Autry's behavior and opinions received such increased public notice that an observation of Lazarsfeld and Merton seemed to hold true: "The audiences of mass media apparently subscribe to the circular belief: 'If you really matter, you will be at the focus of mass attention and, if you *are* at the focus of mass attention, then surely you must really matter.'"[55]

Most certainly, this was the conviction of Archie Levesque, an eighteen-year-old boy from Tunne, Maine, who wrote Autry on December 20, 1933. Levesque traded his German-style accordion for an old guitar that he rebuilt to play. He ordered new guitar strings and a copy of *Cowboy Songs and Mountain Ballads* from the Sears catalog. Archie taught himself to play using the songbook and listening to Autry's records on a Victrola. "I am not sending you this letter to boast about myself but merely trying to make you interested of a boy in Maine whom is enjoying the same work you have done. Your music interests me very much," the young man wrote.[56]

It is important to recognize how Sears supported the creation of "Gene Autry" cultural products and the distribution of the singing cowboy's art, entertainment, and merchandising brands. As Autry's radio and live performance sponsor, Sears determined the quality of the singing cowboy's programming content. As the giant retailer adjusted to the social and economic realities of the Great Depression, Autry maintained his position by aiding corporate advertising efforts through newsworthy appearances that received coverage in magazines and newspapers. He also did guest spots on various radio shows. Confirmation of approval from these additional information outlets verified audience acceptance of the messaging delivered by Sears' "Gene Autry" brands.[57]

It seems ironic that a lowdown singing cowboy persona enabled Autry to rise above his overt associations with American folk culture. Autry transcended his cultural origins by adding sophistication to his Western sound and dress. In the 1934 edition of the *WLS Family Album,* he sported a new Stetson and a fancy Western-style suit in a captioned photograph. A second photograph with the *National Barn Dance* cast showed the singing cowboy wearing a striking, movie-style outfit. WLS billed Autry as the Oklahoma Yodeling Cowboy, claiming authentic cowboy roots. The programming notes made it clear that the singer-songwriter's great success remained predicated on the continued strong sales of "That Silver Haired Daddy of Mine," still a big hit after three years on the charts.[58]

In 1934, *National Barn Dance* and other barn-dance programs fueled the biggest response from radio listeners in advertising history. *Variety* proclaimed: "The greatest box-office attraction in the smaller towns throughout the country. . . . The most loyal audience ever assembled. . . . The top attraction on some dozen of the major stations in the land. . . . A story without precedent in show business, in radio or in the advertising and commercial world." The *Motion Picture Herald* ran stories debating whether radio was a poacher or a provider of potential Western film audiences. The *Herald* published a letter from the advertising manager of the Kerasotes Theatre in Springfield, Illinois, expounding on the benefits of broadcasting live performances of barn-dance-style shows. The theater exhibitor explained: "This type of show is very popular in the Mid-West. We were able to run this show on our stage every Saturday night at seven for almost a year straight."[59]

The use of radio programming as a new medium to draw a crowd for Western and musical-Western films helped small-town exhibitors in the Midwest, South, and Southwest to stay open during the Depression. As national radio networks expanded in the 1930s, this new form of hybridized country-western music grew in popularity with radio listeners. The new musical form gave national advertisers and politicians a medium for reaching the large and underserved audiences. No one understood this market better than Herbert Yates, the head of Republic Pictures, and Nat Levine, the founder of Mascot Pictures and Republic's executive producer.[60]

CHAPTER 2

# Musical-Western Hybrid Film

Representing rural, small-town, and newly urban fans throughout the Midwest, South, and Southwest, Gene Autry's hybridized form of country-western music served the needs of dispossessed people struggling to resist or reshape the flows of mass media that continuously pummeled their cultural heritage. Autry took the electronic media imposed from the outside and made them serve the purposes of rural, small-town, and newly urban Americans. Simultaneously, he served the needs of Herbert Yates, operating from a position of strength. Having consolidated the film processing, record production, and motion picture distribution industries, Yates employed the singing cowboy in a strategy to control the means of transcultural consumption experienced by Gene Autry fans.

As a multiplatform entertainer able to mash up the desires of both rural and urban audiences, Autry blended traditional and modern culture into a corporate strategy that used hybridity to create synergy across multiple information mediums. He played a critical role in developing a potent cultural form recognized by business leaders and politicians as a means for reaching a large and underserved audience. The content of Autry's early films established a precedent for future productions more in tune with President Roosevelt's policies during the Great Depression and the run-up to World War II. Upon closer examination, the singing cowboy's multiplatform entertainment reveals a relationship between the American state and imagery of the American West that remains underreported by historians and political scientists.

Music provided the means for Autry's transmedia storytelling as exemplified by the success of "That Silver Haired Daddy of Mine." This signature song propelled the rising star from Chicago radio to Hollywood motion pictures in 1934. Nat Levine, the head of Mascot Pictures, gave Autry a featured role in his first musical-western, *In Old Santa Fe* (1934). As a follow-up, Levine featured the singing cowboy portraying himself in *The Phantom Empire* (1934), appearing as a recording artist and radio star and singing "That Silver Haired Daddy of Mine" during a live remote broadcast from a mountain valley ranch on the outskirts of Los Angeles. Months later, when Levine merged his Mascot Pictures with Herbert Yates's new Republic Pictures, the filmmaker featured "That Silver Haired Daddy of Mine" a second time in *Tumbling Tumbleweeds* (1935), Autry's first feature film released by Republic Pictures. The singing cowboy starred in 56 films released by Republic Pictures over twelve seasons of the Gene Autry series between 1935 and 1947.[1]

Autry's performance of "That Silver Haired Daddy of Mine" in motion pictures validated the singing cowboy's star quality with a broad and growing fan base. Simultaneously, musical-Western films enabled the performer to introduce his signature song to new moviegoing audiences. The hubbub surrounding the singer-songwriter, recording artist, and radio personality turned movie star created a sensation that Republic Pictures desperately needed to attract audiences reluctant to spend their hard-earned cash during tough times. Adding motion pictures to a repertoire of in-person performances, live radio shows, sound recordings, and name-brand merchandise, Autry extended his reach to another layer of multiplatform entertainment, further emphasizing the values of music as a bonding agent for transmedia storytelling. This history is important because it shows how Herbert Yates assembled a multiplatform entertainment empire during the early years of sound motion pictures and radio broadcasting.

Under Yates's purview, record producer Art Satherley handed the singing cowboy over to film producer Nat Levine in 1934. Yates was familiar with Levine's Mascot Pictures as a financier of several productions dating back to 1927. Pointing to Autry's success selling records and merchandise for ARC, Sears, and WLS, Satherley persuaded Levine to find a place for Autry in his first musical-western, *In Old Santa Fe*. Regular performances with the *WLS Round-Up* had made Autry a household name among rural, small-town, and newly urban moviegoers in the upper Midwest. Moreover, Autry had radio fans tuned in from coast-to-coast to hear him sing on the *National Barn Dance*. Fans could not get enough of Autry's nostalgic hit, "That Silver Haired Daddy of Mine." The introduction of the song to new audiences through motion pictures kept the mountain ballad in rotation at radio stations and in demand among record buyers. The song served as a symbol of synergy and the means of developing a multiplatform entertainment franchise.

The decision to move Gene Autry from Chicago to Hollywood rested largely with Herbert Yates, who wanted to leverage his investments in Mascot Pictures to promote the star qualities of his country-western recording talent in musical-Western films. Concurrently, Levine needed Autry's name recognition from record promotions and radio play to help sell movie tickets. Audiences had seen Autry play on stage before movie screenings in and around Chicago. Now moviegoers nationwide got to see their favorite singing cowboy *in* a musical-Western, alongside Ken Maynard, playing multiple movie theaters on the same day.

Levine envisioned a serial, followed by a feature, edited from the chapter play. The Mascot producer leased the old Mack Sennett lot on Ventura Boulevard in North Hollywood to make musical-Westerns. He approached W. Ray Johnston at Monogram Pictures with a deal to sublet space on the Sennett lot, and he signed Ken Maynard away from Universal Pictures. Levine agreed to match the $10,000-per-picture paid by the big studio to tap Maynard's proven formula for making musical-Western hybrid films. Nevertheless, Maynard's poor singing voice created problems for Levine. To sell movie tickets to music fans, Mascot needed a singing cowboy with a bona fide hit record. Adding Autry to the cast of *In Old Santa Fe* enabled Levine to leverage cross-promotions and create synergy with ARC, NBC, Sears, and other entities, producing and distributing cultural products with the "Gene Autry" name-brand.[2]

Mascot Pictures introduced "The Original Singing Cowboy" with a big build-up and a lengthy musical interlude. *In Old Santa Fe* served as a screen test for the rising star, to the delight of many fans. In his directorial debut, film editor Joseph Kane used a combination of close-ups and wide-angle shots to show Autry as a square dance caller and western balladeer. The folksinger serenaded an audience of easterners as the front man for the Gene Autry Trio, an ensemble that included longtime sidemen Frankie Marvin and Smiley Burnette.

Eastern dudes assembled in the great room of a modern-day dude ranch, somewhere in the Mohave Desert, along the suburban frontier in Southern California, served as stand-ins for emulation by the moviegoing audiences in theaters from coast to coast. In sync with the president's desire to increase travel and tourism in the American West, Levine portrayed the dude ranch as an attractive and adventuresome retreat for newly created worker-tourists considering a caravanning car vacation along Route 66 or another U.S. highway. The picture represented country-western music as a standard form of dude ranch entertainment. Autry sang a siren's song, coaxing his fans to travel westward along the routes of modern-day pioneers.[3]

Levine pushed the boundaries of Ken Maynard's musical-Western formula by adding a gangster element that created a triple-hybrid. The filmmaker produced the musical-Western–gangster movie to mash up fans of different genres. *In Old Santa Fe* dramatized the impact of cultural change experienced by the western ranchers as they adjusted their traditional livestock operations to accommodate the desires of eastern tourists paying to experience a romanticized world of cowboy trappings. Gangsters replaced outlaws as the villains in the film, narrowing the focus of a typical "East versus West" storyline to highlight the tensions between rural communities and the encroaching urban sprawl.[4]

As vacationers headed out to the wide open spaces of the American West, they unknowingly spread the germs of future suburban growth. The process worked by first enticing tourists to make the western journey and then tempting these same travelers to make investments in western real estate. New supplies of water and power made investments in the Southwest, from Los Angeles, California, to Las Vegas, Nevada, and Phoenix, Arizona, particularly attractive. Since the earliest days of cinema, Western films served as come-ons to lure tourists and convince them to relocate as modern pioneers.[5]

*In Old Santa Fe* showed the most physical forms of western work transformed into spectator sports. Tourists and collectors repositioned the trappings of a cowboy's outfit as a stylized fashion connected with an authentic form of American folk culture. Cowboys provided the main attraction for eastern dudes visiting the American West. The cowboy world of work became a spectacle for consumption by touring publics in the form of interactive ranch round-ups, annual rodeo circuits, and high-stakes horseracing. Musical entertainment added to the authenticity of the contemporary western experience sought by vacationers. Western music fit nicely with the ideals of suburban ranch life and adventuresome rodeo sports.[6]

Following the historic precedent established by Ken Maynard with *The Strawberry Roan,* Levine purchased the screen rights for a popular song, "Down in Old Santa Fe," to feature Autry in cross-promotions with ARC. Sears responded by minting a new "Gene Autry-Old Santa Fe" guitar (Supertone Model #257). Similar to the Martin D-45 used by the singing cowboy to perform "That Silver Haired Daddy of Mine," the acoustic archtop came in a super auditorium size, with a maple body, spruce top, and heavy black pick guard. Sears stenciled "Old Santa Fe" on the headstock and a signature endorsement from "Gene Autry" near the tailpiece.[7]

*In Old Santa Fe* provided Nat Levine a blueprint for a series of musical-Westerns starring Gene Autry. The film featured sunshine, scenery, horseback riding, tennis, swimming, music, and horseracing as attractions for the eastern and urban dudes staying at "El Reposo Ranch" (the Restive Ranch). The cattle ranch provided a picturesque component in the otherwise sublime basin and range topography of Southern California. The opportunities for tourism depicted in this film and subsequent "Gene Autry" productions characterized the dude ranch, rodeo arena, and radio broadcast as three focal points for western heritage and cultural tourism promoted by the federal government during the New Deal.[8]

Historian Michael Berkowitz associated mass tourism with the Roosevelt administration in his essay, "A New Deal for Leisure: Making Mass Tourism during the Great Depression" (2001). Describing leisure as "the result of the accretion and confluence of decades-long development," Berkowitz argued that the most significant and revolutionary aspects of the tourism industry culminated during the New Deal for two important reasons.

First, to secure a reliable workforce and counter the rising militancy of labor leaders, American industrialists instituted a policy of annual paid vacations for wage earners. The federal government formalized these policies through a series of legislative acts tied to the National Industrial Recovery Act of 1933, National Labor Relations Act of 1935 (Wagner Act), and the Fair Labor Standards Act of 1938. By 1941, the majority of American workers had access to time off with pay. "Gene Autry" productions reached out to the emerging market of newly urban worker-tourists Berkowitz described as taking advantage of their two-week paid vacations.[9]

*In Old Santa Fe* demonstrated that women were the primary audience for Mascot's musical-western. Youthful male audiences remained important, but secondary to Autry's success until 1938, when the series began incorporating younger sidekicks in ways that echoed the role played by Smiley Burnette. Typifying the female lead of costars in later productions, Levine characterized "Lila Miller" (Evelyn Knapp) as an independent, eastern-educated, highly fashionable, newly urban young woman with western ranch roots. The story dramatized the ways in which Miss Miller learned to navigate the distances between the traditional old world of her rural-western father and the newly urban world of her metropolitan peers. Levine made a point of contrasting the styles and tastes of eastern-urban women with those of rural and western men, circa 1934.[10]

The film opened with "Kentucky" (Ken Maynard) singing a cowboy song while horseback riding with his sidekick, "Cactus" (George "Gabby" Hayes), through a Joshua tree forest in Southern California.

Kentucky and Cactus personified the emergence of a country-western hybrid taking root in the western states. Cowboys survived in this changing environment by turning their traditional crafts into art, entertainment, and recreation. Instead of working as ranch hands, Kentucky and Cactus made their living competing in horseracing spectacles sponsored by local promoters. They also sold authentic cowboy trappings to willing tourists and collectors. When Lila Miller spotted Kentucky selling spurs and saddles, she quipped, "Awe, I thought that you were a real cowboy."

Kentucky replied, "Oh, I am Miss, that's just a sideline."[11]

In *Devil's Bargains: Tourism in the Twentieth Century West* (1998), historian Hal Rothman identified three forms of tourism—cultural/heritage tourism, recreational tourism, and entertainment tourism, which *In Old Santa Fe* represented as "three basic, overlapping, and intertwined types." Rothman demonstrated that travel and tourism in all forms helped define the postmodern, postindustrial New West that Mascot Pictures dramatized. Rothman drew connections between the New West and the New Deal through the activities of Stephen Mather and Horace Albright—the first and second directors of the National Park Service and promoters of western tourism since the 1920s.[12]

Rothman recognized the importance of the dude ranch as a marker of the cultural shift occurring in the 1930s, thrust upward as a result of economic upheaval. With the market for range-fed beef in decline during the Great Depression, the New Deal promoted dude ranches as destinations for tourists visiting the American West. Still, Rothman underestimated the indicators found in country-western music and the symbolism found in musical-Western films. He ignored the appeal of horseback riding for young women and the appeal of rodeos and Wild West shows for adolescent boys and girls. Adding those elements to Rothman's initial work, *New Deal Cowboy* demonstrates more fully how the conversion of cattle ranches into dude ranches served as an indicator of cultural change.

Having legitimized leisure time, the New Dealers joined with community advertising organizations to promote tourism and travel throughout the United States. Public information touting a modern, contemporary culture in a "New West" gained prominence through mass media publications, sound recordings, radio broadcasts, educational filmstrips, newsreels, and Hollywood motion pictures. New Deal administrators encouraged the hype and contributed to it significantly, most notably through agencies in the U.S. Department of the Interior. The National Park Service, National Forest Service, Bureau of Reclamation, Works Progress Administration, Resettlement Administration, and the United States Travel Bureau promoted travel and tourism in the American West.[13]

Assuming a central role in the promotion of travel and tourism, the Roosevelt administration sought to counter the aggressive campaigns of foreign governments that encouraged wealthy Americans to travel abroad. Three factors explain the forceful action of the federal government. First, New Dealers believed in recreational tourism as an antidote for social divisions, radical revolutionary tendencies, right-wing reactionaries, and foreign aggression. Simultaneously, the President regarded travel and tourism as key components in his solution for economic recovery. Moreover, business and civic leaders called for the support of the federal government to help local tourism promotions succeed.[14]

As Mascot Pictures prepared to release *In Old Santa Fe*, publication of the Payne Fund investigations into the psycho-sociological effects of cinema created a backlash against Hollywood. The Motion Picture Research Council (MPRC) joined forces with the Catholic Church to promote a "Legion of Decency" to combat wickedness in the motion picture industry. Catholic bishops and priests threatened to boycott Hollywood films if producers did not make wholesome family entertainment. Priests stood outside of movie box offices and confronted parishioners in lines to buy tickets. The *Hollywood Reporter* expressed alarm in a story warning moviemakers to clean up their act or face the possibility of federal censorship.[15]

Levine exploited the favor shown by the MPRC for smaller, independent moviemakers, film producers, distributors, and theater exhibitors operating outside the Hollywood mainstream. Mascot's musical-Westerns represented the wholesome family entertainment envisioned by the MPRC. Levine welcomed the council's lobbying of President Roosevelt for the inclusion of provisions in the National Recovery Act of 1933 (NRA) to weaken the monopoly of Hollywood's Motion Picture Producers and Directors Association (MPPDA). Critics challenged the production codes created by the NRA to regulate the motion picture industry. Unlike other industry codes, which dealt with labor and management issues, the NRA's motion picture production codes focused on film distribution. Targeting theater exhibitors, the NRA called for the creation of arbitration boards to settle questions about "runs" (the sequencing of different showings of a motion picture in a given geographic zone) and "clearances" (the period of time elapsing between one showing and the next in a given zone). Exhibitors disagreed with MPPDA block booking practices, score charges, and double bills. In response to these unfolding actions, the creative talent in Hollywood established the Screen Writers Guild (SWG), and the Screen Actors Guild (SAG) to represent the actors, screenwriters, and directors in negotiations with motion picture producers and distributors.[16]

President Roosevelt took advantage of this turmoil in the motion picture industry to gain a toe-hold as a motion picture producer. Lacking the support of big-city newspaper publishers, the president wanted motion pictures to augment his radio programming as another means of getting his message out. Harry Hopkins, head of the Works Progress Administration (WPA), introduced a new documentary form of motion picture production. Ralph Steiner and Willard Van Dyke, members of the New York Film and Photo League, presented the new form in a film titled *Hands* (1934). As a reflection of avant-garde cinema in Europe and the Soviet Union, *Hands* drew condemnation from the MPPDA. Hollywood filmmakers viewed the New Deal documentary as a dangerous new form of competition.[17]

Harry Hopkins also contracted with Pathé to produce newsreel films promoting WPA reforms: "A series of New Deal newsreels designed to feature the successes and triumphs of the Roosevelt administration." Newsreels represented a powerful communication format for the president. Popular to the point that some theaters screened nothing else, "The newsreel brings to a modern world a truer picture of itself, and of its people, than any other agency heretofore known to mankind," explained Stephen Early, Roosevelt's press secretary. A former editor of Paramount newsreels, Early understood the power of this remarkable form of visual journalism. Hopkins used newsreels to fundamentally transform the political personalities of the Roosevelt administration into national celebrities.[18]

Nat Levine recognized a niche in making musical-Westerns that reflected rural folk values and promoted western travel and tourism for Midwestern worker-tourists. He decided to drop Ken Maynard in favor of Gene Autry as the star of Mascot's first musical-Western serial. In *The Phantom Empire*, Levine portrayed the singing cowboy as a western siren, beguiling new worker-tourists into spending their two-week paid vacations at dude ranches in the desert or mountain-high vacation camps. By featuring Autry in the chapter play, the Mascot producer targeted large and underserved audiences of country-western music fans familiar with the authentic, real-life recording artist, radio star, and musical performer and the high-volume, low-markup, name-brand merchandise sold by Sears. Autry's move from Chicago to L.A. reinforced traditional quasi-folk beliefs about individual success in American culture. The singing cowboy kept alive the myth of a mobile and classless society for rural, small-town, and newly urban fans coming out of the Great Depression in 1935.[19]

*The Phantom Empire* featured Autry as Radio's Singing Cowboy. The fantastic, twelve-part serial paired the radio star and recording artist with a young rodeo performer, Betsy Ross King, "World's Champion Trick Rider." Levine included the athletic female lead to emphasize rodeos and Wild West shows as attractions for western tourists, an enticement for moviegoers. The film's "Radio Ranch" setting emphasized the close relationships between the artistry of country-western music, the entertainment value of radio broadcasting, and the recreational spectacle of rodeo sport, all encapsulated within the motion picture. These attractions made the American West appealing to American vacationers coming out of the Depression with lots of pent-up purchasing power. Targeting rural, small-town, and newly urban worker-tourists, *The Phantom Empire* demonstrated that vacation camps were accessible to working-class Americans, even if a dude ranch vacation was beyond the reach of most workers.[20]

Similar to the triple hybrid, musical-Western-gangster formula developed by Levine for *In Old Santa Fe*, the producer added another special element to the formula underlying *The Phantom Empire*. Levine envisioned the serial as a triple-hybrid, musical-Western–science fiction film. Playing himself as part owner of Radio Ranch, Autry used live remote broadcasting and radio advertising to promote his Southern California "vacation camp" to lower-income worker-tourists in the Midwest, South, and Southwest. The clothing, accoutrements, and speech of the vacation camp kids, in comparison with the more sophisticated engineers and scientists in the film, mirrored the intended market of the vacation camp. Rustic in comparison to *In Old Santa Fe's* modern dude ranch setting, Radio Ranch did not cater to upper-income easterners and European tourists. The vacation camp offered similar amenities, just not so fancy. The concept appealed more to regional vacationers with large families and worker-tourists with more modest means. Radio Ranch attractions included horseback riding, rodeo sports, western music, live radio broadcasts, and aerial tourism. An added benefit came from a fanciful subterranean tribe, oddly suggestive of Hopi and Zuni cultures, whose origin stories began with the people emerging from beneath the surface in the Grand Canyon of the Colorado River.[21]

Rural and small-town moviegoers may have recognized the word association between the scientific city of Murania introduced in the opening credits of *The Phantom Empire* and the infectious, fast-spreading disease known as the "murrain," a biblical plague of death that affected cattle and other livestock. *The Phantom Empire* associated Murania with modern technology, including a 25,000-foot elevator cutting into the earth's core; various forms of primitive robotics; wireless television broadcasting; a disintegrating-atom–smashing machine; z-ray lithium guns; and radium bombs. By using neutron-induced chain reactions to create explosions, the murderous scientists at work in *The Phantom Empire* illustrated their familiarity with the work of Frederic Joliot-Curie and Irene Joliot-Curie at the Radium Institute in Paris and the studies of critical mass by Hungarian physicist Leo Szilard.[22]

*The Phantom Empire* included a direct reference connecting Autry with President Roosevelt after Betsy Baxter (Betsy Ross King) and her

"Nate Levine Presents Ken Maynard, 'In Old Santa Fe,'" 1934. © Autry Qualified Interest Trust and The Autry Foundation (01-IOSF).

*The Big Show* lobby card, 1936. © Autry Qualified Interest Trust and The Autry Foundation (13-BSHW).

"Gene Autry in Person" press book, 1936. © Autry Qualified Interest Trust and The Autry Foundation (T87-36-249).

brother, Frankie (Frankie Darro), were captured and taken into the depths of Murania for an interview with Queen Tika (Dorothy Christy). When the subterranean monarch threatened to cut off their heads, Frankie responded by evoking Gene Autry, the singing cowboy hero: "He'd telephone the president and before you could wink an eye there'd be a regiment of artillery here knocking the top of this palace, and there'd be airplanes dropping bombs as big as bears, and then what would be left of your Murania?" Typically, President Roosevelt refused to sanction the use of his name or image by any Hollywood studios; thus, making this reference to the head of state significant for moviegoers.[23]

Chapter 2 of the serial opened with Autry singing "That Silver Haired Daddy of Mine" as part of a live remote broadcast from Radio Ranch. Levine framed the song as an explicit radio performance embedded within the narrative of the film. This approach differed from Ken Maynard's method, and the methods of other studios, in which singing cowboys sang spontaneously while riding the trail or sitting around a campfire. Levine's musical scenes included audiences of extras as stand-ins for emulation by moviegoing fans. In subsequent films, the producer developed other strategies to portray the bond between the cowboy hero and his devoted fans. Levine conjured roles for the singing cowboy as a traveling troubadour, medicine show headliner, radio celebrity, and band leader, performing at house parties, barn dances, and fiestas. In addition to the musical performances, Levine used modern record players, radio receiving sets, and futuristic televisions as narrative conceits to help moviegoers break down the distinctions between Autry's film character and his status as a recording artist, radio personality, and movie star.[24]

The successful release of *The Phantom Empire* prompted Herbert Yates to approach Nat Levine with an offer to merge Mascot into Republic Pictures, a new and larger film corporation. Yates wanted to build upon Levine's leadership in the field of chapter plays and serial productions to expand Mascot's feature and musical-Western programs. He also convinced Ray Johnston and Trem Carr to merge Monogram Pictures into the new company. Likewise, Yates eliminated more competition and accumulated additional assets by acquiring outright the Liberty, Majestic, and Chesterfield studios.[25]

Monogram provided Republic Pictures with a syndicate of film exchanges in thirty-six metropolitan markets across the United States and Canada. These exchanges enabled Republic to operate as a major Hollywood studio, packaging its productions into blocks of six or eight films made available exclusively to independent theater owners within specified zones or markets. The difference was that Republic operated mainly outside of Hollywood's major markets. The Monogram exchanges served mostly rural, small-town and newly urban markets in the Ohio River and Mississippi River valleys.[26]

Appealing to heartland audiences, Republic Pictures made a conscious decision to produce films that reinforced traditional American folk values. Unlike other segments of the motion picture market, quasi-folk and lower-culture Americans *preferred* to see "message" films. Evidence of message films' popularity came from Warner Brothers, Republic's principal competitor, and a major supporter of President Roosevelt and the National Recovery Act legislation. Among other techniques, Warner Brothers included the Blue Eagle emblem of the NRA in the background of several pictures.[27]

Herbert Yates controlled Republic Pictures behind the scenes. Levine, Johnston, Carr, and the other studio heads all made deals with Yates because they owed staggering sums of money to CFI for film processing. Yates wanted to make good pictures while keeping exchange and exhibitor costs low. These factors influenced his choice of Johnston to serve as president of the studio. Yates chose Levine as head of studio productions and Trem Carr to handle the executive and financial management decisions. Lindsey Parsons managed publicity, and Bernard Bernbaum took care of advertising and exploitation.[28]

Yates positioned Republic Pictures to monopolize the production of "B" movies for the double feature markets. Republic stimulated production by filling the demand for second features at an inexpensive fixed rate. Having cornered the market for high-volume, low-markup sound recordings with ARC, Yates knew how to dominate the emerging market for "B" movie productions. Stressing quality and economy, Republic quickly became the leading "B" movie producer and distributor. Yates strengthened Levine's production capabilities by adding CFI technical expertise and "Hi-Fidelity" sound from RCA Victor. Republic Pictures had polish that other independent producers lacked. Even so, the studio employed otherwise efficient and often clever means to save money with tight budgets and shooting schedules, no-nonsense writing and directing, judicious use of stock footage, the reuse of individual scenes, and re-releasing some features. Generally, the studio showcased celebrity actors within the Hollywood star system, backed up by an ensemble cast of inexpensive character actors.[29]

Autry played the lead in four pictures for Republic in 1935 and another eight films in 1936. As a follow-up to *The Phantom Empire* serial, Levine featured his singing cowboy star in *Tumbling Tumbleweeds*, the first feature film in the musical-Western genre plotted and sold around the main character's ability to sing. With a contemporary setting and story about ranchers battling nesters over water rights, *Tumbling Tumbleweeds* mirrored the dramatic changes occurring throughout Southern California as the Metropolitan Water District and the Los Angeles Department of Water and Power introduced expansive new water and power resources. Stemming from the opening of Boulder/Hoover Dam, water and power resource development along the Lower Colorado River created opportunities for tremendous growth in Southern California, Arizona, and Southern Nevada. In part, these opportunities reversed the trend of people moving from the countryside into urban areas. More than two million Americans left the cities for rural residences during the New Deal. In unison with New Deal promotions, Republic's Gene Autry series showcased "modern pioneers" leaving the cities to return to a better life in the small towns along the suburban frontiers of the Southwest.[30]

*Tumbling Tumbleweeds* interposed actors populating the fictitious town of Gunstock, a familiar setting for audiences in the theaters of Republic's distribution area in the Midwest and South. Dressed in 1930s work clothes and gathered to watch a traveling medicine show, an audience of extras experienced Autry performing "That Silver Haired Daddy of Mine" in the film, recreating the experience for moviegoers. None of the townsfolk wore cowboy outfits except for the heavies in the film, who taunted Autry with catcalls of "Lavender Cowboy," an obvious insinuation of effeminacy and homosexuality.[31]

In *Horse Opera: The Strange History of the 1930s Singing Cowboy* (2002), Peter Stanfield paid particular attention to the role and importance of the musical performances in *Tumbling Tumbleweeds*. Stanfield argued that Autry's rapid rise to success derived from his ability through song and performance to credibly show that he was a member of the quasi-folk and lower-culture communities that constituted his core audience. Including historical performance traditions—blackface minstrelsy, traveling medicine shows, and traveling troupes—helped fans follow the through-line of traditional American values in Autry's expanded multiplatform entertainment. Stanfield interpreted Autry's singing cowboy persona as a mask worn in an elaborate masquerade to articulate the fears and desires of rural, small-town, and newly urban Americans attempting to deal overtly with issues engendered by the Great Depression. Specifically, the film dealt with modern-day environmental concerns involving water rights throughout the newly irrigated lands of the Lower Colorado River Basin.[32]

The opening scenes of *Tumbling Tumbleweeds* introduced behavioral guidelines familiar to many rural, small-town and newly urban fans. Director Joseph Kane used the first ten minutes of the film as a prologue to establish Autry as the son of a wealthy rancher from Gun Stock. The scenes portrayed a conflict between rural ranchers and Dust Bowl migrants, identified as "nesters," in a classic, native versus newcomers plot device borrowed from traditional western film forms.[33]

The *Tumbling Tumbleweeds* prologue culminated with an epic fight between the ranchers and the nesters that ended with Autry saving his father's life, only to face banishment for stubbornly supporting the civil rights of migrants. A sign posted on the outskirts of town anchored an advance of five years in the story, presumably bridging the gap between the Great Depression and the New Deal. Because the region had not yet modernized—due in large measure to the lack of water and power resources—Autry returned to Gun Stock in 1935, as the singing cowboy headliner of a traveling medicine show, "Dr. Parker's Purveyors of Phun, Phrolic, and Painless Panacea." Autry sang the film's title song, "Tumbling Tumbleweeds," as he rode his horse alongside a traveling troupe, unabashedly playing a "Gene Autry-Old

Santa Fe" guitar sold by Sears. The tone of the song implied a new attitude that accompanied the advance in time. Change was further evidenced in the contemporary dress worn by the townspeople gathered to enjoy the old-time medicine show. A portable, windup phonograph player appeared as another plot device to portray the status quo in the rural and small-town communities of the South and Southwest without electricity.[34]

As the star attraction of Dr. Parker's Medicine Show, Autry wore lightly colored, nicely tailored cowboy suits with neatly creased shirts and pants with piping around the pockets. Autry tucked his tight-fitting pants into highly decorated boots. He wore a neckerchief and Stetson—the kind that the author B. M. Bower described as a "musical comedy brand." He did not appear as a proletarian cowpuncher; instead, Autry portrayed himself as a musical performer. The film emphasized Autry's sartorial distinctiveness in contrast with both working cowhands and the quasi-folk and lower-culture townspeople dressed in contemporary 1930s work wear. Despite the differences in apparel warranted by the singing cowboy's occupation as a showman, Autry nonetheless functioned as a representative of the New Deal, siding with the migrant nesters in opposition to his father, the leader of the ranch-owner establishment.[35]

Republic scored big when Autry's recording of "Tumbling Tumbleweeds" became a huge hit. Written by Bob Nolan in 1929, the song languished until Rudy Vallee performed the piece on his nationally syndicated radio show in 1933. Afterward, Sunset published the music for "Tumbling Tumbleweeds" in May 1934. Sam Fox added a new verse to the song, which the Sons of the Pioneers recorded for Decca on August 8. Autry recorded the song on January 11, 1935, after Republic licensed its use as the title for the first film in the new Gene Autry series. Released by ARC on the Melotone label, "Tumbling Tumbleweeds" delivered Autry his fourth gold record. Autry's version of the song entered *The Billboard's* "Top 100" popular music chart on February 16, 1935. The song stayed on the chart for five weeks, topping out at No. 10.[36]

It did not hurt that the Sons of the Pioneers were *the* musical sensation in Hollywood. Performing together since 1932, the band was on its way to becoming the most profound recording artists in the history of country-western music. Recording with Decca in Hollywood, The Sons of the Pioneers raised the bar in terms of musicianship, harmony singing, and songwriting. Their lyrics and music romanticized the American West as a fierce and lonely place full of tumbling tumbleweeds, timber trails, waterfalls, everlasting hills, open ranges, rippling rills, and cataract spills. They painted portraits of the western landscape in song that remain unrivaled in the history of country-western music.[37]

Including Bob Nolan, Vern Spencer, and Leonard Slye (Roy Rogers), the Sons of the Pioneers anchored a thriving country-western music scene in Los Angeles. Nolan's songs portrayed the American West as a place of ethereal beauty and boundless freedom. His songs featuring the western landscape marked a radical shift in the presentation of Western folk music. Nolan moved cowboy songs away from images of picaresque westerners. The group produced flawless harmonies, and their recordings exhibited technical brilliance far in advance of most contemporary artists.[38]

Autry's performance of "That Silver Haired Daddy of Mine" in *Tumbling Tumbleweeds* provided another big surge for the popularity of his signature song. After the film premiere, ARC re-released the song on its Vocalion label, and it went gold a second time on the *The Billboard* pop chart. "That Silver Haired Daddy of Mine" entered the chart on August 24, 1935, and remained for five weeks, topping out at No. 7. Furthermore, Autry had a third song make *The Billboard* Pop Chart in 1935. "Ole Faithful," released by ARC on the Melotone label, entered the chart on February 9, 1935, and remained popular for seven weeks, topping out at No. 10. Republic's release of *Tumbling Tumbleweeds* demonstrated that Autry could sell movie tickets, sound recordings, and other name-brand merchandise.[39]

The scene in *Tumbling Tumbleweeds* in which Autry sang "That Silver Haired Daddy of Mine" paid tribute to the singing cowboy's deceased father, showing that family was stronger than political affiliations. However, during the performance, a heckler named "Connors" (George Chesboro) shouted out: "Hey, what kind of a fella are you, using your dead father as a build up for a vaudeville act? Hey, we ain't got no use for lavender cowboys in this town." Contemporary audiences understood this surprising reference directed toward Autry's dandified duds as a symbol of sexual orientation. The singing cowboy responded by leaping off the stage to attack the heckler and show his manliness.[40]

Prominent references connecting "lavender" with homosexual men stemmed from Carl Sandburg's use of the term to describe a young Abraham Lincoln in 1926. Cole Porter's reference in the song, "I'm a Gigolo" (1929), included the lyrics: "I'm a famous gigolo, and of lavender, my nature's got just a dash in it." Alfred St. John performed a song titled "The Lavender Cowboy" in *The Oklahoma Cyclone* (1930), a western film by Tiffany Productions, starring Bob Steele. A dictionary of slang published in 1935 defined a "streak of lavender" as a reference to an effeminate man or sissy. No evidence has surfaced concerning Autry's popularity among gay men in the late 1930s. The "lavender cowboy" reference may have served to offset traditional western film fans offended by the musical-Western form; still, it quietly acknowledged the possibility of a larger male fan base.

More than a star vehicle, Republic crafted *Tumbling Tumbleweeds* to mirror the difficulties faced by Autry fans as they confronted the major socio-economic changes in the 1930s. Republic depicted the singing cowboy juggling cultural traditions with modernity, against a backdrop of New Deal responses to the Great Depression. Republic's Gene Autry series represented a broadening of the film genre by defying both stereotypical gender readings and the dominant conception of the "Western" as a frontier narrative. Interpreting Autry's multifaceted public persona as a singer-songwriter, radio star, recording artist, and motion picture celebrity required an understanding of the synchronic operations that drew these activities together and made them coherent to 1930s audiences.[41]

*Tumbling Tumbleweeds* emphasized the same messages as *The Phantom Empire*, although the priorities differed and Republic added some new material. Law and order seemed to be the main theme in the film, coupled with rugged individualism—tempered with cooperation when appropriate. Republic included a strong undercurrent of support for the underdog in American society, a trait rarely found in serial productions. Likewise, the studio incorporated Americanism and patriotism whenever possible.[42]

The musical-Western hybrid emphasized action in combination with leisure, portraying Gene and the boys sitting around playing guitars and singing to relax in the film. This emphasis reinforced the musical heritage of the American folk while suggesting that life on the open range could be peaceful and rewarding in the New West instead of combative, as in traditional Western films depicting frontier scenarios. Musical-Westerns brought about a change in the qualities of the cowboy hero. In addition to traditional features, singing added charm and friendliness to the cowboy-hero's complexion. Singing-cowboy heroes wore theatrical costumes and frequently became involved with heroines, although not on a romantic plane. Heroines included two types: traditional females playing secondary and normally subsidiary roles, and more independent women with important jobs and open camaraderie who helped the cowboy hero bring the plot to a conclusion.[43]

The medicine show in *Tumbling Tumbleweeds* functioned as a symbolic connection to a shared agrarian history in the Midwest, South, and Southwest. The performance sites and rituals of the medicine show suggested a tradition outside of history, a form of entertainment that appeared uncorrupted by the modern media; yet, this medicine show was in fact a product of new media technologies. *Tumbling Tumbleweeds* represented the minstrel and the cowboy as both old and new forms of entertainment in the medicine show. Echoing the radio barn-dance programs that drew upon the idea of rural get-togethers, recreated through new forms of radio broadcasting, the variety show format recreated in *Tumbling Tumbleweeds* belonged wholly to a commercialized system of multiplatform entertainment created around Autry's singing cowboy persona.[44]

CHAPTER 3

# New Deal, New West

The infusion of country-western music into hybridized forms of musical-Western films came about during the Great Depression. As movie attendance dropped from a high of 100 million down to 60 million tickets sold each week, theater exhibitors grappled with ways to stem the tide of slumping sales. Exhibitors borrowed a technique popularized by ARC Records: the marketing of high-volume, low-markup products to quasi-folk and lower-culture music buyers. They lured audiences back into theaters with a "double feature" concept—two movies for the price of one. The idea took hold in the Midwest, South, and Southwest, where Westerns formed the backbone of the movie business.[1]

Exhibitors coupled longer and more expensive "A" features with shorter, cheaper, and more formulaic "B" movies. The economics of the double feature worked because theater owners purchased the rights to show "A" pictures on a percentage basis, while they paid a small flat rate for "B" movies. The move by theater owners to offer double features created a new niche for B-movie film producers, especially the Western filmmakers who managed to overcome the challenges to filming sound motion pictures outdoors.

Herbert Yates gained notoriety during these hard times as a consolidator of film processing laboratories and sound recording companies.

Yates's Consolidated Film Industries (CFI) duplicated high-quality motion pictures with synchronized sound for national distributors. His American Record Company (ARC) made superior sound recordings, also distributed nationally. As events unfolded during President Roosevelt's first term, Yates added motion picture production and distribution companies to this list of consolidated firms. He created Republic Pictures to monopolize the production of B movies for double bills in rural, small-town, and newly urban movie theaters in the Midwest, South, and Southwest.[2]

As a film producer and distributor, Yates used Republic Pictures to create musical-Western star vehicles to promote the country-western recording artists that he signed to the American Record Company. Republic's musical-Westerns offered a contemporary glimpse into the lives of rural, small-town, and newly urban Americans. Musical-Westerns starring Gene Autry mirrored the difficulties faced by moviegoers confronting major social and economic turmoil caused by the Great Depression. For people dealing with significant cultural transformations, "Gene Autry" entertainments reflected mobility in American culture. By showing the singing cowboy moving back and forth between rural and urban environments, Gene Autry pictures helped newly urban fans adjust to the conditions of industrial work, wage dependency, and city life. As a role model, the singing cowboy hero influenced theater audiences directly to modify their behavior. Indirectly, Autry affected a broader public through the diffusion of knowledge. Similarly, discussions about Gene Autry pictures caused additional behavior modification. In studying this mirroring effect in motion pictures, film historian Garth Jowett codified movies as "important artifacts of the twentieth century."[3]

As "The Screen's New Singing Cowboy Star," Autry furnished the archetype for Nat Levine to develop a musical-Western formula that Herbert Yates would apply more broadly at Republic Pictures. Yates targeted consumers buying country-western music from ARC and Sears as the audience for musical-Western films. Republic saturated the quasi-folk and lower-culture markets with new cultural products featuring Autry performing in multiple information media. Republic's cross promotions with theater exhibitors, radio broadcasters, record producers, and giant retailers stimulated a cultural revolution. The ubiquity of Autry's singing cowboy persona illustrated how synergy worked within the art, entertainment, recreation, and information industries.

The delivery of New Deal messaging through the incorporation of country-western music into musical-Western films represented some of the earliest and most advanced forms of soft-power public diplomacy through multiplatform entertainment. During the Roosevelt presidency, Republic developed its Gene Autry series to include twenty-seven films with New Deal themes. Autry's cultural products exemplified support for President Roosevelt's New Deal by underscoring the American West as an attractive destination for travel and tourism.

Also during President Roosevelt's first term, rural electrification sparked tremendous growth in the radio broadcasting industry. Following the advent of rural electrification, in-home radio receiving sets were often the first purchase families made. These same audiences went to see Gene Autry musical-Westerns, in part as a means of comprehending the magnitude of changes foisted upon them, like it or not, through the modern industrial enterprises that accompanied electricity into nearly every household.[4]

Autry's sound recordings and films appealed to a new breed of worker-tourists taking advantage of annual two-week paid vacations granted by industrialists and legislated by the federal government for the first time. The singing cowboy's four gold records, "The Last Round-Up, (1933)" "Ole Faithful," (1935), "Tumbling Tumbleweeds" (1935), and "That Silver Haired Daddy of Mine" (1935), highlighted the appeal of the American West as a destination for travel and tourism. Among the films produced during Republic Pictures' first two seasons, *Melody Trail* (1935), *Red River Valley* (1936), *Guns and Guitars* (1936), *Oh, Susanna!* (1936), *The Big Show* (1936), and *Git along Little Doggies* (1937) stand out as Gene Autry's earliest and best examples of combining entertainment and information into a soft power–public diplomacy strategy reflecting the New Deal and the New West.[5]

Nat Levine transferred Gene Autry's contract, along with the other assets of Mascot Pictures, as part of the merger agreement with Herbert

Yates in 1935. The singing cowboy made mostly low-budget "Jubilee" pictures during his first season with Republic. As head of production for the new studio, Levine slotted his musical cowboy to star in eight pictures. The filmmaker experimented with different formulas before finding the groove for modern musical-Westerns in dude ranch and rodeo settings, where contemporary country-western recording artists might be naturally discovered. Levine distinguished his modern musical-Westerns from traditional Western films by juxtaposing older forms of musical entertainment—traveling medicine shows, traveling troubadours, blackface minstrelsy, and vaudeville novelty acts—with newer forms of sound recordings, record players, radio broadcasts, motion picture productions, and rodeo spectacles.[6]

To emphasize the contemporary nature of Republic's Gene Autry series, Levine incorporated special effects that showed spinning newspapers highlighting front page news. The filmmaker focused the attention of moviegoers on modern-day story objectives ripped from New Deal headlines. Understanding the synergy between advertising and theater audiences, Levine also provided moviegoers with backstage views of radio and television broadcasting stations and the inner workings of advertising agencies. Likewise, Levine juxtaposed open-range roundups and rodeo arena spectacles to illustrate the transformation of nineteenth-century cowboy trappings into professionally organized twentieth-century sporting events. The timeliness of Autry's modern-day, musical-Westerns reflected aspects of President Roosevelt's New Deal in the creation of a New West, especially dude ranching and rodeos, radio broadcasting, aviation, and architecture. Other themes included elections and politics; water for irrigation, electrical power, and flood control; homelessness and migratory labor; and natural resource management.[7]

*Melody Trail* (1935) included scenes of western leisure and recreation that connected Western music and radio broadcasting with the spectacle of rodeo sports and the assembly of large audiences in arenas and stadiums across the country. The film showed modern cowboys leaving their work to compete for prize money in a series of Western sporting events and a group of independent young cowgirls taking over a cattle roundup on the TTT Ranch. Similar to *The Phantom Empire*,

Republic cast Gene Autry as himself in *Melody Trail,* a recording artist and radio personality traveling around the country, making personal appearances and encountering situational adventures. Autry's role as a performer helped explain his dandyish appearance, which women seemed to love, and manly men questioned.[8]

*Melody Trail* appealed to female fans who challenged the notion of patriarchy and the nature of social roles for women and men. Standing in marked contrast to traditional Western films, the musical-Western form confronted modernity head-on, showing audiences how to mediate between the ever-changing world at large and the desires of rural folks to maintain their customs and traditions. Foremost among these changes, critiques concerning the proper roles for women in musical-Western films got caught up with more general critiques of reactionary idealism. Levine leaned heavily toward women writers to develop screenplays for his musical-Western films that mirrored the changing roles of women in western states.

Betty Burbridge stands out among the eighteen women writing Western stories. Burbridge used the musical-Western hybrid form to create cultural mirrors that reflected modernity in the American West. Autry acknowledged this central role that Burbridge gave to young women in his films.

> As written, they gave me a lot of anything-you-can-do-I-can-do-better sass, smoked a lot of Kools—the era's Virginia Slims—and, in general, played a thirties' version of waiting for Gloria [Steinem]. That may have been due in no small part, to the presence of such screenwriters as Betty Burbridge, Luci Ward, and Connie Lee.... those films were about the only ones in the B Western category, up to then, that had a mass appeal to women.[9]

In writing the screenplay for *Melody Trail,* Burbridge positioned Millicent Thomas (Ann Rutherford) as a free agent within a world of cowboy culture. To dramatize the transformations brought about by the New Deal, the writer juxtaposed a representation of modern cowgirls with more traditional female characters. In doing so, the screenplay dramatized the massive economic and social changes that accompanied the shift from rural agrarianism to industrialized urbanism during the 1930s.

Literary critics refused to recognize the work of these women scriptwriters because they considered writing for motion pictures inferior to other forms of literature. Their bias stemmed from the collaborative process required to transfer the written word to the movie screen. Unlike theater productions, in which an author's words remained sacrosanct, screenwriters collaborated with movie directors and producers when they scripted filmic scenes. This collaborative process caused literary institutions to reject the filmmaking process for serious artistic consideration. Many film producers supported this cynical view of screenwriting as a means of neutralizing the salary demands of big-ticket novelists who came to Hollywood looking to make a quick buck.[10]

In addition to Ann Rutherford, costarring as a new breed of contemporary western woman, *Melody Trail* introduced Gene Autry's trick pony, Champion. Billed as "The World's Wonder Horse," Champion provided Autry with a second seasoned sidekick. Autry hired a top trainer for Ringling Brothers-Barnum and Bailey Circus to work with Champion and his other trick horses. John Agee trained the original Champion to do tricks in *Melody Trail* and in subsequent films. Among the mounts trained by Agee and performing under the stage name "Champion," a horse named "Lindy" connected the singing cowboy with the legendary Tom Mix. Born on the day that Charles Lindbergh flew across the Atlantic, Agee originally trained Lindy for Mix to ride in his circus, stage, and rodeo appearances. Lindy went by the stage name "Tony, Jr." when performing with Tom Mix. Agee leased the horse for Mix's tours, and he accompanied Lindy on the road. When Mix retired, the horse trainer convinced Autry to employ Lindy for his stage and rodeo appearances. When Autry agreed to headline the Madison Square Garden Rodeo in September 1939, Lindy-Champion became the first horse to fly from coast to coast for a personal appearance. Agee also trained Champion, Jr., to replace the original Champion in the postwar period.[11]

Champion helped attract young rodeo audiences to see *Melody Trail*. The film showcased the grand spectacle of the imagined American West with humorous commentary from Abe Lefton, rodeo's most famous announcer. Audiences witnessed a series of rodeo scenes, including the grand entry parade, junior calf riding (featuring contestants under ten years of age), bulldogging, bronc riding, calf roping, and bull riding. The action mirrored a real rodeo experience. Lefton spoke from an elevated platform using a state-of-the-art public address system comprised of a microphone, amplifier, and loudspeaker arrangement.

In his introduction from the dais, Lefton referred to Gene Autry as both a rodeo contestant and "star of the phonograph and radio." The association of rodeo sports with country-western music, sound recording, radio broadcasting, and live performance—all *within* the motion-picture medium—demonstrated synergy at work in American media culture. Appealing to large audiences of spectators in stadiums and rodeo arenas across the country, *Melody Trail* put forth "real cowboy" credentials for Gene Autry's singing cowboy persona. Subsequent films continued to build up Autry's rodeo associations. Ultimately, the singing cowboy hero authenticated these sporting credentials by premiering "Gene Autry's Flying A Ranch Rodeo Stampede" in February 1941. After the Second World War, Autry built a reputation as the largest producer of rodeo sports in the world.[12]

The plot of *Melody Trail* involved Autry with Millicent Thomas, the daughter of Timothy Thomas (Wade Boteler), owner of the TTT Ranch. Miss Thomas wore a fashionable knit dress and a stylish beret as the film introduced her to movie audiences. Sitting in the rodeo arena grandstand, she made eye contact with the singing cowboy hero. Moviegoers learned that Millicent was responsible for shipping cattle from her father's ranch and that she lost her cowboys to the arena once the rodeo hit town. She tasked a band of cowgirl friends with responsibility for rounding up the cattle and sending the herd to market. Thus, *Melody Trail* demonstrated women taking on the toughest male-dominated work in the New West of the 1930s.[13]

After participating in the grand entry, Autry joined Lefton on the broadcasting platform to sing "Hold On Little Doggies, Hold On." In this scene, film footage highlighted the modern loudspeaker system amplifying the cowboy crooner's voice to reach the large, assembled rodeo audience. The amplification of music within the context of a rodeo arena represented a new experience for most music fans in 1935. Mirroring real-life audiences responding to amplified musical shows, rodeo spectators in *Melody Trail* roared their applause as Gene Autry sang. The other cowboys seemed to enjoy the singing cowboy's performance, except for Matt Kirby, the TTT Ranch foreman. A favored rodeo contestant and a lowdown cattle rustler, Kirby's loathsome attitude toward Autry's value-laden persona helped identify the dimensions of the debased outlaw. As the singing cowboy hero mounted up in the bucking-bronc event, Lefton commented to the crowd, "If he can ride like he can sing, oh, baby."[14]

Despite the efforts of Republic Pictures to make the West an attractive destination for travel and tourism, Roosevelt did not have broad support from Hollywood. After taking office in 1933, the president rebuffed the movie moguls by denying their requests to use his name and image. Instead, FDR formed his own production company called U.S. Documentary Film. Rexford Tugwell set up this film production unit as part of the Resettlement Administration (RA), a division of the U.S. Department of Agriculture (USDA).[15]

Tugwell hired the filmmaker Pare Lorentz to run U.S. Documentary Film. Lorentz responded by writing, directing, and producing *The Plow That Broke the Plains* (1936). In this film, Lorentz combined populism and patriotism with realism and social commitment to reflect the aspirations of President Roosevelt's New Deal. Lorentz commissioned Virgil Thompson to write an original score to accompany his poetic narration and spectacular images of the Dust Bowl.

U.S. Documentary Film defined the techniques of social realism that inspired a generation of young filmmakers and photographers, especially Walker Evans, Dorthea Lange, and others working for the Resettlement Administration. Lange's exhibition and accompanying publication *American Exodus: A Record of Human Erosion* (1939) showed the techniques of social realism through documentary photographs. Lange showcased her work for the RA and the Farm Security Administration (FSA), another division of the USDA. By mirroring the Great Depression, the imagery of social realism promoted a national identity for American citizens based upon a new set of shared American values connected to Roosevelt's New Deal.[16]

Aesthetic and critical kudos accompanied *The Plow That Broke the Plains*. Lorentz demonstrated the necessity of the New Deal as a means of winning support for President Roosevelt's controversial programs. Lorentz considered the film "good enough technically to bear comparison with commercial films and entertaining enough to draw an audience." Even so, the film provoked negative reactions in Hollywood. The Motion Picture Producers and Distributors Association (MPPDA) considered U.S. Documentary Film a dangerous form of new competition. Studio heads refused to distribute the movie, arguing that Lorentz's documentary style could not draw audiences large enough to pay for distribution through major film exchanges. Moreover, movie moguls thought of social realism as depressing and irreconcilable with the spirit of optimism needed to promote economic recovery. Poor distribution limited the number of people who actually saw *The Plow That Broke the Plains* in theaters after its release in May 1936.[17]

Taking note of *The Plow That Broke the Plains*, Republic Pictures responded by incorporating elements of social realism into the Gene Autry series. To take advantage of the ballyhoo in front of *The Plow That Broke the Plains*, Republic hurried *Red River Valley* (1936) into movie theaters in March 1936. Compared to earlier films, Autry reflected rural and small-town American values with a decidedly political tone in this film. Audiences would not mistake Republic's musical-Western-fantasy as anything but light-hearted entertainment in comparison to *The Plow That Broke the Plains*.[18]

Filmed on location at Laguna Dam on the Lower Colorado River above Yuma, Arizona, *Red River Valley* took advantage of publicity surrounding the state of Arizona and its disputes with the state of California over Colorado River water. The contemporary setting also evoked President Roosevelt's well-publicized dedication of Boulder (Hoover) Dam in May 1935. Likewise, moviegoers learned about construction of the Colorado River Aqueduct (1933–41) and All-American Canal (1934–40) by watching newsreels during the period.

Secretary of the Interior Harold Ickes controlled New Deal plans to create this modern New West. The president put millions of dollars at the disposal of Secretary Ickes to fund Public Works Administration (PWA) projects along the Pacific Slope. East of the Continental Divide, Roosevelt placed Henry A. Wallace in charge of the United States Department of Agriculture (USDA). Wallace instituted strategies for crop reduction, soil conservation, and increased grazing in the Great Plains states. The essence of New Deal programs for the Great Plains called for the end of wheat and cotton production and greater emphasis on livestock grazing. Similarly, government management of livestock grazing left a marked and lasting imprint on the open ranges of the mountain states.[19]

A comparison of *The Plow the Broke the Plains* and *Red River Valley* reveals some differences separating the policies of the agriculture and interior departments. Responding to the Dust Bowl tragedy, the USDA promoted a policy of retrenchment in the Great Plains states. At the same time, the Interior Department focused on modernization in the Southwest, planning an enormous expansion of land use following the construction of major waterworks. The federal government entered into numerous contracts with water and power companies to supply the suburbanizing communities of southern California, central Arizona, and southern Nevada.

Mirroring the point of view at the USDA, *The Plow That Broke the Plains* seized upon a confessional tone to blame the American people for abusing the land. Lorentz conveyed a New Deal promise of government aid and a commitment to resolve the natural catastrophe and resettle the Dust Bowl diaspora in the film's prologue.

> This is a record of land . . . of soil, rather than people—a story of the Great Plains: the 400,000,000 acres of wind-swept grass lands that spread up from the Texas panhandle to Canada . . . A high, treeless, continent, without rivers, without stream . . . A country of high winds, and sun . . . and of little rain . . . By 1880 we had cleared the Indian, and with him, the buffalo, from the Great Plains, and established the last frontier . . . A half million square miles of natural range. . . . This is a picturization of what we did with it.[20]

In contrast, the prologue for *Red River Valley* gave notice to a different view, one that associated more with the rain-rich and reclamation-aided Pacific Slope. In southern California and central Arizona, the water and power infrastructure made possible by the interior department presented an alternative to retrenchment for farmers and ranchers willing to relocate to the Lower Colorado River Basin or the Los Angeles River Basin. "Drought—the grim enemy that devastated once prosperous farm and ranch lands; men have learned the bitter lesson of unpreparedness. Throughout stricken areas today, they are rallying forces to fight back with their only weapon—water."[21]

*Red River Valley* dramatized the concerns of leveraged ranchers desperate to avoid bankruptcy as they waited for the delivery of water promised for the irrigation of arid lands. Storylines in the film dramatized public concerns about sabotage and labor radicalism developing in response to conspicuous wealth and the exploitation of water and power. Expressing the concerns of female moviegoers, Mary Baxter (Frances Grant), the female lead, raised the telling question in the film: "Why would anyone in this country want to keep the canals from being built? That water is our lifeblood. . . . Dad and all the other ranchers, everything they own is invested in this project. If it fails, now . . ."

Given this sentiment, it seemed morally reprehensible to most Autry fans to discover that a double-dealing banker loaned money to the ranchers to improve their properties and then sabotaged the water delivery system he financed. The crooked banker tried to restrict the flow of water temporarily to destroy the seasonal crop and force the cash-strapped landowners to short sale their now valuable property.[22]

Autry played the part of a rancher delivering fresh beef to the Red River Land & Irrigation Company to feed the construction crews building the new canals. Fans saw their singing cowboy hero rounding up steers on the edge of town. When one of the beeves got loose, Gene chased the rampaging bull down Main Street. In the nick of time, he managed to bulldog the critter to the ground before it trampled two small children playing in the street. Mary Baxter ran out to check on the traumatized kids. Then she chastised the cowboy for the near miss. Autry's sidekick Frog Millhouse (Smiley Burnette) approached commenting about his bulldogging technique. Frog emphasized for Mary and movie audiences Autry's rodeo associations, claiming a contrived pedigree as "World's Championship Bulldogger." When Gene learned of the troubles at the dam, he took on the job of ditch rider or *zanjero* (water master) to stop the saboteurs.[23]

*Red River Valley* reflected the emerging markets for agriculture and industry in southern California, central Arizona, and southern Nevada. Filmed against a backdrop of water and power delivery systems under construction, the picture illustrated the expanding prospects for suburban expansion in California's Imperial Valley, Arizona's Salt River Valley, and other locales in the southwestern deserts. The film tied the New Deal response to Dust Bowl resettlement to a growing spirit of labor agitation along the Pacific Coast.

Newsreels and press reports of violent clashes between strikers and strikebreakers held contemporary currency for many Americans in 1936. Some moviegoers remembered the violent opposition experienced during the Carolina Piedmont textile strikes in 1929. Many recalled the coal miner strikes in Harlan and Bell County, Kentucky in 1931. More recently, a wave of strikes across the South by miners and laundry workers and the general strikes in San Francisco had captured the headlines.[24]

Signaling a closer association with proletarian causes, Autry abandoned his elaborate performance outfits in *Red River Valley*. He opted for a pair of Levi's worn over his fancy boots and a plain Western-style shirt. Moreover, the country-western star sang a traditional Western folk song as a tie-up with the movie title. "Red River Valley" marked a departure for the Gene Autry series, which typically relied upon new hit records for eponymous promotions. The traditional folksong appealed to rural and small-town fans who questioned their ability to maintain a traditional lifestyle while facing the onslaught of modernization that transformed the American West during the New Deal. Also in 1936, Republic used other traditional folksongs in eponymous film titles including *Comin' Round the Mountain* and *Oh, Susanna!*[25]

Ultimately, the landowners and the laborers had a showdown in *Red River Valley*. Staged on Laguna Dam, the two sides fought tooth and nail until our cowboy hero arrived with the stolen payroll to fairly

Gene Autry with Martin Guitar, c. 1935. © Autry Qualified Interest Trust and The Autry Foundation (BIO_220).

Autry with new horse trailer, 1937. © Autry Qualified Interest Trust and The Autry Foundation (GA_tour).

compensate the working men. In a failed escape attempt, the crooked banker and his business associate-accomplice accidentally blew themselves up by dramatically crashing a stolen locomotive into a wagon full of dynamite. Afterward, Mr. Baxter (Sam Flint) delivered a speech from the precipice of the dam. Promoting irrigated agriculture, this rancher with water rights proclaimed: "In celebrating the conclusion of our task, we can all feel proud and happy today, because we know that tomorrow, this project will put Red River Valley as one of the richest farming lands in the world. Three cheers for Red River Valley."[26]

Here to, *Red River Valley* provided moviegoers with an image of the American West with new opportunities for agriculture and industry under construction in the Lower Colorado River valley and the Los Angeles River valley. In line with the president's theories about western travel and tourism serving as an antidote for revolutionaries and radicalism, Autry demonstrated music had a civilizing force, even among the roughest of roughnecks. The film reemphasized an association between ranching and rodeo and the relationship of rodeo sports to other forms of Western art and entertainment. All the same, the categorization of *Red River Valley* as a fantasy film served only to dramatize a future for a New West under development in the American Southwest.

Republic released *Guns and Guitars* as a follow up to *Red River Valley* on June 22, 1936. The release coincided with the opening of the Democratic National Convention in Philadelphia. Democrats renominated Franklin Delano Roosevelt as the party's candidate for a second term as president of the United States. A vote for Autry in *Guns and Guitars* suggested a vote for Roosevelt in the fall elections. The film mirrored the efforts needed from women who supported President Roosevelt's reelection campaign in 1936. Republic presented an outstanding dramatization of working ranch women opposing greed, corruption, and violence, women unafraid of using their feminine wiles to influence local elections. Autry later wrote:

> If I had to pick an example of the slice-of-life plots that tended to pop up in my films, *Guns and Guitars* would probably serve. I did not engage, for the most part, in such mundane activities

as saving the old homestead or chasing bank bandits. While my solutions were a little less complex than those offered by FDR, and my methods a bit more direct, I played a kind of New Deal cowboy who never hesitated to tackle many of the same problems: the dust bowl, unemployment, or the harnessing of power. This may have contributed to my popularity with the 1930s audiences.[27]

The New Deal Cowboy provided entertainment to draw a crowd and promote Dr. Parker's Phamous Purveyors of Phun, Phrolic, and Painless Panacea in *Guns and Guitars*. The storyline involved crooked cattlemen trying to move a herd sick with "Texas Fever" across the county line. A professionally trained veterinarian, Professor Parker (Earl Hodges) quoted the *Farmer's Bulletin*, a USDA publication, to reinforce the legitimacy of cattle quarantine laws. Parker's expertise exposed Dave Morgan (J. P. McGowan), the crooked president of the local cattlemen's association, as an unscrupulous civic leader preying upon his constituents.[28]

When Morgan's henchmen bushwhacked the local lawmen, Professor Parker and Marjorie Miller (Dorothy Dix) persuaded Gene Autry to become a candidate for sheriff. In making a nominating speech before an assembly of townsfolk, Dr. Parker proclaimed, "We wish to endorse as candidate for sheriff a man that you all know, a man who has proven his fearlessness in times of danger, Gene Autry." Marjorie Miller encouraged women to vote for Autry. She also asked her friends and neighbors to influence the votes of their husbands. With the polls closed and ballots counted, Autry won the election by a landslide, foreshadowing results that proved true for President Roosevelt in November 1936.[29]

Celebrating the premiere of *Guns and Guitars* during the Republic sales convention at the Drake Hotel in Chicago, Nat Levine announced plans to make six new "Gene Autry Musical Westerns." Upon hearing the news, the singing cowboy demanded a salary increase. Levine agreed to pay his musical-Western star $2,000 per week when filming. Another stipulation required Republic to buy a $2,000 horse trailer to accommodate Champion and make personal-appearance touring more comfortable for Gene. Republic also kept Smiley Burnette under contract as Gene Autry's sidekick. Burnette provided novelty, comic relief, and supporting musical roles in the musical-Western series. Moreover, the longtime sideman remained personally under contract to Autry. Smiley paid Gene 10 percent of his salary, a monthly commission totaling $9.81 in January 1937.[30]

Smiley Burnette's comic genuis and musical talents proved integral to the success of Republic's Gene Autry series. Burnette received a costar billing before the end of the first season. Beginning with *The Singing Vagabond* (1935), the sidekick carried increasingly lengthy segments. Burnette drew on the tomfoolery of the clown tradition in American culture to create a unique character of inestimable importance for fans. Added to Autry's musical interludes, Burnette's vaudevillian comedy and novelty act helped distinguish the musical-Western hybrid film form. Comedy and novelty replaced the fistfights and chase scenes that characterized the traditional Western film formula. "The sidekick's comedic antics punctuated the formulaic narrative of fight, pursuit, capture and escape as much as the music interludes did," explained Peter Stanfield. Smiley acted as a comic foil for Gene.[31]

Autry signed a contract with the M. D. Howe Booking Agency of Hollywood, California, after inking his new deal with Republic. He provided the Howe Agency with exclusive representation to negotiate and procure engagements for live performances on the theatrical and vaudeville circuits, and other places of amusement and entertainment. Howe booked Autry on radio and television broadcasts, negotiated phonographic recording sessions, and managed all other recordings, reproductions, and distributions of the "Gene Autry" likeness by all mechanical means, except for motion pictures. Autry paid Howe a commission of 10 percent of all moneys, properties, and other forms of compensation, including salaries, bonuses, percentages, royalties, shares, and commissions.[32]

A month-long personal appearance tour through Oklahoma was the first engagement the Howe Booking Agency put together for the singing cowboy. In July 1936, Autry left Los Angeles with Smiley Burnette, Frankie Marvin, and Audrey Davis. Howe put together this live performance tour to develop synergy between Gene Autry's singing cowboy persona, his budding film persona, and his successful image as a radio star and recording artist. Performing live sets, Autry had the opportunity to meet personally his growing base of music and movie fans. On the road, the singing cowboy performed live versions of the songs Republic featured in his films. Selling records, sheet music, and songbooks along the way, Gene thanked his fans individually for making him a big star. The actions of citizens in Tulsa, Oklahoma, making Autry an honorary deputy sheriff, typified the response of fans across the state.[33]

Republic opened its second season of Gene Autry musical-Westerns with the August 1936 release of *Oh, Susanna!* The film featured a modern-day dude ranch setting, the fictitious Mineral Springs ranch, set in the spectacular scenery of the eastern Sierra Nevada. Including Mount Whitney, the highest point in the continental United States, and the hoodoos of the Alabama Hills, an otherworldly landscape in the foothills, near Lone Pine, California, these views of Owens Valley were familiar to many residents of southern California because of the controversies surrounding construction of the Los Angeles Aqueduct. Magazines such as *Touring Topics,* published by the Automobile Club of Southern California, promoted the Owens Valley as a destination of choice for automobile tourists. By 1936, the Owens Valley accommodated a landscape filled with vacation camps, dude ranches, and ski lodges amid a host of Indian reservations and infrastructure maintained by the Los Angeles Department of Water and Power.

Because the film promoted the American West as a destination for tourism and recreation, it is likely the Roosevelt administration looked favorably upon *Oh, Susanna!* Tourism and new leisure industries formed an integral part of the New Deal strategy for economic recovery and new development in the western states. Republic gained favor with local business and civic leaders for promoting the Southwest as America's playground through stunning—on location—photography. Local businesses and governments catered to wealthier eastern and foreign tourists who traveled to enjoy spectacular scenery and recreational amenities. Real growth also came from the regional and weekend tourism that accompanied suburbanization.[34]

Nat Levine changed up his musical-Western formula by introducing more musical segments in *Oh, Susanna!* The film showcased three songs by the Light Crust Doughboys, in addition to six songs from Autry, including duets with Smiley Burnette (Frog Millhouse) and Frances Grant (Mary Ann Lee), and a novelty number from Burnette and Earl Hodges (Professor Daniels). Republic created tie-ups with the Burrus Mill and Elevator Company of Fort Worth, Texas, sponsor of the enormously popular Light Crust Doughboys. Company president W. Lee O'Daniel served as the announcer for the Doughboys weekly radio program. Broadcasting throughout Texas and Oklahoma, O'Daniel's Texas Quality Group Network included Radio Station WBAP in Fort Worth; WFAA in Dallas; WOAL in San Antonio; KPRC in Houston; and KOMA in Oklahoma City.[35]

The addition of more onscreen musical talent benefited Herbert Yates as the owner of ARC. Yates featured musicians under contract to ARC in the Gene Autry series. Republic paid the musical groups anywhere from $1,000 to $1,500 for a short engagement in Hollywood. Back home, the musicians helped the studio plug motion pictures by promoting their own appearances in films, live performances, and radio broadcasts. Working in Hollywood added to the resumes of the bands and bolstered their popularity and play dates. Republic benefited from increased box office returns, while Autry gained ever-widening exposure in the major markets of New York, Chicago, Detroit, and Los Angeles, and in the regional markets of Texas, Oklahoma, Tennessee, Missouri, and Iowa.[36]

In combination with leisure time and dude ranch vacations, record players and radio broadcasting added to the elements of modernity reflected in *Oh, Susanna!* Modern forms of transportation also conveyed images of the New West. Early scenes highlighted "Gene Autry, the radio star," as a passenger on the Southern Pacific Railroad's *Sunset Limited,* a deluxe, streamlined train with first-class passenger service from New Orleans to San Francisco via Los Angeles.

Automobiles, too, reflected the modern New West. Frog Millhouse and Professor Daniels drove a late model convertible pulling a travel-trailer designed to look like an old-fashioned covered wagon.[37] The car-and-covered-wagon mash-up provided an entertaining and literal visualization of the transformation of the Old West into the New West in 1936. A sideboard along the wagon read, "Millhouse,

Daniels and Company; Entertainers De Luxe." Another advertisement on the car door, lettered in washable white paint, read: "Now playing The Western Theatrical Circuit, Next Appearance . . . Sage City . . ." These advertisements emphasized the role of entertainers in introducing new ideas and nurturing the development of American media culture.[38]

*Oh, Susanna!* included modern-day gangsters as heavies for Autry to fight. The western outlaw Wolf Bensen (Boothe Howard) teamed up with an urban gangster named Flash Baldwin (Donald Kirke). Backed by a crew of crooked cowboys, they robbed the Mineral Springs Dude Ranch. Baldwin's sport shirt and fedora gave him distinctly eastern-gangster flair in comparison to the western outlaws. The symbolic richness of gangster portrayals in the hybrid, musical-Western-gangster form functioned as an alien interruption in the western landscape. Doubly marked as urban dwellers and ethnic immigrants, the personal mannerisms and artifacts of the gangster's world resonated with movie audiences. Gangsters became the *vade mecum* for Republic Pictures, the scapegoats for all that might be wrong with the New Deal and the New West. Modern-day gangsters made guest appearances as heavies throughout the Gene Autry series as emblems of urban corruption and salutary warnings to rural, small-town, and newly urban Americans as they simultaneously rushed to embrace modernization while continuing to worry about its effects on traditional folkways along the suburban frontier.[39]

In September 1936, after the studio wrapped filming of *Ride, Ranger, Ride*, Gene Autry and Company struck out for Texas, opening at the Liberty Theater in Fort Worth, during the Fort Worth Frontier Centennial Exposition. The singing cowboy handled six more play dates in Texas, Louisiana, and Mississippi, earning an income of $755, about $12,924 in 2015 dollars for the two-week tour. The trio promoted Republic's release of *Oh, Susanna!* and encouraged fans to take part in the Texas Centennial, celebrating the one-hundredth anniversary of Texan independence from Mexico in 1836.[40]

As their tour drew to a close, the cowboy troubadours looped back through Dallas to film portions of *The Big Show* (1936) on location at the Texas Centennial Exposition. Sponsored by the Texas Press Association, the United States Congress matched the $3,000,000 appropriation made by the Texas legislature to kick off fund-raising for the Texas Centennial. The federal government issued commemorative three-cent stamps and commemorative half dollars to support the anniversary events. Government support helped the Central Centennial Exposition in Dallas attracted more than 6.3 million visitors from June to November 1936. During the same six-month run, the Fort Worth Frontier Centennial Exposition brought in nearly one million visitors. New Dealers credited the world's fair and frontier exposition with buffering Dallas and Fort Worth from the worst effects of the Great Depression. Adding 10,000 jobs in construction and the newly emerging leisure and tourism industries, the Texas Centennial contributed more than $50 million to the local economy.[41]

*The Big Show* gave moviegoers an ironic, behind-the-scenes look at moviemaking and radio broadcasting. Simultaneously, the film built desire for leisure travel among Autry fans by highlighting the musicians caravanning across the Southwest on a road trip from Los Angeles to the world's fair in Dallas. Life imitated art for Autry in the filming of *The Big Show*. He played dual roles as a cowboy movie star named Tom Ford (Gene Autry) and the movie star's stunt double, named Gene Autry (Gene Autry). The film opened with Autry leading The Beverly Hillbillies in a traditional version of "The Martins and the Coys," leisurely singing and playing to pass the time on location, backstage with the escapist "Mammoth Pictures" (a euphemism for Republic Pictures) filming near Kernville, California. Revealing a behind-the-scenes view of western location filming, the camera tracked away from the musicians to disclose the group of featured players idly making music for themselves, while a nearby crew filmed a scene with Tom Ford.[42]

In addition to featuring several musical performers, *The Big Show* acknowledged the pleasures of fandom by characterizing a "snooping female" audience that bought tickets to see Autry's musical-Westerns. The film depicted female fans fantasizing about Gene's body and displaying fetishism for his costume. In one scene, women literally consumed the singing cowboy by surrounding him and removing all his clothing. This representation of women in *The Big Show* demonstrated an openness to change brought on by modernization. Here again, the female lead acted as a free agent within a world of work. Implicitly, the film acknowledged the massive economic and social changes accompanying the shift from rural to urban industrial life experienced by most rural and small-town folks. Marion (Kay Hughes) mirrored the modern transformation affecting many women in American culture during the New Deal.[43]

*The Big Show* also illustrated the effects of new technology upon the relationships between labor and capital during the New Deal. The film's setting in the ultramodern Dallas Fair Park displayed the inroads of modernity as fundamental in the American West. The film mirrored modern architecture, petroleum products, and radio communications as aspects of the modern western cityscape. Panning across the Dallas Fair Park, the director showed audiences two golden statues, "Tenor" and "Contralto," representing sound traveling through air and signifying the advances brought by microphones, amplifiers, and loudspeakers in the 1930s. These representations at the Texas Centennial encouraged moviegoers to see the world's fair as a harbinger of a New West, signifying the New Deal in fifty modernist pavilions, built at an average cost of $50,000 each.

Combining tradition with innovation, *The Big Show* included Autry displaying the cowboy arts in the popular "Cavalcade of Texas." His role in the historical pageant depicting four centuries of Texas life showcased some hard riding and stunts with Champion. In a touching final scene, he serenaded his trick pony with the popular ballad, "Ole Faithful." The film explored notions of urban and rural life in complex ways by questioning stasis versus change and the interplay between nostalgia and modernism in contemporary culture. The Texas Centennial did not simply recall the nostalgia of a lost frontier past. As the historicized cavalcade unfolded, the camera lingered on the highly stylized buildings and futuristic statuary juxtaposed around the grandstand. The film emphasized a connection between pageantry in past traditions and modern architecture in the American West. Similarly, the film marked a milestone with The Jones Boys performing "Lady Known as Lulu" to commemorate the "Hall of Negro

Life," the first representation of African American culture at a world's fair.[44]

After filming of *The Big Show* wrapped, Gene Autry and Company embarked upon the largest live performance tour of the young singer-songwriter's career. The *Gene Autry, In–Person* tour played forty-four dates in Texas and Oklahoma from November 1936 to January 1937. Howe developed an elaborate press book for the tour that included predetermined program announcements, a newspaper advertising campaign, special scene mats, press releases, and ballyhoo designed to sell tickets. Publicity included advance features, advance stories, booking stories, and feature stories offering various publicity angles. The press book noted that the Gene Autry Company traveled with its own public address system for special use upon the stages and theaters played. Autry mounted this modern sound system on his truck for street ballyhoo purposes.[45]

During the tour, the singing cowboy star earned $3,591, about $61,472 in 2015 dollars, more than $1,300 per venue, paid through a series of money orders, cashier's checks, and cash en route. A bit discouraging in terms of per-show income, the tour provided enormous exposure for the singing cowboy with core audiences. Over the next twenty years, Autry continuously earned large sums of cash money doing similar tours. A willingness to go out and mingle among his fans distinguished this singing cowboy hero from other Hollywood stars.[46]

George Goodale worked as Autry's advance man during the *Gene Autry, In-Person* tour. As Autry's publicity agent, cashier, and promoter, Goodale traveled in advance to places like Columbia, Tennessee; Wheeling, West Virginia; Steubenville, Ohio; Florence, Alabama; Pine Bluff, Arkansas; and Bowling Green, Kentucky. He prepared the way for the Gene Autry Company to perform a series of one-night stands. *Gene Autry, In-Person* filled the local movie theaters at a buck a head in small towns. The show grossed as much as $1,500 a week. Because banks and most Western Union offices closed on the weekends, Goodale sometimes carried more than a thousand $1 bills on his person. "They'd be in all my pockets, in my socks, under my hat—everyplace.

But I never got mugged," the advance man remembered. Republic Pictures did not share in the proceeds from these live performances.[47]

The headlines made by Gene Autry and the new subgenre of musical-Westerns championed by Republic helped revive the popularity of traditional Western films among mainstream moviegoers. Featuring six to eight musical numbers in each picture, the Gene Autry series proved to be a big hit with female fans. The singing cowboy broke the attendance records of Texas exhibitors and theaters owners in Boston, Massachusetts. Fans confirmed the importance of Burnette's role as Autry's sidekick in films and sideman on tour. Newspapers gave Nat Levine credit for developing the sidekick concept and the singing cowboy innovation.[48]

The Quigley Publishing Company's poll of theater exhibitors in the *Motion Picture Herald* identified George O'Brien as the most popular Western star in January 1936, followed by Buck Jones and then Gene Autry, a comparative newcomer after two seasons. Bill Boyd (Hopalong Cassidy) ranked fourth in the poll, trailed by Ken Maynard, Dick Foran, John Wayne, Tim McCoy, Hoot Gibson and Buster Crabtree. These were the top-ten Western film moneymakers. Autry's rise to prominence received confirmation in the *Los Angeles Times,* which ran a front page story in February 1937, about the singing cowboy being stranded with his film production crew by the spring freshets flooding Kernville.[49]

Autry and company were in Kernville to film *Git along Little Dogies* (1937). The setting for this film resembled the mountain hamlet of the Sierra Nevada, high above the rich oilfields near Bakersfield, California. The film's plot involved a rural radio station owner making a play to strike oil. At first, Autry questioned the environmental impact of oil exploration and the use of radio advertising to promote investment opportunities. He opposed oil drilling, fearing contamination of local water resources. Autry led the ranchers in opposition until he learned that the oil executives could attract a railhead. This new transportation development caused the cowboy hero to have a change of heart and to support oil drilling. Autry justified his flip-flop by arguing in favor of a nearby shipping center. He claimed that the advantages would more than offset the potential of oil drilling to contaminate the water supply. In doing so, Autry mirrored the tradeoffs made by ranchers from Texas, Oklahoma, and California, bearing witness to the enormous expansion of oil industry operations and the resurfacing the western landscape during the New Deal.[50]

To convince his community to support the burgeoning oil industry, Autry staged an afternoon of vaudeville entertainment for locals in the film. Sponsored by a euphemistic Western States Oil Company, the program was broadcast live over the company-owned Radio Station KXB. Autry used the combination of a live show and radio broadcast to sell shares of stock in the hometown oil venture to his fans across the country. Autry demonstrated a desire to solve problems quickly through decisive action. If one solution did not work, he showed pragmatism, trying something new. In this way, the singing cowboy mirrored a comparable New Deal philosophy that called for action over hesitation. New Dealers believed in taking charge to change and perfect society through reform efforts.[51]

*Git along Little Dogies* inspired awe for the raw power of information when combined and communicated through multiplatform entertainment. All who witnessed the spectacle clearly saw the possibilities, so much so that Republic ended the production on an extremely happy note. Promoting Wall Street-style investments by singing the "Stock Selling Song," the final scene showed the Maple City Four asking townsfolk to thank the singing cowboy for the increased value of their Western States Oil Company shares. "Not the banker, nor the landowner," sang the Maple City Four—Autry got the thanks for increasing capital investments. To emphasize Autry's association with FDR, the entire cast broke into a rousing version of "Happy Days Are Here Again." Roosevelt used this tune as his theme song during the 1932 presidential campaign and subsequently, it became the unofficial theme song of the Democratic Party.[52]

CHAPTER 4

# The Second New Deal

During Gene Autry's third season with Republic Pictures, Herbert Yates bought out Nat Levine with a million-dollar offer. Yates brought in Moe Siegel from ARC Records to replace the film producer. Moe's brother, Sol C. Siegel, took over production of the Western serials, including the Gene Autry series. Levine's buyout disquieted the singing cowboy as awareness of his relatively low pay grew. Suddenly realizing his value to the studio, Autry demanded a new deal from Yates. When the movie mogul refused to talk about a new contract, resentment swelled until the singing cowboy waged a one-man strike in May 1937.

Autry walked out on Republic Pictures in protest against the studio's block-booking practices. The job action drew support from theater exhibitors who screened the singing cowboy's motion pictures and staged his live performances. The U.S. Department of Justice took note when Herbert Yates filed legal actions and sent process servers to compel his cowboy crooner to return to the studio. Before the new season got under way, Yates relented and agreed to pay Autry $7,500 per picture. In addition to the salary increase, Autry negotiated a level of script approval.[1]

*Public Cowboy No. 1* became Gene Autry's first film under his new deal with Republic. A milestone in a celebrated career, this film elevated the singing cowboy hero from a Western genre star to a more prestigious ranking as a full-fledged national icon during the Second New Deal. Released on August 23, 1937, *Public Cowboy No. 1* marked a turning point in the career of the yodelin' cowboy and a watershed in American culture.²

Republic Pictures followed up with ever-stronger associations with the Roosevelt Presidency with the releases of *Springtime in the Rockies* (1937), *Gold Mine in the Sky* (1938), *Man from Music Mountain* (1938), *Mountain Rhythm* (1939), and *Colorado Sunset* (1939). Republic's approaches to making the New Deal appear attractive changed somewhat as series scriptwriters worked to accommodate larger and more mainstream audiences. Autry rose to national acclaim in his fifth season starring in *Rovin' Tumbleweeds* (1939). The singing cowboy's ultimate New Deal piece de résistance, *Rovin' Tumbleweeds* featured Autry as a singing cowboy-legislator elected by westerners and sent to Washington, D.C., to introduce measures dealing with dam construction, irrigation, flood control, and the resettlement of migrating refugees.³

The underlying story in *Public Cowboy No. 1* dealt with the desperate need to modernize livestock production in the western states. The film showed Roosevelt's New Deal expansion of livestock production as the primary means of economic development in the rural West. Set against a backdrop of the U.S. Department of the Interior's attempts to implement the Taylor Grazing Act of 1934, the film dealt with issues related to the end to the open range.

The Taylor Grazing Act organized 80 million acres of previously unreserved public lands into grazing districts. The Division of Grazing in the U.S. Department of the Interior (renamed the U.S. Grazing Service in 1939) administered these public lands. The Division of Grazing worked to control erosion through scientific range management. Encountering multiple problems related to low lease fees, opposition from farmers, budget reductions, and unlawful land use, a federal workforce coordinated rehabilitation programs, improved forage, and restrained rodents. Government workers constructed new roads, trails, fences, corrals, and watering places.⁴

Opening with depictions of modern cattle rustlers using aeronautics, short-wave radio communications, and refrigerated trucks to steal livestock from the open range, *Public Cowboy No. 1* showed how influences from outside the region brought corruption and lawlessness as byproducts of economic development in western states. The film scapegoated corrupt executives at the Western Packing Company—a big corporate outfit controlled by outside interests—running a criminal syndicate responsible for the high-tech thievery. Autry fans familiar with the livestock trade interpreted Western Packing as a pseudonym for Swift and Company, a big Colorado meatpacker; Armour and Company or Oscar Mayer in Chicago; or the Cudahy Packing Company in Milwaukee and Los Angeles.

The modern rustlers used techniques of scientific management to baffle Sheriff Matt Doniphan, an elderly, small-town peace officer. Headlines in the *Prairie Junction Courier* declared, "Sheriff Doniphon No Match For Modern Rustlers." A newspaper editorial claimed that "Matt Doniphon Should Be Recalled." These assertions made Deputy Sheriff Gene Autry irate. "If the county would only give us modern equipment to work with, we could get results," Autry contended. "You can't catch high-speed trucks and airplanes with a horse and buggy."[5]

To set the record straight, the cowboy hero paid a visit to the newspaper office to have a word with the antagonistic editor. Upon arrival, Deputy Gene discovered a young woman named Helen Morgan (Ann Rutherford) doing the job. As they faced off, the female publisher bested the young deputy sheriff. Gene made a mess of Helen's typesetting before she chased him out of the office.

Riding horseback on the road out of Prairie Junction, Autry and his sidekick Frog Millhouse (Smiley Burnette) caught up with Helen Morgan. The boys flanked her as they bantered. When Morgan chided the singing cowboys, Autry responded by singing a chorus of "The West Ain't What It Used To Be," backed up by Millhouse's harmonica accompaniment. The song's refrain, "There's a New Deal in the West today," highlighted President Roosevelt's role in the making of a modern New West. The melody reflected the increased leisure made available to American workers by Roosevelt's New Deal. The lyrics imagined a New West where women had greater opportunities and the fewer social constraints.

A couple of lengthy chase scenes that followed included Sheriff Doniphon (William Farnum) getting shot by a crooked meatpacker named Jim Shannon (House Peters, Jr.). Autry caught Shannon and delivered the shooter to the jailhouse. Afterward, the gloating cowboy returned to the newspaper office to warble a second refrain of "The West Ain't What It Used To Be." This time, Miss Morgan appeared more forgiving, which encouraged the cowboy hero to continue serenading his leading lady with "I Picked Up The Trail To Your Heart."

"The West Ain't What It Used To Be" acknowledged changes brought on by independent young women taking part in a modern migration westward. The song celebrated opportunities for professional women to advance in the emerging markets of suburban Los Angeles, Long Beach, Riverside, San Bernardino, and Ontario, California, and other western livestock centers, especially Dallas, Houston, and Phoenix. The New Deal offered freedom for a "cowgirl editor" migrating to the Southwest: freedom to wear dungarees, as Autry put it; freedom from prescribed matrimony.

The most important goal of the New Deal in the American West involved modernization. Much of the West remained a frontier in the 1930s. The overuse of natural resources—grasslands, soil, timber, mining, and watersheds—involved exploitation and serious deterioration. New Dealers sidestepped the question of blame to concentrate on regional planning and strenuous efforts to manage the arid environment. Federal plans called for people living in western states to use the bounty of nature without substantially depleting renewable resources for future generations.[6]

President Roosevelt authorized more planning for the use of natural resources in the American West than in other sections of the country. Public works planning, city, state, and regional planning, and planning with regard to social and economic concerns—all government plans relied upon natural resource development. Permission to develop natural resources on public lands rested with the federal government, further projecting the region into the orbit of a national economy held together by mass media. This is where Gene Autry came into the picture.

A relative newcomer to Hollywood, Autry ranked number one as the biggest box-office earner in the Western film genre in December 1937. Quigley Publishing Company listed the singing cowboy first in its annual poll of theater exhibitors, published in the *Motion Picture Herald*. Autry achieved the top spot among Western film stars in large measure because of *Public Cowboy No. 1*. The singing cowboy unseated a veteran stable of movie cowboys to win the award. He beat out William (Hopalong Cassidy) Boyd, Buck Jones, Dick Foran, George O'Brien, Tex Ritter, Bob Steele, The Three Mesquiteers, Charles Starrett, Ken Maynard, Johnny Mack Brown, Tim McCoy, John Wayne, Bob Allen, Larry Crabtree, Hoot Gibson, Jack Holt, and James Ellison.[7]

Quigley's poll of theater exhibitors and separate ranking of Western film stars signified the importance of the Western genre in American culture during the 1930s and '40s. "Westerns" represented the only film genre tracked by Quigley outside the Hollywood mainstream. Rising with the popularity of its Gene Autry series, Republic Pictures ranked as the number-one producer of Western films in 1937. Autry wore his crown as "Public Cowboy No. 1" for six consecutive years—from 1937 to 1942—giving up the top spot to Roy Rogers after enlisting in the U.S. Army Air Corps.[8]

During his reign at the top, the singing cowboy hero increasingly resonated with larger and more mainstream audiences. Through music and motion pictures, Autry mirrored a deeply ingrained spirit of optimism and hope inspired by President Roosevelt. Republic Pictures managed to harmonize traditional American values with New Deal initiatives in its Gene Autry series. Music proved the key to both synthesis and synergy. Autry's multiplatform entertainments gave his fans an audio-visual representation of the New West and a reason to believe in a future in which leisure and recreation accompanied the development of new water and power resources after the completion of Boulder (Hoover) Dam.[9]

Historians have compared Hoover Dam to the Brooklyn Bridge as a symbol of optimism, marvel of technology, and indicator of modernity in American culture. By connecting Manhattan with Long Island, the Brooklyn Bridge helped transform New York into a world-class city. A half century later, provisions of water and power by Hoover Dam contributed mightily to the conversion of Los Angeles into the grand metropolis of the Pacific Rim and the complete geographic and economic makeovers of southern California, Arizona, and southern Nevada.[10]

Recognizing the promise of local tourism marketing and stimulated by aggressive campaigns of foreign governments encouraging Americans to travel abroad, the Roosevelt administration refocused its efforts in travel promotion. Tourists and travelers accessed the contemporary New West through luxury railcar services, high-speed automobiles, and modern airplanes. New Deal initiatives expanded the vacationing infrastructure in the region to stimulate tourism. A *New York Times* reporter mentioned the "great PWA projects—Muscle Shoals, Norris, Grand Coulee and Bonneville Dam, the Tennessee Valley development, the great Navajo erosion and reclamation project in Arizona and New Mexico, the incredible Boulder Dam" that dotted the itineraries of tourists to the South and West.[11]

An important aid in the development of western tourism came from the publication of an American Guide Series from the Federal Writers Project in the Works Progress Administration (WPA). The Federal Writers Project set out to redefine tourism from the viewpoint of the American state. Before the New Deal, foreign correspondents from France, England, and Germany typically framed the tourist experience in the United States, so much so that the German-based Baedeker's *United States* guide served as the model for the American Guide Series. The first WPA guidebook (Idaho) appeared in January 1937, followed by individual guides for other states.[12]

Interior Secretary Ickes also established the United States Travel Bureau (USTB) with WPA funding in 1937. Secretary Ickes staffed the USTB with Civilian Conservation Corps workers, until Congress authorized an independent appropriation for the agency. To simulate the economy and help bring an end to the Depression, the USTB reshaped the role of the federal government in tourism promotion by imitating foreign competitors.

President Roosevelt encouraged the USTB to launch a "Travel America Year" campaign, followed by a "See the Old West" campaign.

The travel bureau set up a National Travel Advisory Board (NTAB) to distribute information to travel agencies, transportation companies, tour operators, and other service providers. The bureau published and distributed newsletters, bulletins, events calendars, research reports, and promotional aids to encourage travel and tourism. USTB also sponsored lectures, screened motion pictures, staged exhibits, and promoted special radio programs for both government and nongovernment tourist attractions. Additional support came from the Federal Art Project, a WPA program that created dozens of posters to promote tourism and travel to specific national parks and monuments.[13]

As President Roosevelt began his bid for a second term, the popularity of country-western music and musical-Western films made Gene Autry a portent of the New Deal and the New West. As government promotions encouraged worker-tourists to spend their free time traveling in the American West, Republic Pictures mirrored New Deal themes in Autry's music and motion pictures. The attractive cowboy troubadour aided the advertising campaigns of the Roosevelt administration.

Country-western music and musical-Western films made President Roosevelt more attractive to rural, small-town, and newly urban audiences. This support for Roosevelt exemplified a new type of "public diplomacy" defined by the performance of government relations to influence political action through public information media and nongovernmental organizations. These programs demonstrate how the Roosevelt administration developed its tendencies for public diplomacy in foreign policies by garnering support for its New Deal domestic agenda.[14]

To promote *Public Cowboy No. 1* in advance of the film's premiere, Autry left Hollywood for a personal appearance tour in July 1937. The tour began in Dallas, where the Gene Autry Company drew attention to the refreshed and newly reopened Greater Texas and Pan American Exposition, a second season of the Texas Centennial. The singing cowboy's circuit included a stop in New York for a guest appearance on *Rudy Vallee's Varieties*.

The Walter Morris Agency paid the cowboy crooner $667, more than $11,021 in 2015 dollars, to appear on Rudy Vallee's program with Ricardo Cortez, Joe Cook, and the comedy team of Russ Brown and Dorothy Libaire. Originating from New York Radio Station WEAF, audiences heard the nationally syndicated program broadcast over the NBC Radio Network. Back in Los Angeles, Gene's family and friends listened to the program on Radio Station KFI. In October, the J. Walter Thompson Agency booked the singing cowboy for an encore engagement paying $981, about $16,210 in 2015 dollars, for a second appearance on *Rudy Vallee's Varieties*. The national exposure that Autry received from these personal appearances validated for commercial sponsors the singing cowboy's growing appeal among mainstream audiences.[15]

National exposure primed a rumor mill of reports speculating that Autry might leave Republic Pictures. Darryl Zanuck supposedly offered Herbert Yates $500,000 for the singing cowboy's contract, about $8.3 million in 2015 dollars. Other rumors hinted that Autry might leave the studio for a ten-week tour of Brazil. Rumors became so constant that Herbert Yates felt compelled to address them in a press release. Yates refuted all claims that Paramount had signed Gene Autry to a contract. With all the ballyhoo, the movie mogul moved to protect Republic Pictures in the event that Autry did leave. Sol Siegel auditioned musicians for a second singing cowboy series. He signed Leonard Slye of The Sons of the Pioneers to a movie contract. The studio promptly changed the cowboy singer's name to Dick Weston. Later, Dick Weston became Roy Rogers.[16]

Hollywood musicals reached their vogue using song names to inspire new film titles in 1937. The industry finally recognized that a hit song associated with a motion picture release provided the means of integrating sound recordings, radio broadcasting, and live performances. Contemporary accounts credited Autry as one of the first movie stars to achieve success with the eponymous approach. George Burns and Gracie Allen, Bob Hope, and Sonja Henie also received credit for early successes.[17]

Autry's films featured eponymously titled songs in *Boots and Saddles* (1937), *Springtime in the Rockies* (1937), and *Gold Mine in the Sky* (1938). The singing cowboy performed live on the radio and in theaters with his traveling troupe. Autry's association with motion pictures resulted in record sales for the American Record Corporation, three times greater than any other radio crooner. The combination of motion picture features with radio promotions and live performances resulted in some of the biggest record sales in the singing cowboy's career. Hit records dramatically upped Autry's worth to Republic Pictures and theater exhibitors nationwide. The Gene Autry series provided the only proven moneymakers for smaller theater owners in rural, small-town, and newly urban markets.[18]

*Springtime in the Rockies* continued the growing trend of Republic's Gene Autry series to feature New Deal information in the public interest. The singing cowboy demonstrated the value of music as a tool for public diplomacy by diffusing a standoff between cattlemen and sheepherders. Autry succeeded by forcing the opposing ranchers to sing together in harmony, "When It's Springtime in the Rockies." The cowboy hero explained the strategy, saying, "You know it's hard to sing and be mean at the same time." Other New Deal themes showcased the movement of young professional women bringing the techniques of animal husbandry and scientific range management from an eastern university to conduct experiments on western ranchlands inherited by one sorority sister.[19]

Only three years into the motion picture business, Autry outranked seasoned western performers like William Boyd, Buck Jones, George O'Brien, Bob Steele, Charles Starrett, Ken Maynard, Johnny Mack Brown, and John Wayne. Using the advantage that accompanied his enviable position, America's Favorite Cowboy went public for a second time concerning conflicts with Republic Pictures over block booking practices. In January 1938, he complained about Republic using the Gene Autry series to leverage other pictures with exhibitors. "My effort to get a salary raise has met with the statement from the studio that my films don't get much money in the exhibition field, despite the fact that the box-office reports have proved them to be leaders among westerns." Autry complained to the *Los Angeles Times*: "It is known that my pictures are being used as a blackjack to force exhibitors into buying other Republic products, and on this tour I've found out exhibitors are greatly discontented because of the procedure."[20]

Film industry insiders closely watched Autry's dispute with Republic. The singing cowboy's protest against block-booking practices drew attention to similar inquiries by the U.S. Department of Justice. Bringing scrutiny to Republic's block-booking practices demonstrated how the singing cowboy created synergy for New Deal initiatives using multiple forms of art, entertainment, and recreation to influence public opinion. Autry paved the way for people to accept the ideological shifts necessary to adjust to transformative new technology and the global information revolution that accompanied international radio broadcasting and synchronous sound films.[21]

With Autry on strike a second time, Republic assigned the lead in its next musical-Western to Roy Rogers. Hiding his real identity, the studio profiled Leonard Slye as a twenty-five-year-old native of Cody, Wyoming. Sol Siegel claimed he "discovered" Roy Rogers performing on the popular radio program *Hollywood Barn Dance*. Republic paired their new singing cowboy hero with Smiley Burnette to attract fans from the Gene Autry series. The studio recast a film script written for Autry titled "Washington Cowboy" to make the film *Under Western Stars* (1938). Yates spent $100,000 to make and market *Under Western Stars;* more than double the average expenditures for any picture starring Gene Autry.[22]

In a conciliatory gesture, Autry licensed the song "Dust" to the studio for $250. Johnny Mercer originally composed the music and the song lyrics. Autry bought the copyright from Mercer and recorded the song with the intention of featuring it in *Washington Cowboy*. Rogers scored a huge hit with "Dust," garnering Republic's first Academy Award nomination for "Best Song in a Motion Picture." Even so, the name Roy Rogers caused consternation for the studio when a vaudevillian with the same name filed a lawsuit. Perhaps because of the lawsuit or the impermanency of filmmaking, Leonard Slye did not legally change his name to Roy Rogers until after Gene Autry enlisted in 1942.[23]

Autry's ability to attract the attention of mainstream media benefitted from his commitment to appear in full Western regalia at public events like the running of the famous Santa Anita Handicap, featuring "Stagehand" beating "Seabiscuit" by a nose. Reporters commented about the singing cowboy's high-heeled boots, fancy shirt, and ten-gallon hat. They compared the Western hero with Clark Gable, Fred Astaire and other pacesetters modeling the fashions of well-dressed men at Santa Anita. Fans also saw the cowboy crooner at the National Orange Show in San Bernardino, where he appeared with Leo Carrillo, Dick Powell and Dorothy Lamour. Even the cowboy's golf game made the news when Autry's foursome included producer Scott Dunlop, W. Ray Johnston, head of Monogram Pictures, and Trem Carr, now a producer for Universal Pictures. Former executives with Republic, Johnston and Carr helped create the Gene Autry series.[24]

In May 1938, the national press reported that Autry settled his dispute with Herbert Yates. Autry and Yates reached a compromise before Republic's annual convention of sales representatives and exhibitors in New York. They agreed to a gradual increase reaching $10,000 per picture by December 1938, nearly $170,000 in 2015 dollars. To announce the deal, the movie star and movie mogul burst into the convention in a blaze of six-shooters, walking arm-in-arm. Talking to the press at the convention, Autry explained," They [Republic] wanted to settle it because they not only were making money on me, but they were selling their whole product on me. In other words, they'd go to an exhibitor and say, 'Look we've got eight Autrys but in order to get the eight, you're going to have to buy so many of these others.'"[25]

Hollywood's anxiety over block booking practices materialized after several studios went into receivership in the early 1930s. A subsequent contraction affected studios in the industry as they recovered from receivership trauma. Moreover, movies felt pressure from moral censorship codes and new enforcement of a tougher Hays Code by the MPPDA. Movie studios accepted some harsh conditions because the alternative meant government intervention coupled with the assault on block booking practices.[26]

Bankers installed themselves in the top management positions and took charge of distressed companies when motion picture firms went under. These financers set up an assembly line system, heavily dependent on churning out films in proven genres. Burned by economic trauma and threatened with a loss of their own identities, the studios reduced risk by adopting this safer approach to production. Intended to maximize profit, the assembly line system worked, because every successful film not already identified with a specific filmic genre triggered a process of mashing up existing genres and testing the premises of each new series against its specific source of success. When one studio discovered a successful formula, it never escaped other studios, thus leading to the development of an industry-wide genre. At the same time, films were circumscribed by censorship, powerful interests, and predictable for-profit production practices. "The studios exercise maximum control of content," Hanson explained. "But such control could not erase the cultural transactions that went on every day in every movie house in the United States."[27]

Republic timed the 1938 release of *Gold Mine in the Sky* with Autry's participation in a gigantic vaudeville show and Fourth of July celebration with 60,000 American Legion conventioneers at the Los Angeles Coliseum. J. L. Frank lined up the Golden West Cowboys with Pee Wee King as featured entertainers in a costarring musical role. Johnny Marvin and Fred Rose wrote two songs for the picture, "Dude Ranch Cowhands" and "As Long as I Have My Horse." The studio promoted this film more than previous releases in the series. The story highlighted the conflicts between urban-eastern values and rural-western values in a modern dude ranch setting. Tensions underlying *Gold Mine in the Sky* addressed some of the concerns faced by western ranch families attempting to adjust from the old ways to the new tourism and travel industries. Here again, Republic represented a modern New West where eastern gangsters attempted to rustle dude ranch cattle using diesel-powered trucks.[28]

As Autry began a personal appearance tour in Pennsylvania, *Gold Mine in the Sky* broke attendance records in theaters across Texas. The singing cowboy became so popular in the Lone Star State that his hometown of Tioga, Texas, considered changing its name to Autry Springs. The cowboy's musical-Western style inspired Texas Governor James Allred to commission a pair of special boots to celebrate Autry's association as a native Texan. After the summer tour, most of Autry's fan mail came from Pennsylvania, demonstrating the importance of live performances to the maintenance of the singing cowboy's fan base. Texas ranked second among the states, and New York ranked third. Interest in Hollywood was also significant. The Paramount Theater in Los Angeles paid the singing cowboy-movie star $15,000 to appear for one week with Betty Grable in a musical stage production called *Four Star Revue*, more than $250,000 in 2015 dollars.[29]

A memorable stop on the *Gold Mine in the Sky* tour occurred in Kenton, Ohio, home of the Kenton Hardware Company, makers of "Gene Autry" cap pistols. Six thousand people from the town of 7,000 turned out to see America's Cowboy. The mayor of Kenton publicly thanked Gene Autry for providing employment for the citizens of his town. The hardware company produced more than a million "Gene Autry" cap pistols between June and September 1938. Kenton Hardware paid the cowboy crooner $11,589 in fees, more than $195,000 in 2015 dollars, for licensing his name and image. Autry made about one penny for each of the toy guns sold.[30]

With Gene Autry on the verge of national celebrity in May 1938, the singing cowboy's film series proved highly profitable for Republic Pictures. To mainstream the cowboy star, Republic needed to connect Autry more closely with traditional Western film fans, especially adolescent boys. When the studio began a campaign targeting young boys, Autry's fan mail climbed to more than 40,000 letters per month, far greater than any other movie star; yet his movies rarely played in the large downtown theaters of big cities.[31]

A story in the *Los Angeles Times*, "Kids Vote Him Tops," described Republic's attempt to add young boys to the core of female fans championing the musical-Western form. Comparing the singing cowboy to William S. Hart and Tom Mix for previous generations, the cowboy star Harry Carey asked, "Do you know why Autry gets the kids? They see more in him than most of the older folks—He's an eagle that sings!" Film writer E. V. Durling referred to Autry as the "Tom Mix of the talking films," because neither performer ever drank nor smoked on screen. Mix and Autry shared a belief about the bad influences of drinking and smoking upon their young fans.[32]

Affiliation with rodeo sports also helped Gene Autry establish rapport with young boys. To hone this aspect of his singing cowboy persona, Autry appeared as the ringmaster for a charity rodeo at Jim Jeffries Ranch. He also did a guest spot at the World's Championship Rodeo during the Shrine Convention, joining "Hopalong Cassidy" (William Boyd) and Leo Carrillo on stage.[33]

Autry shakes hands with Rudy Vallee, 1937. © Autry Qualified Interest Trust and The Autry Foundation (BIO_244).

*Public Cowboy No. 1* lobby card, 1937. © Autry Qualified Interest Trust and The Autry Foundation (19-PC).

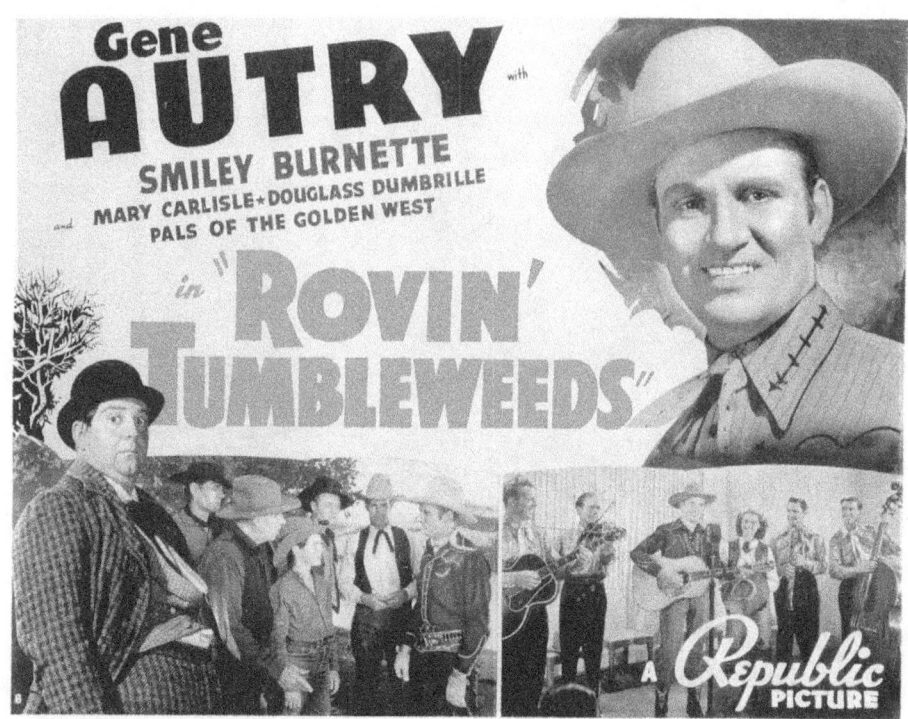

*Rovin' Tumbleweeds* lobby card, 1939. © Autry Qualified Interest Trust and The Autry Foundation (35-RT).

Autry's ability to reach audiences of adolescent boys encouraged more sponsors to license his name and image. The William Morris Agency paid $2,400, more than $40,000 in 2015 dollars, to license the "Gene Autry" name and image for new lines of cap pistols and cowboy hats. The Western Printing and Lithographing Company signed the singing cowboy to a national deal paying $250 per title, more than $4,000 in 2015 dollars, for the use of the "Gene Autry" brand in a "Big Little Book" series. The series included *Gene Autry in Public Cowboy No. 1: retold by Eleanor Parker from the Republic motion picture* (1938), *Gene Autry in Law of the Range* (1939), *Gene Autry, Cowboy Detective* (1940), and *Gene Autry, Special Ranger* (1941). Autry also received a $300 royalty, more than $5,000 in 2015 dollars, from the House of Hollywood to license his name and image for new lines of hair oil, shaving cream, and perfume for men.[34]

Republic Pictures took advantage of all this publicity in releasing *Man from Music Mountain* (1938), a film about the millions of Americans that decided to leave the crowded cities and return to a simpler rural life in the South and West. *Man from Music Mountain* expanded the public understanding of southwestern dude ranch settings in the rural and small-town areas of the Lower Colorado River Basin. The film showed how rural ranch populations dealt with the enormous cultural shift after the opening of Boulder (Hoover) Dam.[35]

*Man from Music Mountain* dramatized the real estate booms that accompanied the distribution of new water and power resources to southern California, central Arizona, and southern Nevada. The studio expanded the notion that "The West Ain't What It Used to Be" to new levels by incorporating dramatic newsreel footage of the Boulder Dam inauguration. Republic used the newsreel footage to set the stage for an escapist story of real estate development and the selling of a dream to make the desert bloom. Twirling newspaper headlines heralded a New West where migrants were portrayed as "Modern Pioneers," heading out west to cash in on a new Gold Rush. The combination of water and power resources on display in the film pitted locals against outsiders to find the accommodations necessary to live and work together as natives and newcomers. Autry's sidekick Frog Millhouse (Smiley Burnette) decided to hang up his spurs and open a new electric appliance store. Frog got the girl and a plethora of new gadgets to sell to newly urban westerners building garden bungalows equipped with running water and electricity.[36]

This film promoted a leisurely New West lifestyle that appeared increasingly attractive to young American voters. Water and power, good roads and modern laborsaving machinery added to the image of the New West. *Man from Music Mountain* showed how the Roosevelt administration was closing the gap in living standards between eastern and western states, between urban and rural lifestyles. Republic went farther than most in the direction of social realism by incorporating newsreel interstitials to portray the hardscrabble conditions that accompanied economic reality throughout much of the rural West. Autry helped audiences believe in the possibilities of a new kind of suburban living, combining the best of town and country. Even so, most of the singing cowboy's fans remained trapped in the foreboding atmosphere of the Great Depression.[37]

In developing Gene Autry's singing cowboy persona to reflect the attitudes and opinions of ticket-buying audiences, Herbert Yates advanced a list of eight rules to follow within the musical-Western formula. Yates associated traditional American values with the New Deal in the construction of these rules. Autry embraced Yates's standards of wholesome family entertainment with a new spirit of Americanism. The singing cowboy followed these eight rules to instill patriotism among tens of thousands of Gene Autry Friendship Club members. The cowboy hero modeled patriotic behavior for fans through heroic portrayals that mirrored rules in a system of cultural values adhered to by tens of millions of Americans.

1. Gene Autry, the cowboy actor, would not hit anyone smaller than himself.
2. The cowboy hero refused to take unfair advantage, even of an enemy.
3. Gene Autry never went back on his word.
4. When representing a government official, Autry never misused the power of his office.

5. Gene Autry always took the side of the oppressed in any conflict.
6. Gene was kind to children, old folks, and, of course, animals.
7. He expressed no racial prejudices whatsoever.
8. His actions were always honorable.[38]

Box office success provided evidence that Gene Autry's evolving "Cowboy Code" resonated with audiences that favored the musical-Western form. Fan support made "the Cowboy" an increasingly valuable spokesperson for sponsors seeking to tap an emerging market of independent female consumers. Girls between the ages of seventeen and twenty formed the bulk of the hundreds of Gene Autry friendship clubs. Republic recognized that Autry's fan base differed from the audiences enjoying traditional Western films. Women wrote more than two-thirds of the letters of support. More importantly, women arranged personal appearances for Autry and his backing band. Local women's organizations played essential roles: renting space for live performances, creating publicity for live events, handling the finances, and dividing profits with the musicians at the end of the night. ARC Records confirmed these findings, as did ARC's deals with Sears and WLS. Women represented the largest and most vocal segment of Autry's fan base.[39]

*Photoplay* discussed the potency of Gene Autry as both a lesson and a promise in 1938. The lesson: never forget the down-to-earth people upon whom the movies have always depended. Films prepared to please lower-culture consumers held the promise of unlimited rewards. The evidence was that Autry sold more movie tickets than other, more famous movie stars. Mostly, Autry sold tickets in movie markets that the major studios ignored. He swelled the returns for Republic while building a name for the studio in the smaller markets of the Midwest, South, and Southwest. Yates understood the desires and needs of these audiences. He appreciated how Autry represented traditional American values to moviegoers. Fans enjoyed seeing the singing cowboy in "message" films. They wanted their cowboy hero to reflect an upfront attitude and reinforce traditional beliefs.[40]

To close the 1938–39 season, the Gene Autry series featured a story of western ranchers battling eastern resort developers over the control of the open range. *Mountain Rhythm* (1939) pitted ranchers against developers in a bid for public lands controlled by the U.S. Department of Grazing. The film showed westerners pooling their money to buy ranchlands at auction that provided access for their cattle to larger holdings within the public domain. In contrast, resort developers competed to buy the same ranchlands to gain the same public access for "The New Pueblo City," a luxury destination for high-rent tourists that arrived via the outside developer's private bus lines. These buses brought "suckers in from every part of the country," explained one resort developer. Another developer clarified, "This ought to send real estate prices in the valley sky high." In a plot twist, *Mountain Rhythm* also characterized life in a refugee camp, reminding audiences of the pervasive homelessness, still abundant in 1938, and the challenges associated with resettling nearly one million Dust Bowl migrants in California.[41]

Further evidence of Autry's affinity for the New Deal appeared in December 1938, when the singing cowboy took part in a radio broadcast to benefit Dust Bowl refugees in the San Joaquin Valley. Melvyn Douglas organized the event after five thousand migrant children petitioned to have Autry and Burnette perform on Christmas Day. When asked which star they wanted to see, a big majority of the youngsters voted for Autry, calling him "The Cowboy." The live radio performance took place at the Farm Security Administration camp in Shafter, California. Sponsors used the broadcast to call attention to the serious problems faced by migratory families. Forced from their homes in the Midwest, South, and Southwest, the refugees lived in subnormal conditions in California. NBC broadcast 45 minutes of the five-hour event over its national radio network.[42]

Overseeing a busy churn of propaganda pictures in 1938, the Roosevelt administration focused on using the film medium to create a national consciousness and compete with the regional and local politicians that historically controlled large blocks of voters. The Western genre in all its forms provided a structured medium for New Dealers seeking to expound a unique sense of national identity based upon the notion of Americanism. Films like *Mountain Rhythm* displayed right thinking, clean living, and a devotion to duty as essential aspects of Americanism. Typically, the Gene Autry series strove for adroitness, preaching in general terms and communicating through inferences about the New Deal. This subtleness disappeared as the specter of wars with Germany and Japan loomed.[43]

Critics attributed the renaissance of "celluloid sage-brushers" to natural causes in 1939, an inevitable cycle following the success of the musical-Western form. Reviewers credited Hollywood with rediscovering the scenic beauty of the American West among the vast panoramas stretching from the Sierra Nevada Mountains to Arizona's spectacular Monument Valley, the location of John Ford's *Stagecoach* (1939). Residents of Kernville and Lone Pine, California, and those in Tombstone, Arizona, offered their towns to Hollywood for a price. These communities maintained permanent western main streets for film companies to use. Merchants and ranchers near filming locations prospered under the arrangements. Ranchers rented their cattle and horses to the moviemakers, and local cowhands found off-season employment. "Quickie" independent film companies operated on shoestring budgets in the rock crags near Chatsworth in the San Fernando Valley and other nearby shooting locations.[44]

Escapism provided the essential philosophy responsible for the success of the Gene Autry series. Herbert Yates explained this philosophy: "The kind of entertainment that we, at least, will stick to will veer away from heavy dramatics or pictures of war. They will have to provide an escape . . . , and until new things develop the company will stand pat on its present plans." *The Film Daily Cavalcade* credited Republic Pictures with successfully reviving the action drama and thus gaining an important place in the Hollywood studio structure. Insiders credited Autry for much of Republic's success with praise for "America's Number One Singing Cowboy, emulated by many, rivaled by no one."[45]

His success proved that Herbert Yates understood "the pulse of the film-going public." Republic recognized its markets for film products, identified its regions, and handled its products well. The studio knew how to read audiences and modify offerings to ensure continued profit. Seeing how direct contact helped Autry build a following and increase market share, Yates demanded that other actors also tour to meet and greet fans personally. In contrast, major stars from the other movie studios rarely traveled to promote new film releases.[46]

*Colorado Sunset* (1939) combined the plot devices of *Guns and Guitars* and *Public Cowboy No. 1* into a story about coded messages in radio programs and the willingness of female fans to "Vote for Autry" in an effort to break a monopoly of milk producers and distributors, sanctioned by legislators in twenty-one states. Highlighting the lack of federal controls over milk and dairy production in the second Agricultural Adjustment Act of 1938, *Colorado Sunset* took aim at the state milk boards that fixed producer prices and provided wholesale and retail price fixing, pooling arrangements, production quotas, and entry controls. Some states justified their laws as protecting public health. In most cases, state laws amounted to little more than a public underwriting of private arrangements between producers and distributors.[47]

The popularity of Autry's singing added capital to his electoral campaign. The singing cowboy targeted women voters who turned admiration into votes by cajoling their menfolk into supporting his candidacy. He attracted diverse audiences by emphasizing music and comedy that appealed to cross-generational, cross-gender, working-class audiences. In a story that emphasized the struggle between agriculture and business, the singing cowboy hero compounded his class-specific address by drawing upon performance traditions that spoke directly to the constituency of his films.[48]

As a follow up to *Colorado Sunset*, Republic elevated Autry into a role as an elected representative in *Rovin' Tumbleweeds* (1939). This film combined the themes of flood control, radio broadcasting, and resettlement with the allure of rodeo sports. Compared with Roy Rogers's *Under Western Stars* (1938) and the Jimmy Stewart classic, *Mr. Smith Goes to Washington* (1939), the political nature of *Rovin' Tumbleweeds* signaled the changing mood and shifting demographics of Autry's increasingly mainstream fan base.[49]

Release of *Rovin' Tumbleweeds* in November 1939 marked the emergence of Autry as a major motion picture star outside the Western film genre. In becoming a national icon, Autry rode a wave of popularity that elevated the entire Western genre outside its traditional niche markets. The *New York Times* marked 1939 as the year that Hollywood recognized the Western as a legitimate film genre. Suddenly, Westerns became adult entertainment and sometimes even high art. Something curious happened, according to reporter Frank Nugent: "Frankly, we don't quite know what to make of it all. We've formed the habit of taking our horse operas in a Class B stride."[50]

*Rovin' Tumbleweeds* provided a portrait of Autry as a congressional representative sent to Washington, D.C., to pass flood control legislation, deal with concerns about migrant workers, and take care of corrupt lobbyists. The film's contemporary New West setting allowed scriptwriters to develop these prominent storylines from the headlines of the western press. Since storylines associated the popular singing cowboy with Roosevelt's political agenda, the approach succeeded with both the public and the president.[51]

As *Rovin' Tumbleweeds* hit the theaters, Boulder (Hoover) Dam became fully functioning in 1939, establishing one of the biggest milestones in the history of the American West. On a tremendous scale, Boulder Dam fulfilled the new multipurpose goals of the New Deal. The United States Bureau of Reclamation also constructed dozens of small earthen dams during the 1930s to catch and store flood waters from smaller streams to help stabilize intermountain and other western states. Nevertheless, hurried agricultural settlement, overgrazing, the plowing of rangelands, speculative farming, and repeated farm failures still characterized the region. Federal reclamation sought to anchor farm families by irrigating areas that were unsuitable for dry farming, thereby supporting an increased number of people living in agricultural valleys of the West and stabilizing many areas. Cooperation between the Bureau of Reclamation, Department of Agriculture, Works Progress Administration, Civilian Conservation Corps, and the National Resources Planning Board made these activities possible.[52]

A great increase in the number of reclamation projects under construction in 1939 relied upon a labor force supported by funds from the Federal Emergency Relief Administration (FERA). Funded by self-liquidating bonds, these projects attracted many investors. Developers ultimately repaid all the monies advanced by the government. Pointing to these efforts to stabilize farm families, Bureau of Reclamation projects helped the Roosevelt administration attract congressional support for its New Deal policies. The future of the Bureau of Reclamation and the integrity of New Deal reclamation policies depended upon repayment by those who benefited directly. Moreover, these projects employed thousands of men and utilized large quantities of machinery, steel, cement, and other supplies, which also stimulated the economy both in the western states and elsewhere. The total of contracts for labor, materials, and machinery in 1939 amounted to $130 million, more than $2.2 billion in 2015 dollars.[53]

*Rovin' Tumbleweeds* reflected the problems faced by the Bureau of Reclamation and the Farm Security Administration in attempting to stabilize migrant farm laborers in California. The film attracted widespread attention to the problem and a deeper understanding of its dimensions. Mirroring the efforts of a Senate subcommittee chaired by Wisconsin Senator Robert M. LaFollette, Jr., Autry brought the problems of California agriculture to public attention in Washington, D.C. Within the context of the film, Congressman Autry appeared to address LaFollette's committee in the nation's capital while focusing attention on the impediments to farm-labor organization. Together with John Steinbeck's novel *The Grapes of Wrath*, Carey McWilliams's *Factories in the Field*, and Dorthea Lange's *American Exodus*, Autry's *Rovin' Tumbleweeds* yielded public information in ways that extended to Americans untouched by prominent literary, intellectual, and artistic figures.[54]

Sentimentalizing the simple life in the American West, the Gene Autry series expressed the desires of more than two million urban residents who took advantage of Farm Credit Act and Emergency Farm Mortgage Act of 1933 to buy properties in southern California and central Arizona within the newly irrigated reclamation areas of the Southwest. By 1940, the rural population of the United States numbered more than 57 million, growing by 6.4 percent during the decade of the 1930s to 43.5 percent of the nation's total population. Part of the increase was due to higher birthrates in rural areas, combined with urban unemployment, which decreased the urge of young people to make good in the city.[55]

Women identified with Gene Autry because he portrayed the New West as safe, law-abiding, and orderly. Respect for law and order permeated the plot of every film in the series. Even so, Autry often committed acts of "heroic" law violations. Reflecting the willingness of many Americans to violate the letter of the law to achieve justice, the ends justified the means for the cowboy hero. Fans expected to see this messaging reinforced in Republic's law-and-order screenplays. Fans patronized movie theaters featuring Republic Pictures because they understood and supported the messaging in the Gene Autry series. People kept buying movie tickets, so Autry remained on board with the approach. He molded an image that championed traditional American values. Voicing support for patriotism, he encouraged the American public to support the federal government while taking voluntary collective action at the state and local levels.

Autry willfully propagandized his name and image to influence his enormous fan base in support of the New Deal. "The West Ain't What It Used To Be" sums up the transformation of the Western star into an internationally known and highly respected iconoclast. Increased media exposure elevated the singing cowboy from a country-western musician performing in musical-Western films to a national icon. The benchmark in this transition from regional to national star was the release of *Public Cowboy No. 1* in 1937.

Between 1935 and 1942, Republic's Gene Autry series incorporated New Deal themes in twenty-seven of fifty-six films. As a westerner with ties to Texas, Oklahoma, and California, the singing cowboy recognized the New Deal as the progenitor of a new western culture, a culture different from and superimposed upon the landscape of the ancient and the Old West. Autry's New Deal filmography showcased stories promoting travel and tourism through performances of Western music, western dude ranch locations, annual rodeo spectacles, and touring Wild West shows.

Autry joined those who believed in the promise of new technologies and the ability of humans to reshape the natural world. He understood the deep and structured role played by the American state in the delivery of water and power in rural and small-town areas. The Gene Autry series offered particular representations of the western New Deal through storylines supporting livestock and range management, water for irrigation and flood control, and rural electricity. A loathing of eastern-establishment types appeared routinely in the musical-Westerns. Republic characterized businessmen and civic leaders as in cahoots with urban gangsters. The gangsters wanted to monopolize western land and cattle companies, meat packers, and trucking firms. Other films in the series took issue with western mining and oil company operations, groundwater contamination, shady stock offerings, short sales, foreclosures, forced migrations, and homelessness.

Republic's musical-Westerns represented modernity through depictions of new media in the American West. Autry's films displayed public address systems broadcasting to large rodeo crowds enjoying supersized stadium shows. The films depicted modern radio broadcasting and futuristic television transmissions combined with behind-the-scenes views of electronic sound recording and motion picture productions. These representations showed how the New Deal connected westerners to the world—and vice versa—through an emerging American media culture. Ultimately, the singing cowboy's support for President Roosevelt appeared most directly in *Guns and Guitars* (1936), *Colorado Sunset* (1939), and *Rovin' Tumbleweeds* (1939). In these films, Republic promoted a "Vote for Autry" in escapist local balloting as the equivalent of a vote for FDR in actual presidential elections.[56]

The notion of Gene Autry as a symbol of the modern, postindustrial New West is consistent with the work of scholars who pegged the emergence of this environment to the New Deal. With Roosevelt at the helm, the economic downturn of the Great Depression occasioned something of a development boom throughout much of the Far West, especially in southern California and central Arizona. New Deal relief and construction programs pulled a flood of unemployed workers from Eastern and Midwestern cities into the region. Western states outpaced all others in per capita share of federal funds for the construction of public works, epitomized by four of the biggest water and hydroelectric power projects in the world to this day, under construction simultaneously in 1936, and built with New Deal money, equipment, and planning. Helping to secure Roosevelt's national agenda for economic recovery, Gene Autry and Republic Pictures contributed to the cultural dialogue about shared national identity that affirmed and legitimized the relationship of the American people to a modern consumer culture in social, economic, and political terms.[57]

Radiating outward from Los Angeles, Gene Autry productions characterized the New West as a place where tradition and innovation converged; a region destined to become the pacesetter for the nation. Autry's singing cowboy persona helped many Americans navigate the material transformation of their lives from rural to urban, from old-fashioned to modern. His entertainments depicted the preconditions necessary to stimulate metropolitan growth, generally in the Southwest and especially in southern California. A basic feature of this New West included the New Deal as a purveyor and promoter of tourism and recreation on public lands.

Autry became a "star" by creating content of lower technical quality for the large audiences that consumed his sound recordings, radio broadcasts, sound motion pictures, and live theater performances. As national advertisers developed an interest in sponsorship, Autry's sound recording and motion picture producers began revising middle-class material to fit working-class values. National advertisers needed to reach audiences with more purchasing power than lower-culture consumers. The shift became apparent when Wrigley's Chewing Gum agreed to sponsor the nationally syndicated *Gene Autry's Melody Ranch* on the CBS radio network. *Melody Ranch* launched on New Year's Eve, December 31, 1939, followed by a movie with the same title released by Republic Pictures in November 1940.[58]

The soft power–public diplomacy represented through Gene Autry productions demonstrated the innovative redefinition of the role played by the U.S. government in formulating a policy of public diplomacy through cultural activities. As the president moved the federal government into the fields of art, entertainment, recreation, and information, Republic Pictures incorporated government information into its cultural products to help combat the Great Depression and promote the New Deal. Increasingly, films in Republic's Gene Autry series appealed to a majority of Americans who did not understand the nuances of government affairs, but who trusted Gene Autry.

CHAPTER 5

# The Good Neighbor Policy

Republic Pictures made fourteen films in its Gene Autry series that promoted Americanism, war preparedness, and friendly relations with Latin America at a time when most of Autry's audience favored separateness. *Comin' Round the Mountain* (April 1936) was the first film in the Gene Autry series to address isolationism. The staging and storyline of the film put forth an attractive portrayal of ethnic Mexicans in California. The film featured Gene Autry as a mail contractor working for the U.S. government while assisting the lovely Dolores Moreno (Ann Rutherford), proprietor of Vista Grande Rancho. Reflecting a principal concern for many Depression-era moviegoers, Moreno faced the prospect of her property being sold at public auction to pay delinquent taxes. As the story opened, Delores sold her cattle to pay the tax bill, and she awaited delivery of the proceeds from the sale via Pony Express. Tasked with delivering the funds, Autry was en route when bandits shot his horse and stole the money.[1]

Vista Grande encompassed the spectacular scenery near Lone Pine, California, in the Eastern Sierra Nevada. In scenes paralleling the contemporary dude ranch settings in Autry's other New Deal pictures, Dolores Moreno hosted a party at her ranch, only this time it was a Mexican fiesta. Disregarding the experimental 1860s setting, fans viewed the fiesta in a modern light, watching dancers in *charreria* outfits performing musical numbers with full orchestral backing. Admirers saw Frog Millhouse (Smiley Burnette) perform a comedic bullfighting novelty song with a chorus of cowboy singers wearing pioneer women's dresses and "Madonna of the prairie" bonnets. The Mexican fiesta featured a marksmanship contest and a horse race, in typical frontier custom for both sides of the U.S.-Mexico border. Autry teaches a young Mexican boy named Pedro (no credit) how to play the guitar and sing "Chiquita." The lesson became a prelude to a serenade when Delores Moreno appeared. Architecture, music, traditions, customs, and dress comprised the elements of the Mexican fiesta displayed positively for the American moviegoers in *Comin' Round the Mountain.*

To combat the Great Depression and prepare the U.S. citizenry for the prospects of global war, FDR encouraged the incorporation of U.S. government information into American cultural products. The president legitimized the use of propaganda in the arts, entertainment, and recreation industries. Roosevelt took advantage of new media to convey optimistic messages of hope to distraught people across the nation and around the world. Anglo-American relations remained the cornerstone of U.S. foreign policy, now combined with a strategy to rebuild trade relations in Latin America. Most commerce between the United States and Latin America had collapsed because of the Depression.[2]

To reestablish markets, Roosevelt reversed much of U.S. foreign policy in the Western Hemisphere. Seeking greater unity as an objective, the president outlined a "policy of the good neighbor" in Latin America during his first inaugural address on March 4, 1933. President Roosevelt intended to ally the twenty-one nations of the Western Hemisphere into a league of nations, with the United States as the dominant stakeholder. As a good neighbor, Roosevelt pledged to eliminate the causes of Latin American complaints against the United States and reopen the channels of trade between the two continents cut off by the Great Depression.[3]

University of California historian Herbert Eugene Bolton contributed significantly to FDR's concept of unity in the Western Hemisphere. During his tenure at Berkeley, Bolton did more than anyone to popularize the teaching of Latin American and borderlands history at the university level. In his 1932 presidential address to the American Historical Association, Bolton presented a theory of Pan-Americanism titled "The Epic of Greater America." Bolton argued that Americans—North, South, and Central—were bound together by a common history and shared New World experience.

The Roosevelt administration used Bolton's theory to anchor its Good Neighbor policy and further the progress of a Western Hemisphere Idea. Defined as a convergence between North, South, and Central America around the values of modernity, gentrification, and market capitalism, the Western Hemisphere Idea promoted an unprecedented degree of amalgamation among democratic republics. Principles of nonintervention and trade reciprocity formed the basis of Good Neighbor policy goals during Roosevelt's first term.

President Roosevelt's reciprocal trade policy set a precedent as the first expression of a modern economic internationalism in the United States. Reciprocal trade underscored the president's understanding of the intimacy between the U.S. economy and the international economy. Prosperity at home depended upon reciprocal trade between the United States and other nations. To inform the public about the need for this new approach, Roosevelt turned to American cultural products and new media to convey the spirit of his Good Neighbor diplomacy. In line with this new approach, Republic Pictures began promoting the common ground between North American cowboys, Mexican vaqueros, and South American gauchos in 1936.[4]

The techniques of public diplomacy the Roosevelt administration learned from the New Deal rolled over into international relations, with new developments in radio broadcasting, sound motion pictures, sound recordings, and live performances. Before 1936, the United States maintained a laissez-faire policy concerning the free flow of two-way cultural relations and public diplomacy. The federal government allowed foreign nations to carry out public information programs in the United States with minimal intervention, excepting the Soviet Union. By 1936, the New Dealers were using public diplomacy to deliver U.S. statements of fact through all the new information media. As war took hold on the European continent, the United States used its public information channels to support Great Britain by countering Axis propaganda with U.S. information. The president trusted the citizens of the world to gauge truthfulness by comparing and contrasting the Axis and Allied information.[5]

Public diplomacy represented an innovative redefinition of the role of government. In formulating a policy of international activity through American cultural and media industries, Roosevelt moved the federal government into the fields of art, entertainment, recreation, and information, disciplines traditionally reserved for states and private industry. Intervening in the American cultural industries became an important part of Roosevelt's overall domestic relief strategy. Creation of the Federal Music Project, Federal Theater Project, Federal Writers' Project and Federal Art Project, signified a major restructuring of American culture stimulated by the American state.[6]

Inter-American radio broadcasting became a major focus for the U.S. government at the first Pan-American Conference in Montevideo, Uruguay. As the U.S. delegation cleared its way through committees, U.S. manufacturers agreed to finance construction of an international broadcasting system to extend the range of American advertising and public diplomacy. A combination of Pan-American conferences, meetings with foreign ministers, and inter-American radio broadcasts enabled President Roosevelt to get the twenty-one republics to adopt widespread policies to join their common interests.[7]

In developing these international bonds, Roosevelt recognized that the citizens of the United States needed a greater appreciation for the different cultures of the Americas. U.S. citizens needed to understand and value the historical experiences that molded the minds of other people in the Western Hemisphere. An informed American citizenry that understood different cultures and appreciated diversity became a national security priority for the president. Republic's Gene Autry series helped President Roosevelt reach this goal by demonstrating the common traits of vaqueros, cowboys, and gauchos through popular country-western music and trendy musical-Western films.[8]

U.S. companies used radio advertising to sell more products in Latin America and recover from the significant declines in U.S.-Latin

American trade caused by the Great Depression. U.S. exporters depended upon Latin American print and broadcasting media to advertise and sell products. Conversely, the Latin American media industry depended upon U.S. advertising dollars to meet its bottom line. Newspapers routinely reported on the popularity of American motion pictures. Foreign news outlets stationed sixty correspondents in Hollywood to cover new releases for consumers abroad. Brazil and Argentina represented the strongest Latin American markets for U.S. goods. U.S. producers purchased 64 percent of the advertising space in prominent daily newspapers and weekly magazines to sell American imports. Likewise, U.S. advertisers bought an estimated one-third of Argentina's total commercial radio time. To stimulate advertising sales, promoters encouraged Gene Autry to tour Brazil and South America, offering the singing cowboy $25,000 in advance and $5,000 a week to make a personal appearance trip.[9]

Radio advertising became increasingly significant to Roosevelt's Good Neighbor strategy in 1936, when NBC launched its network of South American radio affiliates at the Pan-American Conference in Buenos Aries, Argentina. NBC put together an extensive broadcasting apparatus, including local stations and the rebroadcast of shortwave signals originating in the United States. The broadcaster developed new programs for South American markets, including *The Hemisphere Review* and *Good Neighbors* programs. A large advertising firm named Broadcast Abroad secured advertising contracts with forty-seven radio stations in sixteen Latin American countries. Broadcast Abroad specialized in foreign radio advertising for U.S. companies. The company sold U.S.-produced radio programs sponsored by U.S. manufactured goods to local radio stations throughout Latin America. Clients included Parker Pen, Quaker Oats, Standard Oil, Ford Motor Company, Heinz Ketchup, Listerine, and Oxydol.[10]

German advances in Latin America convinced President Roosevelt to double down on efforts to create a network of government-owned shortwave radio stations to broadcast documentary programs like *The American Record*, created to influence public opinion and establish a spirit of hemispheric cooperation. Skeptics labeled Roosevelt's Good Neighbor strategy a smokescreen. Critics argued that domestic propaganda was the real purpose of government radio. Federal control of commercial broadcasting licenses through the Federal Communications Commission (FCC) kept private sector station owners from directly challenging these new forms of government competition. Already, the FCC renewed commercial broadcasting licenses every six months. An indictment of "not operating in the public interest" might limit a broadcaster to a two-month probationary license.[11]

To mend fences with Mexico, the Roosevelt administration targeted southwestern border towns from Los Angeles to San Antonio with soft-power, good neighbor programming. During the Hoover administration, deportations and repatriation of Mexican nationals concentrated Mexican American populations in urban areas. About 57 percent of all ethnic Mexicans in the United States were U.S. citizens. Anxious to succeed by U.S. standards, people of Mexican descent looked forward to the economic upward mobility brought on by the New Deal and the promise that upward social mobility would lead to first-class U.S. citizenship.[12]

Mexican president Lázaro Cárdenas advised Mexican nationals living in the United States to become citizens of their new homeland and to demonstrate loyalty to the United States. This announcement brought forth a rush to U.S. citizenship among Mexican nationals living in the border states of the Southwest. Cardenas's support sped the process of acculturation for Mexicans living in the United States. Americanization campaigns encouraged Mexican immigrants to become more fluent in English. Radio advertisers persuaded Mexican Americans to buy more standardized products from national chain stores. Residents of the barrios tuned in to hear national broadcasts of programs like *The Jack Benny Show* and *Major Bowes' Original Amateur Hour*, but mostly, they listened to daily or weekly Spanish language programming.[13]

Events in Bolivia and Mexico created an international backdrop for the production of *Rootin' Tootin' Rhythm*, released by Republic Pictures in May 1937. Gene Autry portrayed a ranch owner living along the U.S.-Mexico border who had a problem with cattle rustlers. The rustlers drove Autry's stolen herd to a relay ranch owned by Joe Stafford (Monte Blue), head of a local Cattlemen's Protective Association.

Posing as a representative of law and order, Stafford was in cahoots with the rustlers and an outlaw enforcer named the Apache Kid (Max Hoffman, Jr.). Symbolizing the corruption of U.S. business interests, Stafford took advantage of his powerful position to cover up double-dealing and illegal smuggling across the border. When Stafford's niece, Rosa (Armida Vendrell), secretly witnessed her uncle cavorting with criminals, she made a beeline for town to alert the sheriff.[14]

Well known in Los Angeles, Armida Vendrell was a native of Sonora, Mexico. She grew up in a theatrical family, working in a family-owned movie theater in Douglas, Arizona. After the Vendrills moved to Los Angeles, Gus Edwards discovered Armida performing in a vaudeville show with her sister Delores at the Hidalgo Theater on the main plaza. An experienced stage and screen actor, songwriter, and dance instructor, Edwards took Armida to New York and booked her into several theaters. She gained experience performing daily vaudeville routines on Broadway, then returned to Los Angeles to make films like *Mexicana* for Metro-Goldwyn-Mayer (1929) and *Border Romance* (1929) for Tiffany Productions.[15]

Armida portrayed Rosa in *Rootin' Tootin' Rhythm* as a beautiful and talented Mexican American woman with strong moral judgment and good character. Her performance of the best-selling song, "Mexicali Rose," in a duet with Autry, personified the spirit of unity and harmony between Mexico and the United States that President Roosevelt hoped to achieve through the Good Neighbor policy. Autry's attraction to Armida and the suggestive kiss they presumably shared (behind a closed door) conveyed a sense of closeness and intimacy that appealed to young female fans. As Autry fans began to fixate on Armida, they learned something about Mexican culture and Mexican Americans living in the American Southwest. In addition, the singing cowboy received a favorable viewing from the residents of border town barrios that turned out to see Armida.[16]

*Rootin' Tootin' Rhythm* addressed two concerns of FDR's Good Neighbor policy. First, the film introduced Mexican culture to a broad American audience unfamiliar with their neighbors south of the border. In addition, the film positioned Gene Autry to deliver a particular brand of western-style universalism and Americanism designed to appeal to ethnic Mexican audiences. Displaying the soft-power approach sought by President Roosevelt, *Rootin' Tootin' Rhythm* left a favorable impression that attracted audiences in Mexico and the United States.[17]

The impression Gene Autry made emboldened the Mexican film director Fernando De Fuentes to borrow from Republic's musical-Western form to create a new *comedia-ranchera* film genre for the emerging Mexican film industry. De Fuentes combined comedic action on film with *ranchera* music, a genre of rural Mexican folk music comparable to country-western cowboy music in the United States. The filmmaker staged this new genre in a contemporary rural setting on a cattle ranch in northern Mexico.

De Fuentes also copied Republic's method by creating an eponymous film titled, *Allá en el Rancho Grande* (*Over at the Big Ranch*, 1936). The movie title doubled as the title of a popular song performed in the film by Tito Guizar. As the foreman of Rancho Grande, Guizar portrayed José Francisco Ruelas, a singing vaquero hero. Comic relief came from Florentino (Carlos López) a drunken, live-in boyfriend of the wicked godmother in this Cinderella story.[18]

Except for the border separating the Mexican North from the American Southwest, cattle ranchers in the region had a shared history that supported Eugene Bolton's theory and the Western Hemisphere Idea. One glaring difference between Gene Autry pictures and De Fuentes's film involved the reflections of modernity, gentrification, and market capitalism, portrayed as aspects of rural life in the southwestern United States and northern Mexico. Autry's films depicted the American Southwest as a place where elements of modern industrial culture influenced longstanding traditional folkways in the mid-1930s. Smoothing over the rough transitions, the soaring popularity of Autry's music conveyed a sense of romantic agrarianism that encouraged fans in the United States to think kindly about rural Mexican Americans who supposedly remained rooted in the land, uncorrupted by urban vice.

In comparison, De Fuentes's portrayal of rural Mexico incorporated meager references to the Western Hemisphere Idea. The script called for the mention of an automobile a couple of times; yet, no mechanized vehicles ever appeared onscreen. Radios and telephones were also absent from homes and businesses in the contemporary Mexican setting. The only notable reference to market capitalism involved an antithesis of sorts—fleeting references to Communism and the Soviets. Moreover, the opening scene showed a vaquero herding cattle with a looped *reata* (rope) on foot, rather than astride a beautiful mount. De Fuentes showed more grit from daily life on the Mexican rancho compared to Autry films, where the hero never smoked. Moreover, the MPPDA censored scenes of public drunkenness and violence toward women and children in the United States. De Fuentes's *comedia-ranchera* appealed more to adult audiences, unlike the young women and adolescent boys who bought tickets to see Gene Autry.[19]

Even so, Fernando De Fuentes exposed a large and underserved audience among Mexican moviegoers that embraced the *comedia-ranchera* form. President Cárdenas responded by awarding De Fuentes the *Medalla al Mérito Cinematográfico* (Medal of Cinematic Merit). On the strength of popular support for *Allá en el Rancho Grande*, Cárdenas propped up a nascent film industry by creating the first film-workers union in Latin America. In 1938, De Fuentes's film received the first international award ever given to a motion picture from Mexico. The prestigious Venice Film Festival honored Gabriel Figueroa with an award for "Best Cinematography" in the filming of *Allá en el Rancho Grande*. As Cinexport began distribution of *Allá en el Rancho Grande* to Spanish-language movie theaters in the United States, Republic infused the next film in its Gene Autry series with a more complete range of U.S. foreign policy associations.[20]

Rapid developments in world affairs motivated Armand Schaffer and Nat Levine to produce a film with a truly hemispheric storyline. As a follow up to *Rootin' Tootin' Rhythm*, *Boots and Saddles* (1937) added a dimension of Anglo-American relations. This film combined characters that symbolized an alliance between the United States, Great Britain, and Mexico for worldwide moviegoers throughout the Western Hemisphere and the British Empire. Gene Autry portrayed a western ranch foreman managing the work of ethnic Mexicans on a southern California rancho owned by an absentee Englishman, the fictitious Earl of Grandby. When the Englishman died, the rancho passed to his son, Edward (Ra Hould), who journeyed to California with his trustee, Wyndham (John Ward), the solicitor of the estate. The Englishmen came intending to sell the California rancho to relieve its debts, but they changed their minds after spending time with the vaqueros and cowboys inhabiting the wide-open spaces of the American Southwest.[21]

Both vaqueros and cowboys rode out to meet the train carrying Edward and Wyndham as it arrived from the East. These horsemen escorted their English patrons back to the rancho. As the buckboard rolled into the courtyard, the ethnic Mexican rancheros living and working on the estate erupted into a rousing version of "Salud Vaquero," welcoming their patron to a fiesta in his honor. Young Edward stood in the buckboard and thanked the assembly of ethnic Mexican workers. Speaking Spanish, the youthful Englishman conveyed his gratitude and respect for traditional Mexican culture. The opening festivities climaxed with Gene Autry singing the eponymous title song, "Take Me Back to My Boots and Saddles." This folksy Western tune sounded soothing and unthreatening in a gentle, reassuring way, but the subtlety did not overshadow the "Boots and Saddles" association with the standard bugle call used routinely by the U.S. Army to alert cavalrymen to equip themselves and their mounts for immediate action.[22]

Later in the film, Cecilia Callejo performed a classic *ranchera* folksong, "Cielito Lindo," while portraying a singer and dancer at the Spanish Café, a classy nightclub where the cowboy hero entertained his female lead, Bernice Allen (Judith Allen). When combined with other messages conveying a spirit of cooperation built up through the popular press and international radio broadcasting, *Boots and Saddles* persuaded Autry fans to feel positively about the growing alliance between the United States, Great Britain, and Mexico.[23]

With *Rootin' Tootin' Rhythm* and *Boots and Saddles* circulating in the theaters, word spread about Autry considering another South American concert tour. If Grace Dugan's response was typical, the prospect of the cowboy singing south of the border did not make Autry's fans very happy. A teenager from La Crosse, Wisconsin, Grace wrote a letter to Gene dated December 31, 1937, wherein she pleaded with the singing cowboy not to go.

But here's my theme song and lament now———are you REALLY going to South America, as Parsons tells us????????? Why? And where? And when? And for how long? Shhh-h-h, PUL-LEEE-EASE don't go . . . when are you going? Oh, don't stay down there long . . . you don't want another depression in the U.S.A., do you? I know my disposition will hit an all-time low, with the Autry influence far, far away. I do-o-o s-o-o wish you'd stay hyar in the land of stars and strikes—pun intended—but if you must go and do so. . . . WOW 'em, huh? And cash in on all the publicity—farewell parties, bon voyages, et cetera, confetti, and such forth. . . .

P.S. If you can get your tonsils around a South American microphone, I'll be shortwaving from now till then![24]

Rather than following through with the invitation to tour South America, Autry used the offer to leverage more money out of Herbert Yates. Autry threatened to stop making movies and leave the country if Republic did not raise his salary and address concerns about block booking practices. The cowboy complained about the studio using his films to force film exhibitors to rent other pictures.

"It is known that my pictures are being used as a blackjack to force exhibitors into buying other Republic products," Autry explained. In announcing the prospect of a South American concert tour, he claimed to have an offer for $25,000 in advance and $5,000 a week, an advance of more than $413,000 in 2015 dollars, and $82,000 per week. "He may accept, if Republic and he don't agree to agree," Edwin Shallert reported in the *Los Angeles Times*.[25]

Film industry insiders watched Autry's dispute with Republic closely. The U.S. Department of Justice launched an investigation into Hollywood's block booking practices. The department continued to investigate restraint-of-trade allegations until 1940, when the department reduced to five the number of films that distributors could package in a block booking. In 1946, a federal consent decree outlawed the practice altogether. Caving to the pressure, Yates agreed to raise Autry's salary from $2,000 per picture to $5,000 in May 1938, from $33,000 to $82,000 in 2015 dollars. By December, the singing cowboy received another bump, earning $10,000 per picture, more than $165,000 in 2015 dollars.[26]

Gene Autry showed his independence from Republic by siding with the federal government in opposition to the studio's block booking practices and threatening to embark upon the South American concert tour. The timing of these events, following the releases of *Allá en el Rancho Grande* and *Boots and Saddles*, suggested synchronous developments involving Autry's emerging celebrity status and the Roosevelt administration's soft-power approach to influencing public opinion in line with its Good Neighbor policy. As Autry aligned himself with FDR's policies, his motion pictures demonstrated the changing state of world affairs to rural, small-town, and newly urban fans. Autry's films emphasized the role of American cultural industries in facilitating a global information revolution. The performer understood the value of public opinion and the role of opinion-shapers in managing global change.

The Good Neighbor films in the Gene Autry series provided an introduction to Mexican culture for many moviegoers. As the singing cowboy openly embraced Mexican traditions and music on screen, he showed respect by singing traditional folksongs in Spanish. He influenced audiences to think positively about Mexicans Americans, especially in the border states of California, Arizona, New Mexico, and Texas. Similarly, the inclusion of Mexican cultural elements—locations, architecture, traditions, actors, and musicians—made Autry movies more appealing to the large Mexican audiences that enjoyed De Fuentes's *comedia-ranchera* films. American values, put forth through Republic's musical-Western formula and the inclusion of ethnic Mexicans in studio productions, made Autry's brand of Americanization palatable for Mexican American moviegoers while simultaneously meeting the expectations of increasingly larger and more mainstream national and international audiences.[27]

Initially, most filmmakers thought message films were unprofitable, but Autry's success with Republic Pictures changed that opinion. The MPPDA reversed its opposition to controversial subjects and announced plans for Hollywood studios to cooperate with the federal government by producing several shorts and some feature films representing Americanism. The Nazi closure of central Europe to American films provided another stimulus for the MPPDA. The loss of European markets made distribution critical throughout Great Britain and Latin America. Hollywood responded by producing more pro-British–anti-Nazi films and more Good Neighbor pictures.[28]

Newsreel companies cooperated by producing weekly ten-minute news films to accompany virtually every motion picture shown. Newsreels exposed the public to world political leaders and enabled moviegoers to become eyewitnesses to great events. Films of Roosevelt's presidential addresses, particularly his fireside chats, were popular with film audiences and radio listeners. Newsreel companies cultivated goodwill with full and sympathetic coverage. One of Roosevelt's detractors thought the president's head had been turned by flattery. *Baltimore Sun* pundit H.L. Mencken charged, "In the popularity of Roosevelt there has always been something false and meretricious; it is the popularity of a radio crooner or movie actor."[29]

Warner Brothers, Paramount Pictures and Loew's (the parent of MGM) volunteered to assist the White House directly. Warner Brothers eagerly tested the boundaries of tolerance through daring and explicit criticism of Nazi Germany in its films. The execution of the studio's German sales representative keyed the aggressive attitude at Warner Brothers. *Confessions of a Nazi Spy* (1939) is a good example of the studio's approach. Based on a well-publicized espionage trial in New York, the film starred Edward G. Robinson, one of the highest ranking and most aggressive antifascists in Hollywood. Warner Brothers rushed the production to completion after wrestling with the MPPDA for script approval. Released in May 1939, *Confessions of a Nazi Spy* used documentary film techniques to depict a sense of realism in its portrayal of the German-American Bund as a grave threat to U.S. national security. The film ended with the prosecutor at the spy trial delivering a stern speech about the dangers of isolationism.[30]

Contemporary with *Confessions of a Nazi Spy*, Republic Pictures produced and distributed four films in 1939 that connected the Gene Autry series with U.S. foreign policy. The first of these films premiered two weeks after German troops occupied Czechoslovakia. Released on March 29, 1939, *Mexicali Rose* strengthened the associations between Republic's musical-Western formula and De Fuentes's *comedia-ranchera* genre. The movie title came from Autry's golden recording of the duet he performed with Armida in *Rootin' Tootin' Rhythm*. Republic incorporated another song, "Rancho Grande (Allá en el Rancho Grande)," to drive home the associations between the Gene Autry series and De Fuentes's work. Republic acknowledged the growth of its cross-cultural audience by including this song in the film.

*Mexicali Rose* (1939) dramatized the Mexican radio broadcasters that set up powerful stations on the Mexican side of the U.S.-Mexico border. These "border blasters" served all who cared to listen, without regard for race, ethnicity, or nationality. Transmitter power ranged from 100,000 watts to 1,000,000 watts—enough signal strength to reach most of the United States and Canada under normal evening atmospheric conditions. Border radio stations operated on a model similar to Sears, wherein stations measured audience response through direct mail orders for products pitched by radio personalities.[31]

The film opened with Gene Autry and his sidekick Frog Millhouse (Smiley Burnette) racing their horses down a desert road skirted with Joshua trees and framed in the distance by snow-capped mountains. This Old West introduction faded out to the interior of a modern broadcasting booth at a "border blaster" radio station located, presumably, in Mexicali, across the border from Calexico, California, about 250 miles from Los Angeles. A Mexican radio announcer fronting a Mexican band nervously looked at his watch before saying into the microphone, "Buenos tardes amigos, once again the Alta Vista Oil Company brings you Gene Autry and his caballeros, broadcasting from across the border in Old Mexico."[32]

Autry arrived in the nick of time to do the show; but afterwards, he discovered that Alta Vista Oil may be involved in some shady dealings in Mexico that threatened a group of orphans being cared for by the lovely Anita Laredo (Luana Walters) at an old mission overseen by her uncle, Padre Dominic (William Farnsworth), located on an original Spanish land grant handed down within the family since the early nineteenth century. "You ought to be ashamed of yourself, broadcasting for a company like this, helping them sell their worthless stock," Miss Laredo growled, "You and your pretty songs—baiting people for those grafting oil promoters."

The oilman Carruthers (William Royle) countered by offering Autry a new contract to keep performing on the company-owned station. Carruthers and Autry argued about the rights of an entertainer to question a sponsor's product line. The oilman chided the singing cowboy to mind his own business. Autry responded by proclaiming: "A lot of people bought stock in this outfit on my account and I am going to see that they get a square deal!"[33]

Gene and Frog headed for the oil well to check up on things with Carruthers's henchmen trailing along, intending to bushwhack the cowboy heroes. Riding through the Mohave Desert, the boys crossed paths with a Mexican outlaw gang. The bushwhackers shot at Valdez (Noah Beery), the leader of the gang, expecting the outlaw to blame Gene and Frog. Valdez and his men tried to capture the singing cowboys, but they escaped and headed for the Ochenta Mission. Meeting the orphans cared for by the mission, Autry explained to Miss Laredo and Padre Dominic his commitment to investigate the actions of the U.S. oil company.[34]

Valdez turned out to be a music fan. His favorite record, surprise, surprise, the hit Gene Autry song, "Mexicali Rose," played on a modern portable phonograph. When a wood gatherer accidentally broke the noble bandit's record player, Gene calmed things down by singing the song live, in person. Eventually, the entire encampment joined in a symphony of hemispheric unity, a symbolic display of American harmony and the power of music to promote collective action. The harmonizing softened Valdez's disposition. Making music together signaled friendship between the noble Mexican bandit and the gallant American cowboy.[35]

The bond created between Valdez and Autry signified the goodwill and cultural bonds tying Mexico together with the United States. A shared meal and another song sealed the deal. Autry serenaded Valdez with a tune called "Robin Hood," a song about another, much-heralded, noble bandit from English lore. This song introduced an affinity for Great Britain into the budding association between Autry and Valdez, who personified the United States and Mexico in the film.

In this regard, *Mexicali Rose* synergized two principal facets of U.S. foreign policy—Anglo-American relations and the Good Neighbor policy.³⁶

An elaborate fiesta scene featured youthful dancers showcasing a traditional Mexican folk dance, "Chiapanecas," with the accompaniment of a Mexican dance band. Autry covered the popular song, "You're the Only Star in My Blue Heaven," followed by Frog Millhouse singing a comedic, bilingual song, "My Orchestra's Driving Me Crazy," with verses in Spanish and English and the accompaniment of a youthful orphan ensemble. As the partygoers danced, Valdez and his gang strong-armed the wealthy men in the crowd, à la Robin Hood, to raise money to support the poor orphans.³⁷

When Autry and Valdez hatched a plan to foil the corrupt U.S. oilmen, they signified their allegiance by riding together and singing a song from the saddle, "Rancho Grande" ("Allá en el Rancho Grande"). Symbolizing hemispheric unity and harmony through music, the vaqueros and cowboys sang verses from the original Mexican song in Spanish. Then Autry sang new verses of the same song in English. The combination of these Mexican and American verses sung together emphasized for mainstream American audiences the common cattle-ranching heritage of vaqueros and cowboys along the U.S.-Mexico border.

The tight bond between the vaqueros and cowboys in this scene personified the friendly relations between the United States and Mexico, thereby furthering the aims of FDR's Good Neighbor policy. The common heritage of vaqueros and cowboys working on the ranches and ranchos of the border states symbolized the Western Hemisphere Idea as clearly and concisely as any comparable image. Autry and Valdez symbolized the American states of the Western Hemisphere and the bonds made by the people of the Americas to support liberal democracy and individual freedom. Together, these values represented the social ideals that all the American states agreed to protect. *Mexicali Rose* suggested that U.S. business interests, in particular big oil companies like Standard Oil, represented the gravest threat to democracy and freedom in the Western Hemisphere.³⁸

The climactic scene featured a firefight between the oilmen, holed up in a cabin, surrounded by Autry and Valdez and their men, and a company of Mexican *federales*. Valdez was mortally wounded attempting to throw a teargas bomb into the shack. Autry showed off a big-league arm by picking up the bomb and throwing it himself. He literally smoked out the bad guys before turning his attention to the aid and comfort of his good neighbor, Valdez. As the noble bandit lay dying in the cowboy-hero's arms, Valdez asked to be remembered like Robin Hood. In the closing scene, as the assembled Mexican citizenry watched Autry deliver on his promise of oil drilling profits, Padre Dominic expressed his eternal gratitude to Valdez. Autry, in turn, referred to his Mexican *compadre* as a true friend.[39]

*Mexicali Rose* showed sympathy for the positions of the Latin American governments that were anxious to curtail, or at least slow down, the assault of Yankee firms on their natural resources. The film suggested the appropriateness of Roosevelt's decision to side with Mexican President Cárdenas in support of his claims against Standard Oil. In addition, the picture showed Latin American citizens receiving a larger share of the profits derived from U.S. corporations.[40]

Two months later, on May 4, 1939, Republic released a different type of Good Neighbor picture, *Blue Montana Skies.* A now familiar border-smuggling story, this film changed locations from the U.S.-Mexico border to the U.S.-Canada border. The film opened with a close-up of a sign reading "Assiniboia Trading Company." The camera pulled back to reveal a wintry scene with sled dogs barking and men sorting silver fox pelts. The story involved a man named Hendricks, part owner of the "HH Guest Ranch," a dude ranch operating along the Canadian border in northern Montana. Driving cattle across the border to sell in Canada, Hendricks used the HH chuck wagon to smuggle silver fox pelts into the United States. Snow sleds and barking dogs, U.S. and Canadian customs agents, and Canadian Mounties signified the northern border for moviegoers.[41]

Often overlooked as an aspect of the Good Neighbor policy, *Blue Montana Skies* reflected the U.S. desire to build stronger and friendlier relations with neighbors to the north. The film featured Autry driving a dog sled in pursuit of the crooked ranchers turned smugglers and murderers. The singing cowboy hero helped Canadian Mounties by causing an avalanche that pinned the bad guys in their car with the contraband.

In the closing scene, Autry rode with Dorothy (June Storey) singing a reprise of "I Just Want You." As they arrived atop a sublime Rocky Mountain vista, Gene proclaimed to Frog that he liked Montana fine and that he decided to stay on with Dorothy at the HH Guest Ranch for the foreseeable future. Such a nod toward domesticity conveyed a sense of peace and serenity in U.S.-Canadian relations, unlike the chaotic situation in *Mexicali Rose*.

*In Old Monterey* (1939), Republic's third Good Neighbor message film of the season, focused on war preparedness and the likelihood of bombings along the border between the United States and Mexico. This was the first big-budget "Super Western" in the Gene Autry series. Released in first-run theaters in major metropolitan areas on August 14—less than three weeks before the Nazi invasion of Poland and the start of World War II—critics marked this outing as Gene Autry's bid for major representation. The marketing campaign for *In Old Monterey* encompassed a personal appearance tour in and around New York City and an overseas tour of the British Isles and the Irish Free State. Autry spent $18,000 for a 35-foot horse trailer to take his two saddle horses on the overseas tour. British hosts outfitted Champion with a $300 gas mask, making Gene's mount the most stylish and best-prepared horse in Hollywood. Borrowing language from federal propaganda, Jimmie Fidler commented upon the singing cowboy's bon voyage in his Hollywood entertainment column. Fidler wrote, "Bet Gene Autry singing 'Home on the Range' will be the best Good Will Ambassador we ever sent to England."[42]

On the way to London, the Republic Pictures entourage made a stopover in New York on July 21, 1939. Before sailing on the ocean liner *Manhattan*, the singing cowboy appeared on "Gene Autry Day!" at the New York World's Fair. On Monday, July 22, fans got to meet their cowboy hero in person at a reception in the administration building. Afterwards, fan club members escorted their Western singing sensation to a special ceremony at the World's Fair Wild West Show and Rodeo. Ruth Mix, daughter of Tom Mix, crowned Gene Autry "King of the Cowboys." That evening, Gene appeared as guest of honor at a dinner in the Ford Building in the Little Old New York section of the amusement area. On Tuesday, he made a fast tour of eight Loew's theaters throughout New York City, including the Valencia Theater in Jamaica, Pitkin in Brownsville, Boro Park Theater in Brooklyn, Commodore on the East Side, and the Yonkers, Boulevard, Paradise, and Orpheum theaters.[43]

Newspapers billed Gene Autry as an "Ambassador of Good Will" when he landed in London in August 1939. Upon arrival, the cowboy hero was taken by surprise to learn of a ban on firearms. He sent out 100 "Gene Autry" cap pistols as an invitation to tea, but when his guests arrived, a Scotland Yard man confiscated the toy guns at the door. Handguns were reserved for soldiers in England. They served tea in a hall decorated to look like an old-fashioned American saloon. It took an American cowboy to break down the English barriers. The locals seemed to love the Western singer.[44]

Republic continued to broaden its market for Autry films with the release of *In Old Monterey*. The film reflected an increasing shift in the American public away from rural and small-town strongholds into the industrial centers of the United States. As wartime production increased the ranks of newly urban workers, Republic increased its distribution of Autry films in urban areas nationwide. *In Old Monterey* helped smooth the transition for fans moving from rural to urban locales for jobs in wartime industries. The audiences for Autry pictures grew as newly urban workers popularized his films among metropolitan moviegoers.[45]

Republic Pictures released *In Old Monterey* as the Germans prepared to invade Poland, triggering the start of World War II. Republic branded the film a "special," which meant a bigger budget, extra stars, more musical numbers, and other special effects. The film ran seventy-three minutes, longer than the normal "B" Western. In addition to songs by Autry and Burnette, the film featured the Hoosier Hot Shots, a well-known Midwestern musical group. A plot involving the U.S. Army created an opportunity for Autry to appear onscreen in a soldier's uniform. The cowboy hero's delivery of a hard sell, patriotic speech confirmed American resistance to the aggression witnessed during the Spanish Civil War and the Japanese invasion of Manchuria. Autry's performance became a benchmark that foreshadowed future acts of patriotism and the extraordinary efforts necessary for victory.[46]

Republic ballyhoo promoted *In Old Monterey* as a coming attraction during Gene Autry's hugely popular, personal appearance tour of the British Isles and Irish Free State. Upon his return to New York, John Kilpatrick, the operator of Madison Square Garden, booked the singing cowboy to perform in concert at the national finals of Everett Colborn's World's Championship Rodeo (WCR). Autry drew a sold-out crowd of over 17,000 fans in Madison Square Garden. Music at the rodeo proved so popular that Kirkpatrick added Gene Autry as a headliner for the entire nineteen-day run of the 1940 WCR Finals.[47]

Republic had cut Autry's British tour short, just days before the Nazi invasion of Poland on September 1, 1939. As World War II got started, Autry was sailing for New York aboard the ocean liner, *Manhattan*, in the company of Herbert Yates, the head of Republic Pictures. Upon their arrival in New York, B. R. Crisler wrote a *New York Times* feature story referring to Gene Autry as an "omen of world change." Thankful to have escaped the German submarines during their home voyage, the movie star and movie mogul parlayed their experience into an eponymous film version of a new song they discovered in England, "South of the Border (Down Mexico Way)." To prepare for this story about hemispheric cooperation and the prospects of global war spreading to Latin America, Autry signed up for a course to learn Spanish.[48]

*South of the Border* (1939) was the second Gene Autry film to open in first-run movie houses, demonstrating the broadening appeal the singing cowboy generated with mainstream, middle-class audiences. Republic elevated the production values for *South of the Border*, making the film a "special" for play in first-run movie houses. Autry's deepening appeal to the independent sector and its audiences helped the studio amalgamate its understanding of the musical-Western genre. Exploiting the genre as an American art form with the casting and production values of a prestige Western, *South of the Border* appealed across class, gender, generational, and political divisions.[49]

CHAPTER 6

# Western Hemisphere Idea

A quarter century before the Beatles kicked off the British Invasion of the United States, citizens of the British Isles and the Irish Free State generated similar scenes of mass hysteria in London, Glasgow, and Belfast, where tens of thousands of fans mobbed concert halls and movie theaters featuring the personal appearances of Gene Autry, America's Favorite Cowboy. The country-western superstar received a hero's welcome everywhere he appeared to promote his musical-Western film *Colorado Sunset* (1939).[1]

During the tour, Autry met with two songwriters, Michael Carr and Jimmy Kennedy, to purchase a new song titled "South of the Border (Down Mexico Way)." He knew the work of Michael Carr, who had penned "Ole Faithful" with Jimmy's brother, Joseph Hamilton Kennedy. That song went gold for the singing cowboy in 1935, rising to No. 10 on *The Billboard* pop chart. Autry added the new song into a set that included "Rancho Grande" and "Gaucho Serenade," which he performed during a special short-wave transmission from the British Broadcasting Corporation (BBC). "South of the Border (Down Mexico Way)" went viral, becoming a hit instantly with worldwide audiences listening to the international broadcast.[2]

The image of an American cowboy singing a song of Mexico to British and Irish audiences on the verge of global war provided a powerful symbol of harmony and unity for people on three continents. Public response to Autry's live BBC broadcasts piqued the attention of U.S. government officials. The Roosevelt administration recognized the singing cowboy's efforts in its arsenal of new approaches designed to counter German advances. Using motion pictures, sound recordings, live performances, and radio broadcasts to mobilize broad support from the Latin American public, Gene Autry aided the Roosevelt administration by supplanting the cultural diplomacy of academics and educators with an enormous media campaign, supporting war preparedness among lower- and middle-culture Americans.[3]

The press ran wild with the story of Gene Autry's elevation to the Hollywood A-list. Autry's singing cowboy persona succeeded in shifting the Western film genre from the margins of U.S. culture into the mainstream. Pundits marked the singing cowboy's personal appearance tour to Great Britain as the turning point. More specifically, analysts suggested that the American cowboy hero arrived on the world stage the moment he rode Champion into the foyer of the Savoy Hotel in London.[4]

As an advocate for the Roosevelt presidency, Gene Autry symbolized heroism and character, and he offered hope for the millions of people who survived the hardships of the Great Depression to face global war. Support for FDR through public diplomacy elevated Autry from his role as a singing cowboy in low-budget Western films and a moderately successful radio and recording artist to a new level of national and international celebrity. The key to Gene Autry's stardom lay in his ability to create synergy through multiple information media. Because his delivery was simple and direct, people easily understood the information embedded in Gene Autry entertainments. His rising popularity demonstrated an ability to shape public opinion.[5]

Gene Autry's international standing was confirmed during his six-week personal appearance tour of Britain and Ireland. All the daily newspapers reported the cowboy hero's lunch with Champion at the luxurious Savoy. Newspapers noted that Gene Autry sold more than 172 million movie tickets in Britain alone. This extraordinary statistic gained credence from the tumultuous receptions the singing cowboy received from fans in London, Manchester, Birmingham, Cardiff, Leeds, and Newcastle. In Glasgow, 50,000 fans turned out to greet Autry, "an all-time record for public demonstrations of popularity."[6]

Even so, Gene Autry's reception in Dublin eclipsed his Scottish outing. Police estimated that 500,000 to 750,000 people joined in the parade through the city streets. Adoring fans attended Gene Autry shows at Dublin's Theater Royal. They jammed the alley behind the theater after each performance. Fans chanted, "We want Gene!" until their cowboy hero appeared on the fire escape. Remembering how the fans packed the alley his last night at the theater, Autry said: "I never heard anything like it. They sang 'Come Back to Erin,' and weaved back and forth, and it was a very heart-touching scene."[7]

*South of the Border* represented another milestone in Gene Autry's career. Republic released this film about Mexican oil concessions, American espionage, and the rise of foreign powers in Latin America on December 15, 1939, less than two weeks after the Soviets invaded Finland. Two days after the film release, the German battleship *Graf Spee* was scuttled off the coast of Montevideo. Written around the lyrics of the hit song, the film epitomized how the singing cowboy created synergy by integrating motion pictures, radio broadcasting, and sound recording media with advertising tie-ups and personal appearance tours. Autry's eponymous recording of "South of the Border (Down Mexico Way)" resulted in another gold record, topping *The Billboard* popular music chart at No. 12 on November 25, 1939. Additional songs in the film reflected Mexican culture and Good Neighbor themes, including "Come to the Fiesta," "Moon over Mañana," and a novelty song, "Fat Cabellero."

Gene teamed up with costar Mary Lee to produce a second gold record tied up with the film. In July 1940, "Goodbye Little Darlin', Goodbye" reached the No. 20 spot on *The Billboard* popular music chart. Mary Lee also provided the vocals for a song called "Merry-Go-Roundup," a reminder for fans of the New Deal goals and objectives in other Gene Autry pictures. In cowriting the screenplay, Betty Burbridge put Mary Lee front and center as a mirror to the thoughts and opinions of the cowboy hero's female fan base. The young actress reinforced the influence of women in the creation of a New West.[8]

*South of the Border* opened with Gene Autry and Frog Millhouse (Smiley Burnette) riding with their cowboy crew singing, "Come to the Fiesta." The exotic Mohave Desert setting filled with senoritas dancing to the bamba beats of tangos, rumbas, and fandangos depicted "Old Mexico" as a vibrant, attractive culture. Gene and Frog used the cover of the fiesta to meet the U.S. consul. Upon arrival, a gypsy fortune-teller accosted the singing cowboy and begged to tell his fortune. "I see you do secret work for you country," the gypsy exclaimed, while gazing into her crystal ball. The fortuneteller identified Gene Autry as a federal agent and foreshadowed a big job in his near future. Zooming inside the crystal ball, moviegoers saw their singing cowboy-secret agent riding Champion through a forest of Joshua Trees singing, "South of the Border (Down Mexico Way)."[9]

Outside the gypsy's tent, Gene and Frog ran into Patsy (Mary Lee) being chased by the Mexican police. The officers attempted to deport Patsy to an orphanage in the United States after the death of her father. In the midst of this chaos, Gene spotted the senorita foretold by the gypsy woman. He borrowed a guitar to serenade the lovely Delores (Lupita Tovar) singing, "Moon over Mañana." This was enough for Patsy to want Gene to be her new daddy. When the cowboy refused, Patsy commandeered a horse-drawn carriage with Delores and her aunt seated inside. When she took off across the desert, Gene and Champion raced after them. They caught up to the carriage and calmed the horses until the police arrived. Then Gene shared an off-screen kiss with Delores, which made him love-struck. Delores dropped her locket bearing the family crest for Gene to find and use to come calling.

The romance and adventure in Old Mexico carried over in the next scene, featuring Gene and Frog going to the hacienda of Don Diego Mendoza (Frank Relcher) to serenade Delores and return her locket. Climbing a rough-hewn ladder to the balcony outside Delores's window, Gene sang a reprise of "Moon over Mañana" to get her attention. The arrival of a nightrider persuaded Gene and Frog to leave. The rider delivered a note to Aunt Duena (Claire Du Brey) from her husband, Don Diego. "With this revolution threatening, no one is safe in Mexico," the rider proclaimed. Audiences learned that Andreo Mendoza (Duncan Renaldo), Dolores's brother, was a leader of the revolutionaries. Gene and Frog learned that Don Diego owned a big cattle ranch in Palermo that the revolutionaries had threatened. Mendoza had sent his family to northern Mexico for safety. Expressing the viewpoint of U.S. isolationists, Frog responded to this news by urging neutrality. "Look Gene, we've got troubles too, let's don't get mixed up in this. . . ."

Another telling scene opened with a bilingual sign on a door identifying the office of the United States consul in Mexico. Gene Autry, the singing cowboy-secret agent, stood inside the office surveying newspaper headlines that proclaimed "Pan-American Neutrality Menaced" and "Submarines Sighted off American Coast." The consul explained, "We're taking immediate action and the Mexican government is offering its full cooperation. We know that foreign agents are trying to start a revolution in Palermo to gain control of the American oil concessions. . . ." As the diplomat showed the cowboy a map of the fictitious island country off the Mexican coast, he described the Gulf of Mexico as one of the most important oil-producing areas in Latin America.

Viewing the map, Autry noted that Palermo's harbor provided an ideal location for a submarine refueling base. "We're certain that foreign powers have the same idea and it's up to us to put a stop to it," the consul responded. He handed Gene an envelope with instructions inside saying, "Your boat leaves within the hour." Gene expressed concern because he wanted to say goodbye to Dolores, but the consul stopped him by declaring, "You're not telling anybody anything. This is government business."

Gene and Frog and their cowboy crew met Don Diego Mendoza upon their arrival in Palermo via steamship. The cowboy hero was there to learn the identity of foreign agents trying to overthrow the government. As Autry rode with Mendoza in his carriage through a countryside littered with oil derricks, en route to the cattleman's rancho, Mendoza expressed a viewpoint summarizing the aftermath of President Cárdenas's nationalization of the Mexican oil industry.

We have been friendly with your country. Our people were well paid for their work and they were prosperous and happy; all at once, the change.... They listen to propaganda, which teaches them unrest and rebellion. And now, the oil wells lay idle and there is misery and want. My own nephew listened to these lies. Now he believes himself a patriot, a liberator of our country, riding with his band of Americano renegades. Can you blame me if I am bitter?

A few scenes later, Andreo Mendoza expressed the viewpoint of the leftist rebels who agreed to work with the foreign powers (Nazis), because any other nation was better than working with the United States. Suspecting the foreign agent Saunders (Alan Edwards) to double-cross him, Andreo explained: "It is you who must worry, *amigo mio*, you need the submarine base. Your country, she need the oil. You get these things when I take over the government. But the revolution, she costs plenty of money. My army cannot eat promises. Yesterday, you are my good friend. Today, you are just my friend. Tomorrow..." Mendoza punctuated this last statement by blowing smoke into Saunders's face, suggesting a tenuous position for foreign powers in Mexico and the cautiously optimistic outlook in the United States that the revolutionaries might be bought off.

When the vaqueros at Don Diego's rancho learned that the rebels planned to attack Mendoza's herd, they decided to pack up and leave to avoid a fight. Autry and his cowboy band convinced the vaqueros to stay by singing, "When the Cactus Blooms Again," a traditional Western folksong. As the song unfolded, Autry got the cowboys and vaqueros to sing together in harmony, thus expressing unity through music, a recurring theme in the Gene Autry series. Working together, the vaqueros and cowboy drove Mendoza's herd to the beach, where they loaded the livestock into a cattle boat by swimming the herd out to sea and then hoisting the beeves with a crane, a tactic perfected in the Hawaiian cattle trade.

Music also played a role in the singing cowboy's discovery of high-frequency static interfering with a radio broadcast of Gene Autry singing "South of the Border (Down Mexico Way)." The static interfering with the broadcast turned out to be a coded message sent from a clandestine radio station in the abandoned oil fields to the submarines of foreign powers perched offshore from the island. After many attempts, Autry cracked the ciphered code to reveal a secret message: "Notify submarines . . . attempt to obtain oil tonight . . . signal."

Autry tracked the rebels to La Casa Cantina, where he found Andreo Mendoza conspiring with Saunders in the cellar of the saloon. Mendoza and Saunders got the drop on Autry when the cowboy tried to sneak up on their clandestine meeting. Saunders wanted to do away with Autry and Mendoza agreed, until he discovered the locket his sister had given to Gene. Questioning the cowboy hero about the locket, Andreo learned how Gene knew Delores. Autry used the opening to plead with the rebel leader.

> Do you realize what a revolution would do to this country? . . . It will give Saunders and the foreign powers a stranglehold on this entire coast. With their submarines operating in these waters unchallenged, it means the end of Pan-American neutrality. Neither your country nor mine can allow this to happen. And they won't let it happen.

The film reached its climax when Gene and Frog commandeered two oil trucks headed to the beach to refuel the offshore submarine. Andreo Mendoza was killed during the showdown. Newspaper headlines brought the action to its conclusion by heralding, "Submarine Base Smashed! Autry Finishes Job and Leaves Palermo Today, Attempt to Establish Submarine Refueling Station Base is Failure." Passing through northern Mexico on the way back to the United States, Gene returned to the Mendoza safe house. He learned that Delores joined a convent to mourn the death of her brother and atone for the disgrace of his rebellion.

This signifier of a U.S.-Mexico alliance took some of the sting out of President Cárdenas's decision to nationalize Mexican oil fields in 1938 and his decision to sell oil to the Axis powers. The messages in *South of the Border* put the incoming Mexican President Manuel Avila

Camacho on notice that the United States would not tolerate German submarine bases in Mexico. Furthermore, the verses from "South of the Border (Down Mexico Way)" included the refrain, "That's where I fell in love, where the stars at night come out to play," suggested that Americans discomforted by their culture's traditional capitalist credo might turn Mexico into a version of the Left Bank in Paris, where the "Lost Generation" found a home after World War I. More importantly, FDR showed his support for President Camacho by sending Vice President Henry Wallace to represent the United States at his inauguration, the first official vice-presidential trip to any Latin American nation. Wallace's participation conveyed enormous symbolic meaning.[10]

Gene Autry headed the list of moneymaking western stars for a third straight year in December 1939, with William "Hopalong Cassidy" Boyd, Roy Rogers, George O'Brien, Charles Starrett, The Three Mesquiteers, Tex Ritter, Buck Jones, John Wayne, and Bob Baker, rounding out the top ten. Hopalong Cassidy topped the list among the theatrical circuits, while Autry placed first among the independent theater exhibitors. George O'Brien came in second in the circuits with Autry third. The combined voting gave Autry first place overall.[11]

In February 1940, America's Favorite Cowboy experienced his first Hollywood premiere when the industry saw how the allegorical story form in *South of the Border* could be politically expedient in introducing controversial issues without explicit engagement. All the singing cowboy's previous pictures premiered in rural and small-town theaters in the San Fernando Valley and the other hinterlands of Los Angeles. Grace Kingsley recounted that, "The somewhat neglected wild 'westerns' had their innings last night at the Cinema Theater when one of them went swank and had a real premiere, with floodlights, stars in person, ushers in 10-gallon hats and all the rest of it." Gene Autry was the star of stars at the event, taking bows with Smiley Burnette, Lupita Tovar, June Storey, Mary Lee, Duncan Renaldo, and William Farnum. Visiting luminaries called to the stage included Noah Beery, Ray Hatton, and Betty Bradshaw. Roy Rogers, Dick Foran, and Tex Ritter also attended. Burnette proved the cutup of the gang when it came to the speeches.[12]

The song "Rancho Grande (Allá en el Rancho Grande)" inspired the next film to present Mexican culture and themes in the Gene Autry series. Republic used the song to create an eponymous film title for *Rancho Grande*, released on March 22, 1940. Another "special" distributed through first-run movie theaters, *Rancho Grande* incorporated an almost perfect combination of modernity, gentrification, and market capitalism at work in the Western Hemisphere Idea. The film depicted three young Americans, Patsy (Mary Lee), Kay (June Storey) and Tom Dodge (Dick Hogan), as the inheritors of their grandfather's southern California rancho.[13]

*Rancho Grande* emphasized modernity in one scene in which Kay and Tom Dodge flew their own airplane to the California estate. In another scene, Grandfather Dodge communicated the terms of his will via a transcription record, his voice emanating from the grave. Grandpa Dodge left Rancho Grande to his grandchildren with a mortgage held by the Citrus Valley Association. The indebtedness paid for the construction of a dam and irrigation system to open up the southern part of the estate to citrus orchards. In addition, the laborers at Rancho Grande inhabited a Mexican *colonia* that had existed in association with the rancho for generations.

To help promote the film, Autry performed the song "Rancho Grande" on his *Melody Ranch* radio program in May 1940. The broadcast included a chamber reading of the film that tied in with movie theater promotions. June Storey, Autry's co-star in *Rancho Grande*, appeared as Kay Dodge in the radio drama. The story involved the rescue of José, a Mexican laborer trapped under a section of irrigation pipe and threatened by an avalanche. Both the film and radio drama sought to promote Roosevelt's Good Neighbor policy as Wrigley's Doublemint gum pitch made clear.

> Spread a Little Goodwill . . . Say to Your Neighbor, "Have a Stick of Doublemint." You know friends; we Americans like to think of ourselves as friendly folks and it's a real friendly gesture to say to your neighbor, "Have a stick of Doublemint." Just try this easy inexpensive way to sort of spread a little goodwill.[14]

As *Rancho Grande* appeared in movie theaters, hope of containing the war to Europe faded fast. The Nazis invaded Denmark and Norway in April 1940 and, more spectacularly, Holland, Belgium, and France in May. The defeat of France in June 1940 changed the focus of the U.S. policy in Latin America. With Germany in control of western Europe and little chance of Britain surviving, the prior goal of insuring hemispheric neutrality transformed into active organizing against a Nazi threat in the Western Hemisphere. Ominous reports of Nazi subversion in Latin America convinced Roosevelt that the Germans would attempt to overthrow existing Latin American governments. The president expressed concern about German control of Dutch and French possessions in the Caribbean. Moreover, FDR viewed German acquisition of the French fleet and West African naval bases as a prelude to an attack on Brazil and the rest of South America. He initiated secret talks between the United States and Latin American military officials and planned a show of force by the U.S. Navy off the coasts of Brazil and Uruguay.[15]

These U.S. concerns regarding Pan-American neutrality influenced the titling of *Gaucho Serenade*, released by Republic Pictures on May 10, 1940. Use of the term *gaucho* extended Bolton's theory of a shared common heritage from American cowboys and Mexican vaqueros to the South American pampas and Patagonian grasslands of Argentina, Uruguay, southern Chile, and the Rio Grande do Sul province of Brazil. The association with South American gauchos remained tenuous in the film, present mainly in the naming of an otherwise Mexican cantina and in the eponymous title song, but this film got Americans thinking in hemispheric terms. The film opened with a group of independent ranchers, vaqueros, and cowboys disputing the operations of the Western Packing Company, a big firm taking advantage of rural westerners. One of the Mexican rancheros served as the spokesman for the group of cattlemen speaking Spanish and English interchangeably. The leader expressed unity and the will to fight the big packing company through the courts.[16]

Republic promoted the film on *Gene Autry's Melody Ranch* through advertisements and the cowboy singing "Gaucho Serenade" almost every week throughout June and July 1940. In competition with

Gene Autry and Champion at the Savoy Hotel in London, 1939. © Autry Qualified Interest Trust and The Autry Foundation (ABT39098).

"Céad Mile Fáilte, Gene Autry" (A Hundred Thousand Welcomes), 1939. © Autry Qualified Interest Trust and The Autry Foundation (BIO_181).

"Welcome to Dublin, Gene Autry," 1939. © Autry Qualified Interest Trust and The Autry Foundation (ABT39128).

Gene and Ina Autry with Franklin Roosevelt, Jr., Herbert Yates, and Art Satherly on the U.S. Manhattan, sailing from London to New York, 1939. © Autry Qualified Interest Trust and The Autry Foundation (ABT39105).

"South of the Border (Down Mexico Way)" sheet music, 1939. © Autry Qualified Interest Trust and The Autry Foundation (T87-36-28-5).

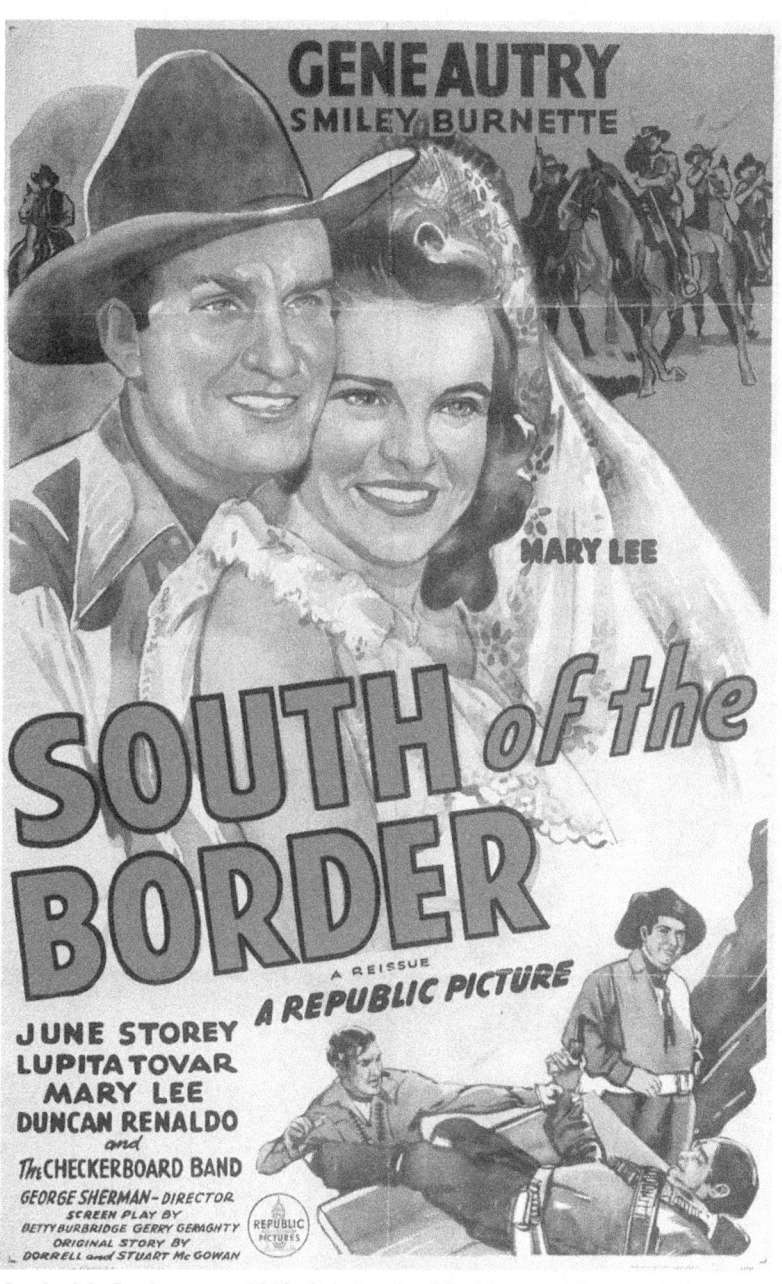

*South of the Border* poster, 1939. © Autry Qualified Interest Trust and The Autry Foundation (T87_36_4696).

*Gene Autry Comics* no. 12, "Down Mexico Way," c. 1941. Courtesy Autry Museum (88.304.1).

Paramount's "Road to . . ." pictures starring Bing Crosby and Bob Hope, *Gaucho Serenade* promoted western tourism by featuring a cross-country road trip on U.S. Route 66, the "Mother Road." The film featured Gene Autry and Frog Millhouse (Smiley Burnette) transporting Ronnie Willoughby (Clifford Sevren, Jr.), Joyce (June Storey) and Patsy (Mary Lee) from Chicago to LA. Midway through the film, a flat tire halted their journey, requiring Autry to earn $25 for a new tire in a singing contest at the Cantina El Gaucho somewhere in northern New Mexico. Carlos (Duncan Renaldo), the proprietor of the cantina, hosted the music contest. Autry scored big with a version of the title song, "Gaucho Serenade," which endeared him to the restaurateur. Autry's competition in the contest included the Mexican specialty dancers Mary and Fred Velasco. Jose Eslava's Orchestra (Jose Estava) performed as El Gaucho's house band.[17]

Gene Autry's second appearance at the New York World's Fair corresponded with the release of *Gaucho Serenade*. The official greeter of the exposition, "Elmer—The Typical American" (Leslie Ostrander), met the singing cowboy when he arrived on horseback. Autry attended a luncheon at the Schaefer Center with officials from Herbert Yates's stomping grounds in Ridgeway, Long Island. Later in the afternoon, Gene made a speech and sang a few songs with a hillbilly band accompaniment. Then he led a mounted parade through the Great White Way.[18]

Returning to Hollywood, Autry headlined the first Southern California Musical Fiesta at the Los Angeles Memorial Coliseum on June 1, 1940. Gene charged into the Coliseum in typical Western array on his prancing sorrel, Champion. He rode straight for the mammoth hacienda stage, where he dismounted and then sang to his own guitar accompaniment the hit song that made him an international celebrity. "South of the Border (Down Mexico Way)" was the highlight of the music program. A cast of 6,000 participated in the spectacular event, sponsored by the *Los Angeles Times*, for the benefit of the Parent-Teacher Association Milk Fund. Autry also performed with Shirley Temple as a headliner for a nationwide Red Cross broadcast from the "Avenue of Mercy" on Sunset Boulevard in Hollywood. In July, he appeared as the honored guest at the Minneapolis Aquatennial.[19]

As the New Deal Cowboy made personal appearances throughout the summer of 1940, the Roosevelt administration dealt with fears of economic destabilization in Latin America and concerns about the possible existence of a "fifth column" in the hemisphere. Capable of exploiting economic troubles, Nazi propaganda in Latin America became more explicitly anti-United States after the fall of France in June 1940. U.S. government officials became quite anxious about the growing Nazi presence. Along with shortwave propaganda and economic activity, many reports about Nazi threats focused on the extent to which the Germans controlled Latin American media culture and influenced public opinion against the United States. In 1940, *Gene Autry's Melody Ranch* radio program routinely featured Good Neighbor songs like "Gaucho Serenade," "It Happened in Monterey," "Trail to Mexico," "Rancho Grande," "Goodbye to Old Mexico," and "Mexicali Rose."[20]

Responding to German aggression, President Roosevelt created the Office of the Coordinator of Inter-American Affairs (CIAA), a government agency set up to assume the largest role in shaping government policy, action, and involvement in cultural and information activities in Latin America. Roosevelt appointed thirty-two-year-old Nelson Rockefeller, grandson of John D. Rockefeller, the founder of the worldwide Standard Oil Empire, to head the CIAA and its subsequent activities. Traveling extensively throughout Latin America while working for Standard Oil, Rockefeller identified cultural misunderstandings as the root of major problems between the United States and Latin America.[21]

The new coordinator set out to address cultural concerns by creating major sections within his office to deal with cultural relations, communications, commercial development, trade, and financing. James Young, former chief of the Bureau of Foreign and Domestic Commerce, headed up the communications section, with radio, movies, and press divisions organized therein. Karle Bickel headed up the press division. John Jay Whitney managed the motion picture division and Don Francisco ran the radio division.[22]

Roosevelt and Rockefeller agreed that cultural exchange programs and grants to support various Latin American cultural figures might result in goodwill toward the United States. The degree to which these cultural investments strengthened hemispheric security had limits, but Rockefeller, whom the president eventually named Assistant Secretary of State for Latin American Affairs, used cultural relations to open the doors for dramatic expansion of economic relations between Latin America and the United States during the war and thereafter. Rockefeller incited the lasting enmity of Pan-American leftists who dismissed the CIAA as a light-weight economic imperialist. Likewise, he aroused the fears of others within Roosevelt's administration who fretted about the CIAA creating an impression that better cultural relations were merely a means to the end of expanding U.S. economic interests. Be that as it may, culture, security, and economics became bound together inseparably in 1940 within a rapidly evolving Good Neighbor policy.[23]

Rockefeller approached Latin America with a reliance on media culture as an invaluable public relations tool. To encourage broad acceptance by Latin Americans of a North American economic presence, the CIAA packaged cultural, economic, and security considerations together by encouraging Hollywood stars and starlets to tour Latin American. Simultaneously, CIAA funds supported touring art exhibitions and tours by symphony orchestras and jazz and swing bands. Rockefeller financed the establishment of binational centers in Latin American cities where local citizens studied English and learned about American institutions. These centers routinely featured American musical and theatrical presentations. Unquestionably, these and other programs heightened mutual understanding between U.S. and Latin American cultural leaders and commoners.[24]

President Roosevelt shared his perspectives with the American public in a Fireside Chat broadcast in December 1940. "There are those who say that the Axis powers would never have any desire to attack the Western Hemisphere. That is the same dangerous form of wishful thinking which has destroyed the powers of resistance of so many conquered peoples." The vast resources of Latin America, Roosevelt assured his listeners, constituted "the most tempting loot in all of the round world."[25]

As these events unfolded, Gene Autry graduated from being number one among Western stars to the select list of the top ten box-office earners in all of Hollywood. Autry's inclusion on Hollywood's top-ten list surprised many industry insiders. Will Rogers was the last cowboy star to make the top-ten list in 1934. Autry finished fourth in the national poll, behind Mickey Rooney, Spencer Tracy, and Clark Gable. Gene placed in front of Tyrone Power, James Cagney, Bing Crosby, Wallace Beery, Bette Davis, and Judy Garland. The annual poll conducted by the *Motion Picture Herald* represented the most comprehensive market research in the industry. Autry and Garland were newcomers to the list. Simultaneously, the singing cowboy headed for the fourth consecutive year the list of the leading Western film personalities. Other stars on the top-ten western star list included William Boyd, Roy Rogers, George O'Brien, Charles Starrett, Johnny Mack Brown, Tex Ritter, The Three Mesquiteers, Smiley Burnette, and Wild Bill Elliott.[26]

In 1941, Gene Autry received unprecedented national and international recognition from major metropolitan newspapers and fan magazines that previously ignored the entire "B" western film genre. *Motion Picture, Picture Play*, and *Screenland* struggled to explain the cowboy's appeal. The magazines recycled claims made in Republic Pictures ballyhoo that the singing cowboy averaged 12,000 pieces of fan mail per week, receiving a record of 50,103 letters in one month. These numbers eclipsed the mail received by other Hollywood stars.[27]

Fanzine writers emphasized Autry's "outsider" status. Gene lived in Hollywood, but he somehow remained separated from the social whirls and shenanigans of Tinsel Town. Photo spreads took readers into the Autry household, where the homey emphasis reinforced the representation of the popular celebrity as a domesticated cowboy—the home was both ranch house and idyllic suburban domicile. Gene's eight-year marriage to Ina Mae, a young woman from a small Oklahoma town, exemplified the rising star's virtuous down-home lifestyle, a further contrast to the love lives of Hollywood's more celebrated citizens. These publications used words like simplicity, sincerity, and warmth most commonly to explain Autry's appeal, unlike the adjectives used to describe other Hollywood stars.[28]

Republic continued to blend Good Neighbor elements in *The Singing Hill* (1941), "a regular humdinger of a western and probably Gene Autry's best, with new story values, new cowboy stunts, extra fine cowboy music and lots of comedy." Modernity, gentrification, and market capitalism remained center stage as the storyline shifted from the issues of the U.S.-Mexico border to the growing influence of Latin jazz. In a birthday celebration scene, the female lead Josephine Adams (Virginia Dale) sang, "Tumbled Down Shack in Havana," with back up from Alfredo's Rumba Band (no credit). A similar scene in *Call of the Canyon* (1942), included female lead Ruth Terry singing "When It's Chilly Down in Chile." In April 1941, promoters bid $16,000 a week for Autry to conduct a personal appearance tour of South America, about $259,000 per week in 2015 dollars.[29]

Concern for Mexican Americans living in the border states returned in the plot of *Under Fiesta Stars*, opening August 25, 1941. Autry starred as a rodeo performer and part owner of a ranch he inherited along the U.S.-Mexico border. As a ranch owner, Gene became responsible for several families of ethnic Mexican *rancheras* living nearby and working a mine located on his property. The Mexican ranchers lost their livestock during the Dust Bowl and Dad Irwin, the original owner of the mine, provided jobs to keep the Mexican families living on their independent ranches until their stock could be replenished and things turned around economically. Through many twists and turns, the singing cowboy hero and the Mexican *rancheras* supported each other as good neighbors. In the closing scene, they celebrated with a fiesta, featuring music and dancing and Gene Autry singing the eponymous movie title song, "Under Fiesta Stars."[30]

Fiesta scenes remained central in *Down Mexico Way* (1941). Autry played a rancher living near the town of Sage City, somewhere along the U.S.-Mexico border in Texas, New Mexico, Arizona, or California. Republic created this film as a reprise to take advantage of the continuing popularity of Gene's gold record, "South of the Border (Down Mexico Way)." Released October 15, 1941, *Down Mexico Way* opened with credits rolling over scenic boulders and Joshua trees in the Mohave Desert and a chorus singing the eponymous movie title song. Republic staged this film with significantly higher production values, designed to support showings in first-run theaters and take advantage of the hugely popular song.

Republic ran afoul of Hayes office regulations in making of *Down Mexico Way*. All Autry pictures had heavies (bad guys), and in this film, which presented Gene and Smiley battling crooks in Mexico, the studio yielded to the MPPDA's concerns about the villain being Mexican. Likewise, producer Harry Grey had difficulty in making the villain an American for fear of upsetting Pan-American amity by instilling suspicion of United States citizens in Latin America. Perhaps reflecting the mood in Hollywood, Grey made movie producers the bad guys in the film, abusing American and Mexican investors equally.[31]

Harold Huber, portraying the character of Pancho Grande, provided Gene Autry with a second sidekick, echoing Republic's successful Three Mesquiteers formula. A reformed outlaw working as an immigrant laborer on Autry's ranch along the U.S.-Mexico border, Pancho became a guide when Gene and Frog decided to make a trip to Mexico after being taken in by a couple of phony movie producers. Autry and the townsfolk of Sage City got duped attempting to showcase their fair city in a motion picture, similar to *Dodge City* (1939) and *Virginia City* (1940).

The folks in Sage City wanted to capitalize on their local history to create tourist attractions that appealed to the travel and recreation industries. Instead, residents got taken in a scam. Gene, Frog, and Pancho followed the sharpies to San Ramon, Mexico, to retrieve $35,000 swindled from Sage City. They also foiled an attempt by the producers to con the honorable Don Carlos Alvarado (Julian Rivero), father of the lovely Maria Elena Alvarado (Fay McKenzie). As the trio crossed the border into Mexico, Autry began to sing his hit song, "South of the Border (Down Mexico Way)."[32]

On the way to San Ramon, Gene and the boys boarded a train for the last leg of the journey. They ran into Maria Elena and the Herrera Sisters, the latter a musical act hired to perform at the fiesta honoring Maria Elena's return home. Entertaining passengers in the club car, the trio sang "La Cachita." Gene followed, singing, "The Cowboy and the Lady." Then came a very elaborate fiesta extravaganza with Mexican bands and a dozen or more dancers. *Down Mexico Way* featured the Herrera Sisters again, singing "Guadalajara." The song and dance numbers benefited from the higher production values in the film. Nothing so elaborate was staged in earlier Gene Autry pictures. In addition, Republic routinely advertised Mexican themes on *Gene Autry's Melody Ranch* radio program. Autry tied together his film and radio productions by entertaining listeners with songs like "Chiquita," "Juanita," "Maria Elena" and "Under Fiesta Stars."[33]

In addition, *Down Mexico Way* featured two other million-selling songs: "Beer Barrel Polka," a song popularized by Will Glahé, who scored No. 1 on *The Billboard* popular music chart in June 1939; and "Maria Elena," a million-seller for the Jimmy Dorsey Orchestra in 1941. Budgeted at $500,000, the film exemplified how the Gene Autry series incorporated increasingly elaborate musical excursions during the run-up to World War II.[34]

A similarly styled grand fiesta scene also graced the screen in *Bells of Capistrano* (1942), another $500,000 special featuring Gene Autry and a group of ethnic Mexican extras, once again singing, "South of the Border (Down Mexico Way). *Bells of Capistrano* involved Gene Autry joining the World Wide Wild West and Rodeo outfit. Setting the climax of the film in San Juan Capistrano combined a rodeo story with the music and dancing of a Mexican fiesta, thereby associating Good Neighbor images more closely with war preparedness themes. For example, the Grand Entry parade sequence featured the regular troupers of Gene Autry's Flying A Ranch Rodeo creating a staged environment for Autry himself to sing, "Don't Bite the Hand that's Feeding You" while a gigantic American flag unfurled behind the assembled troupe.[35]

The type of public diplomacy represented through Gene Autry productions demonstrated the innovative redefinition of the role played by the U.S. government in formulating a policy of international cultural activity. As the president moved the federal government into the fields of art, entertainment, recreation, and information, Republic Pictures incorporated government information into its cultural products to help combat the Great Depression and prepare the United States and its allies for the prospects of global war. Gene Autry films like *Boots and Saddles*, *Mexicali Rose*, and *Gaucho Serenade* stand out as attempts to bridge the gaps between the two major tenets of U.S. foreign policy—Anglo-American allegiance and Pan-Americanism. These films appealed to broad mainstream audiences that did not understand the nuances of foreign affairs, but they trusted Autry as an "ambassador of goodwill."

The focus of Gene Autry's Good Neighbor pictures on U.S. relations with Mexico illustrated the importance of border security issues for the Roosevelt administration and the ability of the singing cowboy to reach cross-cultural audiences. Autry promoted Americanism, war preparedness, and friendly relations with Mexico and Mexican Americans at a time when most of his audience favored isolationism. The need for Mexican cooperation with U.S. war preparedness efforts stimulated attempts through the Gene Autry series to familiarize rural, small town, and newly urban Americans with Mexican culture. Similarly, the singing cowboy's inspiration for Fernando De Fuentes and his work, leading to the establishment of a unique style of Mexican filmmaking, confirmed Autry's influence south of the border.

In the historical figures of the cowboy, vaquero, and gaucho, Herbert Eugene Bolton's idea of a common heritage throughout the Americas found a simple and direct expression in the musical-Western form. Vaqueros and cowboys, working, riding, and singing together in harmony, dramatized this shared experience for tens of millions of music fans and moviegoers worldwide. Music formed the basis for demonstrating unity and harmony between the United States and other nations. The introduction of Mexican songs and traditional folk dances into Autry's films created a positive image of Mexican culture for American fans to embrace.

Autry's British tour cemented the singing cowboy's international standing. Moreover, the decision by Republic Pictures to open Mexican-themed movies in first-run movie houses confirmed Autry's growing appeal among mainstream moviegoers. Further evidence of that attraction came in the form of gold records for "South of the Border (Down Mexico Way)" and "Goodbye Little Darlin', Goodbye." Autry's image as a singing cowboy-secret agent created a metaphor for understanding the significance of soft power to influence public opinion and aid U.S. foreign policy. Similarly, near-perfect encapsulation of the Western Hemisphere Idea in the film *Rancho Grande* demonstrated how modernity, gentrification, and market capitalism served as goals for the Good Neighbor policy. Here again, echoing *Mexicali Rose*, the song "Rancho Grande (Allá en el Rancho Grande)" promoted a symmetry of goals and objectives that influenced audiences on both sides of the U.S.-Mexico border.

Republic Pictures catered to an amalgamating market of U.S. moviegoers to take advantage of the growing mainstream salability of Gene Autry's brand of Americanism. Republic's Gene Autry series reinforced traditional American values of patriotism, conservatism, self-reliance, and justice. The high ratings for Gene Autry in polls of popular stars demonstrated that the series reached beyond western audiences. Still, heavy-handed Americanism on the part of Yates and Autry more than likely dampened support from many Hollywood types. As the United States entered into war, Republic's promotion of the "hundred percenter" suggested a thoroughgoing nationalism that sometimes came off as an extreme or unjustified aspect of Roosevelt's Good Neighbor policy.[36]

CHAPTER 7

# Youth's Model, 1940

After the German invasion of Poland on September 1, 1939, Hollywood began adding war preparedness messaging to the New Deal and Good Neighbor films linked to the Roosevelt presidency. Released in first-run theaters as "Super Westerns," films like *In Old Monterey* and *South of the Border* marked a turning point in Western film productions. As Gene Autry's music and motion pictures moved from the western fringe to the mainstream in American cultural industries, personal appearances provided the catalyst to synergize his multi-platform entertainment.

Live performances drove the sale of sound recordings, movie tickets, and licensed merchandise bearing Gene Autry's image and his signature of authenticity. Radio broadcasting accelerated these processes exponentially. The Wrigley Company of Chicago launched the nationally syndicated *Gene Autry's Melody Ranch* radio program on the CBS Radio Network. A special preview for merchants selling Wrigley's Doublemint gum aired on New Year's Eve, December 31, 1939. *Gene Autry's Melody Ranch* positioned America's Favorite Cowboy to become "Youth's Model, 1940," so named by the *New York Times*.

After the start of World War II, Hollywood incorporated war preparedness messages into the assemblage of films with New Deal and Good Neighbor themes. Republic scriptwriters tried to mash up all these national initiatives in New West stories presented for the Gene Autry series. Films like *Boots and Saddles* (1937), *Western Jamboree* (1938), and *In Old Monterey* (1939) sounded the alarm.

*Boots and Saddles* represented the allied forces of the United Kingdom, Mexico, and the United States working together to save an old *Californio* rancho, now British-owned, from impending sale. Autry led a team of American cowboys and Mexican vaqueros in the effort to save the rancho. They rounded up and broke a herd of wild horses to sell under contract to the U.S. Army. The proceeds of the sale paid the bills of the British owners. The Brits responded by canceling the sale, thereby saving the home of a large Mexican *colonia* residing on the property.[1]

As the plot unfolded, Autry's sidekick Frog Millhouse (Smiley Burnette) inadvertently enlisted in the U.S. Army. Watching Frog's ordeal provided young fans with some comedic food for thought. Millhouse dramatized both the torment of boot camp and the excitement of shooting rapid-fire machine guns. Automatic weapons symbolized modernism in *Boots and Saddles*, along with wireless telephone communications, which enabled soldiers in the field to communicate with HQ. Additional symbolism came from Autry winning a horse race and preserving the ranch for his British and Mexican allies. The cowboy hero symbolized the willingness of the United States to support the United Kingdom and Mexico as the threats of global war increased.

U.S. war preparedness objectives dramatized in *Western Jamboree* (1938) added a new dimension to Republic's Gene Autry series. This quasi-dude ranch drama managed to incorporate New Deal, Good Neighbor, and war preparedness themes. *Western Jamboree* featured a portrayal of Don Carlos (Edward Raquello) as a Mexican nobleman and musical *charro*. Don Carlos appealed to new border town audiences while helping longtime Autry fans gain empathy for ethnic Mexicans living in the United States. A classic version of the Mexican folksong "Ceilito Lindo" featured Gene singing in Spanish and the assembled patrons of the Silver Bow Saloon joining in harmony as the song reached its crescendo. This Spanish serenade probably struck an unusual chord among Autry's rural, small-town, and newly urban fans. Increased movie ticket sales and record sales demonstrated the singing cowboy's effectiveness as a messenger. America's No. 1 cowboy hero also made Hollywood's "Top Ten" list from 1940 to 1942.[2]

Another storyline in *Western Jamboree* involved a search for helium deposits on the Circle J Ranch. Autry worked as foreman for the Circle J, going up against Richard Kimball (Bentley Hewlett), a crooked American businessman. A newspaper in Kimball's hands revealed headlines announcing, "Foreign Powers Still Seek Helium—Recent U.S. Ruling Spurs Efforts to Secure Non-flammable Gas for Lighter-Than-Air Craft." For moviegoers, the spectacle of the notorious Hindenburg disaster remained fresh in 1938. Rumors suggested sabotage, while images of the stunning hydrogen explosion got people thinking about helium as a safer alternative energy source.

*Western Jamboree* encouraged moviegoers to think about the increased sales of American gas and petroleum products as conflicts widened in Europe and Manchuria. Plot points promoted the value of western lands with oil and gas deposits and the challenges of dealing with absentee landowners. The film signaled a transition in the Gene Autry series from films promoting a new leisure in the American West through travel and tourism and western dude ranch vacations. Audiences saw the Circle J transformed from a working cattle ranch into a dude ranch and then an industrial site. Residents and investors understood the value of western rangelands for natural gas and oil extraction. They pointed to the Hugoton gas fields in southwestern Kansas and the panhandles of Texas and Oklahoma, the largest reserves of helium in the United States. The progression from cattle ranching to dude ranching to natural gas extraction showcased the potential for industrial development to reemerge in the western states as war preparedness accelerated the nation's recovery from the Great Depression.[3]

During the winter of 1939, the *New York Times* highlighted a new trend for Hollywood horse operas. Seemingly overnight, consumers of culture reestablished the Western as a popular American film genre. Western films were no longer "the exclusive property of all the little Willies who pranced through preoccupied pedestrian traffic caroling 'Heigh-yo Silver, away!'" Reporter Frank S. Nugent found something curious happening. Gene Autry had propelled the series Western from the fringes into the mainstream of American culture. "Frankly, we don't quite know what to make of it all," Nugent wrote, "We've formed the habit of taking our horse operas in a Class B stride."[4]

The *New York Times* promoted the American West as a region for tourist travel by calling attention to its photogenic qualities. Nugent cited John Ford's *Stagecoach* (1939) to envision the spectacular scenery awaiting photographers willing to travel through the Southwest. He described Ford's Concord Coach carrying a miscellany of passengers past the lonely crags, sculptural sky-mesas, and cloud-shadowed ranges of Arizona's Monument Valley. Ford drew his camera back and then lingered in panoramic mode to let his audiences see the stagecoach cracking off the miles through sublime scenery. "It's something to see," Nugent commented about *Stagecoach*. "We haven't much hesitation in calling it one of the best horse operas ever filmed."[5]

Riding on the success of *Stagecoach*, many critics predicted an announcement from Republic Pictures revealing grand plans for John Wayne. Under contract to Republic, Wayne would become a big box office asset in the postwar era; but in 1939, he could not get past Roy Rogers to challenge Gene Autry for the "No. 1" spot. Autry claimed the title as the biggest box office draw in Western films for six consecutive years, from 1937 to 1942. To tie in with promotions for the government-sponsored "See America First" campaign, Republic set up a special stage at the Golden Gate International Exposition for residents and tourists in the San Francisco Bay area to see Gene Autry and other stars in person.[6]

As the Nazis prepared to invade Poland and trigger the start of World War II, Republic continued to broaden its market for Gene Autry pictures with the release of *In Old Monterey* on August 14, 1939. Republic introduced its star players through a series of screen cameos at the beginning of the film. First Gene Autry, then Smiley Burnette, June Story, George "Gabby" Hayes, The Hoosier Hot Shots, the comedy team of Sarie *and* Sallie, The Ranch Boys and the juvenile actor Billy Lee. Background images for these cameo shots suggested a typical musical-Western adventure until Billy Lee lit a string of firecrackers.[7]

The exploding firecrackers segued into scenes of combat and floating newspapers with headlines announcing, "War Threat Stirs

Europe: World Capitols Agog over War Situation." Superimposed over more footage of aerial bombardments, additional headlines proclaimed, "Powers Increase Armament: Entire World in Arms Race." Scenes of mobile cannon arrays mounted on truck platforms firing rounds skyward served as the backdrop for a third big headline: "Congress Speeds Plans For Defense of U.S.A.: Huge Appropriation Made for Armament Program." These headlines reflected a reality quite obvious throughout the Southwest border states, including Texas, New Mexico, Arizona and California, where construction of flying fields and bombing ranges by the U.S. Army Corps of Engineers facilitated the training of allied pilots from many foreign nations.

The fictitious town of Colby and the ranchers of a fictitious Colby Basin District dramatized local reactions to notices of evacuation and the taking of lands by the federal government. *In Old Monterey* pushed the boundaries of realism in representing the circumstances faced by real westerners dealing with the U.S. Army. Foregoing the typical escapist adventure at the root of the Gene Autry series, the film depicted ranchers resisting attempts by the Army Air Force to establish military bases. The westerners refused to budge despite assurances that the U.S. Army would pay a fair price of rangelands and would help people relocate. Westerners refused to move because they had strong ties to family homesteads and long-established property rights.

George Whittaker (George "Gabby" Hayes) espoused the isolationist sentiment typical of the westerners who resisted war preparedness efforts. As spokesman for the ranchers of Colby Basin, Whittaker responded to a government ultimatum by confronting an army captain (Edward Earle) and explaining that his people were born and raised on the western range: "I guess maybe you don't understand, soldier. We got our homes here. Most of us were born and raised right in this valley. We ain't interested in selling and moving on. This is our land. We fit (fought) Indians, and thieves, and rustlers to get it. By cracky, we'll take on the whole darned United Stated Army to keep it."

Scenes from Camp Kendall, a fictitious army base, included the training of cavalry troops combined with pilot training and bombing ranges. When the captain reported the resistance of the townsfolk to Major Forbes (Robert Warrick), he suggested a deployment of troops to clear the resistors. Major Forbes refused to consider such strong-arm tactics, stating emphatically, "These people are citizens, they pay taxes, and after all, that's what keeps this man's army going." Instead, the major sent Sergeant Gene Autry undercover to convince the ranchers to sell their homes for the benefit of the U.S. war preparedness efforts.

*In Old Monterey* foreshadowed Gene Autry's future as a noncommissioned officer working to recruit two million men and women for the U.S. Army Air Force. The film portrayed the singing cowboy as a working cattleman before he joined the army. Autry's ability to ride and rope and his general ranch experience made him the perfect choice for this special undercover duty. The film connected Gene Autry to the world of rodeo sport by showing him as a trainer working with a group of soldiers learning to break horses for the U.S. Cavalry. As Autry demonstrated his rodeo technique, The Hoosier Hot Shots hit sour notes to spook his fiery mount. Moviegoers got laughs watching Autry handle a bucking bronco to the tune of a playful polka.

Afterward, as Autry confronted his good buddies for their irresponsible behavior, Frog Millhouse (Smiley Burnette) roared upon the scene in a miniature one-man tank. Moviegoers learned that the tour of duty was about over for the boys unless they reenlisted. Gene nudged them all by saying, "You can't quit now!" Then he hatched a scheme to convince the boys to re-up by throwing a party in the mess hall to draw attention to the strong feelings of belonging many soldiers felt. Autry sang "Born in the Saddle" and a sentimental tearjerker, "My Buddy," to convince the boys to reenlist. Directed at young, moviegoing fans, these messages of duty, patriotism, and camaraderie came across loud and clear.

Before Autry signed his own reenlistment papers, he had to complete his secret mission; so technically, he told the truth when passing as a rancher in the Colby Basin. Autry would re-up after completing his undercover assignment. At a town meeting where folks gathered to discuss the army's ultimatum, a greedy mine owner named Stevenson (Jonathan Hale) stirred the people with talk of resisting the federal government. In response, the undercover cowboy reminded the Colby ranchers to think of their wives and families. "What's going to happen to them if you shoot it out with the army?" Autry asked. In an attempt to damage the cowboy's credibility, Stevenson revealed Autry's secret association with the U.S. Army.

Accusations of double-dealing ruined Autry's chance of a peaceable solution, so he created a captive audience by locking down the theater and forcing the assembled audience to watch actual newsreels titled *War in the Far East* and *War in Europe*. Showing scenes of terrible damage and loss of life suffered by civilian populations, actual newsreels being incorporated into the musical-Western format intentionally blurred the line between real life and fantasy for moviegoers. The high demands of war preparedness caused Republic Pictures to blur this line. Only the gravity of the global situation convinced Herbert Yates to support this move.

Americans were not safe or immune from physical danger in modern warfare. Autry declared: "Not a very pretty picture is it? What you saw there could happen right here in this country and will happen unless we have a fighting force so superior that no one would dare attack us. By that I don't mean more men, more guns, and more equipment than anyone else; but better men, and better guns, and better equipment; and to make sure that they are better, we need places where our men can train and our equipment can be tested over and over until every flaw has been found and corrected. That's why the government wants to buy this land and is willing to pay more than a fair price for it. And I don't believe that any of you are such poor Americans that you won't be proud to do your part for such a cause."

Whittaker, the isolationist, jumped up to join Autry on stage to testify to his change of heart. Speaking to isolationists everywhere, Whittaker said: "Folks, I hate to admit it, but Gene here's convinced me that I've been all wrong, Trouble with us is that we have been thinking of our own measly selves so much that we forgot that there is 140 million other people in this country." Then, Whittaker and Autry led the assembly in a rousing version of the nostalgic song "Columbia, the Gem of the Ocean," a patriotic tune that occasionally saw use as an unofficial national anthem, in competition with "Hail, Columbia," and "The Star-Spangled Banner," until the latter's formal adoption as the national anthem in 1931.[8]

Meanwhile, back at Whittaker's ranch, Stevenson's cronies rigged the house with explosives to fake an aerial bombing. Accidentally, they killed little Jimmy Whittaker (Billy Lee) in the blast intended to cast blame upon the U.S. Army Air Force. The killing of little Jimmy turned public opinion away from Gene Autry's position. Whittaker threatened to kill the cowboy hero if he did not leave town. Nevertheless, Gene returned to sing "Vacant Chair" at Jimmy's funeral. He sang a duet with Jill Whittaker (June Storey), Jimmy's older sister.[9]

Aerial photographs taken by the U.S. Army Air Force revealed a car belonging to Gillman (William Hall), Stevenson's partner in crime, hidden behind the barn at the time of the bombing. Further crime scene investigations, including plaster castings of Gillman's tire tread, concluded that the culprits who killed Jimmy were double-dealing business executives from the Atlas Borax Company. To exonerate the Army Air Force, Gene and Frog broke into the Atlas Borax offices and took confidential files that verified the treachery. Apparently, desperate times called for desperate measures and suspension of the rule of law by government agents. Meanwhile, in an act of civil disobedience, the townsfolk built a barricade to fend off an attack from the U.S. Army.

When Autry produced the evidence damning the Atlas Borax Company, the townsfolk, led by Whittaker, rushed to the Atlas Mine to confront Stevenson and Gillman. Frog demonstrated the use of the army's one-man tank by quickly reaching Major Forbes and stopping the assault on Colby. Instead, the army joined with the townspeople in the showdown with the crooked businessmen at the borax mine. Putting the pint-sized tank through its paces, Frog and Gene used this modern war machine to break through a barricade and attempt the capture of the crooks and rabble-rousers. Stevenson and Gillman used an airplane to make their escape, but Autry brought down the plane with a single shot from his Winchester rifle. At the close of the film, Sergeant Gene Autry and The Hoosier Hot Shots (in uniform) performed the title song while they helped the Whittaker family relocate from Colby Basin, making room for the U.S. Army Air Force to prepare the nation for war.

*In Old Monterey* helped inform the nation about the need for air bases and bombing ranges to train pilots and crewmembers for the U.S. Army Air Force. Autry echoed the Roosevelt administration's commitment to a superior air force and long-range bombers to protect the United States from the inevitability of foreign wars. In the process, both the star and studio represented the American West and westerners as supporting a national agenda. America's Favorite Cowboy represented the United States to the world.

Republic ballyhoo promoted *In Old Monterey* as a coming attraction during Autry's hugely popular, personal appearance tour of the British Isles and Irish Free State. Upon his return to New York, John Kilpatrick, the operator of Madison Square Garden, booked the singing cowboy to appear in conjunction with the national finals of Everett Colborn's World's Championship Rodeo (WCR). Drawing a sold-out crowd of over 17,000 fans in Madison Square Garden, Kirkpatrick added Autry as a headliner for the entire nineteen-day run of the 1940 WCR Finals.[10]

Autry's music and motion pictures moved from the western fringe into the mainstream of American cultural industries as the Second World War got underway. The cowboy's ability to sing softly and beat the bad guys attracted attention from the Wrigley Company of Chicago. Familiar with Sears' sponsorship of Gene Autry on WLS and NBC's *National Barn Dance* program, Wrigley offered to sponsor the sing cowboy as the star of a new nationally syndicated program for distribution over the CBS radio network.

Wrigley launched *Gene Autry's Melody Ranch* during a special preview on New Year's Eve, December 31, 1939, exclusively for merchants selling Doublemint Gum. The *Melody Ranch* announcer identified the American cowboy as a romantic hero, comparable to the well-known knight in shining armor astride a powerful charger in Anglo-Saxon culture. The announcer praised the cowboys of the western plains and deserts for self-reliance, and for living a life closer to nature than most Americans. He identified sincerity and authenticity as the calling cards most highly valued by fans.

Wrigley's announcer explained: "Our hero of Melody Ranch is Gene Autry, America's Favorite Singing Cowboy, who is a symbol of the clean thinking, honesty and integrity of the American people. Gene has achieved success through his fine work with Republic Pictures. Millions of picture-goers know him and love him. Much of his success is due to the fact that he personally lives the characters that he depicts. Many of us can still remember the many characters made famous by Horatio Alger. Gene Autry's own history is an Alger story, as you'll hear in a moment."[11]

This *Melody Ranch* inaugural included a radio drama linking the emerging star to the much-beloved Will Rogers. The drama retold an oft-repeated foundational narrative about a meeting between Gene Autry and Will Rogers in a rural Oklahoma town. Autry worked as a telegrapher for the Frisco Line when Rogers dropped in to wire a message. Wrigley promoted Rogers as the source of Autry's inspiration, suggesting that his words of encouragement convinced young Gene to go to New York. The announcer explained that Autry made his way as a singer and succeeded in show business because he contributed something new to American culture. Wrigley asked merchants to celebrate Autry's unique contribution to American life and American song.[12]

Wrigley positioned *Gene Autry's Melody Ranch* as a purely American entertainment that helped audiences forget about the outside world and escape into a modern-day Western fantasy. "You know everybody these days sort of has a hankerin' to escape all this hustle and bustle, and bright lights and all the troubles they think they have on their shoulders, and sort of sink down around the campfire with the boys," Autry surmised. The Wrigley announcer explained:

> Millions go to their favorite theater to see Gene and thrill to his singing in Republic pictures. And now, Gene Autry comes to visit you: to sit around your firesides with you, swapping stories of the colorful West. Telling you his adventures and singing you the grand songs we all love so well, here is a new program. A program to carry you out of yourselves; out of this troubled world of ours; out into the great open plains

of the west; a program that brings you color, America humor and American song by that successful interpreter of our nation's most tuneful folksongs, Gene Autry; so, join Gene and the boys at Melody Ranch next Sunday night and bring your family and friends along too.[13]

*Gene Autry's Melody Ranch* began regular broadcasts on January 7, 1940, and continued in primetime on CBS every Sunday night at 6:30 P.M. The flurry of national and international publicity surrounding the singing cowboy persuaded Wrigley to feature Autry in the national broadcast. Wrigley's Doublemint Gum continued as Autry's product sponsor for the next sixteen years, from 1940 to 1956, through a variety of iterations on radio and television, including *Gene Autry's Melody Ranch*, *Sergeant Gene Autry*, and *The Gene Autry Show*. Wrigley paid its cowboy hero $1,500 per week for appearing on the program in 1940, more than $25,000 per week in 2015 dollars. Over time, Autry's salary for weekly radio work rose to $5,000, about $85,000 per week in 2015 dollars.[14]

Gene Autry's rising star in Republic's stable of "B" Western film stars created the cash flow needed for Herbert Yates to compete within the Motion Picture Producers and Distributors Association (MPPDA). Building upon Autry's success, Yates increased Republic Pictures productions to fifty-six features and four serials in 1940. Yates expected to gross $10,000,000 as a return for his production increases, about $170 million in 2015 dollars. His secret to success involved running the studio like a business. Consequently, Republic made typical Westerns on budgets of $80,000 to $125,000 per picture, about $1.4 to $2.1 million in 2015 dollars. The final costs never missed the mark by more than 5 percent. Yates's formula produced salable Westerns on an assembly line basis, similar to the approach used by P. T. Barnum.[15] Herbert Yates explained:

> The public has always liked Westerns—you know, cowboys, horses and fine scenery—hillbilly comedies and serials. The proof of the pudding is that Gene Autry is one of the best-loved stars in pictures today. Sure, the story is pretty much

the same. There's a hero and the girl and the heavy who's trying to gyp them out of a mortgage or land or cattle. But you change it around a little to give it new trimmings. You've got a formula the public likes and it's as standardized as granulated sugar. If you like sugar in your coffee, why use salt?[16]

Republic's formulaic approach relied upon good stories, according to Yates. Good stories and positive messages mattered to both Yates and Autry. Fans valued Gene's character more than the settings in his films. Again, Yates clarified:

If you have a good yarn you can do it on a low budget and make a picture as entertaining as one costing six times as much. The public doesn't care if your characters are walking around in a set that cost $50,000. The audience is interested in the characters, not the set. Some of those people out on the Coast seem to forget that show business started in a tent. Today they have everything overcapitalized. You don't have to spend $3,000,000 to make a good picture or build a $10,000,000 cathedral to show it in.[17]

Extension of the "Gene Autry" brand through a nationally syndicated radio show increased exponentially the level of synergy produced by the singing cowboy in other American culture industries. Heavy radio promotions helped Republic boost ticket sales and elevate Gene Autry to the top-ten list of Hollywood box office earners. *Gene Autry's Melody Ranch* also increased sales for sound recordings, especially the big hits like "South of the Border (Down Mexico Way)," "Goodbye Little Darlin', Goodbye," "You Are My Sunshine," and "Be Honest with Me."

From the beginning, Wrigley, CBS, and Gene Autry crafted a variety show that promoted Americanism, war preparedness, and hemispheric cooperation through music, drama, advertising, and information about the federal government, presented through public service announcements. Wrigley sponsored the primetime broadcast as part of its overall strategy to show support for U.S. troops and to protect

Autry with members of the Gene Autry Fan Club, c. 1936. © Autry Qualified Interest Trust and The Autry Foundation (BIO_195).

Autry with CBS microphone, 1940. © Autry Qualified Interest Trust and The Autry Foundation (BIO_080).

Doublemint Gum display card for Gene Autry's *Melody Ranch*, 1939. © Autry Qualified Interest Trust and The Autry Foundation (T87-36-354).

*In Old Monterey* poster, 1939. © Autry Qualified Interest Trust and The Autry Foundation (T87-36-2118).

Autry with First Lady Eleanor Roosevelt and Hollywood celebrities at President's Birthday Ball Broadcast, 1940. © Autry Qualified Interest Trust and The Autry Foundation (GAC_046).

Autry and Champion saluting from the Capitol steps, 1941. © Autry Qualified Interest Trust and The Autry Foundation (BIO_273).

the reputation of company brands during an era of wartime rationing. Raw materials for chewing gum came from Malaya, Borneo, and South America. To maintain access to these markets, Wrigley wanted its chewing gum classified as an essential wartime commodity. Company President Phillip Wrigley accomplished this by taking the Spearmint®, Doublemint®, and Juicy Fruit® brands off the civilian market and dedicating the entire output of these products to the U.S. Armed Forces.[18]

Usually, *Gene Autry's Melody Ranch* originated in the studios of CBS Radio Station KNX in Hollywood; however, Wrigley arranged for the program to broadcast live from Washington, D.C., on January 28, 1940. First Lady Eleanor Roosevelt appeared as a special guest on the live broadcast, telling radio listeners that she invited Gene to the nation's capital to celebrate the birthday of Franklin Roosevelt and to raise funds to support the National Foundation for Infantile Paralysis. CBS staged the special broadcast as an all-American musical tribute, harmonizing the often conflicting themes of American unity and diversity through song and melody. This program gave some indication of the close association between Wrigley and the White House. In addition to the festivities in Washington, Americans extended the celebration at another 25,000 local balls, hosted across the country for the benefit of infantile paralysis victims.

From this day forward, a mass of Gene Autry Friendship Club members showed continued support for the president by contributing annually to the March of Dimes. Soon these same fans were buying U.S. defense savings bonds and stamps, promoted by Gene Autry through regular radio pitches, patriotic recordings, jingoistic motion pictures, partisan personal appearances, and licensed merchandise tie-ups.[19]

The presidential birthday broadcast demonstrated how music and radio drama could celebrate diversity as an aspect of American music, while simultaneously promoting unity by harmonizing the different forms within a larger national context. The featured musical groups performed in noticeably different styles, yet they all played American music. The program opened with Autry introducing the musical acts performing live from the CBS studios in Washington, D.C., followed by live simulcasts from St. Louis, Missouri; Fall River, Massachusetts; and Chicago, Illinois.

To symbolize the American West, Gene sang "Carry Me Back to the Lone Prairie"; his theme song, "Back in the Saddle Again"; and a closing number, "The End of the Trail." The performance of a Negro spiritual, "Fly Up/Rise Up," symbolized southern gospel and African American music. A hillbilly song, "Ozark Mountain Home," performed from the CBS studio in St. Louis, represented music from the American heartland. Similarly, a hymn of thanks from Fall River performed in recognition of America's Pilgrim Fathers signified unity through prayer and oneness with God. These songs celebrating regional diversity underscored the differences between local, regional, and national initiatives.[20]

Emphasizing Americanism as a national objective in combination with regionalism, *Gene Autry's Melody Ranch* also included a rendition of "Sweet Adeline," performed by Washington Chapter No. 9 of the Society for the Preservation of Barbershop Quartette Singing in America. Nothing was more "downright American and universal in scope," declared the Wrigley announcer. Showcasing the harmonizing effects of traditional American music, the announcer explained that American popular music was "played all over the world." To emphasize the significance of American music, the big finale featured a popular American dance tune, "Oh, Johnny, Oh," performed live from Chicago by the Orrin Tucker Orchestra, a featured act on *Hit Parade*, another nationally syndicated radio program. At the conclusion of this performance, Autry explained: "Your song brings us right up to date on the media trend of American dance music. Yes, you'll find song and melody wherever men and women gather together. It's a natural form of expression for all of us."[21]

The First Lady thanked Autry for presenting such poignant examples of American songs and melodies. Mrs. Roosevelt pointed out, "So many of us don't realize that in this vast country of ours, each section has songs and traditions peculiar to itself; but at the same time, truly and thoroughly American." These expressions of harmony and unity through music earned Autry a speaking part at a luncheon of Hollywood celebrities at the White House. Newspapers reported that the singing cowboy made a very clever presentation, giving the president and Mrs. Roosevelt a pair of matching cowboy hats.[22]

In sponsoring Autry's radio program, Wrigley invited listeners to a real American get-together at the imaginary Melody Ranch, where freedom of association, freedom of assembly, and freedom of speech provided the cornerstones of American culture and values. Echoing these sentiments through songs like "Dude Ranch Cowhands," "South of the Border (Down Mexico Way)," and "America, the Beautiful," Autry referred to his Melody Ranch get-togethers as "Real American" parties when he said, "Feel the way we do: that life, liberty and the pursuit of happiness are more precious than all of the other riches in this bountiful country of ours. You know, we really are rich, because here in this country people sing because they feel that they have something to sing about. People laugh because they're happy and people work, and they work hard, because we have a lot of pride and faith in the nation we've built, and we're building day after day. So after all, what have we got to worry about when we have things like that? Why, we Americans have less to worry about than any other people on the face of the globe. So if you happen to feel like singing along with us here at Melody Ranch, I don't care where you happen to be, just join right in. It'll help you relax . . ."[23]

Songs recorded in a Los Angeles session on March 12, 1940, marked the beginning of a musical makeover for the singing cowboy. Autry introduced a hot new orchestra with a tangy Western flavor and the breezy feel of a solid jazz combo. The players included Carl Cotner, Spade Cooley, Paul Sells, Frankie Marvin, Oliver E. "Eddie" Tudor, and Walter Jecker. Later known as the "King of Western Swing," Spade Cooley made the greatest impact on Autry's sound. Cooley played fiddle with the Jimmy Wakely Trio at the Venice Pier Ballroom in Venice, California, while Wakely's band was also backing up Autry on the *Melody Ranch* radio program.[24]

Autry's change in musical styling occurred simultaneously with the efforts of Republic Pictures to transition the singing cowboy out of musical-Westerns and into more mainstream Hollywood genres. Aiming to compete with Bing Crosby, Autry's new sound highlighted his maturing vocals. As he abandoned his traditional cowboy sound for more modern popular arrangements, other Western recording artists followed suit. Ten gold records between 1940 and 1942 evidenced Autry's status as a trendsetter in popular music. Many of his finest recordings dated from this period.[25]

Personal appearance tours made Gene Autry different than most other big movie stars in Hollywood. Autry logged almost 100,000 miles on personal appearance tours in 1940. Touring big cities and small hamlets alike, never once did this cowboy hero fail to win friends, not only for himself, but also for his movie studio, radio sponsor, record label, and the licensed merchandise producers and distributors earning income from the "Gene Autry" name and image. The cowboy received letters from theater managers, school superintendents, civic officials, and just plain fans. They all told the same story—Gene Autry came to their town and proved himself a "regular."[26]

Autry always added goodwill stops to his personal appearance jaunts. He visited schools, orphanages, and hospitals on every tour. He believed in setting a good example of clean living for his millions of kid-fans. He never smoked or drank on screen. Autry remained accessible to anyone who wanted to talk with him, and he never refused any demand on his time if he could possibly meet it. American media culture offered few stars with the same friend-making abilities as Gene Autry.[27]

Fans turned out in droves to see the "Gene Autry, In Person" tour in rural, small-town, and neighborhood movie theaters. Autry earned a significant portion of his income from his one-man show and from touring with The Gene Autry Trio. In 1940, the singing cowboy evolved these small shows into a Western musical extravaganza worthy of headliner status with the World's Championship Rodeo Finals at Madison Square Garden. The singing cowboy's experience with huge crowds at Madison Square Garden warranted a bigger presence to match the excitement and intensity of sold out stadium. Gene Autry headlined the nineteen-day WCR Finals ten times between 1939 and 1953. Once he got started, America's Favorite Cowboy toured continuously on the rodeo and Wild West show circuits into the 1960s. His only time out came in 1943–45, while he served as a technical sergeant and pilot for the U.S. Army Air Force.[28]

Borrowing from the Cavalcade of Texas and other displays of pageantry, Autry and his musical sidekicks created a pageant of the Old West to anchor their rodeo performances. Compared to the usual spine-tingling rodeo events, Autry offered a very flossy show. Cross-promotion in Republic pictures and live remote broadcasts of *Gene Autry's Melody Ranch*, originating from different cities during the rodeo tours, enabled the cowboy to fully integrate this purely American form of spectator sport to his repertoire of arts and entertainment.

Headlining for the 1940 World's Championship Rodeo Finals represented one of the biggest breaks Autry received during his long career. John Reed Kilpatrick, president of the Madison Square Garden Corporation, signed Autry to perform during the annual nineteen-day October event. Evertt Johnson's Cowboy Band drove out to La Guardia Field in a bus to welcome the cowboy hero to New York. Autry's arrival by airplane drew the attention of New York media, because Gene brought Champion with him. The decision to plane his famous horse east for personal appearances at the rodeo cost Autry $3,000, more than $50,000 in 2015 dollars. Even so, he must have netted ten times that amount in fan approval.[29]

To kick-start his WCR engagement, America's Ace Cowboy led a parade from Madison Square Garden to the New York City Hall, where the mayor officially welcomed the rodeo participants to the city. America's foremost Western film hero thrilled 2,000 patients and attendants at Bellevue Hospital during the WCR's annual run, appearing at a benefit for incapacitated children. Autry appeared with a contingent of fifteen cowgirls, sixty-five cowboys, and a twenty-piece band. He sang several popular songs from his motion pictures, and he did an imitation of President Roosevelt. At Madison Square Garden, Autry did a free show for 17,000 underprivileged children. *Gene Autry's Melody Ranch* originated from New York during the rodeo finals. Madison Square Garden promoted the singing cowboy's appearance at the WRC in joint advertisements with Republic Pictures, promoting the latest picture in the Gene Autry series, *Ride Tenderfoot Ride* (1940). Boston Garden ran similar promotions then the WCR hit town, following the New York run.[30]

Between performances at the WCR Finals, Autry took part in other special events in New York City. He appeared in two free concerts hosted by the American Society of Composers, Authors, and Publishers (ASCAP) at the Music Hall of the New York World's Fair. Johnny Green led the orchestra that backed up the singing cowboy. These concerts showcased Gene Autry's celebrity status as an American composer and singer of Western folksongs. Autry had many other successes in the years that followed, but none seemed as culturally significant as the respect he earned from ASCAP in 1940.[31]

Gene Autry's singing cowboy persona had evolved since 1931, when Western music first offered a nascent theatrical masquerade for aspiring musicians hoping to carve out recording and radio careers. A decade later, the singing cowboy found himself at the center of the American cultural industries, fueled by a multimillion-dollar American media culture. This combination of Gene Autry productions created a synergy that elevated the "Gene Autry" brand into a true American franchise with an amazing array of license merchandise. In 1940, Gene Autry ushered in an era of respectability and commercial viability for a burgeoning musical genre newly labeled as "country and western."[32]

Tom Mix died suddenly in a car accident, en route from Tucson to Phoenix, Arizona, during the World's Championship Rodeo Finals. Upon learning of the event, Gene Autry lamented: "Now that's terrible news, Tom was the greatest cowboy that ever drew on boots. He was a credit to the American cowboy and was our acknowledged leader. He was also the greatest showman the West ever produced and he brought world attention to cowboys."[33]

To satisfy the throngs of Tom Mix's friends and fans that mourned his passing, Autry added a tribute to his Madison Square Garden rodeo performances. Another tribute called "A New Hand in Heaven" graced *Gene Autry's Melody Ranch* show. "[Tom Mix] contributed a great deal to the betterment of the American cowboy and cowboy sports," Autry proclaimed. The older Western star provided a role model for young Gene as he learned the movie business. Mix earned $17,000 per picture at the height of his career, nearly $290,000 in 2015 dollars.[34]

Gene Autry copied Tom Mix by adopting the custom of routinely dressing Western. Mix knew better than most that cowboy regalia meant good business. Autry's favorite Western outfit was an orangey-yellow number, complete with fancy boots and a 10-gallon hat. His most conservative look came in a delicate, powder-blue ensemble. Gene's dressy Western style provided an ever-present spotlight when he walked down Broadway in New York. The singing cowboy made a statement wherever and whenever he appeared in public.[35]

George A. Mooney's *New York Times* interview of Gene Autry titled "Youth's Model 1940" demonstrated that Autry understood his significance in American culture and media. The radio cowboy recognized that millions of American youngsters typically emulated his every action. Autry consciously obliged his fans by not mixing politics directly into his productions. Nonetheless, he felt differently about Americanism. Having survived the Great Depression only to face the threats of global war, Autry approached kids with sincerity and authenticity to show them the meaning of Americanism. Gene played himself in the movies, on the radio, and on sound recordings.[36]

Autry's fan mail averaged more than 12,000 letters each week, topping that of all other Hollywood stars and proving he had a deep understanding of his youthful audiences. Gene described the many letters received from parents asking him to say a good word so that junior would eat his spinach or take up some other worthy course. Gene Autry Fan Club members pledged to live a good life, following an example set by their cowboy hero. Police departments adopted the "Gene Autry" brand to impress safety campaigns upon school children.[37]

Dressed in a cream-colored shirt edged with brown piping, tight brown breeches, and elaborately tooled boots, "Youth's Model 1940" explained that fans expected their cowboy hero to dress in a Western style. The Western genre figured heavily in his approach to influencing young Americans: "If I can show our youth what it is like to be a real American, then I'm doing a good job. I want to show them that in this country everybody has a chance—just as I did. . . . In the programs we try to keep everything strictly American and down to earth. That's the sort of thing that will do more to knock any Communist, Nazi or other such ideas out of their heads than anything else. As I see it, the way is not to get up and say that the Communists and others are wrong. Instead we should show the young people the decent, good things that are in this country; things that don't exist now in other countries of the world. . . . Acting like a true American is very important, under the circumstances.... These young people watch me very carefully and there are certain things they expect me to do and not to do."[38]

The cowboy refused to express a preference for either motion pictures or radio, because he worked in both media. Gene viewed these two forms of American media culture as complementary. Variety kept him from getting stale in either medium. For the work of spreading Americanism, he preferred radio. "In a single broadcast one can reach more people faster with the American doctrines," declared Autry. Performing live made radio broadcasting more precise—there were no opportunities for "retakes," as in film. A radio broadcast had to be right the first time.[39]

Promoting Americanism through the joint exploitation of live performances, motion pictures, sound recordings, radio broadcasts, and name-brand merchandise, Autry aided the Roosevelt administration through his mastery of mass media. It is no surprise that FDR welcomed support from a singing cowboy who could synergize such a large audience. Autry called himself a "New Deal Cowboy" because he agreed to mix information about public works in western states and issues important to westerners into his diverse cultural productions. By 1940, Autry helped shape public opinion in support of Roosevelt for more than one out of every four Americans.

Emphasizing unity in American culture, Autry said, "You know, a trip east sure opens a fellas eyes to this country's bigness and hustle and to the fact that all these many different cities, rivers, and farms, hills, towns, ranches and shops are actually under one roof—the Great American Sky. You can't beat the prairies and the mountains of the west, but there is something doggoned exciting too in the sight of the sunlight slanting down through city canyons and making all the windows flash and sparkle like a million diamonds."[40]

Every week, millions of fans turned out to see Republic pictures starring Gene Autry. They bought Gene Autry records from the American Record Corporation (ARC) and sheet music and songbooks from the Sears catalogs. They learned to play and sing Gene Autry songs at home on name-brand "Gene Autry" guitars. They chewed Wrigley's Doublemint Gum while listening to *Gene Autry's Melody Ranch,* broadcast live from Hollywood on the CBS radio network, and they went to see Gene Autry perform as a musical headliner on the World's Championship Rodeo Circuit, including the annual WCR Finals at Madison Square Garden in New York City.

The associations between Autry and FDR benefitted both the cowboy and the president. In the annual poll of motion picture exhibitors conducted by the *Motion Picture Herald*, Autry joined a select list of movie stars, earning a spot on the list of top-ten moneymakers for all of Hollywood in 1940. Autry's position on Hollywood's top-ten list surprised critics, while demonstrating the rise of the Western genre in mainstream American cultural industries, during the run up to World War II. What is more, Autry ranked number one for the fourth consecutive year on the *Motion Picture Herald*'s list of biggest Western moneymakers. Not since Will Rogers appeared on both top-ten lists in 1934 had any Western star received similar national recognition.[41]

CHAPTER 8

# Sergeant Gene Autry

Gene Autry fans first heard the song "Melody Ranch" in a film with the same name, released by Republic Pictures on November 15, 1940. Helping to promote the movie, America's Favorite Cowboy sang "Melody Ranch" repeatedly on *Gene Autry's Melody Ranch*, throughout December 1940 and January 1941. Meanwhile, the film *Melody Ranch* gave fans a firsthand look at Autry's live radio broadcasts, sponsored by the Wrigley Company of Chicago on the CBS Radio Network.

*Melody Ranch* opened with Gene and the boys sitting around a campfire singing the eponymous ballad. As the camera pulled back, the scene revealed the staging of the campfire set in a studio at the fictitious Radio Station KRL, a pseudonym for Autry's own CBS affiliate, Radio Station KNX in Hollywood. As Gene sang, moviegoers experienced his performance as if sitting in the back row in the KRL studio. Encountering this scene in panorama, movie theater fans felt as though they were a part of the studio audience.[1]

Jimmy Durante replaced Smiley Burnette as Gene Autry's sidekick in *Melody Ranch*, playing the role of Cornelius J. "Cornie" Courtney. Republic disguised Autry's real radio program sponsor, Wrigley's Doublemint Gum, with a cold remedy called "Nose Posse," so Durante could to do a comedic shtick about his big nose. Station manager Tommy Summerville (Jerome Cowan) showed concern as Autry and his extras launched into their weekly Western drama. Julie (Ann Miller), the drama's leading lady, was a no-show. As the radio drama proceeded, audiences watched the work of the sound effects man attempting to stretch things out to accommodate Julie's late arrival.

Singing a catchy tune called "Rodeo Rose," Autry made a connection to his performances at the World's Championship Rodeo in Madison Square Garden. This storyline developed further when the cowboy received a visit from Pop Laramie (George "Gabby" Hayes) and Penny (Mary Lee), two friends from back home in the western town of Torpedo. Pop and Penny braved their way into the big city to ask Gene to serve as honorary sheriff during Torpedo's annual Frontier Day celebration, an event featuring a rodeo and horse racing, typical of the small-town entertainments promoted by the United States Travel Bureau in 1940–41. Cornie suggested doing a radio show live from Torpedo to boost the sagging ratings of Autry's musical variety show.[2]

Fans got a glimpse of the real life traveling caravan that Autry assembled for his British tour in 1939. *Melody Ranch* included scenes of this live-show rig as it traveled across spectacular scenery along U.S. Highway 395. Seen traveling from Red Rocks State Park through Lone Pine to Mammoth Lakes, California, Autry's troupe included a tour bus, truck and horse trailer combination, and a radio equipment truck for live remote broadcasting.

Autry's outfit set up in a saloon owned by the Wildhack boys to broadcast their Frontier Days show. Midway through the program, the Wildhacks preempted the show, beating up Gene and making him a laughingstock by singing "Go Back to the City Again," a parody of "Back in the Saddle Again." Gene got sore and decided to stick around Torpedo to get even with the Wildhacks. He worked out with Pop Laramie, cowboying at Melody Ranch, to replace the softness of the city with some ranch-hardened manliness. Fan mail received by the singing cowboy in the film showed overwhelming support for the cowboy to fight the Wildhack boys.[3]

*Melody Ranch* featured Gene Autry running for sheriff to clean up the town of Torpedo and clear out the corrupt Wildhacks as a tie-up with President Roosevelt's unprecedented third term campaign for reelection in 1940. Cornie and Penny led the crowd in a rousing reprise of "Vote for Autry," last heard by moviegoers in *Colorado Sunset* (1939). This theme dated back to *Guns and Guitars* (1936), released during Roosevelt's first reelection campaign. In a familiar plot twist, the Wildhacks, in cahoots with the local sheriff, tried to throw the election to favor their candidate. Cornie criticized the barkeeper for denying Gene Autry's constituents their right to vote before the polls closed. He challenged Mark Wildhack (Barton MacLane), saying, "In your attitude, I see the beginnings of cheap totalitarianism."

When a firefight erupted between the Wildhack and Autry factions, a local school teacher named Veronica Whipple (Barbara Allen), ignored the whizzing bullets and overwhelming smell of gunsmoke to crack wise. Whipple made a direct connection between Autry and FDR by saying, "My, the elections seem to get noisier every year. I haven't seen so much excitement since I voted for Roosevelt." Looking directly into the camera and speaking to moviegoing audiences, she added sarcastically, "I mean Theodore, of course." This lighthearted but thinly veiled direct appeal for Autry fans to help reelect Franklin Roosevelt demonstrated how direct government propaganda increasingly wormed its way into American media culture by 1940. Nevertheless, polls showed that Gene Autry's message films resonated with his growing fan base.[4]

More than a simple song giving rise to synergy between radio broadcasting and motion pictures through eponymous titling, the idea of Melody Ranch came to symbolize the source of Autry's uniqueness and the homeland for a new western identity associated with Americanism, war preparedness, and hemispheric cooperation. Emphasizing regional and national objectives, Melody Ranch established a point of origin for Gene Autry's brand of Americanism and its growing mainstream salability. In conjuring an image of Melody Ranch for his radio fans, Autry described his idea of a perfect democracy: "Just picture a congenial, easy-going place to relax and shed your troubles for a while. . . . Just let a few songs and stories that are part and parcel of the wonderful country of ours help you to forget your worries. And all we hope is that these little Sunday get-togethers at Melody Ranch may perhaps remind you that no people anywhere in the world have less to worry about than we do. Because we still have the freedom to get together when we want to as often as we may want to, and to say and do as we please."[5]

In November 1941, the singing cowboy relocated his family to a real-life Melody Ranch after a house fire destroyed the Autry residence in North Hollywood. Gene named his 150-acre ranch, located in the Santa Susana Mountains above Granada Hills, to create a physical setting for the imaginary ranch known to his radio and movie fans. He paid $75,000 for the rolling pasture land located thirty miles from Republic Pictures, hemmed on three sides by steep hills and guarded at the open end by an electrically operated gate, more than $1.2 million in 2015 dollars. Singing birds filled the trees lining the roadway, making apt the name of Melody Ranch. Gene noted, "When I close that gate, I'm cut off from the world. This is a fine place to rest." But rest was one commodity that the cowboy star seemed unable to handle. He stayed on the road for seven months each year, making six pictures for Republic during his five months at home and performing his live radio show 52 weeks a year.[6]

Comparisons with Will Rogers as a Western film star and Hollywood box office sensation continued in 1941. The association garnered Gene Autry unprecedented national and international recognition along the eastern seaboard among middle-income Americans and audiences overseas. Synergy among American media outlets and extension of the "Gene Autry" brand resulted in significant modifications to the organic form of the "Gene Autry" franchise. For example, Republic added increasingly elaborate song and dance numbers to the Gene Autry series to tie up with the Western musical extravaganzas that Autry staged for the World's Championship Rodeo.

To announce the arrival of country-western music and musical-Western film in the American mainstream, Gene Autry and Roy Rogers led a premiere parade down Hollywood Boulevard to the Teleview Theater. In January 1941, Western film fans took in the Hollywood premiere of Republic's musical-Western double feature *Melody Ranch*, starring Gene Autry, and *Robin Hood of the Pecos* (1940), starring Roy Rogers. This was the first time that a first-run theater in Hollywood had featured Western films. Hollywood columnist Hedda Hopper wrote, "You can't beat a good western for entertainment—and an antidote for that super-sophisticated feeling that is beginning to cling to the town."[7]

Republic took advantage of eponymous titling in routine fashion when the studio released *Back in the Saddle* in March 1941. The film opened with actual newsreel film footage of New York's Times Square and the World's Championship Rodeo at Madison Square Garden. A radio announcer broadcasting live discovered the cowboy backstage singing "Back in the Saddle Again," the theme song from *Gene Autry's Melody Ranch* radio show. The incorporation of a hit song attracted a wide audience. Movie fans also experienced Autry performing "In the Jailhouse Now," and "You Are My Sunshine." He sang a contemporary western duet with Patsy (Mary Lee) called "I'm an Old Cowhand," a song with references to the Ford V-eight, radio, and movie stars, a song written by Johnny Mercer for Bing Crosby to sing in *Rhythm on the Range* (1936).[8]

*Back in the Saddle* portrayed Gene Autry to be an actual rodeo contestant, prize money winner, and the foreman of the Bar Cross Ranch near the fictitious town of Solitude, Arizona. Gene and his top hand, Frog Millhouse (Smiley Burnette), went to New York to collect Tom Bennett (Edward Norris), the recently twenty-one-year-old inheritor of the Bar Cross. Bennett was reluctant to leave New York, and it took a fistfight to convince him to make the long railroad journey home to Solitude.

Upon arrival in Arizona, the boys learned that Solitude had been caught up in a copper boom, the biggest in twenty years. Increased wartime production brought about mining booms throughout much of the rural West in the 1940s. Meanwhile, poisonous runoff from the mines polluted streams and rivers with copper sulfate, arsenic, and other nasty chemicals. When mining runoff killed cattle up and down the valley, Arizona cattleman protested the contamination of the water supply.

Gene Autry laid out the situation in a scene with mine owner, E. G. Blaine (Arthur Loft). The cowboy insisted that the mine owner and cattle ranchers find some way to accommodate one another. Autry suggested, "Blaine, that stuff you're dumping in the water is killing stock all over the range. It's got to be stopped.... The boys are getting sore, Blaine, we don't want to have any trouble. We both have to live and work in this valley. There should be some way for us to come to an agreement.... I figure there must be some way for you to use that water without dumping that waste into it. Dig some drainage pits. ... That'd clear up the water and solve both our problems."[9]

Screenwriters Richard Murphy and Jesse Lasky, Jr., may have drawn upon newsworthy stories about the Miami Copper Company to develop the plot for *Back in the Saddle*. Miami Copper made headlines by implementing new leaching techniques designed to extend the life of old mines, allow increased tonnage and the recovery of low-grade ores. The company employed these techniques to develop the Castle Dome copper ore body near Bisbee, Arizona.[10]

The Castle Dome Copper Company, a subsidiary of Miami Copper, entered into an agreement with the U.S. government with financing from the Defense Plant Corporation (DPC), a subsidiary of the Reconstruction Finance Corporation (RFC), tasked with the procurement of mineral products to fuel the wartime expansion of industrial productions in 1941. The government contract supplied $9 million for stripping the overburden and building a concentrating plant that the DPC would own and lease to Castle Dome. Miami Copper supplied additional operating capital needed after completion of the treatment plant. In return, Miami Copper received premium price plan payments for its wartime copper production, a sweetheart deal that paid the company for ore in excess of production quotas from 1941–46.[11]

At the same time, the increased manufacture of airplanes in the San Fernando Valley caused Republic Pictures to rethink its own production methods. Airplanes built for national defense and for service overseas proved challenging for the motion picture producer. Republic faced constant interruptions from planes flying overhead as many as thirty times a day because the studio was situated directly below the air route favored by the test pilots putting new planes through their paces. Each halt in shooting averaged about three minutes. In response, Yates instructed scenarists to confine many scenes to interiors, so the filming could take place on a sound stage. To get away from the airplanes, open air stories filmed by Republic, including all the Gene Autry pictures, began shooting on locations far away from the San Fernando Valley, in Lone Pine and other western towns outside of metropolitan Los Angeles.[12]

Adjusting to the challenges of wartime productions, Herbert Yates made $1,000,000 worth of improvements to the Republic sound stages in 1941, more than $16 million in 2015 dollars. Yates increased Republic's annual budget from $10 million to $15 million, an increase of 50 percent over the previous year. He announced this increase in production at a western regional sales meeting held at the studio. Republic scheduled sixty-six pictures for the 1941–42 season: thirty-two features, thirty Westerns, and four serials. Six features warranted budgets from $750,000 and $1,000,000 each. All this activity made it possible for the studio to become a full-fledged member of the MPPDA. It took Herbert Yates only six years to turn Republic Pictures into a major Hollywood studio. During those same six years, Gene Autry emerged as the Republic's biggest star attraction.[13]

Gene Autry and Smiley Burnette had starred together in forty-six musical-Westerns by 1941, a team record in Hollywood. Their musical-Western films showcasing country-western music in contemporary western settings introduced novel new elements to the traditional western film genre. Autry's serious regard for his fans contributed greatly to the tremendous popularity enjoyed by the duo. Gene gladly sent photographs of himself and Champion without charge to all who asked. Fans considered Gene Autry a personal friend. They really appreciated his sociable demeanor, and they turned out by the millions to enjoy every picture in the Gene Autry series.[14]

Republic's success notwithstanding, many Hollywood insiders detested Westerns because the films targeted lower-culture audiences. Still, Westerns were huge moneymakers. More sophisticated motion pictures won Academy Awards, but film producers knew that the Westerns paid the bills for their artistic triumphs. William S. Hart became the first cowboy-hero to rescue the Western genre from its lower-culture status. Tom Mix followed Hart, along with Hoot Gibson, Art Acord, and J. Warren "Crash" Kerrigan. The tremendous grosses piled up by these colorful and virile cowboy stars covered studio losses on more elegant pictures during the silent film era. That cycle rolled on into the 1930s with such heroes as Buck Jones, George O'Brien, Jack Holt, Charles Starrett, Bill Elliott, Tex Ritter, Bill Boyd, Russell Hayden, Tim Holt and others. Gene Autry and Smiley Burnette provided the most novel new elements to the Western genre by introducing music through a singing cowboy character and humor through the character of the sidekick in a contemporary western setting.[15]

Taking advantage of Autry's rising star, Republic positioned Buck Jones as a rival for America's Favorite Cowboy. Autry's rise to stardom in the mid-1930s came at the expense of Jones, who went from making nine films in 1937 to four in 1938. For all intents and purposes, Autry's popularity forced Jones into early retirement in 1939. Autry's cowboy rival decided to stage a comeback after Tom Mix died. He had retired in disgust at the state of the cow-screen because competing with crooners was not consistent with his code of honor. When the public embraced Gene Autry's "melodious treacle," Jones retreated to his ranch at Sonora, California. There he began to think about the youngsters. "They used to want to grow up to be cowboys," Buck noted. "Now they'll want to grow up to be like Gene Autry."[16]

Buck Jones expressed real concern about the seduction of the young generation growing up with fancy singing cowboys and decadent musical dramas. "Of course, if the public still wants them, there's nothing to be done," he explained, "But I think they've been overdone now and will disappear." Jones accused Republic Pictures of promoting singing cowboys to save money on horses, riders, and ammunition. "Why, you take Gene Autry and lean him up against a tree with his guitar and let him sing three songs and you can fill up a whole reel without spendin' any money," Jones exclaimed! "That's why they've overdone the singing, and that's why it's on the way out."[17]

William Seal, an executive at Republic, added fuel to Buck Jones's fire by listing the five greatest screen cowboys of all time. The studio executive named Bronco Billy Anderson, William S. Hart, Tom Mix, Gene Autry, and Charles "Buck" Jones the favorites of Western film fans. Irked at being ranked fifth behind Autry, Jones could not deny the box-office success of the top four. Nevertheless, he made a class distinction between those who were "real hands" and those who were actors or crooners first and cowboys second. Only Tom Mix rivaled

Buck Jones as a genuine cowhand. "Bronco Bill started in vaudeville, Bill Hart as an actor and Autry as a radio entertainer," Jones noted. He named Gary Cooper as the only other "real hand" working in Westerns. Other real cowpokes on Jones's list included Will Rogers, Hoot Gibson, and Yakima Kanutt.[18]

Buck Jones also worried about succession within a canon of Western cowboy heroes. Jones expressed concern that the breed might die out. He suggested that Gene Autry had led America's children astray. "A dangerous sign of our synthetic times that movie actors should be encouraged to play cowboy," Jones stated, while criticizing the singing cowboy for dressing like a dude. Truth be told, Autry owned at least seventy-five cowboy suits, ranging from vivid colors to the palest yellow. In public, Gene always wore cowboy boots except when playing golf.[19]

The studio's rivalry between Buck Jones and Gene Autry ended tragically in 1942. All Hollywood and the millions of youngsters and adults who loved the typically American, red-blooded Western hero mourned the death of Buck Jones when he died in a disastrous nightclub fire at the Coconut Grove in Boston. Nearly 500 people died in the ghastly blaze. The cowboy hero died of smoke inhalation, burned lungs, and third and second degree burns on his face, neck, and mouth. The fire broke out at a special party hosted by New England motion picture exhibitors honoring Buck Jones. Most of the film executives and their wives also died in the fire.[20]

Bing Crosby ranked as a bigger rival for Gene Autry in 1941. Crosby ranked number one on the music scene, but he placed behind Autry among the top-ten list of Hollywood box office earners. Cultural industry insiders pegged the singing cowboy as a musical contender for the number one spot. The cowboy's work with Republic Pictures and *Gene Autry's Melody Ranch* fueled a resurgence in the sound recording industry. Autry's run of good fortune began with the gold record sales of "South of the Border (Down Mexico Way)," "We're Headin' for the Wide Open Spaces," "Gaucho Serenade," and "Goodbye Little Darlin', Goodbye." His popularity as a recording artist grew intensively with five more gold records in 1941. "Be Honest with Me" and "You Are My Sunshine" made *The Billboard* popular music chart, peaking at number twenty-three. The Motion Picture Academy of Arts and Sciences nominated "Be Honest with Me" for an Oscar in 1941, but Autry lost out to Jerome Kern and Oscar Hammerstein, the composers of "Last Time I Saw Paris." Gene's other gold records that year included "Under Fiesta Stars," "In the Jailhouse Now," and "Ridin' on a Rainbow." Before volunteering for the U.S. Army Air Corps in July 1942, he would score two more gold records for "(I've Got Spurs) Jingle, Jangle, Jingle" with "Clementine" on the B-side. After Autry's enlistment, the record peaked at number fourteen on *The Billboard* pop chart.[21]

This tremendous musical output reinforced the popularity of the singing cowboy and the expansion of the "Gene Autry" franchise through synergy in sound recording, motion picture, radio broadcasting, and live performances. As many of these songs became popular music standards in the postwar period, the range of cultural products associated with Gene Autry's musical output demonstrated the singing cowboy's significance in the history of American media and cultural industries. To take advantage of this music industry renaissance, Autry extended his franchise into music publishing.

Leveraging his musical output, Gene Autry launched Western Music Publishing in 1941 and released the words and music for his many film production numbers in limited editions and folios. "When It's Round Up Time in Texas" became the first big seller for Western Music Publishing. Johnny Marvin, the veteran writer and singer of cowboy ballads, collaborated with Gene Autry on several songs for Western Music.[22]

Taking advantage of the "Gene Autry" franchise to improve its status with the Roosevelt administration, the Wrigley Company used *Gene Autry's Melody Ranch* to promote the sale of U.S. defense savings bonds and stamps. Beginning in June 1941, Autry punctuated his delivery of these public service announcements by repeatedly singing a popular Irving Berlin promotional tune titled, "Any Bonds Today?"[23]

Autry performed this song at state rallies to help boost the sale of defense savings bonds and stamps. Making a whirlwind visit in September 1941, he appeared as the headliner at Taft Stadium in Oklahoma City. At other rallies in Enid, Fort Sill, and Tulsa, Autry kicked off local bond sale campaigns. Nested within a great nationwide effort to sell U.S. defense savings bonds and stamps, these Oklahoma rallies encouraged young fans to purchase defense savings stamps in denominations ranging from 10¢, 25¢, 50¢, $1, and $5. The singing cowboy encouraged Gene Autry Friendship Club members to save their dimes and quarters and to buy the attractive stamp books from their local retailers. When fans filled their stamp books, Autry persuaded them to buy $25 U.S. defense savings bonds. Returning 2.9 percent interest, the popular Series "E" bonds included $25, $50, $100, $500, and $1,000 denominations.[24]

The singing cowboy used a four-point approach to make his patriotic pitches. First, buying defense savings bonds and stamps helped preserve, protect, and defend America's democratic way of life. Autry explained that the U.S. government needed the financial aid of American citizens. Only through the sharing of the task of securing defense could the nation successfully be on guard. Buying government securities represented a partnership with the people owning the best asset in the world. The purchasers of bonds or stamps bought a share in America. He made it clear that each purchase helped make it more certain that Americans could avoid the evils of an increased cost of living. Through the sale of bonds and stamps, the government sought to ensure against inflation and consequent harm to the citizenship. Thrift and savings represented the best defense against inflation. Additionally, bond purchasers built a reserve for the postwar readjustment period. Personal savings, secured upfront through systematic investments, helped Americans protect against distress and build security for the adjustments expected with the coming of peace. Autry described how President Roosevelt's approach to war preparedness reversed the techniques used by Wilson in the Liberty Loan drives during the First World War. The president intended no coercion of any kind and no quotas for cities and states to raise funds. This was strictly a voluntary effort aimed at all types of American citizens.[25]

While touring the Sooner State to sell war bonds, Autry looked in on his growing herd of 1,500 head of prized rodeo stock on his 2,000-acre Flying A Ranch near Berwyn, Oklahoma. The cowboy planned to use the ranch to winter stock for his newest endeavor, Gene Autry's Flying A Ranch Rodeo Stampede. In 1941, more people paid to see rodeo events than any other sport except professional baseball and college football. Autry decided to stage his own Wild West show and rodeo as an extension of the successful formula he had developed in Western music, sound recording, radio broadcasting, motion pictures, and live performances.

Autry planned a knockout show for the World's Championship Rodeo Finals. Incorporating fluorescent costumes, flags, pennants, and emblems that changed color under black lights, he added new stunts and special effects to create a remarkable rodeo sensation. The cowboy needed at least 150 horses and 500 head of cattle and other livestock to launch this new venture. Finding good bucking horses and old-time Texas longhorn steers at a reasonable cost proved to be the biggest problem. Gene considered the production costs a good investment because he expected to clear $2,000 per day during the WCR finals in Manhattan, more than $32,000 in 2015 dollars.[26]

The cowboy implemented a highly innovative black light show as a mainstay of Gene Autry's Flying A Ranch Rodeo to differentiate his extravaganza from the many celebrity rodeos traveling on circuits across the country. Working for Keese Engineering of Hollywood, John T. Shannon designed the "Black-Light Lighting Layout for Traveling Troupe" for use in large stadiums like Madison Square Garden. Beginning in September 1941, Shannon forwarded blueprints and pencil sketches with full details of his black-light lighting system to Eddie Allen, Autry's rodeo manager. The specifications conformed to the usual trouping idea of having individual boxes made for each lighting standard to avoid special packing requirements. Packers merely coiled the wires and put them in the box with the reflectors protected in nesting containers.[27]

While Shannon designed and built Autry's new black light system, the singing cowboy headlined for the third time at the World's Championship Rodeo Finals in Madison Square Garden. The rodeo opened in October 1941 with 200 contestants listed for several events on a nineteen-day program. The WCR decided eight rodeo championships with more than $50,000 in prize money at stake, more than $800,000 in 2015 dollars. A mounted parade routed between the Garden and City Hall opened the show with Gene Autry as the Grand

Marshal. A colorful panoply of 175 cowboys and cowgirls also descended on Bellevue Hospital, to the manifest delight of 3,000 patients and staff members. The singing cowboy hero set the stage by evoking the great open spaces of the American West with the accompaniment of Jimmy Wakely's Melody Ranch Sextette. When the WCR moved to Boston, Autry traveled with the troupe to perform during another thirteen-day run. Afterward, he left the WCR tour to concentrate on launching Gene Autry's Flying A Ranch Rodeo.[28]

By streamlining the rodeo and dressing it up with black-light effects and luminous costumes, Autry added a sparkle of showmanship borrowed from the stage and screen. He envisioned a Western extravaganza, the biggest entertainment spectacle on any amusement circuit in the nation. Announcing the premiere of Gene Autry's Flying A Ranch Rodeo at the Houston Fat Stock Show in February 1942, he planned two eight-week tours in the spring and fall of each year. Future tours kicked off in a new exhibition building in nearby Ardmore, Oklahoma, where the WPA constructed a new indoor arena with seating for 6,500 spectators.[29]

To take advantage of Gene Autry's renown, the citizens of Berwyn—227 inhabitants strong—voted unanimously to change the town's name to Gene Autry, Oklahoma. The Carter County commissioners called a special session to officially approve the name change on November 16, 1941. The Wrigley Company helped stage the event during a live remote broadcast of *Gene Autry's Melody Ranch*. Alvin Bruce presented Gene Autry with the pen used to sign the name change resolution during the national broadcast. J. P. Crowley, General Manager of the Santa Fe Railroad, supervised the changing of the railroad signage. L. M. Cloney represented the Treasury Department from Washington, D.C., promoting the sale of U.S. defense savings bonds and stamps. Juanita Hudson presented the singing cowboy hero with a scroll bearing the name of every person in town.[30]

Berwyn also honored their hero by becoming the first town in the nation to have 100 percent of the residents subscribing to the government's savings bond program. To commemorate the occasion, Gene sang "Don't Bite the Hand that's Feeding You," a patriotic song directed at first-generation Americans, made popular during World War I. Press coverage of the event included a swank layout in *Life* magazine that showcased the re-naming ceremonies.[31]

John Shannon delivered the complete assembly of Gene Autry's black-light stadium show to Eddie Allen in Hollywood on December 30, 1941. The new special effects cost the Western showman a total of $1,890, about $30,000 in 2015 dollars. The final blueprint and complete electrical layout showed a system for twenty black-light units with all the particulars for assembling and disassembling the system as part of a "traveling trouper show," designed for setup in indoor stadiums and arenas. Shannon expressed real excitement for his design, explaining, "Incidentally, all of my boys have been most enthusiastic over the fact that this is the first complete job as large as this in the way of a trouper out-fit that they have worked on." Shannon's system exceeded the cowboy's expectations in every way but one—eight bulbs burned out during the ten-day premiere in Houston.[32]

Black light special effects and luminescent costumes most definitely added color to an already bright entertainment. Gene Autry's Flying A Ranch Rodeo retained the old thrill events while adding some flavor of the New West. The show producer explained: "Rodeo is the second largest attraction in the entertainment field today. It is getting more popular. It is a true western sport. It is getting bigger and bigger. Every large city now has a large building or an arena in which the rodeo can be staged indoors and at night. This makes possible features never before possible in rodeo."[33]

Gene Autry's Flying A Ranch Rodeo retained the events that fans expected to see, specifically, five big rodeo events—bronc-riding, bull-dogging, calf roping, bull roping, and wild-cow milking. Eddie Allen bought rodeo horses, saddle horses, famous bucking horses, rodeo livestock, longhorns, and Brahma steers from all over the United States, Canada, and Mexico. Autry offered large cash purses to assure the stiffest competition for these entry events. He required all the rodeo contestants to ride in a grand entry parade that kicked off each performance. Allen dressed the contestants in bright shirts, big hats, and leather chaps or frontier pants, including the trick riders, trick ropers, and other show personnel carried under contract. Autry hired Phelps-Turkell, a costume house in Los Angeles to make specially

"Gene Autry and Champion in Person" poster, Madison Square Garden, New York, 1941. © Autry Qualified Interest Trust and The Autry Foundation (T87-36-2827-1).

Autry and Champion entering a rodeo arena, 1941. © Autry Qualified Interest Trust and The Autry Foundation (BIO_293).

Fans entering arena to see Gene Autry Rodeo, Fort Worth, Texas, 1941. © Autry Qualified Interest Trust and The Autry Foundation (BIO_291).

Gene Autry with young fans at the rodeo, 1941. © Autry Qualified Interest Trust and The Autry Foundation (GA w KIDS).

Gene Autry changing the name of Berwyn to Gene Autry, Oklahoma, 1941. © Autry Qualified Interest Trust and The Autry Foundation (BIO_192).

Gene Autry's enlistment on the *Melody Ranch* radio program, Chicago, 1942. © Autry Qualified Interest Trust and The Autry Foundation (BIO_011).

Gene Autry signing U.S. savings bonds, 1941. © Autry Qualified Interest Trust and The Autry Foundation (BIO_194).

*Sgt. Gene Autry Presents His Favorite Patriotic and Hillbilly Songs,* songbook, 1941. Courtesy Autry Museum (2003.79.1).

Sergeant Gene Autry broadcasting live from Luke Field, Arizona, 1942. © Autry Qualified Interest Trust and The Autry Foundation (BIO_009).

designed costumes. He placed an order with Ed Gilmore of Hollywood for 160 rodeo saddles, including two elaborately hand-tooled, silver-mounted beauties for personal use.[34]

Gene Autry's Flying A Ranch Rodeo revived an old-time square dancing number with staging under regular floodlights before switching to black-light with stroboscope effects. With the arena blacked out, the dancers continued their routines in luminous costumes that glowed in the dark. Autry built the climax of his own musical performance around another black-light spectacle wherein he serenaded a herd of longhorns rounded up in the arena. Sitting astride his famous horse, Champion, Autry sang to the cattle during a number listed in the program as "The Vanishing Herd." In the postwar period, Gene added a dramatic new hit to this nighthawk routine, featuring the highly acclaimed song, "Ghost Riders in the Sky."[35]

Gold record sales and elaborate rodeo extravaganzas helped Gene Autry make Hollywood's top-ten list for a second consecutive year in 1941. He placed sixth among the ten biggest moneymaking stars. Mickey Rooney, Clark Gable, Abbott and Costello (as a team), Bob Hope, and Spencer Tracy ranked as bigger stars than Gene Autry, but the cowboy landed in front of Gary Cooper, Bette Davis, James Cagney, and Judy Garland. Autry also topped the list of Western stars for a fifth consecutive year. William "Hopalong Cassidy" Boyd, Roy Rogers, Charles Starrett, Smiley Burnette, Tim Holt, Johnny Mack Brown, The Three Mesquiteers (ensemble), Bill Elliott, and Tex Ritter followed in the wake of America's Favorite Cowboy.[36]

Young moviegoers took part in different public opinion polls conducted by *Young America*, a national weekly magazine. The magazine's annual survey of American classrooms showed that average thirteen-year-olds chose Errol Flynn as the number one movie star, followed by Mickey Rooney, Spencer Tracy, Gary Cooper, Deanna Durbin, Gene Autry, and James Stewart. The youth poll revealed that boys in their teens went to the movies 4.3 times per month. They paid an average of 13¢ for movie tickets, and usually they went with a pal. Star power—the name or names of movie stars in a film—remained the final factor for youth deciding which movies to see.[37]

Increasingly throughout 1941, Wrigley sponsored more war-related programming in the broadcasts of Gene Autry's Melody Ranch. In addition to pitches for buying U.S. defense savings bonds and patriotic songs, Doublemint Gum pitches incorporated war references, radio dramas highlighted U.S. military heroes, informative talks focused on the mechanization of the U.S. Cavalry, and the relationship of the cavalry to the Army Air Force. Enlistment pitches profiled contemporary military heroes and special military events, including the program on December 7, 1941, which CBS preempted because of the Japanese attack on Pearl Harbor.[38]

Wrigley promoted Americanism, war preparedness, and hemispheric cooperation through music, radio drama, and advertising. In 1942, the sponsor extended Autry's broadcasts from thirty to forty-five minutes, requiring more thrilling military topics for presentation through Western dramas. Gene told stories about historical military units like George Armstrong Custer's Seventh Cavalry. He conveyed stories about Congressional Medal of Honor awardees such as Lieutenant George Price Hayes, a hero of World War I, and Lieutenant Frank Luke, the namesake of Luke Field near Phoenix, Arizona. Wrigley shifted the tag line used to introduce Gene Autry from "America's Favorite Cowboy" to "America's Ace Cowboy." This change defined the cowboy hero as someone who excelled as an entertainer while associating Gene Autry with the "ace" combat pilots of the U.S. Army Air Force, those who had brought down at least five enemy airplanes.[39]

As the press announced Gene Autry's participation in President Roosevelt's sixtieth birthday celebration, the cover of *The Movie and Radio Guide* for the week of January 25, 1942, featured a beautiful color picture of the singing cowboy astride his famous horse, Champion. Fans learned that Autry attended the president's birthday ball as a member of the "Victory Committee for Stage, Screen and Radio." Gene joined twenty-three other Hollywood film players, including Betty Grable, who had trained east for the event. Autry traveled by airplane to deliver his motion-picture industry tribute. While in the nation's capital, he also appeared at a luncheon hosted by the Texas and Oklahoma congressional delegations.[40]

Soon after this trip to Washington, D.C., Gene Autry's Flying A Ranch Rodeo premiered in the Sam Houston Coliseum at the Houston Fat Stock Show. Republic promoted *Cowboy Serenade* (1942) during

Autry's live remote broadcasts from Radio Station KTRH in Houston. The cowboy continued his promotions of U.S. defense savings bonds and stamp sales from the road. Gene told adventuresome stories of the U.S. Cavalry and sang several songs, including "El Rancho Grande," "Don't Bite the Hand that's Feeding You," "Dude Ranch Cowhands," and "God Must Have Loved America."[41]

During the broadcast on March 1, 1942, Autry began telling his listeners about a transition taking place with the U.S. Cavalry. Gene explained that the U.S. Army Air Force was taking over much of the work formerly done by cavalrymen and their mounts, giving the soldiers more time for fighting. He described a modern cavalry that included thousands of motor vehicles—tanks, armored cars, scout cars, and motorcycles—in addition to plenty of horses. During this transitional phase, the modern U.S. Cavalry employed a "Portee System," using motorized vehicles to quickly transport horses and riders from the scene of one battle to the next. The cowboy hero clarified, "The U.S. Cavalry has always played a prominent part in American history. And every cavalryman looked back with pride on men like Custer and Steward and Sheridan and all of the others who left the glorious tradition upon which the Calvary is founded. And those same cavalrymen are as indispensable part of the model war tank and manpower army fighting for freedom this very minute."[42]

In April 1942, the singing cowboy began using *Gene Autry's Melody Ranch* to promote the launch of Gene Autry's Flying A Ranch Rodeo. Wrigley and CBS expanded the broadcast of *Gene Autry's Melody Ranch* via shortwave broadcasting to reach U.S. soldiers, sailors, and marines serving worldwide. CBS programmed *Gene Autry's Melody Ranch* as part of its new Latin American network of seventy-six stations in twenty countries. Republic Pictures took advantage of this increased exposure to promote Gene Autry's latest films—*Heart of the Rio Grande* and *Home in Wyomin'*—in theaters everywhere. Wrigley joined the bandwagon by promoting Gene Autry's Flying A Ranch Rodeo because the rodeo provided Doublemint Gum chewers with the opportunity to see America's Ace Cowboy in person. As Autry's traveling troupe moved from arenas in Cleveland, Pittsburgh, Philadelphia, Washington, New Haven, and Providence, Wrigley sponsored live remote broadcasts of *Gene Autry's Melody Ranch* from each host city.[43]

Wrigley also sponsored the airing of PSAs for scrap rubber drives that were tied up with a corporation organized by Gene Autry and others named, Records for Our Fighting Men. Kay Kyser, Dr. Sigmund Spaeth, Fritz Reiner, and Kate Smith partnered with Gene Autry to launch this new company. Records for Our Fighting Men salvaged old records for scrap and used the proceeds of the salvage sales to buy new records and phonographs for the enjoyment of men and women in the U.S. Armed Forces. In New York, the American Legion and Auxiliary collected 37,500,000 old and broken phonograph records for the effort. President Roosevelt's Committee on War Relief Agencies approved the project. The Roosevelt administration used the proceeds to buy and install jukeboxes in service posts throughout the United States and overseas.[44]

As these programs launched, Autry began heavy promotion of a U.S. Army Air Force campaign to recruit two million volunteers for all types of duty. In addition to recruitment pitches, Wrigley revamped *Gene Autry's Melody Ranch* radio dramas, adding thrilling stories of modern aviation to the previously recorded stories of military exploits. These stories of heroism featured manly men. According to Autry, "Part of the reward came in the satisfaction of knowing that they were men's men and part of it came from the United States government. Lt. Yarlborough and Lt. O'Brien each received the Distinguished Flying Cross for his heroism. . . . And their action is only a sample of the incentive and loyalty, which is in the heart of every man who wears the uniform of Uncle Sam's Air Force. . . . I am sure Uncle Sam will have no trouble in getting his Air Force of two million, because every man between the ages of eighteen and twenty-six knows that if he is accepted he's automatically classed as one of the best equipped men in the world and he has for his association other real men."[45]

In July 1942, the *New York Times* published a letter written by Frances Morehouse that accused American radio of denying the state of total war that had engulfed the United States. Broadcasters in general took exception to this letter, describing it as a gross misstatement about their war work. CBS pointed out the ignorance of Morehouse's statement: "It would seem that Miss Morehouse is not a radio listener, or she would know how well aware radio is of total war, and how hard it works at the tasks of information, propaganda and morale. If she listened to sponsored programs, how could she have missed *Cheers from the Camps* or the Gene Autry show, which is programmed by the Air Forces?"[46]

Republic Pictures consciously catered to an amalgamating U.S. market. Republic's patriotic escapist entertainment gained traction with a larger moviegoing public as the United States became a combatant in the Second World War. The Gene Autry series reinforced the traditional American values of patriotism, conservatism, self-reliance, and justice. Republic expanded by following the shift in population from rural and small-town regions to industrial centers. Wartime work increased the demand for motion pictures in urban areas. As the studio's audience physically moved and grew larger, moviegoers remained the same in their entertainment habits.[47]

Republic Pictures increasingly sought to take advantage of Gene Autry's popularity as a star of radio and rodeo in its scenarios developed for film. Likewise, the incorporation of pro-government messaging became common currency. Released on April 29, 1942, *Home in Wyomin'* opened with scenes of an attendant sitting behind the reception desk of a New York radio station listening to Gene Autry sing "Be Honest With Me." The camera pulled back to reveal the cowboy-hero singing live in front of an audience in Studio D, when Benson (Fay McKenzie) and Hackett (Chick Chandler), journalists working for *Airwave Review* magazine, strode in with plans for an interview. Making jokes about the cowboy crooner, these reporters characterized the response of the mainstream media to the "Gene Autry" phenomenon in 1942. Hackett asked, "Where's the animal act? The singing milkman? Gene Autry?"[48]

As the reporters enter Studio D, the camera zoomed in on the announcer introducing Gene Autry's next song: "Now, a special musical message from Gene Autry. . . . 'Any Bonds Today?'" Without mentioning Wrigley by name, this scene depicted the chewing gum manufacturer's support for President Roosevelt through sponsorship of *Gene Autry's Melody Ranch*. Inserting this scene logically into the context of *Home in Wyomin'* mirrored Autry's real-life experiences performing on his radio program. Listeners routinely heard the singing cowboy promote efforts for defense savings bond and stamp sales and other means of support for federal government efforts. In movie houses after Pearl Harbor, once the U.S. had entered the war, these messages carried added poignancy without panic. Everything remained under control in Gene Autry's world. His pitches promoting bonds and stamps sales were very matter-of-fact. They blended into the storylines of Republic's contemporary New West dramas. After these initial radio station scenes, the remainder of *Home in Wyomin'* told the story of a fledgling rodeo troupe, intended to dramatize the real-life hardships experienced by those responsible for launching *Gene Autry's Flying A Ranch Rodeo*.[49]

Major film companies simply could not ignore the popularity of musical-Western films by 1942. High ratings for Gene Autry in polls of popular stars demonstrated that the Republic series was not limited to Western audiences. Even so, Hollywood never seemed to embrace Gene Autry, nor did it seem to accept Republic Pictures.

Heavy-handed Americanism on the part of Yates and Autry probably dampened support from many Hollywood types. As the U.S. entered into war, Republic's promotion of the "hundred percenter" suggested a thoroughgoing nationalism that sometimes came off as extreme or unjustified. Patriotism and the values of the "American Way" provided a major impetus in Republic's cultural products. Hence, the topical issues in the studio's message films provided important gauges of popular social thought, as the United States became a combatant in the Second World War.[50]

Patriotism and the American way of life appeared central to Gene Autry's identity after the bombing of Pearl Harbor. Autry's decision to leave a lucrative show business career to join the U.S. Army Air Force verified his status as a "hundred percenter." Completely dedicated to the causes of nationalism under the leadership of Roosevelt's wartime administration, Autry explained his philosophy in an interview widely circulated through newspapers: "Everybody ought to think of winning the war ahead of anything else. . . . Every movie cowboy ought to devote time to the Army winning or to helping win until the war is won—the same as any other American citizen. The Army needs every young man it can get, and if I can set a good example for the young men I'll be mighty proud. Seventeen and eighteen [year olds] are needed, and some of those young boys are my fans. I say to them and to all you young men, every young man should give everything he can for the war effort. If we train young pilots and the war continues for a long stretch, those boys of seventeen or eighteen will be a protectorate over the whole country. I wanted to join the Air Corps rather than the other branches of the services because I felt I could do more good for the war effort there than any other place—because I have been interested in flying for the past ten years."[51]

Arriving in Chicago for a weeklong run with the Gene Autry's Flying A Ranch Rodeo at Soldier Field, the singing cowboy continued his live remote broadcasting of *Gene Autry's Melody Ranch*. The show on July 26, 1942, proved special, when Gene decided to enlist in the U.S. Army Air Force. With millions of people listening across the country and around the world, Orvon Gene Autry took his oath of enlistment. Gene went through his induction ceremony on the air with Lieutenant Colonel Edward Shaifer assigning him the rank of technical sergeant. Afterward, Autry said, "Folks, I am very happy that I've done this and I know that many more real Americans feel the same way that I do. Watching what Hitler and Hirohito and their teammates have been doing since they started running over defenseless countries stealing their food and making slaves of their people, all lovers of liberty have been aroused to do something about it. That's the real reason why I'm proud that I am now a member of Uncle Sam's fighting forces. Come on in, fellas. If you're not in yet, now's the time. Your country needs you more than ever before."[52]

All things considered, using Gene Autry's enlistment as a publicity stunt for recruitment made sense as the U.S. Army Air Forces embarked on a quest to recruit two million young men between the ages of eighteen and twenty-six. Autry inspired thousands of boys listening to his broadcasts to join the army. For millions of listeners, Gene symbolized American righteousness as a protector of the weak and oppressed. His enlistment broadcast kicked off a special campaign of five days called "V-Days" that involved thousands of volunteer war bond salesmen going door to door to meet Illinois's July war bond quota of $85 million.[53]

Autry's efforts were designed to appeal to smaller purchasers buying Series "E" bonds. Higher July quotas calling for a 51 percent increase over June sales spurred the decision to hold the special bond drive. A streetcar painted red, white and blue and advertising war bonds made its initial appearance in the Chicago Loop with drum majorettes from Gene Autry's Flying A Ranch Rodeo. Gene worked the intersection of State Street and Van Buren, known as Treasury corner, serenading bond buyers with a rendition of "Any Bonds Today?" and his most recent gold record, "(I've Got Spurs That) Jingle, Jangle, Jingle." He autographed war stamp boutonnieres to sell for $1.[54]

The PSAs supported by CBS and Wrigley on *Gene Autry's Melody Ranch* contributed to an estimated $62,000,000 in radio time and talent donated by national broadcasters and advertisers for a series of war loan drives beginning May 1, 1941. As the Roosevelt administration turned its attention to radio time and talent to sell U.S. defense savings bonds and stamps, Autry proved especially adept at encouraging young boys and girls to save their nickels and dimes to buy stamps and to convert their stamps books to savings bonds over time. Gene encouraged young Americans to put 10 percent of their income into the popular Series "E" bonds.[55]

Along with the Air Forces recruitment and war bond loan drive efforts, Autry helped the American Legion and the United Service Organization (USO) raise a $1.7 million war fund campaign. Collections for the USO were taken up nightly at Gene Autry's Flying A Ranch Rodeo. In addition, America's singing pal joined other radio and stage stars of Chicago, appearing at USO-American Legion booths in the Loop during the lunch hour to help members of the Legion auxiliary at counters where they received contributions.[56]

The U.S. Army Air Forces allowed Wrigley to continue broadcasting *Gene Autry's Melody Ranch* after the cowboy's induction to recruit radio listeners interested in the aims, needs, and accomplishments of army aviation. Gene kept telling stories of real-life efforts to win the war. He supplemented these inspirational segments with news and information about the officers and men in the Army Air Force and efforts to preserve the American way of life. CBS broadcast the first *Sergeant Gene Autry* program from an imaginary airfield, where the new recruit described a typical day in the life of an Army Air Force corpsman.[57]

The War Department made a point of disclaiming any endorsement of Wrigley's Doublemint Gum, while stating that Autry received no added pay for his radio work. Autry continued to pepper his show with public service announcements, defense savings bond promotions, and recruitment pitches. He sang songs like "Silver Wings on the Moonlight" and "There's a Star-Spangled Banner Waving Somewhere." Wrigley's announcer explained the changes:

> Good afternoon, ladies and gentlemen. Although Gene Autry is no longer appearing on *Melody Ranch* for Doublemint Gum, he will continue to bring his songs and thrilling stories of the exploits of the brave men of the Army Air Forces, because Doublemint Gum has assigned the time formerly used for the *Melody Ranch* program to the United States Army Air Forces. Gene Autry is no longer representing Doublemint Gum. He is now Sergeant Gene Autry and his appearance on the radio is under the supervision of the Army Air Forces. In the interest of supplying *information and entertainment* [emphasis added] to the public and to acquaint young men of America with details of life around Army Air Forces flying fields, Sergeant Autry has been detailed to bring to you dramatizations of true stories from the official records this splendid organization. Sergeant Autry's participation in this radio program for the time being is a part of his regular duties in the Army Air Forces and he receives no compensation for so doing other than his sergeant's pay. Doublemint gum now turns broadcast over the United States Army Air Forces.[58]

The emphasis added to this quotation stresses the admission on the part of Wrigley's announcer that propaganda was now a part of many cultural products, including *Gene Autry's Melody Ranch*, Republic pictures, patriotic songs, and personal appearances. Autry joined the U.S. Army Air Force because he understood the seriousness of the

Second World War. He recognized the war unfolding as a historic event. With enemies threatening the United States from both east and west, Gene explained the need to build modern high-speed, long-range bombers that could safely reach enemy nations: "The future of our lives and homes and the safety of our families depend on our building the superior air force and hitting the enemy faster and harder than he can hit us. We're building the machines and training the men to fly them. The faster we build them and the faster we train men the sooner we are going to make America safe."[59]

In September 1942, Autry settled in for an extended tour of duty at Luke Field, near Phoenix, Arizona. He continued broadcasting *Sergeant Gene Autry* every Sunday evening from the recreation hall at Luke Field. Wrigley invited listeners to take part in the Army Air Forces Sunday night recreation period. Millions listened in each week to learn something about army aviation. Occasionally, Autry traveled to other bases, including Bakersfield, California, and Chicago, Illinois, where he made live remote broadcasts. Autry also broadcast a live remote show from the Burbank Recreation Building, a benefit for the employees of Lockheed and the Vega Aircraft Corporation.

Before enlisting in the U.S. Army Air Force, Autry signed a memorandum of agreement to merge his fledgling rodeo outfit with Everett Colburn's World's Championship Rodeo in exchange for a 20 percent ownership share in the larger sporting spectacle. To promote the rodeos events, Autry allowed the World's Championship Rodeo to use his name, both singularly and in combination with the WCR logo. Gene also agreed not to make any personal appearances with other rodeo outfits unless the WCR gave its written consent. He considered other income derived from personal appearances as separate and of no interest to the WCR. Finally, he pensioned his beloved horse, Champion, until the war was over. Champ got to spend his days sharing a pasture with Tony, Jr., Tom Mix's old horse. The cowboy kept Tony, Jr., in clover after Mix died.[60]

# Conclusion
## New Deal Cowboy

Frank Loesser wrote the lyrics and Joseph Lilley composed the music for "(I've Got Spurs That) Jingle, Jangle, Jingle." Autry recorded the song in Hollywood on June 11, 1942. The American Record Corporation (ARC) released the tune on multiple labels, including Okeh, Columbia (United States and Canada), Regal-Zonophone (England, Australia, and Ireland), and Melody Ranch Records.[1] The song went gold for the western troubadour the week of August 25, 1942, topping out at No. 14 on *The Billboard* popular music chart. Fans heard the singing cowboy perform "Jingle, Jangle, Jingle" live one last time on the *Sergeant Gene Autry* program broadcast October 11 from Luke Field, an air training school near Phoenix, Arizona. Autry served for about a year at Luke Field, training for the Ferry Command or a job as a flight instructor for the U.S. Army Air Forces. After World War II, he included the song as a standard in his shows from 1945 to 1951.[2]

Tex Ritter and Kay Kyser also recorded "Jingle, Jangle, Jingle" in 1942, along with Dick Thomas, who performed the song for Paramount Pictures in *The Forest Rangers* (1942), a film starring Fred MacMurray. Ritter did not score a hit with the song, but it became a standard in his repertoire, reappearing on many albums during a long career lasting until 1976. Kyser performed the song routinely with his orchestra until 1950. More recently, a younger generation of fans gained familiarity with "Jingle, Jangle, Jingle" from a trailer for *Fallout: New Vegas* (2011), unveiled at E3 (Electronic Entertainment Expo), the annual trade fair for the computer and video game industry presented by the Entertainment Software Association.[3]

In the months leading up to the release of *Fallout: New Vegas*, more than 650,000 fans listened to "Jingle, Jangle Jingle" while watching the trailer posted to YouTube by the video game publisher ZeniMax Media. No longer reflecting the optimism and hope of the New Deal, the settings for *Fallout: New Vegas* mirrored the treacherous wastes in the Great Southwest, a post-apocalyptic reimagination of a New West "where you make a name for yourself on a thrilling new journey across the Mojave wasteland." Another 43,000 fans watched the YouTube video of Dick Thomas performing the song in a video clip from *The Forest Rangers*. As a younger generation discovers the arts, entertainment, and recreations created by Gene Autry before World War II, the take-away messages have ironically come to mean something different. Keep in mind that the times were also very bleak for Autry's original fans during the Great Depression. It is all in how one chooses to look at the situation. In the present-day world without singing cowboy heroes, the outlook seems hopeless.[4]

Autry never expanded his multiplatform entertainment into video gaming or the Internet. He stopped performing in 1987, about the time these new media became part of the U.S. information economy. Instead of growing into new electronic entertainment mediums, Autry turned his attention to producing motion pictures and video recordings for television, distributing cultural products as a radio and television broadcaster, and developing new content in the form of spectator sports.

Consolidating several companies, Gene Autry became the largest promoter of American rodeo sports during the 1950s, and then he developed the Los Angeles Angels of the Pacific Coast League into a Major League Baseball franchise. Changing the team name to the California Angels and moving the team to Anaheim, near Disneyland, Autry broadcast every game over his West Coast radio network, and he televised many games on KTLA-TV, his flagship station in Hollywood.

A year after Ina Mae Autry passed in 1980, Gene married Jacqueline Ellam, and together they began divesting his radio and television broadcasting enterprises. With the help of her good friend and founding executive director Joanne Hale, Jackie Autry got her husband into the museum business, opening the Gene Autry Western Heritage Museum in 1988 and guiding its growth and development into the Autry National Center of the American West.

In a lifetime that encompassed most of the twentieth century, Autry offered his fans an incredible variety of cultural products, covering the western genre over much of the Arts, Entertainment, and Recreation spectrum. Music provided the means for Autry to nurture transmedia storytelling. Popularizing songs across multiple information mediums, he created synergy as an independent artist, writer and performer who also worked with performing arts companies and spectator sports as a promoter, agent, and manager for artists, athletes, entertainers, and other public figures. In the 1940s, Autry learned how to inundate American media culture with information in the public interest. At that time, the U.S. information economy included enterprises engaged in the production and distribution of information and cultural products, businesses providing the means to transmit or distribute cultural products, companies transmitting or distributing data and communications, firms involved with data processing, and information services organizations. Autry worked in the motion picture and sound recording industries, broadcasting industries, and publishing industries; simultaneously, he saturated these sizeable subsectors of the U.S information economy with his western-themed cultural products.[5]

When Autry enlisted in the U.S. Army Air Forces on July 26, 1942, the thirty-five-year-old was married with no children, but he had an extended family that remained close and dependent upon him. He entered the U.S. Army as a technical sergeant, a noncommissioned officer. Forsaking his six-shooter for an army rifle, the cowboy patriot left Chicago to report for basic training at the Santa Ana Army Air Base on August 16, 1942. Sergeant Autry was a civilian flyer with more than 200 hours in the air; however, the Army Air Corps thought he could make a greater contribution working special details, raising money to support President Roosevelt's war effort.[6]

Autry continued performing on *Sergeant Gene Autry* until August 1943, providing entertainment each week, targeting young men and women in service to their country from the mess hall at Luke Field. Doing his best to sell U.S. defense savings bonds and stamps, the singing cowboy imported Mary Lee, Judy Canova, and Max Terhune from Hollywood to help entertain the troops in November 1942. He continued working out of Luke Field until 1944, when the Army Air Forces reassigned him to Love Field, near Dallas, Texas.

Autry earned his service pilot wings at Love Field, and the Air Corps promoted him to the position of flight officer with the Ninety-first Ferrying Squadron. He worked repositioning airplanes from one field of battle to another in 1944–45, piloting many types of aircraft during the last year of the war. Autry flew over the famous "Burma Hump" on the eastern end of the Himalayan Mountains, moving military transport aircraft from India to China to resupply the Chinese war effort of Chiang Kai-shek and the units of the U.S. Army Air Forces based in China.[7]

Autry stopped making movies after his enlistment in July 1942, but he continued producing records, performing on the radio, publishing music, and making personal appearances during the war. Even so, the singing cowboy managed to remain on the Hollywood top-ten list for a third consecutive year. The comedy team of Bud Abbott and Lew Costello topped Quigley's annual survey of the ten biggest moneymaking film personalities in 1942, moving up from the third position they held the previous year. Following Abbott and Costello on the top-ten list, Clark Gable placed second, then Gary Cooper, Mickey Rooney, Bob Hope, James Cagney, Gene Autry, Betty Grable, Greer Garson, and Spencer Tracy. Among the Western movie stars, Autry remained the leader for a sixth consecutive year, followed by Roy Rogers, William Boyd, Smiley Burnette, Charles Starrett, Johnny Mack Brown, Bill Elliott, Tim Holt, Don "Red" Barry, and the Three Mesquiteers. Hedda Hopper reported that Abbott and Costello films were wildly popular in occupied France during the war and that their films were being smuggled into Paris, along with Gene Autry's pictures and Julien Duvivier's film, *The Great Waltz*.[8]

Critics predicted that military absorption would affect Gene Autry's position in 1943, despite his great vogue in the hinterland. Republic kept the image of America's Favorite Cowboy in front of fans by rereleasing some of the better-class "oldies" Autry made before the war. Roy Rogers claimed a wrenched back and chronic arthritis to stay out of the war. Republic positioned him to replace Gene Autry as the studio's number one Western star. Nevertheless, the Original Singing Cowboy remained hugely popular, receiving fan mail averaging 50,000 letters per month.[9]

As the nation's economic situation improved, dislocated Southern and Midwestern migrants formed a significant part of the core workforce in the rapidly expanding armament industries emanating outward from Los Angeles. Themes in Republic films shifted from the plight of western migrants and rural social issues more generally to the tastes of newly moneyed and recently established urban hillbillies. The growing popularity of the Western genre during the war years suggested that these audiences did not lose their taste for adventure and romance just because they no longer felt the same fears of dispossession, displacement, and economic insecurity that they experienced during the Depression years. Compared to films produced in the Gene Autry series from 1935–42, Westerns produced during the war addressed a different set of anxieties and desires.[10]

Earlier and more stridently than most entertainers, Gene Autry supported U.S. foreign policy and did what he could to assist the American state. He favored radio broadcasting for spreading Americanism because he could reach more people and reach them more quickly than he could through motion pictures, stating: "In a single broadcast one can reach more people faster with the American doctrines." Still, he knew that Hollywood had a deeper and more meaningful impact on the attitudes of people in other nations toward the United States and toward one another. Autry embraced the fact that capitalism and patriotism went hand in hand with U.S. foreign policy. He understood that global economics motivated the convergence of cultures through mass media. He knew that increased respect and tolerance for the national, cultural, and religious sensitivities of people around the world came about as a consequence of mass media converging cultures. Gene Autry represented the United States of America in this global media market. He joined FDR in an attempt to control mass media as an element of public diplomacy.[11]

The difference from 1942–45 was that Sergeant Gene Autry carried out these activities as a serviceman, not as a private citizen. The singing cowboy helped diffuse radical tensions threatening capitalism in the United States by making it easier for people to feel good about themselves, their situations, and their neighbors both north and south of the border. The key to success for both Autry and FDR lay in their mastery of mass media.

As a live performer, recording artist, radio broadcaster, and movie star, Gene Autry was a real American hero who did not require coercion to support the president, unlike most other Western stars, who generally supported isolationism. Roosevelt did not have to threaten Wrigley and CBS with tighter regulations by the Federal Communications Commission (FCC). Republic Pictures was not the target of intimidating Justice Department lawsuits. In working to promote Americanism, hemispheric cooperation, and war preparedness, Gene Autry's movies influenced audiences on a deeper emotional level, while his sound recordings, radio shows, and live performances elicited more impulsive responses.

Autry's contributions to the cultural and intellectual history of the United States were both timely and significant. His cultural products connected the arts, entertainment, and recreation through multiple information mediums with the policies of the Roosevelt administration. Music endured as the one element common to all the forms of art, entertainment, and recreation featuring the "Gene Autry" brand. Music proved to be a transcendent form of art and entertainment that tied up sound recording, music publishing, live performance, radio broadcasting, motion pictures, rodeo sports, and licensed merchandise into one brand-name enterprise. The coming together of country-western music and musical-Western films created big box office attractions and a story without precedent in the arts, entertainment, and advertising worlds. The growth of radio broadcasting as a new information medium stood out as the greatest influence upon the hybridization of country-western music and the incorporation of this new subgenre into musical-Western films.

Gene Autry chose to become a country-western musician and musical-Western film star because the Western genre appealed to his rural, small-town, and newly urban fans throughout the Midwest, South and Southwest. The singing cowboy represented a quintessential American folk hero, presenting rural American folk values and important working-class behavioral norms as increasingly palatable to a majority of Americans during the Great Depression.

Synergy created a "Gene Autry" brand capable of shaping public opinion, boosting morale, and sparking patriotism within mainstream American culture. Autry's cultural products exemplified support for President Roosevelt's New Deal by underscoring the American West as an attractive destination for travel and tourism. Gene's New Deal films mirrored the creation of a New West, where leisure, recreation, travel, and tourism represented the emerging markets of a post-industrial age. His sound recordings and films appealed to a new breed of worker-tourists taking advantage of annual two-week paid vacations granted by industrialists and legislated by the federal government. The singing cowboy's support for President Roosevelt exemplified a new type of soft-power public diplomacy meant to influence the American public and make the New Deal more appealing to voters, especially women and the men influenced by women.

Reflecting the values of rural, small-town, and newly urban Americans, Gene Autry's musical-Westerns came across as "message" films about law and order, rugged individualism, Americanism, and patriotism. Autry willfully propagandized his name and image to influence his enormous fan base in support of the New Deal. Ultimately, the singing cowboy's support for President Roosevelt appeared most directly in *Guns and Guitars* (1936), *Colorado Sunset* (1939), *Rovin' Tumbleweeds* (1939), and *Melody Ranch* (1940). In these films, Republic promoted a "Vote for Autry" in escapist local balloting as the equivalent of a vote for FDR in actual presidential elections.[12]

Autry joined those who believed in the promise of new technologies and the ability of humans to reshape the natural world. He understood the deep and structured role the American state played in the delivery of information through the arts, entertainment, and recreation. Republic's Gene Autry series offered particular representations favorable to the New Deal, expressed through storylines supporting livestock and range management, water for irrigation and flood control, and rural electricity. A loathing of eastern-establishment types appeared routinely in most Autry films. Some films in the series took issue with western mining and oil company operations, groundwater contamination, shady stock offerings, short sales, foreclosures, forced migrations, and homelessness.

The notion of Gene Autry as a symbol of the modern, postindustrial New West is consistent with the work of scholars who pegged the emergence of this environment to the New Deal. With Roosevelt at the helm, the economic downturn of the Great Depression occasioned something of a development boom throughout much of the far West, especially in southern California and central Arizona. New Deal relief and construction programs drew a flood of unemployed workers from southern and midwestern cities into the region. Helping secure Roosevelt's national agenda for economic recovery, Autry and Republic Pictures contributed to the cultural dialogue about shared national identity that affirmed and legitimized the relationship of the American people to a modern consumer culture.[13]

Gene Autry became a star by creating content of lower technical quality for the large audiences that consumed his sound recordings, radio broadcasts, sound motion pictures, and live theater performances. Followers did not distinguish between Gene Autry the performer and the character he played in the movies.

As national advertisers developed an interest in sponsorship, Autry's sound recording and motion picture producers revised their middle-class material to fit working-class values. National advertisers needed to reach audiences with more purchasing power than lower-culture consumers. The shift became apparent when Wrigley's Chewing Gum agreed to sponsor the nationally syndicated *Gene Autry's Melody Ranch* on the CBS radio network.[14]

The soft-power public diplomacy represented through Gene Autry productions contributed to an innovative redefinition of the role played by the U.S. government in formulating a policy of public diplomacy through cultural activities in the 1940s. As the president moved the federal government into the arts, entertainment, recreation, and information economies, Herbert Yates incorporated government information into cultural products featuring Gene Autry produced by Republic Pictures and the American Record Corporation. Helping to combat the Great Depression and promote the New Deal, films in Republic's Gene Autry series appealed to a majority of Americans who did not understand the nuances of government affairs, but they trusted Gene Autry.

Building upon Autry's success in promoting New Deal themes, Republic began using the singing cowboy's series to draw attention to President Roosevelt's "Good Neighbor" policy, promoting friendly relations throughout the Western Hemisphere. The type of public diplomacy represented through Autry productions also helped redefine the role played by the U.S. government in formulating a policy of international cultural activity. *Boots and Saddles* (1937), *Mexicali Rose* (1939), *South of the Border* (1939), *Gaucho Serenade* (1940), and *Down Mexico Way* (1941) stand out as attempts to bridge the gaps between the two major tenets of U.S. foreign policy—Anglo-American allegiance and Pan-Americanism. These films appealed to broad mainstream audiences that did not understand the nuances of foreign affairs, but they trusted Gene Autry as an "ambassador of goodwill."

The focus of Gene Autry's Good Neighbor pictures on U.S. relations with Mexico illustrated the importance of border security issues for the Roosevelt administration and the ability of the singing cowboy to reach cross-cultural audiences. Autry promoted Americanism, war preparedness, and friendly relations with Mexico and Mexican Americans at a time when most of his audience favored isolationism. The need for Mexican cooperation with U.S. war preparedness efforts stimulated attempts through the Gene Autry series to familiarize Americans with Mexican culture. Similarly, Autry inspired Fernando De Fuentes to establish a unique style of Mexican filmmaking known as *comedia-ranchera*, modeled after Republic's musical-Western form, showing Autry's influence south of the border.

The British tour in 1939 cemented the singing cowboy's international standing. Moreover, the decision by Republic Pictures to open films like *South of the Border* and *Down Mexico Way* in first-run movie houses confirmed Autry's growing appeal within the mainstream of American moviegoers. Further evidence of that attraction came in the form of gold records for "South of the Border (Down Mexico Way)" and "Goodbye Little Darlin', Goodbye."

Gene Autry's image as a singing cowboy-secret agent created a metaphor for understanding the significance of soft power to influence public opinion and aid U.S. foreign policy. Similarly, near-perfect encapsulation of Eugene Bolton's Western Hemisphere Idea in the film *Rancho Grande* (1940) demonstrated how modernity, gentrification, and market capitalism served as goals for the Good Neighbor policy. Here again, echoing *Mexicali Rose*, the song "Rancho Grande (Allá en el Rancho Grande)" promoted symmetry of goals and objectives that influenced audiences on both sides of the U.S.-Mexico border.

Responding to the example set by residents of Gene Autry, Oklahoma, Autry qualified himself as 100 percent committed to preserving, protecting, and defending the American way of life after the Japanese attack on Pearl Harbor on December 7, 1941. Winning the war against the Axis powers took precedence over everything else. Building a superior air force provided the means of achieving victory, so Autry devoted himself to recruiting the two million young men and women that the Army Air Force estimated were necessary to win the war.

To strengthen its association with the Army Air Force, the Wrigley Company rebranded it radio star from being a New Deal Cowboy and ambassador of goodwill into America's Ace Cowboy. Autry codified a brand of American patriotism rooted in a contemporary New West, forged under Roosevelt's Presidency, and adopted internationally as Gene Autry's Cowboy Code.

Music provided the glue that held Autry's multiplatform entertainments together. Synergy elevated the singing cowboy's persona to new heights as an international icon. As Autry reached beyond his traditional audiences to embrace the mainstream in American culture, he changed his musical styling to develop a stronger appeal. Competing for the top spot with Bing Crosby, Autry earned ten gold records and an Oscar nomination from 1940–42. The singing cowboy promoted self-reliance and a life lived close to nature as real American traits. He represented honesty, integrity, sincerity, clean thinking, and authenticity as the elements of Americanism. *Gene Autry's Melody Ranch* embodied the source of Autry's uniqueness. The radio broadcast symbolized Americanism, hemispheric cooperation, and war preparedness as aspects of the American Way.

Melody Ranch remained a part of Autry's identity for the rest of his life. He created a real life Melody Ranch in November 1941, linking his radio show, motion pictures, and sound recordings with the same name. Gene and Ina Autry lived at Melody Ranch until 1949, when they built a new home in the Hollywood Hills.

After moving to Studio City, the Autrys donated their San Fernando Valley home to the St. Vincent de Paul for use as a ranch camp, after relocating Melody Ranch to the old Monogram Pictures movie ranch in Placerita Canyon, near Newhall, California. Autry planned to do something that many in Hollywood were thinking about in 1952. He wanted to give every visitor to Los Angeles an opportunity to see the making of motion pictures and television films. He organized guided tours of the Melody Ranch back lot, where vacationers learned about the various phases and techniques of moviemaking.

As the commander-in-chief's main concerns shifted from the New Deal to Good Neighbor and war preparedness priorities, Gene Autry's cultural products mirrored Roosevelt's move from isolationist to internationalist in music, sound recordings, motion pictures, live performances, radio broadcasts, rodeo sports, and licensed merchandise. Examining the singing cowboy's oeuvre within a context created by the Roosevelt administration policies, *New Deal Cowboy* revealed a process of public diplomacy at work in American media culture from 1932–42. To get at the substance of public diplomacy in Gene Autry's legacy, this book has examined the information included in the singing cowboy's productions and how that information related to presidential politics. Exploring the similarities and differences between Gene Autry's cultural products revealed different ideological operations at work in sound recordings, motion pictures, radio broadcasting, and print media. As President Roosevelt's priorities changed over time, Gene Autry's cultural products reflected these changes from the New Deal to the Good Neighbor policy to war preparedness during the run-up to World War II. American media culture transformed Gene Autry from the New Deal Cowboy of 1936 into an ambassador of goodwill in 1939. As wars raged in Europe and Manchuria, outreach to Great Britain and Latin America increased significantly. The rural, small-town, and newly urban audiences that nurtured Autry's singing cowboy persona in the Midwest, South, and Southwest came to expect message films about the American Way. The New Deal Cowboy codified a brand of American patriotism rooted in a contemporary New West, forged under Roosevelt's presidency, and adopted internationally as Gene Autry's Cowboy Code.

# Notes

### Introduction

1. "Hedda Hopper's Hollywood," *Los Angeles Times* (July 28, 1942): 9; *Bells of Capistrano* (1942; video reissue, Chatsworth, CA: Image Entertainment, 2003).
2. "Cowboys Arrive in City; Rodeo to Open Thursday," *Chicago Daily Tribune* (July 21, 1942): 10.
3. "Special Five Day Bond Drive Will Open Tomorrow," *Chicago Daily Tribune* (July 26, 1942): 15; "Cowboy Autry Gives the Spur to Bond Sales," *Chicago Daily Tribune* (July 25, 1942): 18; "$1,407,642 Total Is Announced in USO Fund Campaign," *Chicago Daily Tribune* (July 25, 1942): 13.
4. "Special Event—Oath of Enlistment and Induction Ceremony of Gene Autry into the U.S. Army Air Forces with Rank of Technical Sergeant by Colonel Edward F. Shaifer [July 26, 1942]," *Melody Ranch,* July 26, 1942, 1761/7921 (these numbers are associated with an iPad of Gene Autry recordings provided by Gene Autry Entertainment. The first number is the number associated with the song on the iPad. The second number is the total number of recordings on the iPad); Gene Autry, introduction to *Bells of Capistrano* (1942), on Nashville Network's *Melody Ranch Theater,* 1987; Magers, *Gene Autry Westerns,* 222; "Listener's Choice," *Chicago Daily Tribune* (July 26, 1942); "Announcer's Closing Plug," *Melody Ranch,* July 19, 1942, 1750/7921; "'Stampede' Rehearsal," *Chicago Daily Tribune* (July 22, 1942): 16; "Listener's Choice," *Chicago Daily Tribune* (July 26, 1942).
5. "Special Event—Oath of Enlistment"; Autry, introduction to *Bells of Capistrano* (1942); Magers, *Gene Autry Westerns,* 222.
6. *Gene Autry's Melody Ranch,* August 23, 1942, 630/9672.
7. Ibid. (emphasis added).
8. Berkowitz, "A 'New Deal' for Leisure," 186.

9. Gans, *Popular Culture and High Culture*, 115–20.

10. Ibid.

11. *Gene Autry's Melody Ranch*, December 31, 1939; *Melody Ranch* (1940), DVD.

12. "Announcer's Opening," *Gene Autry's Melody Ranch*, December 31, 1939, 407/9672.

13. Gene Autry to Franklin D. Roosevelt, September 10, 1943; Franklin D. Roosevelt to Gene Autry, September 15, 1943, both in Franklin D. Roosevelt, Papers as President: The President's Personal File, Part 18: PPF 8501-9000, 1933–1945, Franklin D. Roosevelt Presidential Library & Museum. *The Gene Autry Show*, January 28, 1940; Winifred Mallon, "Nation Observes President's Day," *New York Times* (January 31, 1940): 1.

14. *The Gene Autry Show*, January 28, 1940; Mallon, "Nation Observes President's Day," 1.

15. Jenkins, *Convergence Culture*, location 545.

16. Nye, *Soft Power*, 134–37.

17. Hettinger, "The Future of Radio as an Advertising Medium," 285–87; Marquis, "Written on the Wind," 398.

18. Nye, *Soft Power*, 134–37.

19. Dizard, *Digital Diplomacy*, 1, 21–22.

20. Green, *American Propaganda Abroad*, 15–16.

21. Dizard, *Digital Diplomacy*, 21–22; quote on p. 1. NBC stands for National Broadcasting Company.

22. Price, *Media and Sovereignty*, 248.

23. *Convergence* (Summer 2007).

24. Kavanaugh, *History Curatorship*, 54.

25. Tosh, *The Pursuit of History*, 9–10; Kavanaugh, *History Curatorship*, 63.

26. Tosh, *The Pursuit of History*, 10–11; Kavanaugh, *History Curatorship*, 63–64.

### Chapter 1

1. Gene Autry to "Dear Friend Homer," June 7, 1931, GAC, T87-36-2851-1, Autry National Center of the American West (hereafter cited as GAC). The letterhead on this document stated: "Gene Autry: The Sunny South's Blue Yodeler: Recording Artist: Victor, Velvetone, Champion, and Okeh"; general ledger of Gene Autry's accounts from 1930–33, GAC, T87-36-4613: ledger. Handwritten on WJJD stationary, this ledger included information about the royalties Gene Autry received for his sound recordings; Cusic, *Gene Autry*. 20–22.

2. Autry to "Dear Friend Homer"; general ledger of Gene Autry's accounts from 1930–33, GAC, 87-36-4613: ledger.

3. Art Satherley interview; Cusic, *Gene Autry*, 23–24.

4. Autry to "Dear Friend Homer"; *WLS Family Album* (1934), 94.218.1; Jowett, *Film: The Democratic Art*; Hurst, *Republic Pictures*, pv-pvi.

5. Harkin, *Hillbilly*, 75; Stanfield, *Horse Opera*, 52–54; Green, "Hillbilly Music," 208–9, 215; Fenster, "Preparing the Audience, Informing the Performers," 270.

6. Wilgus, "Country-Western Music and the Urban Hillbilly," The Journal of American Folklore, The Urban Experience and Folk Tradition (Special Issue) 83/328 (Apr.-Jun., 1970) 157.

7. Jenkins, *Convergence Culture*, 2,584. For useful overviews on the literature about hybridity, see Pieterse, "Globalization as Hybridization," in Featherstone (ed.), *Global Modernities*.

8. Hurst, *Republic Studios*, 37–42; Green, *Singing in the Saddle*, 110–13; Aquila, "Introduction," in Aquila (ed.), *Wanted Dead or Alive*, 1–17; Fenster, "Preparing the Audience, Informing the Performers," 264; Stanfield, *Horse Opera*, 1–10.

9. Harkin, *Hillbilly*, 95–96.

10. Green, *Singing in the Saddle*, 49–50.

11. Cusic, *Gene Autry*, 3–8, 26–32; Conqueror Records Catalog, GAC, T87-36-4611; Green, *Singing in the Saddle*; Harkin, *Hillbilly*, 95–96.

12. Photograph, "Round-Up of WLS Radio Stars" (Gene Autry at far left), Chicago, 1934, GAC, BIO_055; Evans, *Prairie Farmer and WLS*, 165; Sorenson, *Sears Roebuck and Co.*, 70.

13. Harmony Database, Supertone 257—Gene Autry "Old Santa Fe" Acoustic archtop—Shaded brown—Distributed by Sears & Roebuck, 1935; Gene Autry-In Old Santa Fe Guitar, GAC, 2004.15.1; "Maynard Returns for New Picture," *Los Angeles Times* (September 17, 1934): 13; Tuska, *Vanishing Legion*, 133–36; Independent Movie Database (hereafter cited as IMDB), *In Old Santa Fe*, Songbook, GAC, T87-36-478-1.

14. U.S. Census Bureau, *Radio Set Ownership 1930*, Population, Volume VI, Families.

15. Jewell, *The Golden Age of Cinema*, 38; Stanfield, *Horse Opera*, 55–56.

16. Berkowitz, "A 'New Deal' for Leisure," in Baranowski and Furlough (eds.), *Being Elsewhere*, 185–212.

17. Stanfield, "Dixie Cowboys and Blue Yodels," in Buscombe and Pearson (eds.), *Back in the Saddle Again*, 100.

18. "Today on the Radio," *New York Times* (November 13, 1931): 28.

19. Harkin, *Hillbilly*, 87–95.

20. Randy Lewis, "Uncle Art Satherley, 96, Recording Industry Pioneer," *Los Angeles Times* (February 12, 1986): 2; Harkin, *Hillbilly*, 87–95; Cox, *American Radio Networks*, 55.

21. Gene Autry balance sheet for month of January 1932, GAC, T87-36-4614.

22. Stanfield, "Dixie Cowboys and Blue Yodels," quote on 100; Harkin, *Hillbilly*, 72, 95–96.

23. *Variety* (December, 29 1926): 1; Green, "Hillbilly Music," 221–22; Harkin, *Hillbilly*, 75.

24. Harkins, *Hillbilly*, 89; Jewell, *The Golden Age of Cinema*, 38–39.

25. Malone, *Singing Cowboys and Musical Mountaineers*, 91.

26. Stanfield, "Dixie Cowboys and Blue Yodels," 103.

27. George-Warren, *Public Cowboy No. 1*, 75–76, 347; Gene Autry balance sheet for month of January 1932, GAC T87-36-4614; "Today on the Radio," *New York*

*Times* (November 13, 1931): 28; Cusic, *Gene Autry*, 3–8, 26–32; Green, *Singing in the Saddle*, 20–68; Conqueror Records Catalog, GAC, T87-36-4611.

28. George-Warren, *Public Cowboy No. 1*, 75–76, 347; Gene Autry balance sheet for month of January 1932, GAC T87-36-4614; "Today on the Radio," 28; Cusic, *Gene Autry*, 20–25; Green, *Singing in the Saddle*, 20–68; Conqueror Records Catalog, GAC, T87-36-4611; Sears Catalog (Spring 1927): 508, 634–42, Sears Archives; Evans, *Prairie Farmer and WLS*, 154.

29. Sears Catalog (Spring 1927): 508, 634–42, Sears Archives; Evans, *Prairie Farmer and WLS*, 154.

30. Sears Catalog (Spring 1927): 508, 634–42, Sears Archives; Evans, *Prairie Farmer and WLS*, 154.

31. Evans, *Prairie Farmer and WLS*, 165; Sorenson, *Sears Roebuck and Co., 100th Anniversary*, 70.

32. Condon, unpublished manuscript, 10; Evans, *Prairie Farmer and WLS*, 165.

33. Condon, unpublished manuscript, 12–15; Jones, "Hollywood's International Relations," 363–64, 373–74; Chanan, "Cinema in Latin America" in Nowell-Smith (ed.), *The Oxford History of World Cinema*, 429; "Daily Theater Guide," *Los Angeles Times* (March 6, 1936): A18; "Daily Theater Guide," *Los Angeles Times* (April 4, 1936): 6; Scheuer, "Foreign Fans Eager for Screen News," C1; Scheuer, "A Town Called Hollywood," 10; "News of the Screen," *New York Times* (December 21, 1937): 28; Harkin, *Hillbilly*, 80.

34. The environment that Autry operated within is described by Hettinger in "The Future of Radio as an Advertising Medium," 283–84; see also, Lornell, "Country Music and the Mass Media in Roanoke, Virginia," 404–8; and Harkin, *Hillbilly*, 80–82.

35. George-Warren, *Public Cowboy No. 1*, 75–76; Gene Autry balance sheet for month of January 1932, GAC, T87-36-4614; "Today on the Radio," 28; Cusic, *Gene Autry*, 3–8, 26–32; Green, *Singing in the Saddle*, 20–68; Conqueror Records Catalog, GAC, T87-36-4611.

36. George-Warren, *Public Cowboy No. 1*, 75–76; Gene Autry balance sheet for month of January 1932, GAC, T87-36-4614; "Today on the Radio," 28; Cusic, *Gene Autry*, 3–8, 26–32; Green, *Singing in the Saddle*, 20–68; Conqueror Records Catalog, GAC, T87-36-4611.

37. Cusic, *Gene Autry*, 26–32.

38. Gene Autry balance sheet for month of January 1932, GAC, T87-36-4614; list of theater dates for January 1932, GAC, T87-36-4618; U.S. Department of Labor, CPI Inflation Calculator.

39. Stanfield, "Dixie Cowboys and Blue Yodels," 101; Cusic, *Gene Autry*, 3–8; Gene Autry-Round Up guitar, GAC, 91.221.659.1. Made in 1932 by the Harmony Company of Chicago and sold by Sears Roebuck and Company. This guitar is serial no. 1 in the line. Made with mother-of-pearl "Gene Autry" inlay on the neck. *Gene Autry's Sensational Collection of Famous Original Cowboy Songs and Mountain Ballads*, 88.216.3;

Photograph, State-Lake Theater, Chicago, 1933, GAC, MARQUEE-BK; Photograph, "Gene Autry, The Oklahoma Yodeling Cowboy," Chicago, 1933, GAC, T87-36-260-1.

40. Hettinger, "The Future of Radio as an Advertising Medium," 286; Landry, "Radio and Government," 568; Ackerman, "The Dimensions of American Broadcasting," 6.

41. Lazarsfeld and Merton, "Mass Communications, Popular Taste and Organized Social Action," in Rosenberg and White (eds.), *Mass Culture*, 457–73.

42. Harkin, *Hillbilly*, 72, 95–96; Stanfield, "Dixie Cowboys and Blue Yodels," 100.

43. Roosevelt, First Inaugural Speech, March 4, 1933; Smith, *FDR*, 275.

44. Hettinger, "The Future of Radio as an Advertising Medium," 283–89; Ackerman, "The Dimensions of American Broadcasting," 6–11; Alice Goldfarb Marquis, "Written on the Wind," 385–88.

45. Hettinger, "The Future of Radio as an Advertising Medium," 283–89; Ackerman, "The Dimensions of American Broadcasting," 6–11; Marquis, "Written on the Wind," 385–88.

46. "Radio Set Ownership 1930," Fifteenth Census of the United States: 1930; Hettinger, "The Future of Radio as an Advertising Medium," 283–89; Ackerman, "The Dimensions of American Broadcasting," 6–11; Marquis, "Written on the Wind, 385–88.

47. Rothel, *The Singing Cowboys*, 21; Stanfield, "Dixie Cowboys and Blue Yodels," 101; Green, *Singing in the Saddle*, 123–27; *WLS Family Album* (1933), T87-36-683.

48. Rothel, *The Singing Cowboys*, 21; Green, *Singing in the Saddle*, 123–27; *WLS Family Album* (1933), T87-36-683; Photograph, "Sears Roebuck Radio Frolic," BIO_055; Lithograph, Sears Roebuck & Company, Chicago, 1933, GAC, 95.184.1; Photograph, State-Lake Theater, Chicago, 1934, GAC, MARQUEE-BK.

49. "Maynard Returns for New Picture," 13; IMDB, *In Old Santa Fe*. .

50. Radio Corporation of America, microphone, Model RCA-44 BX, 1932, GAC, 88.87.1; Atlas Sound Corporation, microphone stand, Brooklyn, New York, c. 1935, GAC, T87-36-4852; C. F. Martin Guitar Company, guitar, Model D-45, Nazareth, Pennsylvania, 1933, GAC, 91.221.620.

51. Copyright Royalty Statement, Southern Music Publishing, Inc., February 15, 1933, T87-36-4602: log; Copyright Royalty Statement, American Record Company, February, 25 1933, GAC, T87-36-4601: log.

52. Gene Autry Royalty Statement, M. M. Cole Publishing Company, March 22, 1933, T87-36-4605: receipt; Gene Autry balance sheet for March 1933, T87-36-4615; Gene Autry list of theater dates for April 1933, T87-36-4619; Robert C. Sahr Political Science Department.

53. George-Warren, *Public Cowboy No. 1*, 350.

54. Gene Autry balance sheet for March 1933, T87-36-4615: ledger; Gene Autry list of theater dates for month of March 1933, T87-36-4619: ledger; Gene Autry list of theater dates for month of April 1933, T87-36-4620: ledger; Gene Autry list of

theater dates for Month of March 1933, T87-36-4619: ledger; invoice, Frontier Publishers, 30 April 1933, T87-36-4608: bill.

55. Lazarsfeld and Merton, "Mass Communications, Popular Taste and Organized Social Action," 457–73.

56. Archie Levesque to Gene Autry, December 20, 1933, T87-36-4596.

57. Lazarsfeld and Merton, "Mass Communications, Popular Taste and Organized Social Action," 457–73.

58. *WLS Family Album* (1934), 94.218.1.

59. *Motion Picture Herald* (February 22, 1936): 99, reprinted in Stanfield, "Dixie Cowboys and Blue Yodels," 102.

60. Stanfield, "Dixie Cowboys and Blue Yodels," 100.

## Chapter 2

1. *In Old Santa Fe* (Mascot Pictures, 1934); *In Old Santa Fe* (Gene Autry Entertainment, 2002); *The Phantom Empire* (Mascot Pictures, 1935); *The Phantom Empire* (Gene Autry Entertainment, 2007); *Tumbling Tumbleweeds* (Republic Pictures, 1935); *Tumbling Tumbleweeds* (Gene Autry Entertainment, 2005).

2. White, "The Good Guys Wore White Hats," in Aquila (ed.), *Wanted Dead or Alive*, 135–59; Green, *Singing in the Saddle*, 131; Cusic, *Gene Autry*, 42–49; Tuska, *Vanishing Legion*, 131; "A. W. Hackel,"; IMDB, "Robert N. Bradbury."

3. "Maynard Returns for New Picture," 13; Tuska, *The Vanishing Legion*; IMDB, "In Old Santa Fe"; Autry and Long, *Cowboy Songs and Mountain Ballads*.

4. *In Old Santa Fe*.

5. Jewell, *The Golden Age of Cinema*, 152; Thomas, "Lovejoy Buttes: Last of the Red Hot Locations," *Los Angeles Times* (September 12, 1967): D1.

6. *In Old Santa Fe*.

7. Harmony Database, Supertone 257—Gene Autry "Old Santa Fe" Acoustic archtop; "Maynard Returns for New Picture," 13; Tuska, *The Vanishing Legion* 133–36; IMDB, "In Old Santa Fe"; Songbook, GAC, T87-36-478-1.

8. *In Old Santa Fe*.

9. Ibid.; Berkowitz, "A 'New Deal' for Leisure," 185–212; quotes on 186.

10. *In Old Santa Fe*.

11. Ibid.

12. Rothman, *Devil's Bargains*, 23.

13. Berkowitz, "A 'New Deal' for Leisure," 193–207.

14. Ibid., 204.

15. Muscio, *Hollywood's New Deal*, 119–28.

16. Hurst, *Republic Pictures*, 41–42; Cusic, *Gene Autry*, 42–49.

17. Muscio, *Hollywood's New Deal*, 82.

18. Ibid, 77.

19. Johnston, "Hollywood Beckons" *Saturday Evening Post* (September 2, 1939); Rothel, *The Singing Cowboys*, 23; White, "The Good Guys Wore White Hats," 135–59; Green, *Singing in the Saddle*, 131; Bergman, *We're in the Money*, pxv-pxvi.

20. *The Phantom Empire*.

21. Ibid.

22. Ibid.

23. "Maynard Returns for New Picture," 13; Rothel, *The Singing Cowboys*, 23; Green, *Singing in the Saddle*, 107, 131; IMDB, *In Old Santa Fe*; IMDB, *Mystery Mountain*; Autry appeared in chapters 6–8 in the role of "Thomas" in the Levine-Maynard serial production *Mystery Mountain*.

24. Stanfield, *Horse Opera*, 102.

25. "Film Groups Consolidate," *Los Angeles Times* (October 15, 1935): A1; Hurst, *Republic Pictures*, 2–3; IMDB, *John Wayne*; Green, *Singing in the Saddle*, 110–13.

26. Hurst, *Republic Pictures*, 2–3.

27. Ibid., 3–4; McCarthy and Flynn, *King of the Bs*, 13–32.

28. "Film Groups Consolidate," A1; Hurst, *Republic Pictures*, 2–3; IMDB, *John Wayne*; Green, *Singing in the Saddle*, 110–13.

29. Hurst, *Republic Pictures*, 3–7.

30. Ibid., 169; Stanfield, "Dixie Cowboys and Blue Yodels," 109.

31. Stanfield, "Dixie Cowboys and Blue Yodels," 109–10.

32. Stanfield, *Horse Opera*, 6–7.

33. *Tumbling Tumbleweeds*.

34. Ibid.

35. Ibid.

36. Green, *Singing in the Saddle*, 131–32.

37. Ibid., 72–75.

38. Ibid.

39. "Gene Autry's Hit Pop and Country Songs by Year," chart assembled by author.

40. *Tumbling Tumbleweeds*. Video recording. Stanfield, "Dixie Cowboys and Blue Yodels," 106–12.

41. Ibid., 110.

42. Hurst, *Republic Pictures*, 214.

43. Ibid, 157–58.

44. Stanfield, *Horse Opera*, 107.

### Chapter 3

1. "Daily Theater Guide," *Los Angeles Times* (March 6, 1936): A18; "Daily Theater Guide," *Los Angeles Times* (April 4, 1936): 6; K. Scheuer, "Foreign Fans Eager for Screen News," *Los Angeles Times* (August 15, 1937): C1; Scheuer, "A Town Called Hollywood," *Los Angeles Times* (December 21, 1937): 10; "News of the Screen," *New York*

*Times* (December 21, 1937): 28; Tan, "The New Deal Cowboy," 90; Green, *Singing in the Saddle*, 94–119; Fyne, *The Hollywood Propaganda of World War II*, 130; Bergman, *We're in the Money*, pxi-pxiii.

2. Tuska, *The Vanishing Legion*, 131.

3. Jowett, *Film*, 14; Hurst, *Republic Pictures*, pv-pvi.

4. Edwin Schallert, "Republic Gets Membership in Hays Group," *Los Angeles Times* (September 25, 1941): A10; White, "The Good Guys Wore White Hats," 135–59.

5. *Melody Trail*; *Red River Valley*; *Guns and Guitars*; *The Big Show*; *Git along Little Doggies*.

6. "Film Groups Consolidate," *Los Angeles Times* (October 15, 1935): A1; Schallert, "Republic Gets Membership in Hays Group," *Los Angeles Times* (September 25, 1941): A10; Republic display ad, *Los Angeles Times* (December 20, 1938): B26; Stanfield, "Dixie Cowboys and Blue Yodels," 96.

7. Gene Autry's New Deal filmography includes the following motion pictures: *Guns and Guitars*, *The Big Show*, *Git along Little Doggies*, *Public Cowboy No. 1*, *Man from Music Mountain*, *Mountain Rhythm*, *Colorado Sunset*, *Rovin' Tumbleweeds*, *Sunset in Wyoming*, and *Sierra Sue*.

8. *Melody Trail*.

9. Francke, *Script Girls*, 172; Stanfield, "Dixie Cowboys and Blue Yodels," 111; quote from Autry and Herskowitz, *Back in the Saddle Again*, 66.

10. Schulberg, "The Writer in Hollywood," 135; Schultheiss, "The Eastern Writer in Hollywood," 22–25.

11. Rothel, *The Singing Cowboys*, 28.

12. Films in Republic Pictures' Gene Autry series with rodeo themes and settings from 1934–42 include *Melody Trail*, *Red River Valley*, *Rhythm of the Saddle*, *Rovin' Tumbleweeds*, *Carolina Moon*, *Ride Tenderfoot Ride*, *Back in the Saddle*, and *Bells of Capistrano*.

13. *Melody Trail*.

14. Ibid.

15. Muscio, *Hollywood's New Deal*, 85–91.

16. Ibid.

17. Ibid.

18. IMDB, *Red River Valley*.

19. Lowitt, *The New Deal and the West*, 64–80; Nash, *The American West: Transformed*, 31.

20. *The Plow That Broke the Plains*.

21. *Red River Valley*.

22. Ibid.

23. Ibid.

24. Stanfield, *Horse Opera*, 139–40.

25. *Red River Valley*; *Comin' Round the Mountain*; *Oh, Sussana!*

26. *Red River Valley*.

27. Autry and Herskowitz, *Back in the Saddle Again*, 53.

28. *Guns and Guitars.*

29. Ibid.

30. "Republic Gives Schedule," *New York Times* (June 5, 1936): 16; Schallert, "The Pageant of the Film World," *Los Angeles Times* (July 10, 1936): A11; Read Kendall, "Around and About in Hollywood," *Los Angeles Times* (July 11, 1936): A7; "Never Bores Self," *Los Angeles Times* (July 17, 1936): 17; ledger of cash receipts and cash disbursements from September 1, 1936 through December 31, 1938.

31. Stanfield, *Horse Opera*, 117–18.

32. Contract between Gene Autry and M. D. Howe for the M. D. Howe Booking Agency, 1 July 1936.

33. "Republic Gives Schedule: Company Lists the Titles of 50 Films It Will Produce," *New York Times* (June 5, 1936): 16; Schallert, "Pageant of the Film World," A11; "Never Bores Self," 17; Schallert, "Pageant of the Film World," 19; Read Kendall, "Odd and Interesting Hollywood Gossip," *Los Angeles Times* (July 28, 1936): 13; Kendall, "Odd and Interesting," *Los Angeles Times* (August 9, 1936): C1.

34. Berkowitz, "A 'New Deal' for Leisure," 204; Duchemin, "Destinations of Choice," in *Scenic View Ahead*, 76.

35. Texas State Historical Association, "Texas Centennial," in *Handbook of Texas History Online*.

36. David Hanna, "The Little Acorn Has Grown," *New York Times* (February 2, 1941): X4.

37. *Oh Susanna!*

38. Ibid.

39. Stanfield, *Horse Opera*, 140–41.

40. "Texas Centennial."

41. Ibid.

42. Schallert, "Accidents Delay Western Feature," *Los Angeles Times* (August 11, 1936): 13; ledger of cash receipts and cash disbursements from September 1936 through December 31, 1938; Scheuer, "Pageant of the Film World," *Los Angeles Times* (August 27, 1936): 15; Schallert, Pageant of the Film World," *Los Angeles Times* (September 16, 1936): 15; Stanfield, *Horse Opera*, 115–16; Hurst, *Republic Pictures*, 170.

43. Stanfield, *Horse Opera*, 126–27.

44. Ibid, 137.

45. Press Book.

46. Press Book; ledger of cash receipts and cash disbursements from September 1936 through December 31.

47. Earl Gustkey, "Life with Autry Turns out Fine for Goodale," *Los Angeles Times* (April 30, 1970): F8; ledger of cash receipts and cash disbursements from September 1936 through December 31, 1938, GAC, T87-36-4623; David Hanna, "The Little Acorn Has Grown," *New York Times* (February 2, 1941): X4.

48. Shallert, "Ridin' Buckaroos of Cinema Win New Triumphs at Box Office," *Los Angeles Times* (February 14, 1937): C1.

49. Ibid.; Schallert, "The Pageant of the Film World," *Los Angeles Times* (April 20, 1937): 12; IMDB, "Buck Jones."

50. *Git Along Little Doggies*.

51. White, "The Good Guys Wore White Hats," 135–59.

52. "Valley Fights Flood Threat," *Los Angeles Times* (February 7, 1937): 1; Schallert, "The Pageant of the Film World," *Los Angeles Times* (April 20, 1937): 12.

**Chapter 4**

1. Hurst, *Republic Pictures*, 171; Green, *Singing in the Saddle*, 120–48; ledger, GAC, T87-36-4623: ledger; Schallert, "Autry to Get $7500 per Film," *Los Angeles Times* (June 16, 1937): 10; "Hedda Hopper's Hollywood," *Los Angeles Times* (June 21, 1938): 11.

2. Schallert, "Autry to Get $7500 Per Film," *Los Angeles Times* (June 16, 1937): 10; *Public Cowboy No. 1*.

3. *Springtime in the Rockies*; *Gold Mine in the Sky*; *Man from Music Mountain*; *Mountain Rhythm*; and *Colorado Sunset*.

4. Lowitt, *The New Deal and the West*, 64–80; Koppes, "Efficiency/Equity/Esthetics," 127–46.

5. *Public Cowboy No. 1*.

6. Lowitt, *The New Deal and the West*.

7. Schallert, "Gene Autry Western Champ," *Los Angeles Times* (December 27, 1937): 11.

8. Philip K. Scheuer, "A Town Called Hollywood," *Los Angeles Times* (December 21, 1937): 10; "News of the Screen," *New York Times* (December 21, 1937): 28; Schallert, "Gene Autry Western Champ," 11.

9. White, "The Good Guys Wore White Hats," in Aquila (ed.), *Wanted Dead or Alive*, 145–46. Republic Pictures produced five films in the Gene Autry series with storylines involving water rights and the development of water and power resources in the New West: *Tumbling Tumbleweeds*; *Red River Valley*; *Man from Music Mountain*; *Rovin' Tumbleweeds*; and *Sunset in Wyoming*.

10. The federal government recognized the Brooklyn Bridge in 1964, crediting its status as the longest suspension bridge in the world and the world's first steel-wire suspension bridge when it opened in 1883. Duchemin, "Water, Power, and Tourism," 60; Billington and Jackson, *Big Dams of the New Deal Era*, 11, 177, 217; *National Park Service Landmarks Program*. See also White, "The Good Guys Wore White Hats," 145–46.

11. Berkowitz, "A 'New Deal' for Leisure," 202; Aron, *Working at Play*, 246; *New York Times*, 9 June 1935; Duchemin, "Water, Power, and Tourism," 74.

12. Taylor, *American-Made*, 292–93; Duchemin, "Water, Power, and Tourism," 74.

13. Berkowitz, "A 'New Deal' for Leisure," 203–5.

14. Nye, *Soft Power*, 134–37. The identification of twenty-seven New Deal-themed films in Republic Pictures' Gene Autry series comes from my own screening and rating of all fifty-six prewar films.

15. Parker, *Gene Autry in Public Cowboy No. 1*, 287; Dale Armstrong, "Various and Sundry," *Los Angeles Times* (October 21, 1937): 18; Carrol Nye, "Varieties," *Los Angeles Times* (July 27, 1937): 11; ledger, GAC, T87-36-4623: ledger; Schallert, "The Pageant of the Film World," *Los Angeles Times* (July 17, 1937): A7; "Today on the Radio," *New York Times* (July 22, 1937): 28; "Hedda Hopper's Hollywood," *Los Angeles Times* (June 21, 1938): 11.

16. Schallert, "Gleanings from Studio Citadel," *Los Angeles Times* (December 30, 1937): 11; Scheuer, "Foreign Fans Eager for Screen News," *Los Angeles Times* (August 15, 1937): C1; Schallert, "The Pageant of the Film World," *Los Angeles Times* (September 23, 1937): A9. Scheuer, "Singing Cowboy Assigned," *Los Angeles Times* (August 21, 1937): A7. Kendall, "Around and About in Hollywood," *Los Angeles Times* (October 4, 1937): A9; Rothel, *The Singing Cowboys*, 118–19.

17. Kay Campbell, "Song Names Inspire New Film Titles," *Los Angeles Times* (September 18, 1938): C4; Green, *Singing in the Saddle*, 120–48.

18. *Boots and Saddles*; *Springtime in the Rockies*; *Gold Mine in the Sky*.

19. *Springtime in the Rockies*.

20. Schallert, "Gene Autry Battles Studio," *Los Angeles Times* (January 27, 1938): 10.

21. Schallert, "Pageant of the Film World," *Los Angeles Times* (March 16, 1938): 10; Schallert, "Autry May Be Replaced," *Los Angeles Times* (February 15, 1938): 10.

22. Schallert, "Autry Sells Song Numbers," *Los Angeles Times* (February 25, 1938): 10; ledger, GAC, T87-36-4623: ledger; David Rothel, *The Singing Cowboys*, 118–19.

23. Schallert, "Autry Sells Song Numbers," *Los Angeles Times* (February 25, 1938): 10; ledger, GAC, T87-36-4623: ledger; Rothel, *The Singing Cowboys*, 118–19. Rogers claimed the number one spot in Quigley's Western film poll in 1943, and he held onto that ranking as America's favorite western star until 1954. The reign ended when the Walt Disney Company starred Fess Parker as the lead in the hugely popular *Davy Crockett* series. Remaining on top from 1937–54, the longevity of the singing cowboy era was pronounced in Western film history, and it deserves further study. Likewise, the ability of Autry and Rogers to rank among the Hollywood A-list of biggest box office earners (Autry from 1940 to 1942; Rogers from 1945 to 1946) showed the influence of the singing cowboy in the American mainstream. A majority of Americans considered themselves fans of Autry or Rogers during the Second World War.

24. Read Kendall, "Hollywood Fans Wager on Stagehand," *Los Angeles Times* (March 6, 1938): A16; "Stagehand Beats Seabiscuit by Nose in $137,300 Stake," *New York Times* (March 6, 1938): 63; "Band and Musical Star on Orange Show Program," *Los Angeles Times* (March 13, 1938): A7; "Orange Show Books Stars," *Los Angeles Times* (March 14, 1938): A19; "Record Orange Show Exhibits Placed for Opening

Thursday," *Los Angeles Times* (March 15, 1938): A5; Kendall, "Around and About in Hollywood," *Los Angeles Times* (April 15, 1938): 15.

25. Schallert, "Next Autry Feature Selected," *Los Angeles Times* (May 18, 1938): A10; Rothel, 28; ledger, GAC, T87-36-4623: ledger.

26. Hanson, *This Side of Despair*, 19–20.

27. Ibid, 20.

28. *Gold Mine in the Sky*; "Veterans See Stars Shine at Coliseum," *Los Angeles Times* (September 22, 1938): 1.

29. "Screen and Stage Bill Announced," *Los Angeles Times* (October 3, 1938): 26; Jones, "Gene Autry to Headline Stage Show," *Los Angeles Times* (October 4, 1938): 10; Scheuer, "Gene Autry Clicks in Local Bow," *Los Angeles Times* (October 7, 1938): A18; "Bob Keneston Risks Crown," *Los Angeles Times* (October 10, 1938): A18; "Telephone Benefit Card at Legion," *Los Angeles Times* (October 15, 1938): 8; Kendall, "Around and About in Hollywood," *Los Angeles Times* (December 17, 1938): A7; Maxine Bartlett, "Helpers Plan Holiday Ball," *Los Angeles Times* (October 30, 1938): D6; Kendall, "Celebrities Assist Shrine Charity," *Los Angeles Times* (November 21, 1938): 24.

30. Schallert, "Next Autry Feature Selected," *Los Angeles Times* (May 18, 1938): A10; John Scott, "Autry Western Previewed," *Los Angeles Times* (June 30, 1938): 12; Tully, "Kids Vote Him Tops"; Kendall, "Odd and Interesting," *Los Angeles Times* (June 19, 1938): C4; "Hedda Hopper's Hollywood," *Los Angeles Times* (September 26, 1938): A16; ledger, GAC, T87-36-4623: ledger; Isabel Morse Jones, "Cowboy Star's Fans," *Los Angeles Times* (March 17, 1938): 10.

31. Tully, "Kids Vote Him Tops," *Los Angeles Times* (May 29, 1938): H6.

32. Ibid.

33. Ibid.; E. V. Durling, "On the Side with E. V. Durling," *Los Angeles Times* (November 15, 1938): A1; ledger, GAC, T87-36-4623: ledger; Kendall, "Around and About in Hollywood," *Los Angeles Times* (March 24, 1938): A10; Schallert, "Movieland Jottings and Castings," *Los Angeles Times* (June 6, 1938): A14.

34. Parker, *Gene Autry in Public Cowboy No. 1*, 287; Dale Armstrong, "Various and Sundry," *Los Angeles Times* (October 21, 1937): 18; Carrol Nye, "Varieties," *Los Angeles Times* (July 27, 1937): 11; ledger, GAC, T87-36-4623: ledger; Schallert, "The Pageant of the Film World," *Los Angeles Times* (July 17, 1937): A7; "Today on the Radio," *New York Times* (July 22, 1937): 28; "Hedda Hopper's Hollywood," *Los Angeles Times* (June 21, 1938): 11

35. *Man from Music Mountain*.

36. Ibid.

37. "Back to the Farm," *Pittsburgh Press* (July 27, 1940): 4; Bergman, *We're in the Money*, 70–72.

38. "Gene Autry Anecdotes," June 1947.

39. John L. Scott, "Horse-Opera Vogue Revived: Singing Cowboy has Revolutionized Western Pictures," *Los Angeles Times* (March 5, 1939): C4; Stanfield, "Dixie Cowboys and Blue Yodels," 111.

40. Hurst, *Republic Pictures*, 212–13.

41. *Mountain Rhythm*.

42. "Film Folk Entertain Dust Bowl Children," *New York Times* (December 25, 1938): 13; "Hedda Hopper's Hollywood," *Los Angeles Times* (December 21, 1938): 11.

43. Douglas W. Churchill, "'We'll Head 'Em Off at Eagle Pass,'" *New York Times* (April 23, 1939): 108.

44. Ibid.

45. Hurst, *Republic Pictures*, 13, 60.

46. Ibid., 60.

47. Stanfield, "Dixie Cowboys and Blue Yodels," 111–13; Stanfield, *Horse Opera*, 141–145, 154.

48. Stanfield, "Dixie Cowboys and Blue Yodels," 111–13; Stanfield, *Horse Opera*, 141–45, 154; Hawley, *The New Deal and the Problem of Monopoly*, 192–94.

49. Hurst, *Republic Pictures*, 172.

50. Frank S. Nugent, "A Horse of Another Color," *New York Times* (March 12, 1939): 154.

51. *Rovin' Tumbleweeds*.

52. Lowitt, *The New Deal and the West*, 81–99.

53. Ibid.

54. Steinbeck, *The Grapes of Wrath*; McWilliams, *Factories in the Field*; Lange, *An American Exodus*; *Rovin' Tumbleweeds*.

55. "Table 3—Urban and Rural Population, for the United States: 1790 to 1940," Sixteenth Census of the United States, 18.

56. Ibid.

57. Schivelbusch, *Three New Deals*; Billington and Jackson, *Big Dams of the New Deal Era*. The big western dams included the Boulder Canyon Project on the Colorado River in Nevada; the Columbia River Control Plan-Bonneville and Grand Coulee Dams in Washington; Fort Peck Dam on the Missouri River in Montana; and California's Central Valley Project: Shasta Dam on the Sacramento River and Friant Dam on San Joaquin River.

58. Gans, *Popular Culture and High Culture*, 115–19.

## Chapter 5

1. Six of the fourteen films are featured in this book: *Comin' Round the Mountain* (1936): Ranch Vista Grande. Season 1: 1935–36: No. 6 of 8; *Rootin' Tootin' Rhythm* (1936): U.S.-Mexico border. Season 2: 1936–37: No. 7 of 8; *Boots and Saddles* (1937): Anglo-American-Mexican relations. Season 3: 1937–38: No. 2 of 5; *Mexicali Rose* (1939): U.S. oil interests in Mexico. Season 4: 1938–39: No. 7 of 8; *Blue Montana Skies* (1939): U.S.-Canada border. Season 4: 1938–39: No. 8 of 8; *In Old Monterey* (1939): International pilot training in Southwest. Season 4: 1939–40: No. 2 of 7.

2. Fejes, *Imperialism, Media, and the Good Neighbor*, 32–33.

3. Pike, *FDR's Good Neighbor Policy*, 211–12; Whitaker, "The Origin of the Western Hemisphere Idea," 323–26; Whitaker, *The Western Hemisphere Idea*; Worcester, "Herbert Eugene Bolton," in Etulain (ed.), *Writing Western History*, 207.

4. Pike, *FDR's Good Neighbor Policy*, 211–12; Whitaker, "The Origin of the Western Hemisphere Idea," 323–26; Whitaker, *The Western Hemisphere Idea*; Worcester, "Herbert Eugene Bolton," 207.

5. Aikman, "The Machinery for Hemisphere Cooperation," 550–54; Morrison, "Josephus Daniels—Simpatico," 277; Meyer, "Toscanini and the Good Neighbor Policy," 247.

6. Fejes, *Imperialism, Media, and the Good Neighbor*, 77.

7. Philip K. Scheuer, "Foreign Fans Eager for Screen News," *Los Angeles Times* (August 15, 1937): C1; Fejes, *Imperialism, Media, and the Good Neighbor*, 25–27, 73; Aikman, "The Machinery for Hemisphere Cooperation," 550–54; Morrison, "Josephus Daniels—Simpatico," 277; Meyer, "Toscanini and the Good Neighbor Policy," 247. Familiarity with radio broadcasting and a lack of support from newspaper publishers and motion picture producers convinced FDR to use shortwave radio broadcasting as a principal means of creating friendlier relations between the U.S. and Latin America. Developments and innovations in shortwave radio technology piqued the president's interest in international broadcasting. High-powered transmitters and directional antennas made north-south communications feasible by 1936.

8. Aikman, "The Machinery for Hemisphere Cooperation," 550–54; Morrison, "Josephus Daniels—Simpatico," 277; Meyer, "Toscanini and the Good Neighbor Policy," 247. The need for greater understanding and appreciation for the people of the Americas took on new meaning after Adolph Hitler, Germany's president and chancellor, rejected the Treaty of Versailles. Hitler withdrew Germany from the League of Nations and busied the Third Reich with the expansion and rearming of the German military. Benito Mussolini, the Italian prime minister, followed suit by starting a war of aggression against Ethiopia. The Italian assault further exposed the league's inability to guarantee world peace. Antiwar sentiment permeated the United States as these events unfolded. Isolationists in Congress confirmed an American desire for nonaggression by passing the Neutrality Act of 1935. President Roosevelt responded by "Pan-Americanizing" the Monroe Doctrine. He got the other nations of the Western Hemisphere to agree that an attack on one country equaled an attack on all the twenty-one nations in the Americas. Closer relations in the Western Hemisphere helped increase national security for the United States by enabling American companies to maintain control of raw material supplies and access to markets for manufactured goods in Latin America.

9. Scheuer, "Foreign Fans Eager for Screen News," C1; Scheuer, "Singing Cowboy Assigned"; Edwin Schallert, "Gleanings From Studio Citadel," *Los Angeles Times* (December 30, 1937): 11; Schallert, "Gene Autry Battles Studio," *Los Angeles Times* (January 27, 1938): 10; Fejes, *Imperialism, Media, and the Good Neighbor*, 25–27, 73.

10. Meyer, "Toscanini and the Good Neighbor Policy," 247; Landry, "Radio and Government," 557–65; Pollard, "Words Are Cheaper than Blood," 286; Carson, "Notes toward an Examination of the Radio Documentary," 69; Morrison, "Josephus Daniels—Simpatico," 284–89. NBC competed in South America with German and Italian radio broadcasters offering sixteen hours of programming per day. Germany launched advertising and public relations campaigns designed to edge out British and U.S. business interests. German trade with Brazil grew substantially from 1933 to 1938. Brazilian exports climbed from 12 percent to 25 percent, while German imports rose from 8 percent to nearly 20 percent. Mexican trade with Germany jumped 12 percent in the first quarter of 1938, after the Mexican President Lázaro Cárdenas nationalized the oil industry. German economic strength increased chatter concerning the prospects of a military invasion in Latin America. As U.S. citizens contemplated this possibility, President Roosevelt used the potential threat to unnerve isolationists in Congress and gain support for Great Britain in a war against Germany.

11. Meyer, "Toscanini and the Good Neighbor Policy," 247; Landry, "Radio and Government," 557–65; Pollard, "Words Are Cheaper than Blood," 286; Carson, "Notes toward an Examination of the Radio Documentary," 69; Morrison, "Josephus Daniels—Simpatico," 284–89.

12. Muscio, *Hollywood's New Deal*, 66; Pike, *FDR's Good Neighbor Policy*, 106.

13. Muscio, *Hollywood's New Deal*, 66; Pike, *FDR's Good Neighbor Policy*, 106; Schwoch, *The American Radio Industry and Its Latin American Activities*, 143. Latin American broadcasters like Emilio Azcarraga helped the Roosevelt administration and U.S. advertisers reach additional large audiences in Mexico. Cooperation with the U.S. government enabled Azcarraga to enter an international arena and make connections with NBC and radio capitalists in the U.S. Working closely with NBC, the Mexican broadcaster developed new markets by helping to finance regular program exchanges for his powerful stations. Azcarraga organized a talent agency to book Mexican musicians to perform on his radio stations. He also formed a music publishing company to control the copyright of the playlists at his stations. Another company distributed records in Mexico City for the RCA and Victor labels.

14. *Rootin' Tootin' Rhythm*.

15. "Theatre Activities," *Bedford Gazette* (May 23, 1930): 10; "Cinderella Story," *Charleston Gazette* (September 22, 1929): 7; "Armida Is Gay, Young Discovery," *Los Angeles Times*, (October 21, 1928): B13; "Wave of Popularity Sweeping Mexican Stars to the Top Keeps Going On," *Los Angeles Times* (January 27, 1929): C11; http://en.wikipedia.org/wiki/Armida_Vendrell.

16. *Rootin' Tootin' Rhythm*.

17. Ibid.

18. Cinemateca—Condor Media, Inc., *Allá en el Rancho Grande (Over at the Big Ranch)*.

19. Ibid.

20. *Mexicali Rose*; Chanan, "Cinema in Latin America," in Nowell-Smith (ed.), *The Oxford History of World Cinema*, 431; Sklar, *A World History of Films*; Katz and Nolan, *The Film Encyclopedia*; Riera, *Fernando De Fuentes*.

21. *Boots and Saddles*.

22. Ibid.

23. Ibid.

24. Grace Dugan to Gene Autry, December 31, 1937.

25. Schallert, "Gene Autry Battles Studio," *Los Angeles Times* (January 27, 1938): 10.

26. Ibid.; Schallert, "Autry May Be Replaced," *Los Angeles Times* (February 15, 1938): 10; Schallert, "Pageant of the Film World," *Los Angeles Times* (March 16, 1938): 10; Green, *Singing in the Saddle*, 120–48.

27. Good Neighbor–themed films in Republic's Gene Autry series included *Comin' Round the Mountain* (1936); *Rootin' Tootin' Rhythm* (1936); *Boots and Saddles* (1937); *Mexicali Rose* (1939); *Blue Montana Skies* (1939); *In Old Monterey* (1939); *South of the Border* (1939); *Rancho Grande* (1940); *The Singing Hill* (1941); *Under Fiesta Skies* (1941); *Down Mexico Way* (1941); *Call of the Canyon* (1942); and *Bells of Capistrano* (1942).

28. Steele, "The Great Debate: Roosevelt, the Media, and the Coming of the War, 1940–1941," 79–80.

29. Ibid, 72–73; Pike, *FDR's Good Neighbor Policy*, 147; *Baltimore Sun* (November 10, 1940).

30. Steele, "The Great Debate," 74–75; Rostron, "'No War, No Hate, No Propaganda,'" 88.

31. Schwoch, *The American Radio Industry and its Latin American Activities*, 144.

32. *Mexicali Rose*.

33. Ibid.

34. Ibid.

35. Ibid.

36. Ibid.

37. Ibid.

38. Fejes, *Imperialism, Media, and the Good Neighbor*, 77.

39. *Mexicali Rose*.

40. Pike, *FDR's Good Neighbor Policy*, 178.

41. *Blue Montana Skies*.

42. *In Old Monterey*; "Jimmie Fidler in Hollywood," *Los Angeles Times* (July 4, 1939): A8; "Jimmie Fidler in Hollywood," *Los Angeles Times* (September 18, 1939): A16; "Jimmie Fidler in Hollywood," *Los Angeles Times* (July 12 1939): 13.

43. Churchill, "Screen News Here and in Hollywood," *New York Times* (July 20, 1939): 24; "The Coming Week at the World's Fair: A Page of Information for the Sightseer," *New York Times* (July 22, 1939): 5; "Named 'King of the Cowboys,'" *New York Times* (July 23, 1939): 28; Churchill, "Screen News Here and in Hollywood," *New York Times* (July 24, 1939): 15.

44. "Hedda Hopper's Hollywood," *Los Angeles Times* (August 18, 1939): A11.

45. Hurst, *Republic Pictures*, 171.

46. Ibid.

47. Douglas W. Churchill, "News of the Screen," *New York Times* (October 13, 1939): 30; Al Wolf, "Louis-Baer Bout Here Awaits Public Reaction," *Los Angeles Times* (August 28, 1949): A10; "Rodeo Show to Open at Garden Tomorrow," *New York Times* (October 8, 1940): 31; "Jimmie Fidler in Hollywood," *Los Angeles Times* (October 2, 1940): 15.

48. Ibid.

49. Stanfield, *Horse Opera*, 150.

**Chapter 6**

1. Gene Autry, conversation with Pat Buttram, televised on *Melody Ranch Theater*, included with *South of the Border*; George-Warren, *Public Cowboy No*, 182–83; *Glasgow Herald*, "Actor Mobbed in Glasgow" (August 21, 1939); *Daily Record* (Glasgow), "50,000 Welcome Cowboy Gene" (August 21, 1939); *Belfast News-Letter*, "Cowboy Star Mobbed" (August 15, 1939); *Evening Dispatch*, "Singing Cowboy Star Admires Our Golf Links" (August 7, 1939); "Studios Call Stars Back from War-Menaced Europe," *Los Angeles Times* (August 26, 1939): A19.

2. Gene Autry, conversation with Pat Buttram; "Studios Call Stars Back from War-Menaced Europe," *Los Angeles Times* (August 26, 1939): A19; Churchill, "Screen News Here and in Hollywood," *New York Times* (September 7, 1939): 35; Churchill, "Screen News Here and in Hollywood," *New York Times* (September 8, 1939): 32; B. R. Crisler, "Alarms and Discursions," *New York Times* (September 24, 1939): 131; "Jimmie Fidler in Hollywood," *Los Angeles Times* (October 6. 1939): 28.

3. Fejes, *Imperialism, Mexico, and the Good Neighbor*, 5–8.

4. Stanfield, *Horse Opera*, 7, Lynette Tan and Philip Loy mention Gene Autry's role as a supporter of U.S. foreign policy, but neither developed the idea. See Tan, "The New Deal Cowboy," 89–101; and Loy, "Soldiers in Stetsons," 197–205.

5. Stanfield, *Horse Opera*, 7. Lynette Tan and Philip Loy mention Gene Autry's role as a supporter of U.S. foreign policy, but neither developed the idea. See Tan, "The New Deal Cowboy," 89–101; and Loy, "Soldiers in Stetsons," 197–205.

6. Stanfield, *Horse Opera*, 151–52; Rothel, 29.

7. Ibid.

8. Hurst, *Republic Pictures*, 172.

9. *South of the Border*. The following paragraphs summarize and quote from this movie.

10. Loy, "Soldiers in Stetsons," 198; Pike, *FDR's Good Neighbor Policy*, 185, 195.

11. Schallert, "Gene Autry Leads Western Money-Makers," *Los Angeles Times* (December 22, 1939): 13.

12. Review 1—No title. *Los Angeles Times* (February 3, 1940): A7; "Premiere of Western Due," *Los Angeles Times* (February 5, 1940): 15; Grace Kingsley, "Autry Film in Premiere at Cinema," *Los Angeles Times* (February 6, 1940): A10.

13. *Rancho Grande.*

14. *Melody Ranch* (May 19, 1940).

15. Fejes, *Imperialism, Media, and the Good Neighbor*, 121.

16. *Gaucho Serenade.*

17. *Gaucho Serenade; Melody Ranch* (June 9, 1940: 159/7921; June 23, 1940: 205/9672; July 7, 1940: 206/9672; July 28, 1940: 280/9672).

18. "Today's Program at the Fair," *New York Times* (May 14, 1949): 20; Sidney M. Shalett, "Lily Pons, Tibbett Thrill Fair Crowd," *New York Times* (May 14, 1940): 20.

19. "Jimmie Fidler in Hollywood," *Los Angeles Times* (July 5, 1940): A14; "Headliners to Broadcast," *Los Angeles Times* (June 20, 1940): 8; "Gene Autry to Aid Fiesta," *Los Angeles Times* (May 19, 1940): A1.

20. Friedman, *Nazis and Good Neighbors*, 52–57; Fejes, *Imperialism, Media, and the Good Neighbor*, 122; *Melody Ranch* (May 19, 1940: 156/7921; June 9, 1940: 4093/9672; June 23, 1940: 205/9672; June 30, 1940: 5995/9672; October 27, 1940: 252/9672; November 10, 1940: 5992/9672; November 24, 1940: 7504/9672; December 8, 1940: 4239/9672; December 22, 1940: 6409/9672).

21. Fejes, *Imperialism, Media, and the Good Neighbor*, 131–35.

22. Fejes, *Imperialism, Media, and the Good Neighbor*, 131–35; Pike, *FDR's Good Neighbor Policy*, 252.

23. Pike, *FDR's Good Neighbor Policy*, 253.

24. Ibid.

25. Ibid, 231.

26. Schallert, "Autry Joins Select List," *Los Angeles Times* (December 27, 1940): 11; "Autry Joins First Ten," *New York Times* (December 27, 1940): 23.

27. Stanfield, *Horse Opera*, 150–51.

28. Ibid.

29. Grace Kingsley, "Autry Westerns," *Los Angeles Times* (May 15, 1941): A10; Jimmie Fidler in Hollywood," *Los Angeles Times* (April 23, 1941): 24.

30. *Under Fiesta Stars.*

31. Schallert, "Gleams From Stellar Galaxy," *Los Angeles Times* (April 5, 1941): A9; "More Hollywood Notes," *New York Times* (July 6, 1941): X4.

32. *Down Mexico Way.*

33. *Melody Ranch* (various programs throughout 1941).

34. Pike, *FDR's Good Neighbor Policy*, 112.

35. "Republic's Busy Program," *New York Times* (February 10, 1942): 25.

36. Edwin Schallert, "Drama," *Los Angeles Times* (January 9, 1942): 25.

## Chapter 7

1. *Boots and Saddles.*

2. *Western Jamboree.*

3. Ward and Pierce, "Helium," 285–90.

4. Frank S. Nugent, "A Horse of Another Color," *New York Times* (March 12, 1939): 154.

5. Ibid.

6. "Republic to Make 50 Feature Films," *New York Times* (April 6, 1939): 34; "Jimmie Fidler in Hollywood," *Los Angeles Times* (April 18, 1940): A10; "Jimmie Fidler in Hollywood," *Los Angeles Times* (April 26, 1939): 13.

7. *In Old Monterey*.

8. Beginning in 1942, the U.S. Department of State used the song's melody as the interval signal for the Voice of America. Holsinger (ed.), *War and American Popular Culture*, 67; http://en.wikipedia.org/wiki/Columbia,_Gem_of_the_Ocean.

9. *In Old Monterey*.

10. George A. Mooney, "Youth's Model 1940," *New York Times* (October 27, 1940): 140.

11. "Announcer's Opening: Our Hero of Melody Ranch is Gene Autry—America's Favorite Singing Cowboy, Who Is a Symbol of the Clean Thinking, Honesty and Integrity of the American People," *Melody Ranch* (December 31, 1939; 1 of 7921 radio show segments.

12. Ibid.

13. "Announcer's Opening, *Melody Ranch* (December 31, 1939; 407/9672 song tracks.

14. Mooney, "Youth's Model 1940," 140; Stanfield, *Horse Opera*, 151; Rothel, 29.

15. Theodore Strauss, "Littlest Doggies Git Along," *New York Times* (August 4, 1940): 105.

16. Ibid.

17. Ibid.

18. *The Gene Autry Show*, December 31, 1939; Blum, *V Was For Victory*, 108–10; The Wrigley Company, "Wrigley's Gum Production Dedicated to U.S. Armed Forces," http://www.wrigley.com/global/about-us/heritage-timeline.aspx.

19. Letter from Gene Autry to Franklin D. Roosevelt, dated September 10, 1943; letter from Franklin D. Roosevelt to Gene Autry, dated September 15, 1943, both in Franklin D. Roosevelt Library; *The Gene Autry Show,* January 28, 1940; Winifred Mallon, "Nation Observes President's Day," *New York Times* (January 31, 1940): 1.

20. *The Gene Autry Show,* January 28, 1940.

21. *Melody Ranch* (January 28, 1940; 679/9672); Delbert Clark, "President Goes to Birthday Play," *New York Times* (January 29, 1940): 10; "Fifty-Eighth Birthday," *New York Times* (February 4, 1940): 111; Winifred Mallon, "Nation Observes President's Day," *New York Times* (January 31, 1940): 1; Schallert, "While the Films Reel By," *Los Angeles Times* (April 7, 1940): C2.

22. *Melody Ranch* ( January 28, 1940; 679/9672); Delbert Clark, "President Goes to Birthday Play," *New York Times* (January 29, 1940): 10; "Fifty-Eighth Birthday," *New*

*York Times* (February 4, 1940): 111; Winifred Mallon, "Nation Observes President's Day," *New York Times* (January 31, 1940): 1; Schallert, "While the Films Reel By," *Los Angeles Times* (April 7, 1940): C2.

23. *Melody Ranch* (February 11, 1940; 547/9672).

24. "Jimmie Fidler in Hollywood," *Los Angeles Times* (October 7, 1941): 13; Green, *Singing in the Saddle*, 156–57; George-Warren, *Public Cowboy No. 1*, 191–92, 361; Gilmore, *LA Despair*, 313.

25. "Jimmie Fidler in Hollywood," *Los Angeles Times* (October 7, 1941): 13; Green, *Singing in the Saddle*, 156–57; George-Warren, *Public Cowboy No. 1*, 361.

26. "Jimmie Fidler in Hollywood," *Los Angeles Times* (August 11, 1940): 8.

27. Ibid.

28. Roy Rogers appeared as Autry's surrogate during the off years.

29. Churchill, "News of the Screen," *New York Times* (October 13, 1939): 30; Al Wolf, "Louis-Baer Bout Here Awaits Public Reaction," *Los Angeles Times* (August 28, 1949): A10; "Rodeo Show to Open at Garden Tomorrow," *New York Times* (October 8, 1940): 31; "Jimmie Fidler in Hollywood," *Los Angeles Times* (October 2, 1940): 15.

30. "Rodeo Entertains Bellevue Patients," *New York Times* (October 16, 1940): 20; "17,000 Child Guests, Whoop It Up of Rodeo; Bronco-Busting Is a Hit and Autry Is 'Swell,'" *New York Times* (October 22, 1940): 22; *Melody Ranch* (October 20, 1940: 253/9672; October 27, 1940: 252/9672; November 3, 1940: 214/9672).

31. "News and Notes of the Advertising Field," *New York Times* (October 14, 1940): 32; "ASCAP to Give Concerts," *New York Times* (October 23, 1940): 26; Stanfield, *Horse Opera*, 152–54.

32. "News and Notes of the Advertising Field," *New York Times* (October 14, 1940): 32; "ASCAP to Give Concerts," *New York Times* (October 23, 1940): 26; Stanfield, *Horse Opera*, 152–54.

33. "Tom Mix, Rider, Dies Under Auto," *New York Times* (October 13, 1940): 1; "Friends Pay Actor Tribute," *Los Angeles Times* (October 13, 1940): 6; *Melody Ranch* (October 13, 1940: 7891/9672).

34. "Tom Mix, Rider, Dies under Auto," 1; "Friends Pay Actor Tribute," 6; *Melody Ranch* (October 13, 1940: 7891/9672).

35. "Tom Mix, Rider, Dies under Auto," 1; "Friends Pay Actor Tribute," 6; *Melody Ranch* (October 13, 1940: 7891/9672).

36. Mooney, "Youth's Model 1940," 140.

37. Ibid.

38. Ibid.

39. Ibid.

40. *Melody Ranch* (May 5, 1940; radio show segment 128/7921).

41. Edwin Schallert, "Autry Joins Select List," *Los Angeles Times* (December 27, 1940): 11; "Autry Joins First Ten," *New York Times* (December 27, 1940): 23.

## Chapter 8

1. *Melody Ranch*; *Melody Ranch* (December 1, 1940; December 29, 1940; January 5, 1941: 249/9672; January 19, 1941: 219/9672.

2. *Melody Ranch*; *Melody Ranch* (January 5, 1941: 249/9672; January 19, 1941: 212/9672; January 26, 1941: 1795/9672).

3. *Melody Ranch*.

4. Ibid.

5. *Melody Ranch* (February 4, 1940; 546/9672).

6. "Fire Ruins Home of Gene Autry," *Los Angeles Times* (November 9, 1941): 3; Lirtley Baskette, "Home, Home on the Ranch," *Los Angeles Times* (June 14, 1942): H14; Hedda Hopper, "Autry Can't Get Around to Resting," *Los Angeles Times* (July 31, 1949): D1; "Camp Run Like Real Ranch, but More Fun," *Los Angeles Times* (August 9, 1970): SF_B1.

7. "Hedda Hopper's Hollywood," *Los Angeles Times* (January 22, 1941): 12.

8. *Back in the Saddle*.

9. Ibid.

10. "Film Info" for *Back in the Saddle*; Burgin, *Time Required in Developing Selected Arizona Copper Mines*, 18, 37, 78–79.

11. "Film Info" for *Back in the Saddle* (1941) Gene Autry Entertainment: http://www.geneautry.com/geneautry/motionpictures/filmography/backinthesaddle.html; Burgin, *Time Required in Developing Selected Arizona Copper Mines*, 18, 37, 78–79.

12. "Armadas of Defense Planes Prove Headache for Films," *Los Angeles Times* (January 26, 1941) A6.

13. Ibid.

14. "Hedda Hopper's Hollywood," *Los Angeles Times* (June 7, 1941): A9; "Hedda Hopper's Hollywood," *Los Angeles Times* (January 26, 1941): C3; "Jimmie Fidler in Hollywood," *Los Angeles Times* (May 4, 1941): C2; "Jimmie Fidler in Hollywood," *Los Angeles Times* (May 15, 1941): A11; "Putting Guffaws Into the Western," *New York Times* (October 12, 1941): X4.

15. "Jimmie Fidler in Hollywood," *Los Angeles Times* (May 4, 1941): C2; "Putting Guffaws Into the Western," *New York Times* (October 12, 1941): X4.

16. "Jimmie Fidler in Hollywood," *Los Angeles Times* (June 12, 1941): A10; Thomas Brady, "The Unmusical Mr. Jones," *New York Times* (July 20, 1941): X4.

17. Thomas Brady, "The Unmusical Mr. Jones," *New York Times* (July 20, 1941): X4.

18. Ibid.

19. "Hedda Hopper's Hollywood," *Los Angeles Times* (January 28, 1941): 10; Thomas Brady, "The Unmusical Mr. Jones," *New York Times* (July 20, 1941): X4.

20. Schallert, "Fans Mourn Buck Jones in Dramatic Fire Death," *Los Angeles Times* (December 1, 1942): 8.

21. Hedda Hopper, "Rackin to Remake Classic Western," *Los Angeles Times* (February 4, 1965): C10; Green, *Singing in the Saddle*, 120–48.

22. Harry MacPherson, "Tin Pan Hollywood," *Los Angeles Times* (March 24, 1940): 19; Ron Ryan, "Hillbilly Music," *Los Angeles Times* (March 3, 1940): H9; "Republic Studio Announces $15,000,000 Film Budget," *Los Angeles Times* (February 26, 1941): A3; Schallert, "Republic Gets Membership in Hays Group," *Los Angeles Times* (September 25, 1941): A10; Hurst, *Republic Pictures*, 10–11.

23. Melody Ranch (June 29, 1941: 9100/9672; July 6, 1941: 9097/9672; July 20, 1941: 9095/9672; July 27, 1941: 9098/9672; August 24, 1941: 1008/9672; September 14, 1941; 1010/9672; November 16, 1941: 3291/9672; June 14, 1942: 1011/9672).

24. Melody Ranch (June 29, 1941: 9100/9672; July 6, 1941: 9097/9672; July 20, 1941: 9095/9672; July 27, 1941: 9098/9672; August 24, 1941: 1008/9672; September 14, 1941; 1010/9672; November 16, 1941: 3291/9672; June 14, 1942: 1011/9672); "Oklahoma Defense Savings Bond Rally featuring Gene Autry, September 6–7, 1941. Newspaper clipping: "Autry's Songs to Give Boost For Bonds at State Rallies," GAC, T87-36-4629.

25. Ibid.

26. "Jimmie Fidler in Hollywood," *Los Angeles Times* (February 1, 1941): 9; Treanor, "The Home Front," *Los Angeles Times* (July 30, 1941): A1; "Jimmie Fidler in Hollywood," *Los Angeles Times* (August 4, 1941): 8; "Jimmie Fidler in Hollywood," *Los Angeles Times* (August 12, 1941): A10; "Hedda Hopper's Hollywood," *Los Angeles Times* (September 12, 1941): 19.

27. Letter from John T. Shannon to Eddie Allen, October 3, 1941, Warwick Hotel, NYC, GAC, T87-36-2922-18; letter from John T. Shannon to Eddie Allen, December 29, 1941, Gene Autry Co. GAC, T87-36-2922-4; blueprint. "The Shannon Line" of Black Light designed by John T. Shannon, chief engineer, and manufactured by Keese Engineering Co., Hollywood, especially for Gene Autry. GAC, T87-36-2922-2.

28. "Rodeo Will Open Tonight," *New York Times* (October 8, 1941): 25; "Bellevue Patients Get Taste of West," *New York Times* (October 15, 1941): 19.

29. Newspaper clipping. "Autry Rodeo Will Have Beauty, Sparkle: Western Film Star Will Take Part in Sunday Ceremonies," *Oklahoma City Times* (November 14, 1941): 15, GAC, T87-36-502.

30. "Town Named for Gene Autry," *New York Times* (November 6, 1941): 12; "Jimmie Fidler in Hollywood," *Los Angeles Times* (November 12, 1941): A10; *Melody Ranch* (November 16, 1941); Rothel, 29.

31. "Town Named for Gene Autry," *New York Times* (November 6, 1941): 12; "Jimmie Fidler in Hollywood," *Los Angeles Times* (November 12, 1941): A10; *Melody Ranch* (November 16, 1941); Rothel, 29.

32. Shannon to Allen, December 29, 1941, Gene Autry Co., GAC, T87-36-2922-4; John T. Shannon to Gene Autry, February 18, 1942; Gene Autry to John T. Shannon, February 20, 1942. GAC, T87-36-2922-7.

33. Newspaper clipping, "Autry Rodeo Will Have Beauty, Sparkle: Western Film Star Will Take Part in Sunday Ceremonies," *Oklahoma City Times* (November 14, 1941): 15, GAC, T87-36-502.

34. Ibid.

35. Ibid.

36. Schallert, "Rooney Tops 10-Best List; Gable in Second," *Los Angeles Times* (December 26, 1941): A10; "Those Box Office Champions," *New York Times* (December 28, 1941): X4.

37. Philip K. Scheuer, "Poll Reveals Flynn Favorite of Juveniles," *Los Angeles Times* (September 16, 1941): A10.

38. *The Gene Autry Show*, 1939–45.

39. Ibid.

40. *Melody Ranch* (December 21, 1941: 4087/9672; January 11, 1942: 245/9672; January 25, 1942: 9153/9672); "Film Trio Leaves of Roosevelt Fete," *Los Angeles Times* (January 29, 1942): A1; "Film Stars Will Participate in President's Birthday Ball," *Los Angeles Times* (January 26, 1942): 8; "Gene Autry Feted," *Los Angeles Times* (May 6, 1942): 11; *Melody Ranch* (February 1, 1942: 8379/9672).

41. *Melody Ranch* (February 2, 1942: February 8, 1942; February 15, 1942; February 22, 1942).

42. *Melody Ranch* (March 15, 1942: 8413/9672).

43. *Melody Ranch* (March 29, 1942; April 12, 1942; April 19, 1942; April 26, 1942; May 3, 1942; May 10, 1942; May 17, 1942; May 24, 1942); "Jimmie Fidler in Hollywood," *Los Angeles Times* (December 15, 1941): A14; "Hedda Hopper's Hollywood," *Los Angeles Times* (April 10, 1942): A10.

44. "One Thing and Another," *New York Times* (November 30, 1941): X12; "New Drive Aids Troops," *New York Times* (June 3, 1942): 25; "Legion In Records Drive," *New York Times* (July 16, 1942): 21; *Melody Ranch* (April 19, 1942; May 17, 1942; June 14, 1942; June 21, 1942).

45. *Melody Ranch* (June 28, 1942: 8502/9672).

46. "Radio War Effort Defended," *New York Times* (July 28, 1942): 16.

47. Hurst, *Republic Pictures*, 61.

48. *Home in Wyomin'*.

49. Ibid.

50. Schallert, "Drama," *Los Angeles Times* (January 9, 1942): 25; "Hedda Hopper's Hollywood," *Los Angeles Times* (April 27, 1942): 8; Hurst, *Republic Pictures*, 203–5.

51. Hurst, *Republic Pictures*, 168–69.

52. *Melody Ranch* (July 26, 1942: 174/9672).

53. "Special Five Day Bond Drive Will Open Tomorrow," *Chicago Daily Tribune* (July 26, 1942): 15.

54. "Cowboy Autry Gives the Spur to Bond Sales," *Chicago Daily Tribune* (July 25, 1942): 18.

55. Melody Ranch (June 29, 1941: 9100/9672; July 6, 1941: 9097/9672; July 20, 1941: 9095/9672; July 27, 1941: 9098/9672; August 24, 1941: 1008/9672; September 14, 1941; 1010/9672; November 16, 1941: 3291/9672; June 14, 1942: 1011/9672); "Oklahoma Defense Savings Bond Rally featuring Gene Autry, September 6–7,

1941. Newspaper clipping: "Autry's Songs to Give Boost For Bonds at State Rallies." GAC, T87-36-4629.

56. "$1,407,642 Total Is Announced in USO Fund Campaign," *Chicago Daily Tribune* (July 25, 1942: 13; "Stars of Stage, Radio Help Drum Up Cash For USO," *Chicago Daily Tribune* (July, 1942).

57. *Melody Ranch* (August 2, 1942: 190/9672).

58. *Melody Ranch* (August 23, 1942: 630/9672).

59. Ibid.

60. Gene Autry to Everett Colborn, July 12, 1942. GAC, T87-36-2921; "Gene Autry Goes into Army Aug. 1," *Los Angeles Times* (July 9, 1942): A1; "Gene Autry Takes Army Oath," *New York Times* (July 28, 1942): 13; "Hedda Hopper's Hollywood," *Los Angeles Times* (July 28, 1942): 9.

### Conclusion

1. George-Warren, *Public Cowboy No. 1*, 365; Cowboy Autry Give the Spur to Bond Sales," *Chicago Daily Tribune* (July 25, 1942): 18.

2. "Gene Autry Leaves Horse Behind When He Joins Army," *Los Angeles Times* (October 12, 1942): A2; "Hedda Hopper's Hollywood," *Los Angeles Times* (November 16, 1942): 22; Green, *Singing in the Saddle*, 168.

3. "Kay Kyser," *iTunes*; Tex Ritter, "(I Got Spurs That) Jingle, Jangle, Jingle"; "Fallout Soundtrack—Jingle, Jangle, Jingle," *YouTube*.

4. "Fallout Soundtrack—Jingle, Jangle, Jingle"; "Jingle Jangle Jingle Dick Thomas 1942."

5. Since the 1980s, telecommunications companies, Web search portals, software publishers, including those publishing exclusively over the Internet, and companies broadcasting exclusively over the Internet have transformed and expanded the information economy. *North American Industry Classification System*.

6. "Gene Autry Joins Army Air Forces," *Los Angeles Times* (August 17, 1942): 16.

7. "Gene Autry Leaves Horse Behind When He Joins Army," *Los Angeles Times* (October 12, 1942): A2; "Hedda Hopper's Hollywood," *Los Angeles Times* (November 16, 1942): 22.

8. George-Warren, *Public Cowboy No. 1*, 365; "Hedda Hopper's Hollywood," *Los Angeles Times* (July 24, 1942): 17; "Abbott and Costello Top at Box Office," *New York Times* (December 26, 1942): 12.

9. Edwin Schallert, "While the Films Reel By," *Los Angeles Times* (June 20, 1943): C3; Lucy Greenbaum, "'A Sinatra in a Sombrero,'" *New York Times* (November 4, 1945): SM21; Thomas M. Pryor, "By Way of Report," *New York Times* (November 28, 1943): X3.

10. Stanfield, *Horse Opera*, 154.

11. Quote from George A. Mooney, "Youth's Model 1940," *New York Times* (October 27, 1940): 140; Phillips, *Singing Cowboy Stars*; Sherman, *Legendary Singing Cowboys*;

Stanfield, "Dixie Cowboys and Blue Yodels," 96–118; Tan, "The New Deal Cowboy"; Loy, *Westerns and American Culture, 1930–1955*; Stanfield, *Horse Opera*; Loy, "Soldiers in Stetsons."

12. Ibid.

13. Schivelbusch, *Three New Deals*; Billington and Jackson, *Big Dams of the New Deal Era*.

14. Gans, *Popular Culture and High Culture*, 115–19.

# Bibliography

### Archival Sources

Autry, Gene. Papers. Autry National Center of the American West. Los Angeles, California.
Autry, Gene. Papers. Gene Autry Entertainment. Studio City, California.
Carlin, Esther. Papers. Gene Autry Oklahoma Museum Collections. Gene Autry Oklahoma Museum. Gene Autry, Oklahoma.
Condon, Edward J. Unpublished manuscript. n.d. Sears Foundation Collection. Sears. Chicago, Illinois.
Preisler, Dennis. "Sears Public Relations Goes Electronic: The Birth of Radio Station WLS." Unpublished manuscript. Author's collection.
Roosevelt, Franklin D. Papers as President: The President's Personal File, Part 18: PPF 8501-9000, 1933-1945. Franklin D. Roosevelt Presidential Library & Museum.
Satherly, Art. Interview. n.d. Oral History Project. Country Music Hall of Fame & Museum, Nashville, Tennessee.

### Public Documents

#### United States

U.S. Bureau of Agricultural Economics. *Changing Technology and Employment in Agriculture.* New York: Da Capo Press, 1973.
U.S. Bureau of Mines. *Time Required in Developing Selected Arizona Copper Mines.* Washington, D.C.: Government Printing Office, 1976.

U.S. Bureau of the Census. Economics and Statistics Administration. *Radio Set Ownership, 1930.* Prepared by the Geography Division. Bureau of the Census. Washington, D.C.: Government Printing Office, 1930.

U.S. Congress. House. Committee on Natural Resources. *Consumer Incomes in the United States: Their Distribution in 1935–1936.* New York: Da Capo Press, 1972.

———. *The Structure of the American Economy.* New York: Da Capo Press, 1972.

———. *Regional Factors in National Planning and Development.* New York: Da Capo Press, 1974.

———. *The Changing Needs of the West: Oversight Hearing before the Committee on Natural Resources, House of Representatives, One Hundred Third Congress, Second Session . . . Hearing Held in Salt Lake City, UT, April 7, 1994.* Washington, DC: Government Printing Office, 1994.

———. *The Evolving West: Oversight Hearing Before the Committee on Natural Resources, U.S. House of Representatives, One Hundred Tenth Congress, First Session, February 28, 2007.* Washington, D.C.: Government Printing Office, 2007.

U.S. Congress. House. Select Committee to Investigate the Interstate Migration of Destitute Citizens. *Interstate Migration: Report of the Select Committee to Investigate the Interstate Migration of Destitute Citizens.* New York: Da Capo Press, 1976.

U.S. Congress. Senate. Committee on Foreign Relations. *American Foreign Policy: Basic Documents, 1941–1949.* 1950. Reprint, New York: Arno Press, 1971.

U.S. Federal Emergency Relief Administration. *Final Statistical Report of the Federal Emergency Relief Administration.* New York: Da Capo Press, 1972.

U.S. Federal Theatre Project. *Federal Theatre Plays.* 1938. Reprint, New York: Da Capo Press, 1973.

U.S. National Resources Planning Board. Committee on Long-range Work and Relief Policies. *Security, Work, and Relief Policies; Report.* New York: Da Capo Press, 1973.

U.S. National Resources Planning Board. Public Works Committee. *The Economic Effects of the Federal Public Works Expenditures, 1933–1938.* New York: Da Capo Press, 1975.

U.S. Work Projects Administration. *Urban Workers on Relief.* New York: Da Capo Press, 1971.

———. *Changing Aspects of Urban Relief.* New York: Da Capo Press, 1974.

## United Kingdom

Great Britain. United States Embassy. *Confidential Dispatches; Analyses of America by the British Ambassador, 1939–1945.* 1973. Reprint, Evanston, Ill.: New University Press 1974.

## State and Local Governments

Collins, William S. *The New Deal in Arizona.* Phoenix: Arizona State Parks Board, 1999.

Texas. Good Neighbor Commission. *Handbook compiled by Myrtle L. Tanner, Acting Executive Director in Collaboration with Mrs. George W. Stevens, Consultant and President of the Local Good Neighbor Council of Forth Worth.* Austin, Texas, 1954.

———. *Texas Migrant Labor: A Special Report to the Governor and Legislature.* Austin: The Commission, 1977.

Texas. Inter-agency Task Force on Migrant Labor. *Special Report: Prepared for Governor Preston Smith by the Good Neighbor Commission of Texas.* Austin, Texas, 1970.

## Books

Abbott, Carl. *The Metropolitan Frontier: Cities in the Modern American West.* Tucson: University of Arizona Press, 1993.

———. *How Cities Won the West: Four Centuries of Urban Change in Western North America.* Albuquerque: University of New Mexico Press, 2008.

Aden, Roger C. *Popular Stories and Promised Lands: Fan Cultures and Symbolic Pilgrimages.* Tuscaloosa: University of Alabama Press, 1999.

Adkinson, Burton W. *Two Centuries of Federal Information.* Stroudsburg, Penn.: Dowden, Hutchinson & Ross, 1978.

Albarran, Alan B. *The Radio Broadcasting Industry.* Boston, Mass.: Allyn and Bacon, 2001.

Allen, Michael. *Rodeo Cowboys in the North American Imagination.* Reno: University of Nevada Press, 1998.

Allmendinger, Blake. *Imagining the African American West.* Lincoln: University of Nebraska Press, 2005.

Alter, Jonathan. *The Defining Moment: FDR's Hundred Days and the Triumph of Hope.* New York: Simon & Schuster, 2006.

Alvarez, David J. *Secret Messages: Codebreaking and American Diplomacy, 1930–1945.* Lawrence: University Press of Kansas, 2000.

Ambrose, Stephen E. *Rise to Globalism: American Foreign Policy since 1938.* New York: Penguin Books, 1997.

Amenta, Edwin. *Bold Relief: Institutional Politics and the Origins of Modern American Social Policy.* Princeton, N.J.: Princeton University Press, 1998.

American Historical Association. Historical Service Board. *Canada, Our Oldest Good Neighbor . . .* Madison, Wis.: United States Armed Forces Institute, 1946.

Anderson, Mark Cronlund. *Cowboy Imperialism and Hollywood Film.* New York: Peter Lang, 2007.

Anderson, Tim J. *Making Easy Listening: Material Culture and Postwar American Recording.* Minneapolis: University of Minnesota Press, 2006.

Aquila, Richard, ed. *Wanted Dead or Alive: the American West in Popular Culture.* Urbana: University of Illinois Press, 1996.

———. "Introduction." *Wanted Dead or Alive: The American West in Popular Culture,* edited by Richard Aquila. Urbana and Chicago: University of Illinois Press, 1996.

Arndt, Richard T. *The First Resort of Kings: American Cultural Diplomacy in the Twentieth Century.* Washington, D.C.: Potomac Books, 2005.

Arnold, Joseph L. *The New Deal in the Suburbs; A History of the Greenbelt Town Program, 1935–1954.* Columbus: Ohio State University Press, 1971.

Arnold, Oren, ed. *Roundup, a Collection of Western Stories, Poems, Articles for Young People.* Dallas, Texas: B. Upshaw and Company, 1937.

Aron, Cindy S. *Working at Play: A History of the United States.* New York: Oxford University Press, 1999.

Arrington, Leonard J. *Utah, the New Deal and the Depression of the 1930s.* Ogden, Utah: Weber State College Press, 1983.

Austin, Gene. *Gene Austin's ol' Buddy.* Phoenix, Ariz.: Augury Press, 1984.

Autry, Gene. *Western Stories.* New York: Dell, 1947.

———. *Gun Smoke Yarns.* New York: Dell Pub. Co., 1948.

Autry, Gene, and Mickey Herskowitz. *Back in the Saddle Again.* New York: Doubleday and Co., 1978.

Badger, Anthony J. *FDR: The First Hundred Days.* New York: Hill and Wang, 2008.

Bakken, Gordon Morris, ed. *Icons of the American West: From Cowgirls to Silicon Valley.* Westport, Conn.: Greenwood Press, 2008.

Balio, Tino. *Grand Design: Hollywood as a Modern Business Enterprise, 1930–1939.* Berkeley: University of California Press, 1995.

Balk, Alfred. *The Rise of Radio, from Marconi through the Golden Age.* Jefferson, N.C.: McFarland & Co., 2006.Banta, Martha. *Imaging American Women: Idea and Ideals in Cultural History.* New York: Columbia University Press, 1987.

Barber, William J. *Designs within Disorder: Franklin D. Roosevelt, the Economists, and the Shaping of American Economic Policy, 1933–1945.* New York: Cambridge University Press, 1996.

Barnard, Rita. *The Great Depression and the Culture of Abundance: Kenneth Fearing, Nathanael West, and Mass Culture in the 1930s.* New York: Cambridge University Press, 1995.

Barnum, Fred. *"His Master's Voice" in America: Ninety Years of Communications Pioneering and Progress: Victor Talking Machine Company, Radio Corporation of America, General Electric Company.* Camden, N.J.: General Electric Co., 1991.

Bataille, Gretchen M., and Charles L. P. Silet, eds. *The Pretend Indians: Images of Native Americans in the Movies.* Ames: Iowa State University Press, 1980.

Baughman, James L. *The Republic of Mass Culture: Journalism, Filmmaking, and Broadcasting in America since 1941.* 3rd ed. Baltimore: Johns Hopkins University Press, 2006.

Bauman, John F. *In the Eye of the Great Depression: New Deal Reporters and the Agony of the American People.* DeKalb: Northern Illinois University Press, 1988.

Baxter, John. *Hollywood in the Thirties.* New York: A. S. Barnes, 1968.

Beard, Charles Austin. *American Foreign Policy in the Making, 1932–1940; A Study in Responsibilities.* New Haven: Yale University Press, 1946.

———. *President Roosevelt and the Coming of the War, 1941: Appearances and Realities.* 1948. Reprint, New Brunswick, N.J.: Transaction Publishers, 2003.
Bennett, G. H., ed. *Roosevelt's Peacetime Administrations, 1933–41: A Documentary History of the New Deal Years.* New York: Manchester University Press, 2004.
Benson, Thomas W., ed. *American Rhetoric in the New Deal Era, 1932–1945.* East Lansing: Michigan State University Press, 2006.
Berger, Jason. *A New Deal for the World: Eleanor Roosevelt and American Foreign Policy.* Social Science Monographs Series. New York: Columbia University Press, 1981.
Bergman, Andrew. *We're in the Money: Depression America and Its Films.* New York: New York University Press, 1971.
Berkowitz, Michael. "A 'New Deal' for Leisure: Making Mass Tourism during the Great Depression." In Shelly Baranowski and Ellen Furlough, eds., *Being Elsewhere: Tourism, Consumer Culture, and Identity in Modern Europe and North America.* Ann Arbor: University of Michigan Press, 2001.
Bermingham, Peter. *The New Deal in the Southwest, Arizona and New Mexico.* Tucson: University of Arizona Museum of Art, 1980.
Beschloss, Michael R. *The Conquerors: Roosevelt, Truman, and the Destruction of Hitler's Germany, 1941–1945.* New York: Simon & Schuster, 2002.
Best, Gary Dean. *The Critical Press and the New Deal: The Press Versus Presidential Power, 1933–1938.* Westport, Conn.: Praeger, 1993.
———. *The Nickel and Dime Decade: American Popular Culture during the 1930s.* Westport, Conn.: Praeger, 1993.
———. *The Retreat from Liberalism: Collectivists Versus Progressives in the New Deal Years.* Westport, Conn.: Praeger, 2002.
———. *Peddling Panaceas: Popular Economists in the New Deal Era.* New Brunswick, N.J.: Transaction Publishers, 2007.
Billington, David P., and Donald C. Jackson. *Big Dams of the New Deal Era: A Confluence of Engineering and Politics.* Norman: University of Oklahoma Press, 2006.
Black, Conrad. *Franklin Delano Roosevelt: Champion of Freedom.* New York: Public Affairs, 2003.
Blatanis, Konstantinos. *Popular Culture Icons in Contemporary American Drama.* Madison, N.J.: Fairleigh Dickinson University Press, 2003.
Blew, Mary Clearman. *Bone Deep in Landscape: Writing, Reading, and Place.* Norman: University of Oklahoma Press, 1999.
Blonsky, Marshall. *American Mythologies.* New York: Oxford University Press, 1992.
Blue, Howard. *Words at War: World War II Era Radio Drama and the Postwar Broadcasting Industry Blacklist.* Lanham, Md.: Scarecrow Press, 2002.
Blum, John Morton. *V Was for Victory: Politics and American Culture during World War II.* New York: Harcourt Brace Jovanovich, 1976.
Bodnar, John E. *Blue-Collar Hollywood: Liberalism, Democracy, and Working People in American Film.* Baltimore: Johns Hopkins University Press, 2003.
Bogue, Allan G., Thomas D. Phillips, and James E. Wright., eds. *The West of the American People.* Itasca, Ill.: F. E. Peacock Publishers, 1970.

Boorstin, Daniel J. *The Image: A Guide to Pseudo-Events in America.* New York: Vintage Books, 1992.

Borg, Dorothy. *The United States and the Far Eastern Crisis of 1933–1938; From the Manchurian Incident through the Initial Stage of the Undeclared Sino-Japanese War.* Cambridge: Harvard University Press, 1964.

Bold, Christine. "Malaeska's revenge; or, The Dime Novel Tradition in Popular Fiction." In Richard Aquila, ed., *Wanted Dead or Alive: The American West in Popular Culture.* Urbana: University of Illinois Press, 1996.

Borne, Lawrence R. *Dude Ranching: A Complete History.* Albuquerque: University of New Mexico Press, 1983.

Brant, Irving. *Adventures in Conservation with Franklin D. Roosevelt.* 1988. Reprint, Flagstaff, Ariz.: Northland Publishing, 1989.

Brennan, John A. *Silver and the First New Deal.* Reno: University of Nevada Press, 1969.

Brewer, Stewart. *Borders and Bridges: A History of U.S.-Latin American Relations.* Westport, Conn.: Praeger Security International, 2006.

Bridger, Bobby. *Buffalo Bill and Sitting Bull: Inventing the Wild West.* Austin: University of Texas Press, 2002.

Brigham, Jay L. *Empowering the West: Electrical Politics before FDR.* Lawrence: University Press of Kansas, 1998.

Brillembourg, Carlos. *Latin American Architecture, 1929–1960: Contemporary Reflections.* New York: Monacelli Press, 2004.

Brinkley, Alan. *Liberalism and Its Discontents.* Cambridge, Mass.: Harvard University Press, 1998.

———. *Culture and Politics in the Great Depression.* Waco, Texas: Markham Press Fund, 1999.

Brock, William Ranulf. *Welfare, Democracy, and the New Deal.* New York: Cambridge University Press, 1988.

Brogan, D. W. *The Era of Franklin D. Roosevelt; A Chronicle of the New Deal and Global War.* New Haven: Yale University Press, 1950.

Browder, Laura. *Rousing the Nation: Radical Culture in Depression America.* Amherst: University of Massachusetts Press, 1998.

Brown, Michael K. *Race, Money, and the American Welfare State.* Ithaca, N.Y.: Cornell University Press, 1999.

Brown, Robert J. *Manipulating the Ether: The Power of Broadcast Radio in Thirties America.* Jefferson, N.C.: McFarland & Co., 1998.

Browne, Ray B., and Marshall W. Fishwick, eds. *The Hero in Transition.* Bowling Green, Ohio: Bowling Green University Popular Press, 1983.

Brownlow, Kevin. *The War, the West, and the Wilderness.* 1978. Reprint, New York: Random House, 1979.

Bryant, Adam. *Canada, Good Neighbor to the World.* Parsippany, N.J.: Dillon Press, 1997.

Buhite, Russell D., and David W. Levy, eds. *FDR's Fireside Chats.* Norman: University of Oklahoma Press, 1992.

———. *Douglas MacArthur: Statecraft and Stagecraft in America's East Asian Policy.* Lanham, Md.: Rowman & Littlefield Publishers, 2008.

Burbick, Joan. *Rodeo Queens and the American Dream.* New York: Public Affairs, 2002.

Burke, Robert E. *Olson's New Deal for California.* 1953. Reprint, Westport, Conn.: Greenwood Press, 1982.

Buscombe, Edward. *The BFI Companion to the Western.* London: Andre Deutsch, 1993.

Buscombe, Edward, and Roberta E. Pearson, eds. *Back in the Saddle Again: New Essays on the Western.* London: British Film Institute, 1998.

Bushnell, David. *Eduardo Santos and the Good Neighbor, 1938–1942.* Gainesville: University of Florida Press, 1967.

Butler, Anne M. *The American West: A Concise History.* Malden, Mass.: Blackwell 2008.

Butsch, Richard, ed. *For Fun and Profit: The Transformation of Leisure into Consumption.* Philadelphia: Temple University Press, 1990.

Calder, Jenni. *There Must Be a Lone Ranger: The American West in Film and in Reality.* 1974. Reprint, New York: McGraw-Hill, 1977.

Campbell, Neil. *The Cultures of the American New West.* Edinburgh: Edinburgh University Press, 2000.

Canclini, Nestor Garcia. *Consumers and Citizens: Globalization and Multicultural Conflicts.* Minneapolis:: University of Minnesota Press, 2001.

Cannon, Brian Q. *Remaking the Agrarian Dream: New Deal Rural Resettlement in the Mountain West.* Albuquerque: University of New Mexico Press, 1996.

Cantelon, Hart., and Robert Hollands, eds. *Leisure, Sport, and Working-Class Cultures: Theory and History.* Toronto, Ont.: Garamond Press, 1988.

Carlson, Paul H., ed. *The Cowboy Way: An Exploration of History and Culture.* Lubbock, Texas: Texas Tech University Press, 2000.

Carmichael, Deborah A., ed. *The Landscape of Hollywood Westerns: Ecocriticism in an American Film Genre.* Salt Lake City: University of Utah Press, 2006.

Carothers, Doris. *Chronology of the Federal Emergency Relief Administration, May 12, 1933, to December 31, 1935.* New York: Da Capo Press, 1971.

Carpenter, Ronald H. *Father Charles E. Coughlin: Surrogate Spokesman for the Disaffected.* Westport, Conn.: Greenwood Press, 1998.

Cary, Diana Serra. *The Hollywood Posse: The Story of a Gallant Band of Horsemen Who Made Movie History.* Norman: University of Oklahoma Press, 1996.

Casey, Steven. *Cautious Crusade: Franklin D. Roosevelt, American Public Opinion, and the War against Nazi Germany.* New York: Oxford University Press, 2001.

Cawelti, John G. *The Six-Gun Mystique.* Bowling Green, Ohio: Bowling Green State University Popular Press, 1984.

———. *The Six-Gun Mystique Sequel.* Bowling Green, Ohio: Bowling Green State University Popular Press, 1999.

Ceplair, Larry. *The Inquisition in Hollywood: Politics in the Film Community, 1930–1960.* Garden City, N.Y.: Anchor Press/Doubleday, 1980.

Chafe, William H., ed. *The Achievement of American Liberalism: The New Deal and Its Legacies.* New York: Columbia University Press, 2003.

Chanan, Michael. "Cinema in Latin America." In Geoffrey Nowell-Smith, ed., *The Oxford History of World Cinema.* New York: Oxford University Press, 1996.

Charles, Douglas M. *J. Edgar Hoover and the Anti-Interventionists: FBI political surveillance and the rise of the domestic security state, 1939–1945.* Columbus: Ohio State University Press, 2007.

Chesnar, Lynne. *February Fever: Historical Highlights of the First Sixty Years of the Houston Livestock Show and Rodeo, 1932–1993.* Houston, Texas: Houston Livestock Show and Rodeo, 1991.

Chierichetti, David. *Hollywood Costume Design.* New York: Harmony Books, 1976.

Childs, Marquis W. *The Farmer Takes a Hand; The Electric Power Revolution in Rural America.* 1952. Reprint, New York: Da Capo Press, 1974.

Clarke, Jeanne Nienaber. *Roosevelt's Warrior: Harold L. Ickes and the New Deal.* Baltimore: Johns Hopkins University Press, 1996.

Clawson, Marion. *New Deal Planning: The National Resources Planning Board.* Resources for the Future Series. Baltimore: Johns Hopkins University Press, 1981.

Clayton, Lawrence. *Vaqueros, Cowboys, and Buckaroos.* Austin: University of Texas Press, 2001.

Cole, Wayne S. *Senator Gerald P. Nye and American Foreign Relations.* Minneapolis: University of Minnesota Press, 1962.

———. *Roosevelt & the Isolationists, 1932–45.* Lincoln: University of Nebraska Press, 1983.

Coleman, John J. *Party Decline in America: Policy, Politics, and the Fiscal State.* Princeton, N.J.: Princeton University Press, 1996.

Corkin, Stanley. *Cowboys as Cold Warriors: The Western and U.S. History.* Philadelphia, Penn.: Temple University Press, 2004.

Corn, Joseph J. *Yesterday's Tomorrows: Past Visions of the American Future.* Baltimore: Johns Hopkins University Press, 1996.

Cotner, Thomas E., ed. *Essays in Mexican History; The Charles Wilson Hackett Memorial Volume.* Austin: University of Texas, Institute of Latin-American Studies, 1958.

Cox, Jim. *Say Goodnight, Gracie: The Last Years of Network Radio.* Jefferson, N.C.: McFarland & Co., 2002.

———. *Frank and Anne Hummert's Radio Factory: The Programs and Personalities of Broadcasting's Most Prolific Producers.* Jefferson, N.C.: McFarland Co. Publishers, 2003.

———. *Music Radio: The Great Performers and Programs of the 1920s through Early 1960s.* Jefferson, N.C.: McFarland & Co., 2005.

———. *Sold on Radio: Advertisers in the Golden Age of Broadcasting.* Jefferson, N.C.: McFarland & Co., 2008.

———. *American Radio Networks: A History.* Jefferson, N.C.: McFarland & Co., 2009.

Coyne, Michael. *The Crowded Prairie: American National Identity in the Hollywood Western.* New York: I. B. Tauris, 1997.

Craig, Douglas B. *Fireside Politics: Radio and Political Culture in the United States, 1920–1940*. Baltimore: Johns Hopkins University Press, 2000.Crawley, Andrew. *Somoza and Roosevelt: Good Neighbor Diplomacy in Nicaragua, 1933–1945*. New York: Oxford University Press, 2007.

Creel, George. *How We Advertised America: The First Telling of the Amazing Story of the Committee on Public Information that Carried the Gospel of Americanism to Every corner of the Globe*. New York: Harper & Brothers Publishers, 1920.

Cross, Robin. *The Big Book of B Movies, or, How Low Was My Budget*. New York: St. Martin's Press, 1982.

Crownover, A. Blair. *Franklin D. Roosevelt and the Primary Campaigns of the 1938 Congressional Election*. Princeton: Princeton University Press, 1955.

Culver, John C. *American Dreamer: The Life and Times of Henry A. Wallace*. New York: Norton, 2000.

Currell, Susan., and Christina Cogdell, eds. *Popular Eugenics: National Efficiency and American Mass Culture in the 1930s*. Athens: Ohio University Press, 2006.

Cusic, Don. *Gene Autry: His Life and Career*. Jefferson, N.C.: McFarland & Co., 2007.

———. *Discovering Country Music*. Westport, Conn.: Praeger, 2008.

Cutler, Phoebe. *The Public Landscape of the New Deal*. New Haven: Yale University Press, 1985.

Dallek, Robert. *Lone Star Rising: Lyndon Johnson and His Times, 1908–1960*. New York: Oxford University Press, 1991.

———. *Franklin D. Roosevelt and American Foreign Policy, 1932–1945: With a New Afterword*. 1979. Reprint, New York: Oxford University Press, 1995.

Daniel, Cletus E. *Chicano Workers and the Politics of Fairness: The FEPC in the Southwest, 1941–1945*. Austin: University of Texas Press, 1991.

Dary, David. *Cowboy Culture: A Saga of Five Centuries*. Lawrence: University Press of Kansas, 1989.

Das, Taraknath. *Foreign Policies of President Franklin D. Roosevelt*. Calcutta, India: Calcutta University Press, 1934.

Davis, Ronald L. *The Glamour Factory: Inside Hollywood's Big Studio System*. Dallas, Texas: Southern Methodist University Press, 1993.

Davis, Robert Murray. *Playing Cowboys: Low Culture and High Art in the Western*. Norman: University of Oklahoma Press, 1992.

Dawley, Alan. *Struggles for Justice: Social Responsibility and the Liberal State*. Cambridge, Mass.: Belknap Press of Harvard University Press, 1991.

Dawson, Patrick. *Mr. Rodeo: The Big Bronc Years of Leo Cremer*. Livingston, MT: Cayuse Press, 1986.

Day, Timothy. *A Century of Recorded Music: Listening to Musical History*. New Haven, Conn.: Yale University Press, 2000.

De Voto, Bernard Augustine. *The Western Paradox: a Conservation Reader*. New Haven, Conn.: Yale University Press, 2000.

Dean, Frank E. *Cowboy Fun*. New York: Sterling Publishing Co., 1980.

Dick, Bernard F. *The Star-Spangled Screen: The American World War II Film*. Lexington, KY: University Press of Kentucky, 1996.

Dinerstein, Joel. *Swinging the Machine: Modernity, Technology, and African American Culture between the World Wars*. Amherst: University of Massachusetts Press, 2003.

Divine, Robert A. *The Illusion of Neutrality*. Chicago: University of Chicago Press, 1962.

———. *Roosevelt and World War II*. Baltimore: Johns Hopkins Press, 1969.

Dixon, Wheeler Winston. ed. *American Cinema of the 1940s: Themes and Variations*. New Brunswick, N.J.: Rutgers University Press, 2006.

Dizard, Wilson P., Jr. *Old Media, New Media: Mass Communications in the Information Age*. 3rd ed. New York: Longman, 2000.

———. *Digital Diplomacy: U.S. Foreign Policy in the Information Age*. Published with the cooperation of the Center for Strategic and International Studies. Westport, Conn.: Praeger Publishers, 2001.

———. *Inventing Public Diplomacy: The Story of the U.S. Information Agency*. Boulder, Colo.: Lynne Rienner, 2004

Dizikes, John. *Britain, Roosevelt, and the New Deal: British Opinion, 1932–1938*. New York: Garland Publishing, 1979.

Doenecke, Justus D. *From Isolation to War: 1931–1941*. Wheeling, Ill.: Harlan Davidson, 2003.

———. *Debating Franklin D. Roosevelt's Foreign Policies, 1933–1945*. Lanham, Md.: Rowman & Littlefield, 2005.

Doherty, Thomas Patrick. *Projections of War: Hollywood, American Culture, and World War II*. New York: Columbia University Press, 1999.

Dorst, John Darwin. *Looking West*. Philadelphia: University of Pennsylvania Press, 1999.

Douglas, Susan J. *Inventing American Broadcasting, 1899–1922*. Baltimore: Johns Hopkins University Press, 1987.

———. *Listening In: Radio and the American Imagination*. Minneapolis: University of Minnesota Press, 2004.

Drucker, Susan J., and Robert S. Cathcart. *American Heroes in a Media Age*. Cresskill, N.J.: Hampton Press, 1994.

Drummond, Donald Francis. *The Passing of American Neutrality, 1937–1941*. Ann Arbor: University of Michigan Press, 1955.

Druxman, Michael B. *The Musical: From Broadway to Hollywood*. South Brunswick N.J.: A. S. Barnes, 1980.

Duchemin, Michael. "Destinations of Choice: National Parks, Auto Tourism, and *Westways* Magazine." In Matthew Roth, ed., *Scenic View Ahead: The* Westways *Cover Art Program, 1928–1981*. Los Angeles: Automobile Club of Southern California.

Dulles, Foster Rhea. *America Learns to Play: A History of Popular Recreation* (New York: D. Appleton-Century Company, 1940.

Dutton, Monte. *True to the Roots: Americana Music Revealed*. Lincoln: University of Nebraska Press, 2006.

Edsforth, Ronald. *The New Deal: America's Response to the Great Depression.* Malden, Mass.: Blackwell Publishers, 2000.

Elkins, Andrew. *Another Place: An Ecocritical Study of Selected Western American Poets.* Fort Worth: Texas Christian University Press, 2002.

Erickson, John R. *The Modern Cowboy.* Denton, Texas: University of North Texas Press, 2004.

Escott, Colin. *Lost Highway: The True Story of Country Music.* Washington, D.C.: Smithsonian Books, 2003.

Eskenazi, Gerald. *I Hid It Under the Sheets: Growing Up with Radio.* Columbia: University of Missouri Press, 2005.

Esperdy, Gabrielle M. *Modernizing Main Street: Architecture and Consumer Culture in the New Deal.* Chicago: University of Chicago Press, 2008.

Etulain, Richard W., ed. *Myths and the American West.* Manhattan, Kan.: Sunflower University Press, 1998.

———. *The American West: a Modern History, 1900 to the Present.* Lincoln: University of Nebraska Press, 2007.

Etulaine, Richard W., and Ferenc Morton Szasz, eds. *The American West in 2000: Essays in Honor of Gerald D. Nash.* Albuquerque: University of New Mexico Press, 2003.

Evans, James. *Prairie Farmer and WLS: The Burridge D. Butler Years.* Urbana: University of Illinois Press, 1969.

Fagette, Paul. *Digging for Dollars: American Archaeology and the New Deal.* Albuquerque: University of New Mexico, 1996.

Farnham, Barbara. *Roosevelt and the Munich Crisis: A Study of Political Decision-Making.* Princeton, N.J.: Princeton University Press, 1997.

Farnham, Rebecca Tufts. *Effects of the Works Program on Rural Relief; A Survey of Rural Relief Cases Closed in Seven States, July through November, 1935.* New York: Da Capo Press, 1971.

Feinman, Ronald L. *Twilight of Progressivism: The Western Republican Senators and the New Deal.* Baltimore: Johns Hopkins University Press, 1981.

Fejes, Fred. *Imperialism, Mexico, and the Good Neighbor: New Deal Foreign Policy and United States Shortwave Broadcasting to Latin America, 1900–1939.* Norwood, N.J.: Ablex Publishing Corporation, 1986.

Fellow, Anthony R. *American Media History.* Belmont, Calif.: Thomson/Wadsworth, 2005.

Fenin, George N. *The Western, from Silents to Cinerama.* New York: Orion Press, 1962.

———. *The Western, from Silents to the Seventies.* 1973. Reprint, New York: Penguin Books, 1977.

Fernlund, Kevin J., ed. *The Cold War American West, 1945–1989.* Albuquerque: University of New Mexico Press, 1998.

Fife, Austin E. *Heaven on Horseback: Revivalist Songs and Verse in the Cowboy Idiom.* Logan: Utah State University Press, 1989.

Finegold, Kenneth. *State and Party in America's New Deal.* Madison: University of Wisconsin Press, 1995.

Finer, Herman. *The T.V.A.: Lessons for International Application.* New York: Da Capo Press, 1972.

Fishwick, Marshall William. *Seven Pillars of Popular Culture.* Westport, Conn.: Greenwood Press, 1985.

Flynn, Kathryn A. *The New Deal: A 75th Anniversary Celebration.* Layton, Utah: Gibbs Smith, 2008.

Folkerts, Jean. *Voices of a Nation: A History of Mass Media in the United States.* 5th ed. Boston: Pearson/Allyn and Bacon, 2008.

Forrest, Suzanne. *The Preservation of the Village: New Mexico's Hispanics and the New Deal.* 1989. Reprint, Albuquerque: University of New Mexico, 1998.

Fox, Claire F. *The Fence and the River: Culture and Politics at the U.S.-Mexico Border.* Minneapolis: University of Minnesota Press, 1999.

Francke, Lizzie. *Script Girls: Women Screenwriters in Hollywood.* New York: British Film Institute, 1994.

Fredriksson, Kristine. *American Rodeo: From Buffalo Bill to Big Business.* College Station: Texas A & M University Press, 1985.

French, Philip. *Westerns: Aspects of a Movie Genre.* New York: Oxford University Press, 1977.

Frezza, Daria. *The Leader and the Crowd: Democracy in American Public Discourse, 1880–1941.* Athens: University of Georgia Press, 2007.

Friedman, Max Paul. *Nazis and Good Neighbors: The United States Campaign against the Germans of Latin America in World War II.* New York: Cambridge University Press, 2003.

Friedrich, Otto. *City of Nets: A Portrait of Hollywood in the 1940s.* Berkeley: University of California Press, 1997.

Fry, Phillip L. *Texas Country Singers.* Ft. Worth, Texas: TCU Press, 2008.

Funigiello, Philip J. *Toward a National Power Policy; The New Deal and the Electric Utility Industry, 1933–1941.* Pittsburgh, Penn.: University of Pittsburgh Press 1973.

Furia, Philip. *The Poets of Tin Pan Alley: A History of America's Great Lyricists.* New York: Oxford University Press, 1990.

Fusfeld, Daniel Roland. *The Economic Thought of Franklin D. Roosevelt and the Origins of the New Deal.* 1954. Reprint, New York: Columbia University Press, 1956.

Fyne, Robert. *The Hollywood Propaganda of World War II.* Metuchen, N.J.: Scarecrow Press, 1994.

Gaard, Greta Claire. *The Nature of Home: Taking Root in a Place.* Tucson: University of Arizona Press, 2007.

Gamson, Joshua. *Claims to Fame: Celebrity in Contemporary America.* Berkeley: University of California Press, 1994.

Gans, Herbert J. *Popular Culture and High Culture: An Analysis and Evaluation of Taste.* 1974. Revised edition, New York: Basic Books, 1999.

García, Mario T. *Mexican Americans: Leadership, Ideology & Identity, 1930–1960.* New Haven: Yale University Press, 1989.

Garrett, Charles Hiroshi. *Struggling to Define a Nation: American Music and the Twentieth Century*. Berkeley: University of California Press: The Roth Family Foundation Music in American Endowment imprint, 2008.
Garrett, Garet. *Salvos against the New Deal: Selections from the Saturday Evening Post, 1933–1940*. Caldwell, ID: Caxton Press, 2002.
———. *Defend America First: the Antiwar Editorials of the Saturday Evening Post, 1939–1942*. Caldwell, ID: Caxton Press, 2003.
Gary, Brett. *The Nervous Liberals: Propaganda Anxieties from World War I to the Cold War*. New York: Columbia University Press, 1999.
Gellman, Irwin F. *Roosevelt and Batista; Good Neighbor Diplomacy in Cuba, 1933–1945*. Albuquerque: University of New Mexico Press, 1973.
———. *Good Neighbor Diplomacy: United States Policies in Latin America, 1933–1945*. Baltimore: Johns Hopkins University Press, 1979.
———. *Secret Affairs: Franklin Roosevelt, Cordell Hull, and Sumner Welles*. Baltimore: Johns Hopkins University Press, 1995.
George-Warren, Holly. *Public Cowboy No. 1: The Life and Times of Gene Autry*. New York: Oxford University Press, 2007.
Gilmore, John. *LA Despair: A Landscape of Crime & Bad Times*. Los Angeles: Amok Books, 2005.
Glantz, Mary E. *FDR and the Soviet Union: the President's Battles over Foreign Policy*. Lawrence: University Press of Kansas, 2005.
Goodale, Thomas L., and Geoffrey C. Godbey. *The Evolution of Leisure: Historical and Philosophical Perspectives*. State College, Penn.: Venture Publishing, 1988.
Goodwin, Doris Kearns. *No Ordinary Time: Franklin and Eleanor Roosevelt: The Home Front in World War II*. New York: Simon & Schuster, 1994.
Gordon, Colin. *New Deals: Business, Labor, and Politics in America, 1920–1935*. New York: Cambridge University Press, 1994.
Gourley, Catherine. *Rosie and Mrs. America: Perceptions of Women in the 1930s and 1940s*. Minneapolis: Twenty-First Century Books, 2008.
Graff, Frank Warren. *Strategy of Involvement: A Diplomatic Biography of Sumner Welles*. New York: Garland, 1988.
Green, David. *The Containment of Latin America; A History of the Myths and Realities of the Good Neighbor Policy*. Chicago: Quadrangle Books, 1971.
Green, Douglas B. *Singing in the Saddle: History of the Singing Cowboys*. Nashville, Tenn.: The Country Music Foundation Press and Vanderbilt University Press, 2002.
———. *Singing Cowboys*. Layton, Utah: Gibbs Smith, 2006.
Green, Fitzhugh. *American Propaganda Abroad*. New York: Hippocrene Books, 1988.
Greer, Thomas H. *What Roosevelt Thought: The Social and Political Ideas of Franklin D. Roosevelt*. East Lansing, Mich.: Michigan State University Press, 2000.
Gressley, Gene M., ed. *The American West: A Reorientation*. Laramie: University of Wyoming, 1966.
———. *The Twentieth-Century American West: A Potpourri*. Columbia: University of Missouri Press, 1977.

Groves, Melody. *Ropes, Reins, and Rawhide: All about Rodeo*. Albuquerque: University of New Mexico Press, 2006.

Grow, Michael. *The Good Neighbor Policy and Authoritarianism in Paraguay: United States Economic Expansion and Great-Power Rivalry in Latin America during World War II*. Lawrence: Regents Press of Kansas, 1981.

Grubbs, Donald H. *Cry from the Cotton: The Southern Tenant Farmers' Union and the New Deal*. Fayetteville: University of Arkansas Press, 2000.

Gruber, Jonathan. *Faith-Based Charity and Crowd Out during the Great Depression*. Cambridge, Mass.: National Bureau of Economic Research, 2005.

Guerrant, Edward O. *Roosevelt's Good Neighbor Policy*. Albuquerque: University of New Mexico Press, 1950.

Hair, William Ivy. *The Kingfish and His Realm: the Life and Times of Huey P. Long*. Baton Rouge: Louisiana State University Press, 1991.

Halper, Donna L. *Radio Music Directing*. Boston: Focal Press, 1991.

Halverson, Cathryn. *Maverick Autobiographies: Women Writers and the American West, 1900–1936*. Madison: University of Wisconsin Press, 2004.

Hamilton, David E. *From New Day to New Deal: American Farm Policy from Hoover to Roosevelt, 1928–1933*. Chapel Hill: University of North Carolina Press, 1991.

Handel, Leo A. *Hollywood Looks at Its Audience: A Report of Film Audience Research*. 1950. Reprint, New York: Arno Press, 1976.

Handlin, Oscar. *The Distortion of America*. Boston: Little, Brown, 1981.

Hanson, Philip. *This Side of Despair: How the Movies and American Life Intersected during the Great Depression*. Madison, N.J.: Fairleigh Dickinson University Press, 2008.

Hareven, Tamara K. *Eleanor Roosevelt: An American Conscience*. New York: Da Capo Press, 1975.

Hariman, Robert. *No Caption Needed: Iconic Photographs, Public Culture, and Liberal Democracy*. Chicago: University of Chicago Press, 2007.

Hark, Ina Rae, ed. *American Cinema of the 1930s: Themes and Variations*. New Brunswick, N.J.: Rutgers University Press, 2007.

Harkin, Anthony. *Hillbilly: A Cultural History of an American Icon*. New York: Oxford University Press, 2005.

Harris, Jonathan. *Federal Art and National Culture: The Politics of Identity in New Deal America*. New York: Cambridge University Press, 1995.

Harris, Neil. *Cultural Excursions: Marketing Appetites and Cultural Tastes in Modern America*. Chicago: University of Chicago Press, 1990.

Hart, David M. *Forged Consensus: Science, Technology, and Economic Policy in the United States, 1921–1953*. Princeton, N.J.: Princeton University Press, 1998.

Haslam, Gerald W. *Workin' Man Blues: Country Music in California*. Berkeley: Heyday Books, 2005.

Hawley, Ellis W. *The New Deal and the Problem of Monopoly: A Study in Economic Ambivalence*. New York: Fordham University Press, 1995.

Hayes, Dade. *Open Wide: How Hollywood Box Office Became a National Obsession*. New York: Miramax Books/Hyperion, 2004.

Hayes, Lynton R. *Energy, Economic Growth, and Regionalism in the West.* Albuquerque: University of New Mexico Press, 1980.
Heale, M. J. *Franklin D. Roosevelt: The New Deal and War.* New York: Routledge, 1999.
Hearden, Patrick J. *Architects of Globalism: Building a New World Order during World War II.* Fayetteville: University of Arkansas Press, 2002.
Heide, Robert. *Home Front America: Popular Culture of the World War II Era.* San Francisco: Chronicle Books, 1995.
Heil, Alan L., Jr. *Voice of America.* New York: Columbia University Press, 2003.
Henderson Henry L., and David B. Woolner, eds. *FDR and the Environment.* New York: Palgrave Macmillan, 2005.
Hendrickson, Jr., Kenneth E. *The Life and Presidency of Franklin Delano Roosevelt: An Annotated Bibliography.* Lanham, Md.: Scarecrow Press, 2005.
Herzberg, Bob. *Shooting Scripts: From Pulp Western to Film.* Jefferson, N.C.: McFarland & Co., 2005.
Hill, Edwin G. *In the Shadow of the Mountain: The Spirit of the CCC.* Pullman: Washington State University Press, 1990.
Hilmes, Michele. *Hollywood and Broadcasting: From Radio to Cable.* Urbana: University of Illinois Press, 1990.
———. *Radio Voices: American Broadcasting, 1922–1952.* Minneapolis: University of Minnesota Press, 1997.
Hirschhorn, Clive. *The Hollywood Musical.* New York: Crown, 1981.
Hitt, Jim. *The American West from Fiction (1823–1976) into Film (1909–1986).* Jefferson, N.C.: McFarland & Co., 1990.
Hoefer, Jacqueline. *A More Abundant Life: New Deal Artists and Public Art in New Mexico.* Santa Fe, N.M.: Sunstone Press, 2003.
Hogeboom, Amy. *The Boys' Book of the West.* New York: Lothrop, Lee and Shepard Company, 1946.
Holbo, Paul Sothe, ed. *Isolationism and Interventionism, 1932–1941.* Chicago: Rand McNally, 1967.
Holley, Donald. *Uncle Sam's Farmers: The New Deal Communities in the Lower Mississippi Valley.* Urbana: University of Illinois Press, 1975.
Holli, Melvin G. *The Wizard of Washington: Emil Hurja, Franklin Roosevelt, and the Birth of Public Opinion Polling.* New York: Palgrave, 2002.
Holmes, Thom, ed. *The Routledge Guide to Music Technology.* New York: Routledge, 2006.
Holsinger, Paul, ed. *War and American Popular Culture: A Historical Encyclopedia.* Santa Barbara, Calif.: Greenwood Publishing Group, 1999.
Hoopes, Townsend. *FDR and the Creation of the U.N.* New Haven: Yale University Press, 1997.
Horkheimer, Max., Theodor W. Adorno and Gunzelin Schmid Noerr. "The Culture Industry: Enlightenment as Mass Deception." In *Dialectic of Enlightenment: Philosophical Fragments.* Palo Alto, Calif.: Stanford University Press, 2002.
Horowitz, David., and Laurence Jarvik, eds. *Public Broadcasting and the Public Trust.* Los Angeles, Calif.: Center for the Study of Popular Culture, 1995.

Horten, Gerd. *Radio Goes to War: The Cultural Politics of Propaganda during World War II.* Berkeley: University of California Press, 2002.

Houck, Davis W. *FDR and Fear Itself: the First Inaugural Address.* College Station: Texas A&M University Press, 2002.

Hough, Emerson. *The Story of the Cowboy.* New York: D. Appleton, 1897.

Hull, Cordell. *The Memoirs of Cordell Hull.* New York: Macmillan Co., 1948.

Hurst, Robert M. *Republic Pictures: Between Poverty Row and the Majors.* Updated edition, Lanham, Md.: The Scarecrow Press, 2007.

Hurt, R. Douglas, ed. *The Rural West since World War II.* Lawrence: University Press of Kansas, 1998.

Ibrahim, Hilmi. *Leisure and Society: A Comparative Approach.* Dubuque, Iowa: Wm. C. Brown Publishers, 1991.

Ike, Roberto Marie. *Advocacy Coalition and Welfare Policy: Analyzing Coalition Consensus.* Lanham, Md.: University Press of America, 2007.

Jablon, Howard. *Crossroads of Decision: The State Department and Foreign Policy, 1933–1937.* Lexington: University Press of Kentucky, 1983.

Jacobs, Del. *Revisioning Film Traditions: The Pseudo-Documentary and the NeoWestern.* Lewiston, N.Y.: Mellen Press, 2000.

Jakle, John A. *The Tourist: Travel in Twentieth-century North America.* Lincoln: University of Nebraska Press, 1985.

Jarvie, I. C. *Hollywood's Overseas Campaign: The North Atlantic Movie Trade, 1920–1950.* New York: Cambridge University Press, 1992.

Jeansonne, Glen. *Messiah of the Masses: Huey P. Long and the Great Depression.* New York: HarperCollins College Publishers, 1993.

———. *Women of the Far Right: the Mothers' Movement and World War II.* Chicago: University of Chicago Press, 1996.

Jenkins, Henry. *Convergence Culture: Where Old and New Media Collide.* New York: New York University Press, 2006.

Jensen, Joli. *The Nashville Sound: Authenticity, Commercialization, and Country Music.* Nashville, Tenn.: Vanderbilt University Press, 1998.

Jewell, Richard B. *The Golden Age of Cinema: Hollywood, 1929–1945.* Malden, Mass.: Blackwell Publishing, 2007.

Johnson, Michael L. *New Westers: The West in Contemporary American Culture.* Lawrence: University Press of Kansas, 1996.

———. *Hunger for the Wild: America's Obsession with the Untamed West.* Lawrence: University Press of Kansas, 2007.

Johnston, William M. *Celebrations: The Cult of Anniversaries in Europe and the United States Today.* New Brunswick, N.J.: Transaction Publishers, 1991.

Jonas, Manfred. *Isolationism in America, 1935–1941.* Ithaca, N.Y.: Cornell University Press, 1966.

Jones, Alfred Haworth. *Roosevelt's Image Brokers; Poets, Playwrights, and the Use of the Lincoln Symbol.* Port Washington, N.Y.: Kennikat Press, 1974.

Jones, Jesse H. *Fifty Billion Dollars: My Thirteen Years with the RFC, 1932–1945*. New York: Macmillan, 1951.
Jones, Ken D. *Hollywood at War, the American Motion Picture and World War II*. South Brunswick, N.J.: A. S. Barnes, 1973.
Joseph, Peniel E., ed. *Freedom North: Black Freedom Struggles Outside the South, 1940–1980*. 2003. Reprint, New York: Routledge, 2006.
Jowett, Garth. *Film: The Democratic Art: Social history of American Film*. Boston: Little, Brown and Co., 1976.
Justman, Stewart. *Fool's Paradise: The Unreal World of Pop Psychology*. Chicago: Ivan R. Dee, 2005.
Kalfatovic, Martin R. *The New Deal Fine Arts Projects: A Bibliography, 1933–1992*. Metuchen, N.J.: Scarecrow Press, 1994.
Kammen, Michael G. *American Culture, American Tastes: Social Change and the 20th Century*. New York: Knopf, 1999.
Kane, Kathryn. *Visions of War: Hollywood Combat Films of World War II*. Ann Arbor, Mich.: UMI Research Press, 1982.
Karl, Barry Dean. *Executive Reorganization and Reform in the New Deal: The Genesis of Administrative Management, 1900–1939*. 1963. Reprint, Chicago: University of Chicago Press, 1979.
Katz, Ephraim., and Ronald Dean Nolan. *The Film Encyclopedia*. Sixth edition, New York: Harper Collins, 2003.
Kavanaugh, Gaynor. *History Curatorship*. Washington, D.C.: Smithsonian Institution Press, 1990.
Keith, Michael C. *Sounds in the Dark: All-Night Radio in American Life*. Ames, Iowa: Iowa State University Press, 2001.
Kennedy, David M. *Freedom from Fear: The American People in Depression and War, 1929–1945*. New York: Oxford University Press, 2004.
Kenney, William Howland. *Recorded Music in American Life the Phonograph and Popular Memory, 1890–1945*. New York: Oxford University Press, 1999.
Kiewe, Amos. *FDR's First Fireside Chat: Public Confidence and the Banking Crisis*. College Station: Texas A&M University Press, 2007.
Kilpatrick, Carroll, ed. *Roosevelt and Daniels, a Friendship in Politics*. Chapel Hill: University of North Carolina Press, 1952.
Kimball, Warren F. *The Juggler: Franklin Roosevelt as Wartime Statesman*. Princeton, N.J.: Princeton University Press, 1991.
King, Frank M. *Mavericks; The Salty Comments of an Old-time Cowpuncher*. Pasadena, Calif.: Trail's End Publishing Co., 1947.
Kingrea, Nellie Ward. *History of the First Ten Years of the Texas Good Neighbor Commission, and Discussion of Its Major Problems*. Fort Worth: Texas Christian University Press, 1954.
Kirk, John M. *Canada-Cuba Relations: The Other Good Neighbor Policy*. Gainesville: University Press of Florida, 1997.

Kitch, Carolyn L. *The Girl on the Magazine Cover: The Origins of Visual Stereotypes in American Mass Media*. Chapel Hill: University of North Carolina Press, 2001.

Knapp, Raymond. *The American Musical and the Performance of Personal Identity*. Princeton, N.J.: Princeton University Press, 2006.

Knobloch, Frieda. *The Culture of Wilderness: Agriculture as Colonization in the American West*. Chapel Hill: University of North Carolina Press, 1996.

Knowles Thomas W., and Joe R. Lansdale, eds. *Wild West Show!* New York: Random House Value Publishing, 1994.

Kraemer, Sylvia K. *Science and Technology Policy in the United States: Open Systems in Action*. New Brunswick, N.J.: Rutgers University Press, 2006.

Krugler, David F. *The Voice of America and the Domestic Propaganda Battles, 1945–1953*. Columbia: University of Missouri Press, 2000.

La Chapelle, Peter. *Proud to Be an Okie: Cultural Politics, Country Music, and Migration to Southern California*. Berkeley: University of California Press, 2007.

Lange, Dorthea. *An American Exodus: A Record of Human Erosion*. New York: Reynal & Hitchcock, 1939.

Langer, William L. *The Challenge to Isolation; The World Crisis of 1937–1940 and American Foreign Policy*. 1952. Reprint, Gloucester, Mass.: Peter Smith, 1970.

Larsen, Lawrence Harold. *The Urban West at the End of the Frontier*. Lawrence: Regents Press of Kansas, 1978.

Lawhn, Juanita Luna, ed. *Mexico and the United States: Intercultural Relations in the Humanities*. San Antonio, Texas: San Antonio College, 1984.

Lawrence, Elizabeth Atwood. *Rodeo, an Anthropologist Looks at the Wild and the Tame*. 1982. Reprint, Chicago: University of Chicago Press, 1984.

Lawson, R. Alan, *A Commonwealth of Hope: The New Deal Response to Crisis*. Baltimore: Johns Hopkins University Press, 2006.

Lazarfeld, Paul F., and Frank N. Stanton, eds. *Radio Research, 1942–1943*. New York: Arno Press, 1979.

Lee, Katie. *Ten Thousand Goddam Cattle: A History of the American Cowboy in Song, Story, and Verse*. Albuquerque: University of New Mexico, 2001.

Leighninger, Robert D. *Long-range Public Investment: The Forgotten Legacy of the New Deal*. Colombia: University of South Carolina Press, 2007.

Lenihan, John H. *Showdown, Confronting Modern America in the Western Film*. Urbana: University of Illinois Press, 1980.

Lenthall, Bruce. *Radio's America: The Great Depression and the Rise of Modern Mass Culture*. Chicago: University of Chicago Press, 2007.

Leonelli, Elisa. *Robert Redford and the American West: A Critical Essay*. Philadelphia: Xlibris, 2007.

Lester, DeeGee. *Roosevelt Research: Collections for the Study of Theodore Franklin, and Eleanor*. Westport, Conn.: Greenwood Press, 1992.

Leuchtenburg, William Edward. *The FDR Years: on Roosevelt and his Legacy*. New York: Columbia University Press, 1995.

———. *The White House Looks South: Franklin D. Roosevelt, Harry S. Truman, Lyndon B. Johnson*. Baton Rouge: Louisiana State University Press, 2005.
Levine, Rhonda F. *Class Struggle and the New Deal: Industrial Labor, Industrial Capital, and the State*. Lawrence: University Press of Kansas, 1988.
Levy, Alan Howard. *Musical Nationalism: American Composers' Search for Identity*. Westport, Conn.: Greenwood Press, 1983.
Lewis, C. Jack. *White Horse, Black Hat: A Quarter Century on Hollywood's Poverty Row*. Lanham, Md.: Scarecrow Press, 2002.
Lewis, George H., ed. *All that Glitters: Country Music in America*. Bowling Green, Ohio: Bowling Green State University Popular Press, 1993.
Lindenmeyer, Kriste. *The Greatest Generation Grows Up: American Childhood in the 1930s*. Chicago: Ivan R. Dee, 2005.
Lingenfelter, Richard E., comp. *Songs of the American West*. Berkeley: University of California Press, 1968.
Lipsitz, George. *Time Passages: Collective Memory and American Popular Culture*. Minneapolis: University of Minnesota Press, 1990.
———. *Rainbow at Midnight: Labor and Culture in the 1940s*. Urbana: University of Illinois Press, 1994.
Locke, Ralph P., and Cyrilla Barr, eds. *Cultivating Music in America: Women Patrons and Activists Since 1860*. Berkeley: University of California Press, 1997.
Lord, Barry., and Gail Dexter Lord, eds. *The Manual of Museum Exhibitions* (Walnut Creek, Calif.: AltaMira Press, 2002.
Lorence, James J. *Organizing the Unemployed: Community and Union Activists in the Industrial Heartland*. Albany: State University of New York Press, 1996.
Louchheim, Katie. *The Making of the New Deal: The Insiders Speak*. Cambridge, Mass.: Harvard University Press, 1983.
Loviglio, Jason. *Radio's Intimate Public: Network Broadcasting and Mass-Mediated Democracy*. Minneapolis: University of Minnesota Press, 2005.
Lowitt, Richard. *The New Deal and the West*. 1984. The West in the Twentieth Century Series. Reprint, Norman: University of Oklahoma Press, 1993.
———. *Politics in the Postwar American West*. Norman: University of Oklahoma Press, 1995.
———. *American Outback: The Oklahoma Panhandle in the Twentieth Century*. Lubbock: Texas Tech University Press, 2006.
Loy, R. Philip. *Westerns and American Culture, 1930–1955*. Jefferson, N.C.: McFarland & Co., 2001.
———. *Westerns in a Changing America, 1955–2000*. Jefferson, N.C.: McFarland & Co., 2004.
Maciel, David R., and María Herrera-Sobek, eds. *Culture across Borders: Mexican Immigration & Popular Culture*. Tucson: University of Arizona Press, 1998.
MacCann, Richard Dyer. *The People's Films: A Political History of U.S. Government Motion Pictures*. New York: Hastings House, 1973.

MacCannell, Dean. *The Tourist: A New Theory of the Leisure Class*. 1979. Reprint, Berkeley: University of California Press, 1999.

MacKinnon, Kenneth. *Hollywood's Small Towns: An Introduction to the American Small-Town Movie*. Metuchen, N.J.: Scarecrow Press, 1984.

Magers, Boyd. *Gene Autry Westerns*. Madison, N.C.: Empire, 2007.

Maher, Neil M. *Nature's New Deal: Franklin Roosevelt, the Civilian Conservation Corps, and the Roots of the American Environmental Movement*. New York: Oxford University Press, 2007.

Mahoney, Sylvia Gann. *College Rodeo: From Show to Sport*. College Station: Texas A&M University Press, 2004.

Malden, Gregory A., ed. *Moviegoing in America: A Sourcebook in the History of Film Exhibition*. Malden, Mass.: Blackwell Publishers, 2002.

Malone, Bill C. *Singing Cowboys and Musical Mountaineers: Southern Culture and the Roosts of Country Music*. Athens: University of Georgia Press, 1993.

———. *Country Music, U.S.A.* Austin: University of Texas Press, 2002.

Malone, Michael P. *The American West: A Twentieth-Century History*. Lincoln: University of Nebraska Press, 1989.

Maney, Patrick J. *The Roosevelt Presence: The Life and Legacy of FDR*. Berkeley: University of California Press, 1998.

Marcus, Greil. *The Dustbin of History*. Cambridge, Mass.: Harvard University Press, 1995.

Marquis, Alice Goldfarb. *Hopes and Ashes: the Birth of Modern Times, 1929–1939*. New York: Free Press, 1986.

Marshall, P. David. *Celebrity and Power: Fame in Contemporary Culture*. Minneapolis: University of Minnesota Press, 1997.

Mather, Christine. *True West: Arts, Traditions, and Celebrations*. New York: C. Potter, 1992.

Matsumoto, Valerie J., and Blake Allmendinger, eds. *Over the Edge: Remapping the American West*. Berkeley: University of California Press, 1999.

Matteson, Donald W. *The Auto Radio: A Romantic Genealogy*. Jackson, Mich.: Thornridge Publishing, 1987.

McCann, Sean. *Gumshoe America: Hard-Boiled Crime Fiction and the Rise and Fall of New Deal Liberalism*. Durham, N.C.: Duke University Press, 2000.

McCarthy, Todd., and Charles Flynn. *King of the Bs: Working within the Hollywood System: An Anthology of film History and Criticism*. New York: E. P. Dutton and Company, 1975.

McClelland, Doug. *The Golden Age of "B" Movies*. 1978. Reprint, New York: Crown Publishers, 1981.

McConathy, Dale. *Hollywood Costume: Glamour, Glitter, Romance*. New York: H. N. Abrams, 1976.

McCusker, Kristine M. *Lonesome Cowgirls and Honky-tonk Angels: The Women of Barn Dance Radio*. Urbana: University of Illinois Press, 2008.

McDonald, Archie P., ed. *Shooting Stars: Heroes and Heroines of Western Film*. Bloomington: Indiana University Press, 1987.

McGee, Patrick. *From Shane to Kill Bill: Rethinking the Western.* Malden, Mass.: Blackwell Pub., 2007.
McJimsey, George T. *Harry Hopkins: Ally of the Poor and Defender of Democracy.* Cambridge, Mass.: Harvard University Press, 1987.
———. *The Presidency of Franklin Delano Roosevelt.* Lawrence: University Press of Kansas, 2000.
McKenna, Marian C. *Franklin Roosevelt and the Great Constitutional War: The Court-Packing Crisis of 1937.* New York: Fordham University Press, 2002.
McKercher, B. J. C. *Transition of Power: Britain's Loss of Global Pre-eminence to the United States, 1930–1945.* New York: Cambridge University Press, 1999.
McMahon, Kevin J. *Reconsidering Roosevelt on Race: How the Presidency Paved the Road to Brown.* Chicago: University of Chicago Press, 2004.
McWilliams, Carey. *Factories in the Field: The Story of Migratory Farm Labor in California.* 1939. Reprint, Berkeley: University of California Press, 2000.
Mertz, Paul E. *New Deal Policy and Southern Rural Poverty.* Baton Rouge: Louisiana State University Press, 1978.
Mettler, Suzanne. *Dividing Citizens: Gender and Federalism in New Deal Public Policy.* Ithaca, N.Y.: Cornell University Press, 1998.
Mickelson, Sig. *America's Other Voice: The Story of Radio Free Europe and Radio Liberty.* New York: Praeger, 1983.
Milkman, Paul. *PM: A New Deal in Journalism, 1940–1948.* New Brunswick, N.J.: Rutgers University Press, 1997.
Miller, Edward D. *Emergency Broadcasting and 1930s American Radio.* Philadelphia, Penn.: Temple University Press, 2003.
Mink, Gwendolyn. *The Wages of Motherhood: Inequality in the Welfare State, 1917–1942.* Ithaca, N.Y.: Cornell University Press, 1995.
Mitchell, Lee Clark. *Westerns: Making the Man in Fiction and Film.* Chicago: University of Chicago Press, 1996.
Mix, Tom. *The West of Yesterday, by Tom Mix, and Tony's Story, by Himself.* Los Angeles: The Times-Mirror Press, 1923.
Mooney, Booth. *Roosevelt and Rayburn; A Political Partnership.* Philadelphia, Penn.: Lippincott, 1971.
Moos, Dan. *Outside America: Race, Ethnicity, and the Role of the American West in National Belonging.* Hanover, N.H.: Dartmouth College Press, 2005.
Mora, Joseph, Jacinto. *Trail Dust and Saddle Leather.* 1946. Reprint, Lincoln: University of Nebraska Press, 1987.
Mordden, Ethan. *The Hollywood Musical.* New York, N.Y.: St. Martin's Press, 1981.
Morey, Anne. *Hollywood Outsiders: The Adaptation of the Film Industry, 1913–1934.* Minneapolis: University of Minnesota Press, 2003.
Morgan, Neil Bowen. *Westward Tilt; the American West Today.* New York: Random House, 1963.
Morris, Gregory L. *Talking Up a Storm: Voices of the New West.* Lincoln: University of Nebraska Press, 1994.

Mullen, Bill., and Sherry Lee Linkon, eds. *Radical Revisions: Rereading 1930s Culture.* Urbana: University of Illinois Press, 1996.

Murdoch, David Hamilton. *The American West: The Invention of a Myth.* Reno: University of Nevada Press, 2001.

Murray, John A. *Cinema Southwest: An Illustrated Guide to the Movies and Their Locations.* Flagstaff, Ariz.: Northland Publishing, 2000.

———. *Mythmakers of the West: Shaping America's Imagination.* Flagstaff, Ariz.: Northland Publishing, 2001.

Muscio, Giuliana. *Hollywood's New Deal.* Philadelphia, Penn.: Temple University Press, 1996.

Myers, James M. *The Bureau of Motion Pictures and Its Influence on Film Content during World War II: The Reasons for Its Failure.* Lewiston, N.Y.: Edwin Mellen Press, 1998.

Nachman, Gerald. *Raised on Radio: In Quest of the Lone Ranger. . . .* Berkeley: University of California Press, 2000.

Nareau, Bob. *Kid Kowboys: Juveniles in Western Films.* Madison, N.C.: Empire Publishing, 2003.

Nash, Gerald D. *The American West in the Twentieth Century; A Short History of an Urban Oasis.* 1973. Reprint, Englewood Cliffs, N.J.: Prentice Hall, 1977.

———. *The American West: Transformed: The Impact of the Second World War.* Lincoln: University of Nebraska Press, 1985.

Nash, Gerald D., and Richard W. Etulain, eds. *The Twentieth Century West: Historical Interpretations.* Albuquerque: University of New Mexico Press, 1989.

Nash, Gerald D. *World War II and the West: Reshaping the Economy.* Lincoln: University of Nebraska Press, 1990.

———. *The Federal Landscape: an Economic History of the Twentieth-Century West.* Tucson: University of Arizona Press, 1999.

———. *A Brief History of the American West since 1945.* Fort Worth, Texas: Harcourt College Publishers, 2001.

Neal, Steve. *Happy Days Are Here Again: The 1932 Democratic Convention, the Emergence of FDR—and How America was Changed Forever.* New York: William Morrow, 2004.

Newman, Kathy M. *Radio Active: Advertising and Consumer Activism, 1935–1947.* Berkeley: University of California Press, 2004.

Nevins, Allan. *The New Deal and World Affairs; A Chronicle of International Affairs, 1933–1945.* New Haven: Yale University Press, 1950.

Nicholas, John H. *Tom Mix, Riding Up to Glory.* Oklahoma City: National Cowboy Hall of Fame and Western Heritage Museum, 1980.

Nicholas, Liza., Elaine M. Bapis, and Thomas J. Harvey, eds. *Imagining the Big Open: Nature, Identity, and Play in the New West.* Salt Lake City: University of Utah Press, 2003.

Ninkovich, Frank A. *The Diplomacy of Ideas: U.S. Foreign Policy and Cultural Relations, 1938–1950.* New York: Cambridge University Press, 1981.

Nixon, Edgar B., ed. *Franklin D. Roosevelt and Foreign Affairs.* Cambridge, Belknap Press of Harvard University Press, 1969.

Nugent, Walter T. K. *Into the West: The Story of Its People.* New York: Random House, 1999.
Nye, Jr., Joseph S. *Soft Power: The Means to Success in World Politics.* New York: Public Affairs, 2004.
O'Brien, Charles. *Cinema's Conversion to Sound: Technology and Film Style in France and the U.S.* Bloomington: Indiana University Press, 2004.
Ohrlin, Glenn. *The Hell-Bound Train: A Cowboy Songbook.* Urbana: University of Illinois Press, 1973.
Oliker, Michael A., and Walter P. Krolikowski, eds. *Images of Youth: Popular Culture as Educational Ideology.* New York: P. Lang, 2001.
Olson, James Stuart. *Saving Capitalism: The Reconstruction Finance Corporation and the New Deal, 1933–1940.* Princeton, N.J.: Princeton University Press, 1988.
O'Meara, Doc. *The Guns of the Gunfighters: Lawmen, Outlaws & Hollywood Cowboys.* Iola, Wis.: Krause Publications, 2003.
Orgill, Roxane. *Dream Lucky: When FDR was in the White House, Count Basie Was on the Radio, and Everyone Wore a Hat.* New York: Smithsonian Books, 2008.
Orvell, Miles. *After the Machine: Visual Arts and the Erasing of Cultural Boundaries.* Jackson: University Press of Mississippi, 1995.
Paine, Jefferey Morton. *The Simplification of American Life: Hollywood Films of the 1930's.* 1972. Reprint, New York: Arno Press, 1977.
Parker, Eleanor. *Gene Autry in Public Cowboy No. 1: Retold by Eleanor Parker from the Republic Motion Picture* (Racine, Wis.: Whitman Publishing Company, 1938.
Parks, Rita. *The Western Hero in Film and Television: Mass Media Mythology.* Ann Arbor, MI: University of Michigan Research Press, 1982.
Parman, Donald Lee. *The Navajos and the New Deal.* New Haven: Yale University Press, 1976.
Parrish, Michael E. *Securities Regulation and the New Deal.* New Haven: Yale University Press, 1970.
Pasachoff, Naomi E. *Frances Perkins: Champion of the New Deal.* New York: Oxford University Press, 1999.
Patenaude, Lionel V. *Texans, Politics, and the New Deal.* New York: Garland, 1983.
Patterson, James T. *The New Deal and the States; Federalism in Transition.* Princeton, N.J.: Princeton University Press, 1969.
Pecknold, Diane. *The Selling Sound: The Rise of the Country Music Industry.* Durham, N.C.: Duke University Press, 2007.
Perkins, Dexter. *The New Age of Franklin Roosevelt, 1932–1945.* Chicago: University of Chicago Press 1957.
Perkins, Van L. *Crisis in Agriculture; The Agricultural Adjustment Administration and the New Deal, 1933.* Berkeley: University of California Press, 1969.
Perras, Galen Roger. *Franklin Roosevelt and the Origins of the Canadian-American Security Alliance, 1933–1945: Necessary, but Not Necessary Enough.* Westport, Conn.: Praeger, 1998.
Persico, Joseph E. *Roosevelt's Secret War: FDR and World War II Espionage.* New York: Random House, 2001.

Peters, Charles. *Five Days in Philadelphia: The Amazing "We want Wilkie!" Convention of 1940 and How it Freed FDR to Save the Western World.* New York: Public Affairs, 2005.

Peterson, Richard A. *Creating Country Music: Fabricating Authenticity.* Chicago: University of Chicago Press, 1997.

Pettit, Arthur G. *Images of the Mexican American in Fiction and Film.* College Station: Texas A&M University Press, 1980.

Phillips, Robert W. *Singing Cowboy Stars.* Salt Lake City, Utah: Gibbs Smith, 1994.

Phillips, Sarah T. *This Land, This Nation: Conservation, Rural America, and the New Deal.* New York: Cambridge University Press, 2007.

Pidgeon, Mary Elizabeth. *Women in the Economy of the United States of America; Employed Women under NRA Codes.* New York: Da Capo Press, 1975.

Pierce, Paul. *Take an Alternate Route.* Los Angeles: Sherbourne Press, 1968.

Pieterse, Jan Nederveen. "Globalization as Hybridization." In Michael Featherstone, ed., *Global Modernities.* New York: Sage, 1995.

Pike, Fredrick B. *FDR's Good Neighbor Policy: Sixty Years of Generally Gentle Chaos.* Austin: University of Texas Press, 1995.

Pointer, Larry. *Rodeo Champions: Eight Memorable Moments of Riding, Wrestling, and Roping.* Albuquerque: University of New Mexico Press, 1985.

Pomerance, Murray., and John Sakeris, eds. *Popping Culture.* Boston: Pearson/Education, 2007.

Poole, Mary. *The Segregated Origins of Social Security: African Americans and the Welfare State.* Chapel Hill: University of North Carolina Press, 2006.

Porter, David L. *The Seventy-Sixth Congress and World War II, 1939–1940.* Columbia: University of Missouri Press, 1979.

Potter, Claire Bond. *War on Crime: Bandits, G-men, and the Politics of Mass Culture.* New Brunswick, N.J.: Rutgers University Press, 1998.

Poulsen, Richard C. *The Landscape of the Mind: Cultural Transformations of the American West.* New York: P. Lang, 1992.

Prats, A. J. *Invisible Natives: Myth and Identity in the American.* Ithaca, N.Y.: Cornell University Press, 2002.

Price. Monroe E. *Media and Sovereignty: The Global Information Revolution and Its Challenge to State Power.* Cambridge, Massachusetts: The MIT Press, 2002.

Prover, Jorja. *No One Knows Their Names: Screenwriters in Hollywood.* Bowling Green, Ohio: Bowling Green State University Popular Press, 1994.

Puddington, Arch. *Broadcasting Freedom.* Lexington, University of Kentucky Press, 2003.

Pusateri, C. Joseph. *Enterprise in Radio: WWL and the Business of Broadcasting in America.* Washington, D.C.: University Press of America, 1980.

Pustz, Matthew. *Comic Book Culture: Fanboys and True Believers.* Jackson: University Press of Mississippi, 1999.

Rabinowitz, Harold. *Black Hats and White Hats: Heroes and Villains of the West.* New York: MetroBooks, 1996.

Radford, Gail. *Modern Housing for America: Policy Struggles in the New Deal Era.* Chicago: University of Chicago Press, 1996.
Rand, Yardena. *Wild Open Spaces: Why We Love Westerns.* Manville, RI: Maverick Spirit Press, 2005.
Randall, Stephen J. *The Diplomacy of Modernization: Colombian-American Relations, 1920–1940.* Toronto, Ont.: University of Toronto Press 1977.
Range, Willard. *Franklin D. Roosevelt's World Order.* Athens: University of Georgia Press, 1959.
Reagan, Patrick D. *Designing a New America: The Origins of New Deal Planning, 1890–1943.* Amherst: University of Massachusetts Press, 2000.
Reedstrom, Ernest Lisle. *Historic Dress in the Old West: Authentic Costumes & Characters of the Wild West.* New York: Sterling Publishing Co., 1992.
Reiman, Richard A. *The New Deal & American Youth: Ideas & Ideals in a Depression Decade.* Athens: University of Georgia Press, 1992.
Renov, Michael. *Hollywood's Wartime Woman: Representation and Ideology.* Ann Arbor, Mich.: University of Michigan Research Press, 1988.
Rice, Rondall Ravon. *The Politics of Air Power: From Confrontation to Cooperation in Army Aviation Civil-Military Relations.* Lincoln: University of Nebraska Press, 2004.
Richard, Alfred Charles. *Censorship and Hollywood's Hispanic Image: An Interpretive Filmography, 1936–1955.* Westport, Conn.: Greenwood Press, 1993.
Richter, William A. *Radio: A Complete Guide to the Industry.* New York: P. Lang, 2006.
Riera, Emilio Garcia, ed. *Fernando De Fuentes.* Mexico: Cineteca Nacional, 1984.
Ritchie, Donald A. *Electing FDR: The New Deal Campaign of 1932.* Lawrence: University Press of Kansas, 2007.
Robbins, William G. *Colony and Empire: The Capitalist Transformation of the American West.* Lawrence: University Press of Kansas, 1994.
Roberts, John W. *Putting Foreign Policy to Work: The Role of Organized Labor in American Foreign Relations, 1932–1941.* New York: Garland Publishing, 1995.
Robinson, Edgar Eugene. *They Voted for Roosevelt; The Presidential Vote, 1932–1944.* Stanford, Calif.: Stanford University Press, 1947.
Rock, William R. *Chamberlain and Roosevelt: British Foreign Policy and the United States, 1937–1940.* Columbus: Ohio State University Press, 1988.
Rofe, J. Simon. *Franklin Roosevelt's Foreign Policy and the Welles Mission.* New York: Palgrave Macmillan, 2007.
Roffman, Peter. *The Hollywood Social Problem Film: Madness, Despair, and Politics from the Depression to the Fifties.* Bloomington: Indiana University Press, 1981.
Rogers, Jimmie N. *The Country Music Message, Revisited.* Fayetteville: University of Arkansas Press, 1989.
Rollin, Lucy. *Twentieth-Century Teen Culture by the Decades: A Reference Guide.* Westport, Conn.: Greenwood Press, 1999.
Rollins, Jr., Alfred B. *Roosevelt and Howe.* New Brunswick, N.J.: Transaction, 2002.
Roorda, Eric. *The Dictator Next Door: The Good Neighbor Policy and the Trujillo Regime in the Dominican Republic, 1930–1945.* Durham, N.C.: Duke University Press, 1998.

Roosevelt, Eleanor. *This I Remember.* 1949. Reprint, Westport, Conn.: Greenwood Press, 1975.
Rosen, Elliot A. *Hoover, Roosevelt, and the Brains Trust: From Depression to New Deal.* New York: Columbia University Press, 1977.
Rosenberg, Bernard., and David Manning, eds. *Mass Culture: The Popular Arts in America.* Glencoe, Ill.: The Free Press, 1957.
Rosenberg, Bruce A. *The Code of the West.* Bloomington: Indiana University Press, 1982.
Ross, Stewart Halsey. *How Roosevelt Failed America in World War II.* Jefferson, N.C.: McFarland & Co., 2006.
Rothel, David. *The Singing Cowboys.* San Diego, Calif.: A. S. Barnes & Company, 1978.
———. *The Gene Autry Book.* Madison, N.C.: Empire Publishing Co., 1988.
———. *Those Great Cowboy Sidekicks.* Madison, N.C.: Empire Publishing Co., 2001.
Rothman, Hal K. *Devil's Bargains: Tourism in the Twentieth-Century West.* Lawrence: University of Kansas Press, 1998.
Rubin, Joan Shelley. *The Making of Middlebrow Culture.* Chapel Hill: University of North Carolina Press, 1992.
Rudzitis, Gundars. *Wilderness and the Changing American West.* New York: Wiley, 1996.
Russell, Tony. *Country Music Originals: The Legends & the Lost.* New York: Oxford University Press, 2007.
Ryan, Jim. *The Rodeo and Hollywood: Rodeo Cowboys on Screen and Western Actors in the Arena.* Jefferson, N.C.: McFarland & Co., 2006.
Ryfe, David Michael. *Presidents in Culture: The Meaning of Presidential Communication.* New York: Peter Lang, 2005.
Sackett, Susan. *The Hollywood Reporter Book of Box Office Hits.* New York: Billboard Books, 1990.
Sadlier, Darlene J. *Brazil Imagined: 1500 to the Present.* Austin: University of Texas Press, 2008.
Sagala, Sandra K. *Buffalo Bill on Stage.* Albuquerque: University of New Mexico Press, 2008.
Salmond, John A. *The Civilian Conservation Corps, 1933–1942: A New Deal Case Study.* Durham, N.C.: Duke University Press, 1967.
Saloutos, Theodore. *The American Farmer and the New Deal.* Ames: Iowa State University Press, 1982.
Sherman, Samuel M. *Legendary Singing Cowboys.* New York: Friedman/Fairfax Publishers, 1995.
Sanjek, Russell. *American Popular Music Business in the 20th Century.* New York: Oxford University Press, 1991.
Sarf, Wayne Michael. *God Bless You, Buffalo Bill: A Layman's Guide to History and the Western Film.* Rutherford, N.J.: Fairleigh Dickinson University Press, 1983.
Savage, Sean J. *Roosevelt, the Party Leader, 1932–1945.* Lexington: University Press of Kentucky, 1991.
Savage, William W. *Commies, Cowboys, and Jungle Queens: Comic Books and America, 1945–1954.* Hanover, N.H.: Wesleyan University Press, 1998.

Scharff, Virginia. *Twenty Thousand Roads: Women, Movement, and the West*. Berkeley: University of California Press, 2003.
Schatz, Thomas, *Hollywood Genres: Formulas, Filmmaking, and the Studio System*. New York: Random House, 1981.
———. *The Genius of the System: Hollywood Filmmaking in the Studio Era*. New York: Pantheon Books, 1988.
———. *Boom and Bust: American Cinema in the 1940s*. Berkeley: University of California Press, 1999.
Schechter, Harold. *Savage Pastimes: A Cultural History of Violent Entertainment*. New York: St. Martin's Press, 2005.
Schewe, Donald B., ed. *Franklin D. Roosevelt and Foreign Affairs, Second series, January 1937-August 1939*. New York: Clearwater Publishing, 1979–1983. Microform.
Schickel, Richard. *Intimate Strangers: The Culture of Celebrity in America*. Chicago: Ivan R. Dee, 2000, 1985.
Schiller, Herbert I. *Culture, Inc.: The Corporate Takeover of Public Expression*. New York: Oxford University Press, 1989.
Schivelbusch, Wolfgang. *Three New Deals: Reflections on Roosevelt's America, Mussolini's Italy, and Hitler's Germany, 1933–1939*. New York: Metropolitan Books, 2006.
Schlesinger, Arthur M. *The New Deal in Action, 1933–1939*. Folcroft, Penn.: Folcroft Library Editions, 1977.
———. *The Coming of the New Deal, 1933–1935*. Boston: Houghton Mifflin, 2003.
———. *The Politics of Upheaval, 1935–1936*. Boston: Houghton Mifflin, 2003.
Schlesinger, Robert. *White House Ghosts: Presidents and their Speechwriters*. New York: Simon & Schuster, 2008.
Schmitz, David F. *The Triumph of Internationalism: Franklin D. Roosevelt and A World in Crisis, 1933–1941*. Washington, D.C.: Potomac Books, 2007.
Schneider, James C. *Should America Go to War?: The Debate over Foreign Policy in Chicago, 1939–1941*. Chapel Hill: University of North Carolina Press, 1989.
Schrader, Robert Fay. *The Indian Arts & Crafts Board: An Aspect of New Deal Indian Policy*. Albuquerque: University of New Mexico Press, 1983.
Schrum, Kelly. *Some Wore Bobby Sox: The Emergence of Teenage Girls' Culture, 1920–1945*. New York: Palgrave Macmillan, 2004.
Schubart, Rikke, and Anne Gjelsvik, eds. *Femme Fatalities: Representations of Strong Women in the Media*. Goeteborg, Sweden: Nordicom: Goeteborg University, 2004.
Schwantes, Carlos Arnaldo. *Going Places: Transportation Redefines the Twentieth-Century West*. Bloomington: Indiana University Press, 2003.
Schwartz, Andrew J. *America and the Russo-Finnish War*. 1960. Reprint, Westport, Conn.: Greenwood Press, 1975.
Schwartz, Nancy Lynn. *The Hollywood Writers' Wars*. 1982. Reprint, New York: McGraw-Hill, 1983.
Schwartz, Rosalie. *Flying Down to Rio: Hollywood, Tourists, and Yankee Clippers*. College Station: Texas A & M University Press, 2004.

Schwoch, James. *The American Radio Industry and Its Latin American Activities, 1900–1939.* Urbana and Chicago: University of Illinois Press, 1990.
Scott, Barbara Kerr. *New Deal Art—The Oklahoma Experience, 1933–1943.* Lawton, OK: Cameron University, 1983.
Scroop, Daniel. *Mr. Democrat: Jim Farley, the New Deal, and the Making of Modern American Politics.* Ann Arbor: University of Michigan Press, 2006.
Seidman, Steve. *Comedian Comedy: A Tradition in Hollywood Film.* Ann Arbor, Mich.: University of Michigan Research Press, 1981.
Sellnow, Les. *The Journey of the Western Horse: From the Spanish Conquest to the Silver Screen.* Lexington, KY: Eclipse Press, 2003.
Sennett, Robert S. *Hollywood Hoopla: Creating Stars and Selling Movies in the Golden Age of Hollywood.* New York: Billboard Books, 1998.
Sennett, Ted. *Hollywood Musicals.* New York: H. N. Abrams, 1981.
———. *Hollywood's Golden Year, 1939: A Fiftieth Anniversary Celebration.* New York: St. Martin's Press, 1989.
Serrell, Beverley. *Exhibit Labels: An Interpretive Approach.* Walnut Creek, Calif.: AltaMira Press, 1996.
Shamir, Ronen. *Managing Legal Uncertainty: Elite Lawyers in the New Deal.* Durham, N.C.: Duke University Press, 1995.
Sherman, Robert G. *Quiet on the Set: Motion Picture History at the Iverson Movie Location Ranch.* Chatsworth, Calif.: Sherway Publishing Co., 1984.
Sherman, Samuel M. *Legendary Singing Cowboys.* New York: Friedman/Fairfax Publishers, 1995.
Sherry, Michael S. *In the Shadow of War: The United States since the 1930's.* New Haven: Yale University Press, 1995.
Sherwood, Robert E. *Roosevelt and Hopkins, an Intimate History.* New York: Harper, 1950.
Shindler, Colin. *Hollywood Goes to War: Films and American Society, 1939–1952.* Boston: Routledge & K. Paul, 1979.
Shivers, Jay Sanford. *Leisure and Recreation Concepts: A Critical Analysis.* Boston: Allyn and Bacon, 1981.
———. *The Story of Leisure: Context, Concepts, and Current Controversy.* Champaign, Ill.: Human Kinetics, 1997.
Shlaes, Amity. *The Forgotten Man: A New History of the Great Depression.* New York: HarperCollins Publishers, 2007.
Simmon, Scott. *The Invention of the Western Film: A Cultural History of the Genre's First Half-Century.* New York: Cambridge University Press, 2003.
Sitkoff, Harvard. *A New Deal for Blacks: The Emergence of Civil Rights as a National Issue: The Depression Decade.* New York: Oxford University Press, 2008.
Sklar, Robert. *A World History of Films.* New York: Abrams, 1993.
Slatta, Richard W. *Cowboy: The Illustrated History.* New York: Sterling Publishing, 2006.
Slotkin, Richard. *Gunfighter Nation: The Myth of the Frontier in Twentieth-Century America.* Norman: University of Oklahoma Press, 1998.

Smith, Andrew Brodie. *Shooting Cowboys and Indians: Silent Western Films, American Culture, and the Birth of Hollywood.* Boulder: University Press of Colorado, 2003.

Smith, Henry Nash. *Virgin Land; the American West as Symbol and Myth.* 1950. Reprint, Cambridge: Harvard University Press, 1971.

Smith, Jason Scott. *Building New Deal Liberalism: The Political Economy of Public Works, 1933–1956.* New York: Cambridge University Press, 2006.

Smith, Jean Edward. *FDR.* New York: Random House, 2007.

Smith, Leon. *Hollywood Goes on Location.* Los Angeles: Pomegranate Press, 1988.

Smulyan, Susan. *Selling Radio: The Commercialization of American Broadcasting, 1920–1934* Washington, D.C.: Smithsonian Institution Press, 1994.

Sobel, Robert. *The Origins of Interventionism; The United States and the Russo-Finnish War.* 1960. Reprint, New York: Bookman Associates, 1961.

Solomon, William S., and Robert W. McChesney, eds. *Ruthless Criticism: New Perspectives in U.S. Communication History.* Minneapolis: University of Minnesota Press, 1993.

Solomon, William. *Literature, Amusement, and Technology in the Great Depression.* New York: Cambridge University Press, 2002.

Sorenson, Lorin. *Sears Roebuck and Co., 100$^{th}$ Anniversary.* St. Helena, Calif.: Silverado Publishing Company, 1985.

Sorensen, Todd. *Migration Creation, Diversion, and Retention: New Deal Grants and Migration: 1935–1940.* Bonn, Germany: IZA, 2007.

Sparrow, Bartholomew H. *From the Outside In: World War II and the American State.* Princeton, N.J.: Princeton University Press, 1996.

Spring, Joel H. *Educating the Consumer: A History of the Marriage of Schools, Advertising, and Media.* Mahwah, N.J.: Lawrence Erlbaum, 2002.

Spurgeon, Sara L. *Exploding the Western: Myths of Empire on the Postmodern Frontier.* College Station: Texas A&M University Press, 2005.

Stanfield, Peter. "Dixie Cowboys and Blue Yodels: The Strange History of the Singing Cowboy." In Edward Buscombe and Roberta E. Pearson, eds., *Back in the Saddle Again: New Essays on the Western.* London: British Film Institute Publishing, 1998.

———. *Horse Opera: The Strange History of the 1930s Singing Cowboy.* Urbana: University of Illinois Press, 2002.

Starr, Paul. *The Creation of the Media: Political Origins of Modern Communications.* New York: Basic Books, 2004.

Steffen, David J. *From Edison to Marconi: The First Thirty Years of Recorded Music.* Jefferson, N.C.: McFarland, 2005.

Steinbeck, John. *The Grapes of Wrath.* 1939. Reprint, New York: Bantam Books, 1972.

Steindl, Frank G. *Understanding Economic Recovery in the 1930s: Endogenous Propagation in the Great Depression.* Ann Arbor: University of Michigan Press, 2004.

Stegner, Wallace Earle. *The Sound of Mountain Water.* 1969. Reprint, Garden City, N.Y.: Doubleday, 1980.

———. *Where the Bluebird Sings to the Lemonade Springs: Living and Writing in the West.* New York: Modern Library, 2002.

Sternsher, Bernard. *Rexford Tugwell and the New Deal.* New Brunswick, N.J.: Rutgers University Press, 1964.

Sternsher, Bernard, ed. *Hope Restored: How the New Deal Worked in Town and Country.* Chicago: Ivan R. Dee, 1999.

Steward, Dick. *Trade and Hemisphere: The Good Neighbor Policy and Reciprocal Trade.* Columbia: University of Missouri Press, 1975.

Stewart, Polly, ed. *Worldviews and the American West: The Life of the Place Itself.* Logan: Utah State University Press, 2000.

Stoler, Mark A. *Allies and Adversaries: The Joint Chiefs of Staff, the Grand Alliance, and U.S. Strategy in World War II.* Chapel Hill: University of North Carolina Press, 2000.

Storrs, Landon R. Y. *Civilizing Capitalism: The National Consumers' League, Women's Activism, and Labor Standards in the New Deal Era.* Chapel Hill: University of North Carolina Press, 2000.

Stout, Janis P. *Coming Out of War: Poetry, Grieving, and the Culture of the World Wars.* Tuscaloosa: University of Alabama Press, 2005.

Swift, Will. *The Roosevelts and the Royals: Franklin and Eleanor, the King and Queen of England, and the Friendship that Changed History.* Hoboken, N.J.: John Wiley & Sons, 2004.

———. *The Kennedys amidst the Gathering Storm: A Thousand Days in London, 1938–1940.* Washington, D.C.: Smithsonian Books, 2008.

Synder, Robert L. *Pate Lorentz and the Documentary Film.* Norman: University of Oklahoma Press, 1968.

Szalay, Michael. *New Deal Modernism: American Literature and the Invention of the Welfare State.* Durham, N.C.: Duke University Press, 2000.

Szwed, John F. *Crossovers: Essays on Race, Music, and American Culture.* Philadelphia: University of Pennsylvania Press, 2005.

Talbert, Robert H. *Spanish-Name People in the Southwest and West; Socioeconomic Characteristics of White Persons of Spanish Surname in Texas, Arizona, California, Colorado, and New Mexico.* Fort Worth, Texas: Leo Potishman Foundation, Texas Christian University, 1955.

Taylor, Graham D. *The New Deal and American Indian Tribalism: The Administration of the Indian Reorganization Act, 1934–45.* Lincoln: University of Nebraska Press, 1980.

Taylor, Lonn, and Ingrid Maar. *The American Cowboy.* Washington, D.C.: American Folklife Center, Library of Congress, 1983.

Taylor, Nick. *American-Made: The Enduring Legacy of the WPA: When FDR Put the Nation to Work.* New York: Bantam Books, 2008.

Taylor, Quintard. *In Search of the Racial Frontier: African Americans in the American West, 1528–1990.* New York: Norton, 1998.

Thomas, Selma., and Ann Mintz. eds. *The Virtual and the Real: Media in the Museums* (Washington, D.C.: American Association of Museums, 1998.

Thorp, Margaret Farrand. *America at the Movies.* New Haven, Conn.: Yale University Press, 1939.

Tichi, Cecelia. *High Lonesome: The American Culture of Country Music.* Chapel Hill: University of North Carolina Press, 1994.

Tichi, Cecelia, ed. *Reading Country Music: Steel Guitars, Opry Stars, and Honky-Tonk Bars.* Durham, N.C.: Duke University Press, 1998.

Tierney, Dominic. *FDR and the Spanish Civil War: Neutrality and Commitment in the Struggle that Divided America.* Durham, N.C.: Duke University Press, 2007.

Tischler, Barbara L. *An American Music: The Search for An American Musical Identity.* New York: Oxford University Press, 1986.

Tobey, Ronald C. *Technology as Freedom: The New Deal and the Electrical Modernization of the American Home.* Berkeley: University of California Press, 1996.

Tompkins, Jane P. *West of Everything: The Inner Life of Westerns.* New York: Oxford University Press, 1992.

Tosh, Jon. *The Pursuit of History: Aims, Methods and New Directions in the Study of Modern History.* 1984. Revised 3rd edition, New York: Longman, 2002.

Tugwell, Rexford G. *In Search of Roosevelt.* Cambridge: Harvard University Press, 1972.

Turner, Barnard Edward. *Cultural Tropes of the Contemporary American West.* Lewiston, N.Y.: Edwin Mellen Press, 2005.

Tuska, Jon. *The Filming of the West.* Garden City, N.Y.: Doubleday, 1976.

———. *The Vanishing Legion: A History of Mascot Pictures, 1927–1937.* Jefferson, N.C.: McFarland & Co., 1982.

———. *The American West in Film: Critical Approaches to the Western.* Westport, Conn.: Greenwood Press, 1985.

Tuttle, Dwight William. *Harry L. Hopkins and Anglo-American-Soviet Relations, 1941–1945.* New York: Garland Publishing, 1983.

Tyson, James L. *U.S. International Broadcasting and National Security.* New York: Ramapo Press, 1983.

Underhill, Robert. *FDR and Harry: Unparalleled Lives.* Westport, Conn.: Praeger, 1996.

Utley, Jonathan G. *Going to War with Japan, 1937–1941.* New York: Fordham University Press, 2005.

Van Nuys, Frank. *Americanizing the West: Race, Immigrants, and Citizenship, 1890–1930.* Lawrence: University Press of Kansas, 2002.

Varenne, Herve. *Symbolizing America.* Lincoln: University of Nebraska Press, 1986.

Verstraten, Peter. *Screening Cowboys: Reading Masculinities in Westerns.* Nijmegen: Vantilt, 1999.

Victor, George. *The Pearl Harbor Myth: Rethinking the Unthinkable.* Washington, D.C.: Potomac Books, 2007.

Vittoz, Stanley. *New Deal Labor Policy and the American Industrial Economy.* Chapel Hill: University of North Carolina Press, 1987.

Von Glahn, Denise. *The Sounds of Place: Music and the American Cultural Landscape.* Boston: Northeastern University Press, 2003.

Waddell, Brian. *Toward the National Security State: Civil-Military Relations during World War II.* Westport, Conn.: Praeger Security International, 2008.

Walker, Frank C., ed. *FDR's Quiet Confidant: The Autobiography of Frank C. Walker.* Niwot, Colo.: University Press of Colorado, 1997.
Walker, J. Samuel. *Henry A. Wallace and American Foreign Policy.* Westport, Conn.: Greenwood Press, 1976.
Walker, Janet, ed. *Westerns: Films through History.* New York: Routledge, 2001.
Wallace, Henry Agard. *Democracy Reborn.* 1944. Reprint, New York: Da Capo Press, 1973.
―――. *The Price of Vision; The Diary of Henry A. Wallace, 1942–1946.* Boston: Houghton Mifflin, 1973.
Walle, Alf H. *The Cowboy Hero and Its Audience: Popular Culture as Market Derived Art.* Bowling Green, Ohio: Bowling Green State University Popular Press, 2000.
Wallmann, Jeffrey M. *The Western: Parables of the American Dream.* Lubbock: Texas Tech University Press, 1999.
Walsh, Margaret. *The American West: Visions and Revisions.* New York: Cambridge University Press, 2005.
Ward, Fay E. *The Cowboy at Work: All about his Job and How He Does It.* Mineola, N.Y.: Dover Publications, 2003.
Ware, Susan. *Beyond Suffrage, Women in the New Deal.* Cambridge, Mass.: Harvard University Press, 1981.
Warren, Donald I. *Radio Priest: Charles Coughlin, the Father of Hate Radio.* New York: Free Press, 1996.
Warren, Frank A., *Noble Abstractions: American Liberal Intellectuals and World War II.* Columbus: Ohio State University Press, 1999.
Warren, Louis S. *Buffalo Bill's America: William Cody and the Wild West Show.* New York: Alfred A. Knopf, 2005.
Webb, John Nye. *Migrant Families.* New York: Da Capo Press, 1971.
―――. *The Migratory-Casual Worker.* New York: Da Capo Press, 1971.
Weed, Clyde P. *The Nemesis of Reform: The Republican Party during the New Deal.* New York: Columbia University Press, 1994.
Weeks, Gregory Bart. *U.S. and Latin American Relations.* New York: Pearson Longman, 2008.
Weigold, Auriol. *Churchill, Roosevelt, and India: Propaganda during World War II.* New York: Routledge, 2008.
Weiland, Victoria Carlyle. *100 Years of Rodeo Stock Contracting.* Reno, Nev.: Professional Rodeo Stock Contractors Association, 1997.
Welles, Benjamin. *Sumner Welles: FDR's Global Strategist: A Biography.* New York: St. Martin's Press, 1997.
Wertheim, Arthur Frank, and Barbara Bair, eds., *The Papers of Will Rogers.* 5 vols. Norman: University of Oklahoma Press, 1996–2006.
Westbrook, Robert B. *Why We Fought: Forging American Obligations in World War II.* Washington, D.C.: Smithsonian Books, 2004.
Westermeier, Clifford P. *Man, Beast, Dust: The Story of Rodeo.* 1947. Reprint, Lincoln: University of Nebraska Press, 1987.

Westfahl, Gary. *Science Fiction, Children's Literature, and Popular Culture: Coming of Age in Fantasyland*. Westport, Conn.: Greenwood Press, 2000.

Whitaker, Arthur P. *The Western Hemisphere Idea: Its Rise and Decline*. Ithaca, N.Y.: Cornell University Press, 1954.

White, G. Edward, *The Eastern Establishment and the Western Experience: The West of Frederic Remington, Theodore Roosevelt, and Owen Wister*. Austin: University of Texas Press, 1989, 1968.

White, Graham J. *FDR and the Press*. Chicago: University of Chicago Press, 1979.

———. *Harold Ickes of the New Deal: His Private Life and Public Career*. Cambridge, Mass.: Harvard University Press, 1985.

———., *Henry A. Wallace: His Search for a New World Order*. Chapel Hill: University of North Carolina Press, 1995.

White, John Franklin, ed. *Art in Action: American Art Centers and the New Deal*. Metuchen, N.J.: Scarecrow Press, 1987.

White, John I. *Git Along, Little Dogies: Songs and Songmakers of the American West*. Urbana: University of Illinois Press, 1975.

White, Mark J. *Against the President: Dissent and Decision-Making in the White House: A Historical Perspective*. Chicago: Ivan R. Dee, 2007.

White, Richard D. *Kingfish: The Reign of Huey P. Long*. New York: Random House, 2006.

White, Ray. "The Good Guys Wore White Hats: The B Western in American Culture." In Richard Aquila, ed., *Wanted Dead or Alive: The American West in Popular Culture*. Urbana: University of Illinois Press, 1996.

White, William Allen. *The Changing West; An Economic Theory about Our Golden Age*. New York: The Macmillan Company, 1939.

Williamson, Judith. *Consuming Passions: The Dynamics of Popular Culture*. New York: Scribner, 1986.

Wills, Matthew B. *Wartime Missions of Harry L. Hopkins*. 1996. Reprint, Bloomington, Ind.: Author House, 2004.

Wilson, Robert A., ed. *Power and the Presidency*. New York: Public Affairs, 1999.

Winfield, Betty Houchin. *FDR and the News Media*. New York: Columbia University Press, 1994.

Winn, J. Emmett., and Susan L. Brinson, eds. *Transmitting the Past: Historical and Cultural Perspectives on Broadcasting*. Tuscaloosa: University of Alabama Press, 2005.

Witcomb, Andrea. *Re-Imagining the Museum: Beyond the Mausoleum*. New York: Routledge, 2003.

Wolfe, Charles K., and James E. Akenson, eds. *Country Music Goes to War*. Lexington, Ky.: University Press of Kentucky, 2005.

Woll, Allen L. *The Latin Image in American Film*. Los Angeles: UCLA Latin American Center Publications, University of California, 1980.

———. *The Hollywood Musical Goes to War*. Chicago: Nelson-Hall, 1983.

Wood, Bryce. *The Making of the Good Neighbor Policy*. New York: Columbia University Press, 1961.

———. *The Dismantling of the Good Neighbor Policy*. Austin: University of Texas Press, 1985.
Wooden, Wayne S. *Rodeo in America: Wranglers, Roughstock & Paydirt*. Lawrence: University Press of Kansas, 1996.
Woods, John A. *Roosevelt and Modern America*. London: English Universities Press 1959.
Woods, Randall Bennett. *The Roosevelt Foreign-Policy Establishment and the "Good Neighbor": The United States and Argentina, 1941–1945*. Lawrence: Regents Press of Kansas, 1979.
———. *A Changing of the Guard: Anglo-American Relations 1941–1946*. Chapel Hill: University of North Carolina Press, 1990.
Woolner, David B., Warren F. Kimball, and David Reynolds, eds. *FDR's World: War, Peace, and Legacies*. New York: Palgrave Macmillan, 2008.
Worster, Donald. *Rivers of Empire: Water, Aridity, and the Growth of The American West*. New York: Pantheon Books, 1985.
———. "Herbert Eugene Bolton: The Making of a Western Historian." In Richard W. Etulain, ed., *Writing Western History: Essays on Major Western Historians*. 1991. Reprint, Reno & Las Vegas: University of Nevada Press, 2002.
———. *Under Western Skies: Nature and History in the American West*. New York: Oxford University Press, 1992.
Wright, Will. *Six Guns and Society: A Structural Study of the Western*. Berkeley: University of California Press, 1975.
Wrobel, David M., and Michael C. Steiner, eds. *Many Wests: Place, Culture & Regional Identity*. Lawrence: University Press of Kansas, 1997.
Wynter, Leon E. *American Skin: Pop Culture, Big Business, and the End of White America*. New York: Crown Publishers, 2002.
Yagoda, Ben. *Will Rogers: A Biography*. Norman: University of Oklahoma Press, 2000.
Zeitz, Joshua. *Flapper: The Notorious Life and Scandalous Times of the First Thoroughly Modern Woman*. New York: Crown Publishers, 2006.

## Journal Articles

Ackerman, William C. "The Dimensions of American Broadcasting." *Public Opinion Quarterly* 9, no. 1 (Spring 1945): 1–18.
Aikman, Duncan. "The Machinery for Hemisphere Cooperation." *Public Opinion Quarterly* 6, no. 4 (Winter 1942): 550–54.
Belli, Melvin M. "The Adequate Award." *California Law Review* 39, no. 1 (March 1951): 1–41.
Bentinck, Henry. "The Nation's Barn Dance." *Radio Guide* 4, no. 2 (11 November 1934).
Boatright, Mody C. "The Formula in Cowboy Fiction and Drama." *Western folklore* 28, no. 2 (April 1969): 136–45.
Boddy, William. "The Studios Move into Prime Time: Hollywood and the Television Industry in the 1950s." *Cinema Journal* 24, no. 4 (Summer 1985): 23–37.

Carson, Saul. "Notes toward an Examination of the Radio Documentary." *Hollywood Quarterly* 4, no. 1 (Autumn 1949): 69–74.
Chester, Giraud. "The Press-Radio War: 1933–35." *Public Opinion Quarterly* 13, no. 2 (Summer 1949): 252–64.
Cohen, Norman. "Computerized Hillbilly Discography: The Gennett Project." In *Commercialized Folk Music*. Special issue, *Western Folklore* 30, no. 3 (July 1971): 182–93.
Davis, David B. "Ten-Gallon Hero." *American Quarterly* 6, no. 2 (Summer 1954): 111–25.
Doordan, Dennis P. "Design at CBS." *Design Issues* 6, no. 2 (Spring 1990): 4–17.
Duchemin, Michael. "Mr. Autry Goes to Washington: The Cowboy and the New Deal." *Convergence* (Summer 2007): 14–23.
———. "Water, Power, and Tourism: Hoover Dam and the Making of the New West." *California History* 86, no. 4 (2009): 60–79.
Elkin, Frederick. "The Psychological Appeal of the Hollywood Western." *Journal of Educational Sociology* 24, no. 2 (October 1950): 72–86.
Etzkorn, K. Peter. "Social Contexts of Songwriting in the United States." *Ethnomusicology* 7, no. 2 (May 1963): 96–106.
Fenster, Mark. "Preparing the Audience, Informing the Performers: John A. Lomax and Cowboy Songs and Other Frontier Ballads." *American Music* 7, no. 3 (Autumn, 1989): 260–77.
Fishwick, Marshall. "The Cowboy: America's Contribution to the World's Mythology." *Western Folklore* 11, no. 2 (April 1952): 77–92.
———. "American Heroes: Columbia's Path." *Western Folklore* 13, no. 2/3 (1954): 153–59.
Freire-Medeiros, Bianca. "Hollywood Musicals and the Invention of Rio de Janeiro, 1933–1953." *Cinema Journal* 41, no. 4 (Summer 2002): 52–67.
"Gallop and Fortune Polls." *The Public Opinion Quarterly* 4, no. 1 (March 1940): 83–115.
Green, Archie. "Hillbilly Music: Source and Symbol." *The Journal of American Folklore* Hillbilly Issue 78, no. 309 (July–September, 1965): 204–28.
———. "Vernacular Music: A Naming Compass." *Musical Quarterly* 77, no. 1 (Spring 1993): 35–46.
Griffin, Sean. "The Gang's All Here: Generic versus Racial Integration in the 1940s Musical." *Cinema Journal* 42, no. 1 (Autumn 2002): 21–45.
Henderson, Brian. "Romantic Comedy Today: Semi-tough or Impossible?" *Film Quarterly* 31, no. 4 (Summer 1978): 11–23.
Herzog, Herta. "Radio: The First Post-War Year." *The Public Opinion Quarterly* 10, no. 3 (Autumn 1946): 297–313.
Hettinger Herman S. "The Future of Radio as an Advertising Medium." *The Journal of Business of the University of Chicago* 7, no. 4 (October 1934): 283–84.
Johnston, Alva. "Hollywood Beckons." *Saturday Evening Post* (September 2, 1939).
Jones, Dorothy B. "Hollywood's International Relations." *The Quarterly of Film Radio and Television* 11, no. 4 (summer 1957): 362–74.

Kollin, Susan. "Genre and the Geographies of Violence: Cormac McCarthy and the Contemporary Western." *Contemporary Literature* 42, no. 3 (Autumn 2001): 557–88.

Koppes, Clayton R. "Efficiency/Equity/Esthetics: Toward a Reinterpretation of American Conservation." *Environmental Review: ER* 11, no. 2 (Summer 1987): 127–46.

Kremenliev, Boris. "Background Music for Radio Drama." *Hollywood Quarterly* 4, no. 1 (Autumn 1949): 75–83.

Landry, Robert J. "Radio and Government." *The Public Opinion Quarterly* 2, no. 4 (October 1938): 557–69.

Leicester, Jr., H. Marshall. "Discourse and the Film Text: Four Readings of 'Carmen.'" *Cambridge Open Journal* 6, no. 3 (November 1994): 245–82.

Lewis, Grover. "True to the West after 26 years and $34 Million, Gene Autry Gets His Dream Museum." *Los Angeles Times Magazine* (November 20, 1988): 8.

Leyda, Julia. "Black-Audience Westerns and the Politics of Cultural Identification in the 1930s." *Cinema Journal* 42, no. 1 (Autumn 2002): 46–70.

"Liabilities of Advertising Endorsers." *Stanford Law Review* 2, no. 3 (April 1950): 496–514.

Locke, Ralph P. "Paradoxes of the Women Music Patrons in America." *The Musical Quarterly* 78, no. 4 (Winter 1994): 798–825.

Logan, Rayford W. "Negro Youth and the Influence of the Press, Radio, and Cinema." In *The Negro Adolescent and His Education*. Special issue, *The Journal of Negro Education* 9, no. 3 (July 1940): 425–34.

Lornell, Kip. "Country Music and the Mass Media in Roanoke, Virginia." *American Music* 5, no. 4 (Winter 1987): 404–08.

Loy, Jane M. "The Present as Past: Assessing the Value of Julien Bryan's Films as Historical Evidence." *Latin American Research Journal* 12, no. 3 (1977): 103–28.

Loy, R. Philip. "Soldiers in Stetsons: B-Westerns go to war." *Journal of Popular Film and Television* (Winter 2003): 197–205.

Luther, Rodney. "Television and the Future of Motion Picture Exhibition." *Hollywood Quarterly* 5, no. 2 (Winter 1950): 164–77.

MacCann, Richard Dyer. "Film and Foreign Policy: The USIA, 1962–67." *Cinema Journal* 9, no. 1 (Autumn 1969): 23–42.

Manheim, James M. "B-Side Sentimentalizer: 'Tennessee Waltz' in the History of Popular Music." *The Musical Quarterly* 76, no. 3 (Autumn 1992): 337–54.

Marquis, Alice Goldfarb. "Written on the Wind: The Impact of Radio during the 1930s." *Journal of Contemporary History* 19, no. 3 (July 1984): 385–88.

Martin, Darryl. "Innovation and the Development of the Modern Six-String Guitar." *The Galpin Society Journal* 51, no. 9 (July 1998): 86–109.

McDowell, Linda. "Off the Road: Alternative Views of Rebellion, Resistance and 'The Beats.'" *New Series*. Special issue, *Transactions of the Institute of British Geographers* 21, no. 2 (1996): 412–19.

Mchaffy, Marilyn Maness. "Advertising Race/Racing Advertising: The Feminine Consumer(-Nation), 1876–1900." *Signs* 23, no. 1 (Autumn 1997): 131–74.

McKenzie, Vernon. "United Nations Propaganda in the United States." *The Public Opinion Quarterly* 6, no. 3 (Autumn 1942): 351–66.

McLure, Helen. "The Wild, Wild Web: The Mythic American West and the Electronic Frontier." *The Western Historical Quarterly* 31, no. 4 (Winter 2000): 457–76.

Meerse, David E. "To Reassure a Nation: Hollywood Presents World War II." *Film and History* 6, no. 4 (December 1976): 79–80.

Mercey, Arch A. "Films by American Governments: The United States." *Films* 1 (Summer 1940): 5–11.

Meyer, Donald C. "Toscanini and the Good Neighbor Policy: The NBC Symphony Orchestra's 1940 South American Tour." *American Music* 18, no. 3 (Autumn 2000): 233–56.

Mooney, Hughson F. "Songs, Singers and Society, 1890–1954." *American Quarterly* 6, no. 3 (Autumn 1954): 221–32.

Moore, John Norton. "The Secret War in Central America and the Future of World Order." *The American Journal of International Law* 80, no. 1 (January 1986): 43–127.

Morrison, Joseph L. "Josephus Daniels—Simpatico." *Journal of Inter-American Studies* 5, no. 2 (April 1963): 277–89.

Noriega, Chon A. "Sacred Contingencies: The Digital Deconstruction of Raphael Montanez Ortiz." *Video Art*. Special issue, *Art Journal* 54, no. 4 (Winter 1995): 36–40.

Ogilvie, John W. "The Potentialities of Inter-American Radio." *The Public Opinion Quarterly* 9, no. 1 (Spring 1945): 19–28.

Padelford, Norman J. "Regional Organization and the United Nations." *International Organization* 8, no. 2 (May 1954): 203–16.

Pollard, John A. "Words Are Cheaper Than Blood." *The Public Opinion Quarterly* 9, no. 3 (Autumn 1945): 283–304.

Price, Charles Gower. "Sources of American Styles in the Music of the Beatles." *American Music* 15, no. 2 (Summer 1997): 208–32.

Riegel, O. W. "Press, Radio, Films." *The Public Opinion Quarterly* 4, no. 1 (March 1940): 136–50.

Rivadulla, Jr., Eladio, and Jessica Gibbs. "The Film Poster in Cuba (1940–1959)." *Design Issues* 16, no. 2 (Summer 2000): 36–44.

Roberts, Shari. "'The Lady in the Tutti-Frutti Hat': Carmen Miranda, a Spectacle of Ethnicity." *Cinema Journal* 32, no. 3 (Spring 1993): 3–23.

Ross, Andrew. "Intellectuals and Ordinary People: Reading the Rosenberg Letters." *Cultural Critique* 9 (Spring 1988): 55–86.

Rostron, Allen. "'No War, No Hate, No Propaganda': Promoting Films about European War and Fascism during the Period of American Isolationism." *Journal of Popular Film & Television* 30, no. 2 (Summer 2002): 85–96.

Sayre, Jeanette. "Radio." *The Public Opinion Quarterly* 5, no. 2 (June 1941): 301–05.

Schulberg, Bud. "The Writer in Hollywood." *Harper's Magazine*, (October 1959): 135.

Schultheiss, John. "The Eastern' Writer in Hollywood." *Cinema Journal* 11, no. 1 (Autumn 1971): 13–47.

Scott, Derek B. "Incongruity and Predictability in British Dance Band Music of the 1920s and 1930s." *The Musical Quarterly* 78, no. 2 (Summer 1994): 290–315.

Scott, James F. "Beat Literature and the American Teen Cult." *American Quarterly* 14, no. 2 (Summer 1962): 150–60.

Seagoe, May V. "Children's Television Habits and Preferences." *The Quarterly of Film Radio and Television* 6, no. 2 (Winter 1951): 143–53.

Shusterman, Richard. "Moving Truth: Affect and Authenticity in Country Musicals." *Aesthetics and Popular Culture*. Special issue, *The Journal of Aesthetics and Art Criticism* 57, no. 2 (Spring 1999): 221–33.

Steele, Richard W. "The Great Debate: Roosevelt, the Media, and the Coming of the War, 1940–1941." *The Journal of American History* 71, no. 1 (June 1984): 73–74.

Stoeltje, Beverly J. "Rodeo: From Custom to Ritual." *Western Folklore* 48, no. 3 (July 1989): 244–55.

———. "Power and the Ritual Genres: American Rodeo." *Theorizing Folklore: Toward New Perspectives on the Politics of Culture*. Special issue, *Western Folklore* 52, no. 2/4 (Apr.-Oct. 1993): 135–56.

Tan, Lynette. "The New Deal Cowboy: Gene Autry and the Antimodern Resolution." *Film and History* 13, no. 1 (2001): 89–101.

*Variety* (29 December 1926): 1.

Ward, Dwight E., and Arthur P. Pierce. "Helium." In *United States Mineral Resources*. US Geological Survey, Professional Paper 820 (1973): 285–90.

Weales, Gerald. "Popular Theatre of the Thirties." *The Tulane Drama Review* 11, no. 4 (Summer 1967): 51–69.

Whitaker, Arthur P. "The Origin of the Western Hemisphere Idea." *Proceedings of the American Philosophical Society* 98, no. 5 (October 15, 1954): 323–26.

Whitehall, Richard. "The Heroes Are Tired." *Film* 20, no. 2 (Winter 1966–67): 12–24.

Wilgus, D. K. "Country-Western Music and the Urban Hillbilly." *The Urban Experience and Folk Tradition*. Special issue, *The Journal of American Folklore*. 83, no. 328 (April-June, 1970): 157–79.

Yamasaki, Mitch. "Using Rock 'N' Roll to Teach the History of Post-World War II America." *The History Teacher* 29, no. 2 (February 1996): 179–93.

Zarlengo, Kristina. "Civilian Threat, the Suburban Citadel, and Atomic Age American Women." *Institutions, Regulation, and Social Control*. Special issue, *Signs* 24, no. 4 (Summer 1999): 925–58.

Zingg, Paul J. "Diamond in the Rough: Baseball and the Study of American Sports History." *The History Teacher* 19, no. 3 (May 1986): 385–403.

## Newspapers

*Bedford Gazette*. 1930.
*Belfast News-Letter*. 1939.
*Charleston Gazette*. 1929.

*Chicago Daily Tribune.* 1942.
*Daily Record* (Glasgow). 1939.
*Evening Dispatch.* 1939.
*Los Angeles Times.* 1928–87.
*Glasgow Herald.* 1939.
*Motion Picture Herald.* 1936–42.
*New York Times.* 1931–84.
*Pittsburgh Press.* 1940.

**Nonbook Materials**

Internet

Laurie. "A. W. Hackel: A Producer Supreme and the Pulp Western's Best Friend." Part 12. *Movies in the Santa Clarita Valley* (blog). November 12, 2009. http://lauriepowerswildwest.blogspot.com/2009/11/aw-hackel-producer-supreme-and-pulp.html.

Harmony Database. "Supertone 257—Gene Autry 'Old Santa Fe' Acoustic archtop—Shaded brown—Distributed by Sears & Roebuck, 1935." http://harmony.demont.net/model.php?id=743.

Texas State Historical Association. "Texas Centennial." *Handbook of Texas History Online.* http://www.tshaonline.org/handbook/online/articles/LL/xgl1.html.

"Wave of Popularity Sweeping Mexican Stars to the Top Keeps Going On." *Los Angeles Times.* January 27, 1929: C11. http://en.wikipedia.org/wiki/Armida_Vendrell.

Gene Autry Entertainment. *Back in the Saddle.* 1941. http://www.geneautry.com/geneautry/motionpictures/filmography/backinthesaddle.html.

Independent Movie Database. *"Buck Jones."* http://www.imdb.com/name/nm0427659/#Actor.

———. *In Old Santa Fe.* http://www.imdb.com/.

———. "John Wayne." http://www.imdb.com/name/nm0000078/?fr=c2l0ZT1kZnxteD0yMHxzZz0xfGxtPTIwMHxwbj0wfHE9am9obiB3YXluZXxodG1sPT-F8bm09b24_;fc=1;ft=20;fm=1#actor1920.

———. *Mystery Mountain.* http://www.imdb.com/title/tt0025544/fullcredits.

———. *Red River Valley.* http://www.imdb.com/title/tt0028163/.

———. "Robert N. Bradbury." http://www.imdb.com/name/nm0102908/maindetails.

Robert C. Sahr Political Science Department, Oregon State University, Corvallis, Oregon, 2009. http://oregonstate.edu/cla/polisci/faculty-research/sahr/cv2006.pdf.

Roosevelt, Franklin D. "First Inaugural Speech 4 March 1933." *The History Place—Great Speeches Collection.* http://www.historyplace.com/speeches/fdr-first-inaug.htm.

U.S. National Park Service. *National Park Service Landmarks Program.* http://www.nps.gov.

The Wrigley Company. "Wrigley's Gum Production Dedicated to U.S. Armed Forces." *Heritage Timeline.* http://www.wrigley.com/global/about-us/heritage-timeline.aspx.

U.S. Department of Labor. Bureau of Labor Statistics. "CPI Inflation Calculator." http://146.142.4.24/cgi-bin/cpicalc.pl?cost1=460&year1=1932&year2=2011.

## Radio Transcriptions

Autry, Gene. "The Complete Recordings of Gene Autry." Studio City, Calif.: Gene Autry Entertainment, 2009. iPod.

*Gene Autry's Melody Ranch.* Studio City, Calif.: Gene Autry Entertainment, 2009. iPod.

*Sergeant Gene Autry.* Studio City, Calif.: Gene Autry Entertainment, 2009. iPod.

## Videorecordings

*Allá en el Rancho Grande (Over at the Big Ranch).* 1936. Reprint, Buenos Aries, Argentina: Cinemateca—Condor Media, Inc., 2007.

Autry, Gene. "Introduction to *Bells of Capistrano.* Nashville Network's *Melody Ranch Theater.*" 1987. Reprint, Chatsworth, Calif.: Image Entertainment, 2003. Videorecording.

Autry, Gene. "Introduction to *South of the Border* on Nashville Network's *Melody Ranch Theater.*" 1987. Reprint, Studio City, Calif.: Gene Autry Entertainment, 2001. Videorecording.

*Back in the Saddle* 1941. Reprint, Chatsworth, Calif.: Image Entertainment, 2003. Videorecording.

*Bells of Capistrano* 1942. Reprint, Chatsworth, Calif.: Image Entertainment, 2003. Videorecording.

*Blue Montana Skies.* 1939. Reprint, Studio City, Calif.: Gene Autry Entertainment, 2004. Videorecording.

*Boots and Saddles* 1937. Reprint, Studio City, Calif.: Gene Autry Entertainment, 2002. Videorecording.

*Carolina Moon* 1940. Reprint, Studio City, Calif.: Gene Autry Entertainment, 2004. Videorecording.

*Colorado Sunset* 1939. Reprint, Chatsworth, Calif.: Image Entertainment, 2006. Videorecording.

*Comin' Round The Mountain* 1936, Reprint, Studio City, Calif.: Gene Autry Entertainment, 2004. Videorecording.

*Down Mexico Way* 1941. Reprint, Chatsworth, Calif.: Image Entertainment, 2005. Videorecording.

*Gaucho Serenade* 1940. Reprint, Chatsworth, Calif.: Image Entertainment, 2003. Videorecording.

*Git Along Little Doggies.* 1937. Reprint, Studio City, Calif.: Gene Autry Entertainment, 2002. Videorecording.

*Gold Mine in the Sky* 1938. Reprint, Chatsworth, Calif.: Image Entertainment, 2007. Videorecording.

*Guns and Guitars* 1936. Reprint, Chatsworth, Calif.: Image Entertainment, 2005. Videorecording.

*Home in Wyomin'* 1942. Reprint, Chatsworth, Calif.: Image Entertainment, 2007. Videorecording.
*In Old Monterey.* 1939. Reprint, Chatsworth, Calif.: Image Entertainment, 2005. Videorecording.
*In Old Santa Fe.* 1934. Reprint, Studio City, Calif.: Gene Autry Entertainment, 2002. Videorecording.
*Man Fran Music Mountain,* 1938. Reprint, Studio City, Calif.: Gene Autry Entertainment, 2004. Videorecording.
*Melody Ranch* 1940. Reprint, Chatsworth, Calif.: Image Entertainment, 2003. Videorecording.
*Melody Trail,* 1935. Reprint, Studio City, Calif.: Gene Autry Entertainment, 2004. Videorecording.
*Mexicali Rose.* 1939. Reprint, Chatsworth, Calif.: Image Entertainment, 2006. Videorecording.
*Mountain Rhythm,* 1939. Reprint, Studio City, Calif.: Gene Autry Entertainment, n.d., Videorecording.
*Oh, Susana!* 1937. Reprint, Studio City, Calif.: Gene Autry Entertainment, 2005. Videorecording.
*Public Cowboy No. 1* 1937. Reprint, Studio City, Calif.: Gene Autry Entertainment, 2004. Videorecording.
*Rancho Grande.* 1949. Reprint, Studio City, Calif.: Gene Autry Entertainment, 2004. Videorecording.
*Red River Valley* 1936. Reprint,. Studio City, Calif.: Gene Autry Entertainment, 2005. Videorecording.
*Rhythm of the Saddle* 1938. Reprint, Studio City, Calif.: Gene Autry Entertainment, 2004. Videorecording.
*Ride Tenderfoot Ride* 1940. Reprint, Studio City, Calif.: Gene Autry Entertainment, 2003. Videorecording.
*Rootin' Tootin' Rhythm* 1937. Reprint, Studio City, Calif.: Gene Autry Entertainment, 2005. Videorecording.
*Rovin' Tumbleweeds* 1939. Reprint, Studio City, Calif.: Gene Autry Entertainment, 2001. Videorecording.
*Sierra Sue* 1941. Reprint, Studio City, Calif.: Gene Autry Entertainment, 2002. Videorecording.
*South of the Border* 1939. Reprint, Studio City, Calif.: Gene Autry Entertainment, 2001. Videorecording.
*Springtime in the Rockies* 1937. Reprint, Studio City, Calif.: Gene Autry Entertainment, 2003. Videorecording.
*Sunset in Wyoming.* 1941. Reprint, Chatsworth, Calif.: Image Entertainment, 2006. Videorecording.
*The Big Show* 1936. Reprint, Studio City, Calif.: Gene Autry Entertainment, 2002. Videorecording.

*The Phantom Empire*. 1934. Reprint, Studio City, Calif.: Gene Autry Entertainment, 2007. Videorecording.
*The Plow That Broke The Plains*. 1936. Reprint, Franklin, Tenn.: Naxos, 2007. Videorecording.
*Tumbling Tumbleweeds* 1935. Reprint, Chatsworth, Calif.: Image Entertainment, 2006. Videorecording.
*Under Fiesta Stars* 1941. Reprint, Chatsworth, Calif.: Image Entertainment, 2003. Videorecording.
*Western Jamboree* 1938. Reprint, Studio City, Calif.: 2002. Videorecording.
*Wide Wide World: The Western*. 1955. Reprint, Studio City, Calif.: Gene Autry Entertainment. Videorecording.

# Index

*References to illustrations appear in italic type.*

Abbott and Costello, 227–28
African American culture and music, 87–88, 183
Agee, John, 71
Agriculture, U.S. Department of (USDA), 73, 75, 81
Air Force. *See* Army Air Forces, U.S.
*Allá en el Rancho Grande (Over at the Big Ranch)*, 125–26
All-American Canal, 74
Allen, Eddie, 203, 204
*American Exodus* (Lange), 73
American Guide Series, 96
Americanism, 110–11, 130, 183–84, 188–89, 193–94, 219, 228. *See also* national identity; tourism; traditional values
Americanization campaigns, 129
American Legion, 4, 102, 221
*American Propaganda Abroad* (Green), 11
*American Record, The*, 122
American Record Corporation (ARC), 18–19, 21, 25, 27, 35, 48, 98–99. *See also* Yates, Herbert J.

American Society of Composers, Authors, and Publishers (ASCAP), 187
Anderson, Broncho Billy, 198–99
Anglo-American relations, 126–27, 132–33, 135–36, 161, 232, 233
"Any Bonds Today?" 200, 218, 221
Appalachia region, 21, 37
apparel/clothing. *See* clothing and appearance
Army Air Forces, U.S., 4–5, 216, 217–18, 219–20, 224, 226–27
*Art of Writing Songs and How to Play the Guitar, The*, 35, 40, 41
Autry, Ina Mae, *151*, 158, 226, 234
Autry, Jacqueline (née Ellam), 226
Autry, Orvon Gene: early career, 18–19; homes, 194, 234; hometown, 102; military service, 4–5, *210*, 219–20, 226–27; retirement from performing, 225
Autry National Center of the American West, 13, 226
Azcarraga, Emilio, 251n13

305

*Back in the Saddle*, 195–96
"Back in the Saddle Again," 183, 195
*Baltimore Sun*, 130
"barn dance" radio format, 22, 28, 33–34, 38, 42–43, 100
baseball, 225
"Beer Barrel Polka," 161
*Bells of Capistrano*, 3, 161
benefits. *See* charity/benefit appearances
Berkowitz, Michael, 49
Berwyn, Okla., 201, 203–4, *209*
Beverly Hillbillies, 21, 24–25, 86
Big Little Book series, 107
*Big Show, The*, *56*, 68, 85–88
*Billboard, The*, charts, 41, 62, 63, 138, 140, 161, 199–200, 224
black-light system, 4, 202–3, 204
black propaganda, 11
block booking disputes, 52, 91, 99–100, 101, 128
*Blue Montana Skies*, 134–35
blues music, 7, 26, 159, 184. *See also* hillbilly music, evolution of
"B" movie production specialty, 59–60, 66, 67
Bolton, Herbert Eugene, 16, 119–20, 125, 162
bonds, war, promotion of, 4–5, 182, 200–201, 203, *211*, 218, 221, 227
boots, Autry's, 35, 62, 102. *See also* clothing and appearance
*Boots and Saddles*, 126–27, 165
"border blasters," 131
border-culture themes, 16, 119–20, 123–24, 130–35, 159–60, 165–66, 232–33
Boulder (Hoover) Dam, 23, 60, 74, 95–96, 107, 113
Bower, B. M., 62
Boyd, William (Hopalong Cassidy), 89, 103, 145
branding and marketing, 6, 35–36, 41–42, 46–47, 68, 107, 194, 223, 230.
*See also* clothing and appearance; merchandising; multiplatform media
British Broadcasting Corporation (BBC), 16, 138–39
Brooklyn Bridge, 95–96
Burbridge, Betty, 70–71, 140
Burnette, Smiley, 47, 76–77, 82, 89, 100, 169, *179*, 197–98

Camacho, Manuel Avila, 144–45
Canada and Good Neighbor Policy themes, 134–35
cap pistols, Autry branded, 103, 136
Cárdenas, Lázaro, 123, 126, 144
Carey, Harry, 103
Carr, Trem, 58, 59, 101
Cassidy, Hopalong. *See* Boyd, William (Hopalong Cassidy)
Cavalry, U.S., 215–16
censorship issues, 51–52, 101, 126, 129–30
C. F. Martin Guitar Company, 39, *78*, *104*
Champion (horse), 71–72, 135, 139, 186, 223
chapter plays, 46, 53, 58. *See also* serial film format
charity/benefit appearances, 110, 155, 182, 186, 223. *See also* war support efforts
"Chiapanecas," 133
*Chicago Daily Tribune*, 3
clear-channel radio, 34, 39
clothing and appearance, 24, 42, 48, 62, 70, 77, 100–101, 187–88, 199
*Colorado Sunset*, 112, 116, 138, 230
Columbia Broadcasting System (CBS), 4–5, 8, 9, 117, 164, 172, 175, 182, 216, 217
*comedia-ranchera* film genre, 125–26, 131, 233
*Comin' Round the Mountain*, 118–19
concert/appearance tours: in 1933, 40–41; in 1936, 82–83, 85–86; in

INDEX   307

1936–37, 88–89; in 1937, 97–98; in 1938, 102–3; in 1939, 135–36; Britain/Irish Free State, 135–36, 138–40, *148–51*, 162, 233; marketing value of, 111–12, 185; New York City, 135–36, 155, 186–88; South America offers, 122, 127–28, 159. *See also* Round-Up of WLS Radio Stars
Condon, Edward, 33
*Confessions of a Nazi Spy*, 130
*Conqueror Record Time*, 22, 34, 35
Consolidated Film Industries (CFI), 59–60, 67
*Convergence Culture* (Jenkins), 20
Cooley, Spade, 184
Coordinator of Inter-American Affairs (CIAA), 11–12, 156–57
corporate corruption themes, 76, 112, 116, 124, 131–32, 133
country-western music, evolution of, 19–27, 37, 187, 230. *See also* "barn dance" radio format; hillbilly music, evolution of
Cowboy Code, 108–9, 233, 235. *See also* cowboy culture and mythos
cowboy culture and mythos, 21, 24–26, 35–36, 37, 65, 108–9, 115, 172, 198–99. *See also* Cowboy Code; dude ranch themes; hero image; rodeo sport
*Cowboy Serenade*, 215–16
cowboy songs, 20, 35, 40, 63. *See also* country-western music, evolution of
*Cowboy Songs and Other Frontier Ballads* (Lomax), 20
Crisler, B. R., 137
Crosby, Bing, 155, 184, 195, 199, 234
cultural convergence, 9, 16, 20–22, 125, 132, 133, 162, 228–29. *See also* Good Neighbor Policy of FDR; hemispheric unity; Western Hemisphere Idea

decency issues, 51–52, 101, 126
Defense Plant Corporation (DPC), 196
De Fuentes, Fernando, 125–26, 131, 232–33
de-urbanization and New West opportunities, 60, 107, 114
*Devil's Bargains* (Rothman), 50
*Digital Diplomacy* (Dizard), 11–12
diplomacy, public. *See* public diplomacy
Dizard, Wilson, 11–12
documentary film format, 52–53, 73–74, 122–23, 130
Donovan, William "Wild Bill," 11
"Don't Bite the Hand That's Feeding You," 161, 203, 216
double feature concept, 66
"Down in Old Santa Fe," 48
*Down Mexico Way*, 159–60
dude ranch themes, 47–50, 83, 102, 107, 166
Dugan, Grace, 127–28
Durante, Jimmy, 191
Durling, E. V., 103
"Dust," 100
Dust Bowl, 61, 74–76, 110, 114

Early, Stephen, 52–53
easterners *vs.* westerners themes, 47, 102, 110, 231. *See also* rural *vs.* urban culture themes
Edwards, Gus, 124
electricity, availability of, 23, 68, 231. *See also* water/power development
Ellam, Jacqueline, 226
enlistment and recruiting efforts, wartime, 4–5, 169, 215, 217, 219–20, 233
"Epic of Greater America, The," 120
eponymous approach to movie/song titles, 17, 98–99
escapism in entertainment, 111, 173–74, 218

Evans, James, 28
Everett Colborn's World's Championship Rodeo (WCR). *See* World's Championship Rodeo (WCR)

Fair Labor Standards Act, 49
*Fallout: New Vegas* (game), 225
fans of Autry: Autry's accessibility, 83, 112, 139–40, 197; fan club/friendship club, *176*, 182; fan mail, amount of, 33, 103, 158, 188, 228; shifting demographic, late 30s, 112; targeting strategies, 103, 104, 107, 109; and war bond campaigns, 200–201; women, 70, 86–87, 109
Farm Security Administration (FSA), 73, 110, 114
Federal Communications Commission (FCC), 123
federal cultural projects, 121
Federal Emergency Relief Administration (FERA), 113–14
Fidler, Jimmie, 135
Figueroa, Gabriel, 126
*Film Daily Cavalcade*, 111
film exchanges, 59. *See also* block booking disputes
film locations and scenic West, 53, 111, 118
"fireside chats," 130, 157
first-run "specials," 135, 137, 146, 159, 164, 194–95
Fitzpatrick, Rita, 3, 4
flood control, 69, 92, 112, 113, 115, 231
Flying A Ranch (Autry ranch), 201–2
Flying A Ranch Rodeo Stampede, 3–4, 72, 161, 201–4, 214, 215–16
folk songs and culture, 6–9, 14, 21, 26, 35, 42, 77, 230. *See also* traditional values
foreign policy. *See* Good Neighbor Policy of FDR

*Forest Rangers, The*, 224, 225
*Four Star Revue*, 103
Frank, Joseph Lee, 34, 102
Frontier Publishers, 40–41

gangster themes, 47, 85, 102, 116
Gans, Herbert J., 6–7
*Gaucho Serenade*, 147, 155
"Gaucho Serenade," 138, 147, 155
gender roles, changing, 70–71, 72, 87, 94
*Gene Autry, In-Person* tour, 88–89
Gene Autry, Okla., 203–4, *209*
*Gene Autry and the Twentieth Century West: The Centennial Exhibition, 1907–2007*, 13
Gene Autry's Flying A Ranch Rodeo Stampede. *See* Flying A Ranch Rodeo Stampede
*Gene Autry's Melody Ranch. See* Melody Ranch
*Gene Autry's Sensational Collection of Famous Original Cowboy Songs and Mountain Ballads*, 35, 40
Gene Autry Western Heritage Museum, 226
gentrification and Western Hemisphere Idea, 125, 158, 233
George-Warren, Holly, 14
*Git Along Little Dogies*, 68, 89–90
*Gold Mine in the Sky*, 102–3
gold records, *32*, 62, 63, 68, 138, 140, 161, 199–200, 224, 233, 234
Goodale, George, 88–89
"Goodbye Little Darlin', Goodbye," 140
Good Neighbor Policy of FDR: Anglo-American/Mexican alliance, 126–27; inter-American radio, 11–12, 121–23; Mexican *comedia-ranchero* film genre, 125–26; public diplomacy through cultural products, 118–19, 120–21, 123–25, 129, 130–37, 141–45, 146–47,

155, 157–62, 232–33. *See also* Mexico; public diplomacy; Western Hemisphere Idea
Grable, Betty, 103, 215
grazing and open range issues, 92, 110, 231
Great Britain, 126–27. *See also* Anglo-American relations; concert/appearance tours
Great Depression, impact of, 21, 26–27, 35–36, 66, 67, 70–71. *See also* Dust Bowl
Great Plains recovery programs, 74–76
Green, Fitzhugh, 10–11
Gross, Ben, 10
guitars, Autry branded, 22, 35, 39, 48, 62, *78, 104*
*Guns and Guitars*, 68, 80–81, 116, 230

*Hands*, 52
Hanson, Philip, 102
"Happy Days Are Here Again," 90
Hart, William S., 103, 197, 198
Hays Code, 101, 159–60
*Heart of the Rio Grande*, 216
hemispheric unity, 147, 156–57, 250n8. *See also* Western Hemisphere Idea
hero image, 7–8, 21, 35–36, 53, 108–9, 115, 173, 220, 230. *See also* cowboy culture and mythos; role model, Autry as
hillbilly music, evolution of, 20–21, 24–26, 37, 38. *See also* folk songs and culture
history museum exhibition context and value, 13–15
"Hold On Little Dogies, Hold On," 72
*Hollywood Reporter*, 51
*Home in Wyomin'*, 216, 218–19
Hoover Dam. *See* Boulder (Hoover) Dam
Hopalong Cassidy. *See* Boyd, William (Hopalong Cassidy)

Hopkins, Harry, 52–53
Hopper, Hedda, 194–95, 227–28
*Horse Opera* (Stanfield), 61
horses, 71, 223. *See also* Champion (horse)
Houston Fat Stock Show, 215–16
Howe Booking Agency, 82
Huber, Harold, 160
hybridity in cultural industry, 19–24, 37, 230

Ickes, Harold, 74–75, 96
image, Autry's. *See* hero image; role model, Autry as
income, Autry's: Autry's demands for increases, 81–82, 91, 99–100, 101; examples, 25, 40, 41, 85, 88, 97–98, 101, 102–3, 128–29; *Melody Ranch*, 174; of Tom Mix, 187
industrialization, reemergence of, 166, 196, 231
information sharing and public diplomacy, 9–12, 37–38, 52–53, 66–69, 114, 129–30. *See also* public diplomacy
*In Old Monterey*, 135–37, 167–70, *179*
*In Old Santa Fe*, 46–50, 55
inter-American radio, 121–22
Interior, U.S. Department of, 51, 74–75, 92, 96–97
internationalism, 6, 10, 234. *See also* Anglo-American relations; Pan-Americanism; Western Hemisphere Idea
irrigation programs, 60, 61, 113–14. *See also* water/power development
isolationism, 118, 168–69, 229, 250n8
"(I've Got Spurs That) Jingle, Jangle, Jingle," 4, 200, 221, 224–25

jazz music, 26, 159, 184
Jenkins, Henry, 20

"Jingle, Jangle, Jingle." *See* "(I've Got Spurs That) Jingle, Jangle, Jingle"
Johnston, Ray, 58, 59
Jones, Charles "Buck," 89, 198–99
Jowett, Garth, 67

Kane, Joseph, 47, 61
Kenton Hardware Company, 103
Kilpatrick, John R., 137, 172, 186. *See also* World's Championship Rodeo (WCR)
King, Betsy Ross, 53
Kingsley, Grace, 145
Kyser, Kay, 224–25

labor issues, 23, 49, 51, 76–78
LaFollette, Robert M., Jr., 114
land recovery and redevelopment projects, 74–76, 113–14. *See also* resource management and redevelopment projects; water/power development
Lange, Dorothea, 73, 114
"Last Roundup, The," 41, 68
Latin America. *See* Good Neighbor Policy of FDR; Mexico; Western Hemisphere Idea
"lavender cowboy," 60, 64
"Lavender Cowboy, The," 64
law and order themes, 64, 73, 115, 123–24, 230
Lazarsfeld, Paul F., 41
League of Nations, 250n8
Lee, Mary, 140
Lefton, Abe, 71–72
leisure/recreation themes, 69, 83, 86, 93, 95, 108, 166. *See also* tourism
Levesque, Archie, 41
Levine, Nat, 45–49, 51–54, 58–59, 68–69, 81, 89, 91, 126
*Life* (magazine), 10, 203
Light Crust Doughboys, 83, 84

live performances. *See* concert/appearance tours
locals *vs.* outsiders themes. *See* natives *vs.* newcomers themes
Lone Pine, Calif., 83, 111, 118, 192, 197
Long, Jimmy, 18–19
Lorentz, Pare, 73–74
Los Angeles Angels, 225
*Los Angeles Times*, 89, 99, 103, 128, 155
Lower Colorado River Basin, 60, 61, 74, 80, 107
lower-culture audiences, 6–8, 11, 61, 109, 197
Luke Field, Ariz., *213*, 215, 223, 224, 227

Madison Square Garden, 137, 172, 186. *See also* World's Championship Rodeo (WCR)
mail, fan. *See under* fans of Autry
*Man from Music Mountain*, 107
"Maria Elena," 161
market capitalism and Western Hemisphere Idea, 125, 158, 233
Martin Guitar Company, 39, 78, 104
Marvin, Johnny, 82, 102, 200
Mascot Pictures, 45, 46, 58–59. *See also* Levine, Nat
Maynard, Ken, 39, 46, 53, *55*
M. D. Howe Booking Agency, 82
*Media and Sovereignty* (Price), 12
Melody Ranch (Autry homestead), 194, 234
*Melody Ranch* (film), 191, 194, 230
*Melody Ranch* (radio program): Americanist messaging, 182–84; Autry's enlistment and induction, 4–5, *210*; Berwyn, Okla., show, 203; and cultural convergence, 8–9, 117, 175; expansion and reach, 216; and hemispheric unity, 146, 156, 160; launch and overview, 172–75; New York City broadcast, 186; theme

song, 195; Tom Mix tribute, 187; war support, 200–201, 214–15, 221–23
"Melody Ranch," 191
*Melody Trail*, 68, 69–73
Mencken, H. L., 130
Mercer, Johnny, 100, 195
merchandising: Big Little Book series, 107; cap pistols, 103, 136; comic books, *154*; guitars, 22, 35, 39, 48, 62, *78, 104*; licensing of Autry branded products, 22, 107; songbooks and sheet music, 34, 35, 40–41, *152, 212. See also* branding and marketing
Merton, Robert K., 41
"message" films, 59, 109, 129, 193, 230
*Mexicali Rose*, 131–34
"Mexicali Rose," 124, 132
Mexico: *comedia-ranchero* film, 125–26; cultural diplomacy and movie themes, 118–19, 123–25, 126–27, 129, 130–37, 141–45, 146–47, 155, 159–62, 232–33; New Deal efforts and Americanization campaign, 123; U.S.–Great Britain–Mexico alliance, 126–27, 138–39, 162, 165
Miami Copper Company, 196
military service, Autry's, 4–5, *210*, 219–20, 226–27
Millhouse, Frog, 76–77
mining industry, 195–96
Mix, Ruth, 135
Mix, Tom, 71, 103, 187–88, 197, 198, 223
M. M. Cole Publishing Company, 35, 40
modernization: expansion and suburbanization, 75, 77; oil industry expansion, 89–90; range management issues, 92, 110, 231; themes in movies, 84–85, 87, 92–94, 116, 231; and Western Hemisphere Idea, 125, 158, 165, 233

Monogram Pictures, 58–59
Mooney, George A., 188
"Moon over Mañana," 141
Morehouse, Frances, 214–18
*Motion Picture Herald*, 42, 89, 158, 190
Motion Picture Producers and Directors Association (MPPDA), 52, 74, 101, 126, 129–30, 160
Motion Picture Research Council (MPRC), 51–52
mountain music. *See* hillbilly music, evolution of
*Mountain Rhythm*, 110–11
*Movie and Radio Guide*, 215
multiplatform media: as marketing strategy, 20–21, 44–46, 140, 164, 175, 187, 229–30; and popular appeal, 7–9, 72; and public diplomacy, 5–12, 97, 117, 121, 189–90, 228–29
musical-Western movie genre, evolution of, 39, 43, 46, 66–69, 197–98, 229–30
music genres: blues music, 7, 26, 159, 184; jazz music, 26, 159, 184; *ranchera* music, 125, 127; Western Swing, 24, 184–85. *See also* country-western music, evolution of; hillbilly music, evolution of

*National Barn Dance*, 22, 38, 42
National Broadcasting Company (NBC), 22, 122
National Foundation for Infantile Paralysis, 9, 182
national identity, 73–74, 110–11, 116, 143, 183, 231. *See also* Americanism
National Industrial Recovery Act, 49
nationalism. *See* national identity
National Labor Relations Act, 49
National Recovery Act (NRA), 52, 59

National Travel Advisory Board (NTAB), 97
natives *vs.* newcomers themes, 61, 107. *See also* rural *vs.* urban culture themes
natural gas industry, 166
natural resource development. *See* resource management and redevelopment projects
Nazi subversion in Latin America, fear of, 142–43, 147, 156–57, 250n8, 251n10
New Deal: Autry's support of, overviews, 115–16, 189–90, 230; and documentary film production, 52–53, 73–74; messaging through media, overviews, 66–69, 92–94; and tourism, promotion of, 23–24, 47–51, 83, 96–97. *See also* Good Neighbor Policy of FDR; water/power development
"New Deal for Leisure, A" (Berkowitz), 49
newsreel format, 52–53, 130, 170, 195
New West, overviews, 6, 50–51, 65, 117, 230–31
*New York Daily News*, 10
*New York Times*, 96, 113, 137, 164, 166–67, 188, 217
New York World's Fair, 135, 155
Nolan, Bob, 62, 63
Nugent, Frank S., 113, 166–67
Nye, Joseph S., 9–10

O'Brien, George, 89, 145
O'Daniel, W. Lee, 84
*Oh, Susanna!* 68, 83–85
oil and gas industry, 89–90, 131, 142–43, 144–45, 166
"Oklahoma Yodeling Cowboy," 19, 22, 25, *29*, 34, 38
"Ole Faithful," 63, 68, 87
open range, control of, 92, 110, 231

"Original Singing Cowboy, The," 19, 47
Owens Valley, California, 83

Pacific Slope recovery programs, 74–76
Pan-American Conferences, 121, 122
Pan-Americanism, 120, 144, 161, 232–33, 250n8. *See also* Western Hemisphere Idea
patriotism themes, 73, 108, 115, 163, 168–72, 219. *See also* Americanism; national identity; traditional values; war preparedness themes and public diplomacy
*Phantom Empire, The*, 45, 53–54, 58
*Photoplay*, 109
*Plow That Broke the Plains, The*, 73–74, 75
political themes in movies, 112–13, 114
*Popular Culture and High Culture* (Gans), 6–7
Porter, Cole, 64
*Prairie Farmer and WLS* (Evans, J.), 28
Price, Monroe, 12
"Private Buckaroo," 5
propaganda, 10–12, 110–11, 119–21, 129–30, 168–70, 193. *See also* public diplomacy
*Public Cowboy No. 1* (film), 91–95, 97, *105*, 115
*Public Cowboy No. 1: The Life and Times of Gene Autry* (George-Warren), 14
public diplomacy: and information sharing, 9–12, 37–38, 52–53, 66–69, 114, 129–30; and musical-Western film genre, 67–69; and radio broadcasting, 37–38; through cultural products, 5–12, 97, 117, 119, 121–23, 232; and war preparedness, 135–37, 139, 161–63, 164–65, 167–72. *See also* Americanism; Good Neighbor Policy of FDR

public opinion, manipulation of, 36–37, 157
Public Works Administration (PWA), 75, 96

"quasi-folk" audiences, 6–8, 11, 61. *See also* folk songs and culture
Quigley Publishing Company, 89, 95

radio: border stations, 131; broadcasting models, evolution of, 28; clear-channel, 34, 39; and FDR's public diplomacy, 10–12, 37–38; and Good Neighbor Policy, 122; government, and international diplomacy, 122–23; growth of, 22–24, 68; inter-American, 121–22; value of exposure on, 33–34, 164, 189, 228; and war support, 216–17. *See also names of individual radio programs*
*ranchera* music, 125, 127
*Rancho Grande*, 146–47
"Rancho Grande (Allá en el Rancho Grande)," 131, 133, 138, 146
real estate boom and water/power development, 107–8
Reclamation, U.S. Bureau of, 113–14
Records for Our Fighting Men, 217
recruiting efforts, wartime, 4–5, 169, 215, 217, 219–20, 233
*Red River Valley*, 68, 74–77
"Red River Valley," 77
Republic Pictures, 45; air traffic and location issues, 196–97; Autry's disputes with, 81–82, 91, 99–100, 101, 128–29; "B" movie production specialty, 59–60, 66, 67; growth and expansion of, 197; number one producer of Western films, 95; Republic-Mascot-Monogram merger, 58–59; strategy for musical-Western genre, 66–69; war support movies, 218–19; and Western Hemisphere unity themes, 120. *See also* Yates, Herbert J.
Resettlement Administration (RA), 73
resource management and redevelopment projects, 74–76, 92, 94, 113–14. *See also* water/power development
Rice, Glen, 24
*Ride, Ranger, Ride*, 85
*Ride, Tenderfoot, Ride*, 186
Ritter, Tex, 224
"Robin Hood," 132
*Robin Hood of the Pecos*, 194
Robinson, Edward G., 130
Rockefeller, Nelson, 11–12, 156–57
rodeo sport: Autry's involvement in, 72, 225; and cowboy culture, evolution of, 53, 69; movie themes, 71–72, 161, 195; popularity of, 201–2, 204; and young boy fan development, 103. *See also* Flying A Ranch Rodeo Stampede; Wild West shows; World's Championship Rodeo (WCR)
Rodgers, Jimmie, 18
Rogers, Roy, 63, 95, 98, 100, 194, 228
Rogers, Will, 158, 173, 194
role model, Autry as, 67, 172, 185, 188–90. *See also* hero image
Roosevelt, Eleanor, 9, *180*, 182–83
Roosevelt, Franklin Delano (FDR): Autry's support of, overviews, 5, 116, 192–93, 201, 229–30; birthday celebrations, 9, *180*, 182–83, 215; motion picture production by, 52–53, 73–74; radio broadcasting, use of, 37–38. *See also* Good Neighbor Policy of FDR; New Deal
Roosevelt, Franklin, Jr., *151*
*Rootin' Tootin' Rhythm*, 123–25
Rose, Fred, 102

Rothman, Hal, 50
*Round-Up of WLS Radio Stars*, 22, 28, *30, 31*, 38–39
Route 66, 23, 155
*Rovin' Tumbleweeds*, 92, *106*, 112–14, 116, 230
royalties, 18–19, 35, 40
*Rudy Vallee's Varieties*, 97–98
rural *vs.* urban culture themes, 20, 49, 60, 102, 107–8. *See also* easterners *vs.* westerners themes; natives *vs.* newcomers themes

Sandburg, Carl, 64
Satherley, Art, 18–19, 24, 25, *32*, 46, *151*
scenic appeal of American West, 83, 111, 118, 167, 192
science/science fiction themes, 54–55
Screen Actors Guild (SAG), 52
Screen Writers Guild (SWG), 52
Sears, Roebuck and Company, 21–22, 27–28, 33, 35, 38, 41–42, 48
*Sergeant Gene Autry*, 5, 174, 222, 224, 227
serial film format, 46, 53, 58, 62, 174–75
Shaifer, Edward F., 5, 220
Shallert, Edwin, 128
Shannon, John T., 202, 204
Shay, Jeff, 27–28, 34
sheet music and songbooks, 34, 35, 40–41, *152, 212*
sidekick concept, 82, 89, 160
Siegel, Sol C., 10, 91
*Singing Hill, The*, 158–59
*Singing Vagabond, The*, 82
Slye, Leonard (Roy Rogers), 63, 98. *See also* Rogers, Roy
social realism, 73–74, 108, 125–26
*Soft Power* (Nye), 10
soft-power diplomacy, 10–11, 68, 117, 123–25, 129, 230, 232
songbooks and sheet music, 34, 35, 40–41, *152, 212*

Sons of the Pioneers, 62–63
*South of the Border*, 137, 140–45, *153*
"South of the Border (Down Mexico Way)," 137, 138–39, 140, *152*, 155, 159, 161
Spanish language song/radio, 133, 165–66
"specials," 136, 137, 146. *See also* first-run "specials"
*Springtime in the Rockies*, 99
*Stagecoach*, 111, 167
stamps, war. *See* bonds, war, promotion of
Stanfield, Peter, 25–26, 61, 82
stardom, achievement of, 139, 157–58. *See also* top-ten lists
state and imagery, 12, 45. *See also* soft-power diplomacy
St. John, Alfred, 64
submarines, German, 137, 142–45
suburbanization, 47–48, 75, 77, 108
"Sunny South's Blue Yodeler, The," 18–19
"Super Westerns," 135, 164. *See also* "specials"

"Take Me Back to My Boots and Saddles," 127
technology themes, 54, 72–73, 87, 116
Texas, Autry's popularity in, 102
Texas Centennial Exposition, 85–88, 97
"That Silver Haired Daddy of Mine," 18–19, 21, 22, 25, 40, 45–46, 58, 60, 63, 68
Thomas, Dick, 224, 225
Tony, Jr. (horse), 71, 223
top-ten lists: Hollywood stars, 157–58, 166, 190, 199, 214, 227; Western stars, 89, 95, 145, 158, 167, 190, 214, 227
tourism: dude ranch themes, 47–50, 83, 102, 107, 166; and economic recovery, 6, 23–24, 51, 96; and New West culture, 49–51, 65, 230;

INDEX    315

promotion of, and New Deal, 23–24, 47–51, 83, 96–97; promotion of in movie themes, 86, 155, 167; scenic appeal of American West, 83, 111, 118, 167, 192; vacationing, paid, 49, 68, 230. *See also* leisure/recreation themes; rodeo sport
tours. *See* concert/appearance tours
*Tower Topics*, 22, 34, 35
trade, international, 119, 120, 121–22
traditional values, 25–26, 53, 59, 61, 108–9, 230. *See also* national identity; working-class values
travel. *See* tourism
"Travel America Year" campaign, 96
Travel Bureau, U.S. (USTB), 96–97
Tugwell, Rexford, 73
*Tumbling Tumbleweeds*, 45, 60–65
"Tumbling Tumbleweeds," 61, 62, 68

underdog themes, 61, 64
*Under Fiesta Stars*, 159
*Under Western Stars*, 100
United Service Organization (USO), 4, 221
"urban hillbillies," 20–21, 25, 228
urbanization, Depression Era, 20, 23, 25, 67, 136, 230
urban *vs.* rural culture themes. *See* rural *vs.* urban culture themes
U.S.-Canada relations, 134–35
U.S. Documentary Film, 73–74

vacation camps, 53–54. *See also* dude ranch themes
vacationing, paid, 49, 68, 230
Vallee, Rudy, 62, 97–98, *104*
*Variety*, 42
"V-Days" campaign, 4
Vendrell, Armida, 124
Voice of America (VOA), 11

"Vote for Autry" metaphor for FDR, 80, 112, 116, 193, 230

Wakely, Jimmy, 184, 203
Wallace, Henry A., 75, 145
Warner Brothers, 59, 130
war preparedness themes and public diplomacy, 135–37, 139, 161–63, 164–66, 167–72. *See also* propaganda; war support efforts
war support efforts: bonds, promotion of, 4–5, 182, 200–201, 203, *211*, 218, 221, 227; loan drives, 221; materials drives, 217; movie themes, 218–19; radio shows, 200–201, 214–16; recruiting campaigns, 4–5, 217, 233; war fund campaigns, 221. *See also* war preparedness themes and public diplomacy
*Washington Cowboy*, 100
water/power development: expansion and opportunities, 23, 48, 74–77, 95–96, 107, 116, 231; flood control, 69, 92, 112, 113, 115, 231; water rights/disputes, 61, 74, 83. *See also* Boulder (Hoover) Dam
Wayne, John, 167
"West Ain't What It Used to Be, The," 93, 94, 115
westerners *vs.* easterners themes. *See* easterners *vs.* westerners themes
Western film genre, mainstream recognition of, 112–13, 139, 166–67, 172, 190, 194–95, 228
Western Hemisphere Idea, 119–21, 125, 132, 133, 161–63, 162, 233. *See also* hemispheric unity
*Western Jamboree*, 165–66
Western Swing music, 24, 184–85
"When It's Round-Up Time in Texas," 200
"When It's Springtime in the Rockies," 99

Wild West shows, 53, 185–86. *See also* Flying A Ranch Rodeo Stampede; World's Championship Rodeo (WCR)
"Wizard of Washington," 11
*WLS Barn Dance*, 22, 28, 33
*WLS Family Album*, 40, 42
WLS radio, 22, 28, 33–34
*WLS Roundup*. *See* Round-Up of WLS Radio Stars
women: characterization of, modern Mexican culture, 124; characterization of and evolution of New West, 49, 53, 65, 87, 93, 94, 99, 140; electoral power of, 80, 81, 112; fan base, 70, 86–87, 109; screenwriters, 70–71, 140. *See also* gender roles, changing
working-class values, 7–8, 95, 109, 117, 231. *See also* folk songs and culture; national identity; traditional values
Works Progress Administration (WPA), 52, 96, 97
World's Championship Rodeo (WCR), 103, 172, 185, 186, 195, 202–3, 223

"World's Wonder Horse, The," 71
World War II. *See* war preparedness themes and public diplomacy
World Wide Wild West and Rodeo, 3, 161
Wrigley Company sponsorship, 4–5, 8, 117, 146, 164, 172, 174, 175, 182, 200, 214–15, 216, 222, 231

Yates, Herbert J., *32, 151*; Autry cultural values "rules," 108–9; buyout of Levine, 91; influence on Autry, 21; marketing strategies, 84, 109, 111–12, 174–75; multiplatform dynasty, 44–45, 66–69; Republic-Mascot-Monogram merger and leadership, 58–60; Roy Rogers, signing of, 98. *See also* Republic Pictures
yodeling, 18
*Young America*, 214
"Youth's Model, 1940," 164, 188

Zanuck, Darryl, 98

www.ingramcontent.com/pod-product-compliance
Lightning Source LLC
Chambersburg PA
CBHW020738160426
43192CB00006B/231